# US–SANDINISTA DIPLOMATIC RELATIONS

# US–Sandinista Diplomatic Relations

## Voice of Intolerance

David Ryan
*Lecturer, Department of Historical and International Studies*
*De Montfort University, Leicester*

First published in Great Britain 1995 by
**MACMILLAN PRESS LTD**
Houndmills, Basingstoke, Hampshire RG21 6XS
and London
Companies and representatives
throughout the world

A catalogue record for this book is available
from the British Library.

ISBN 0–333–61463–1

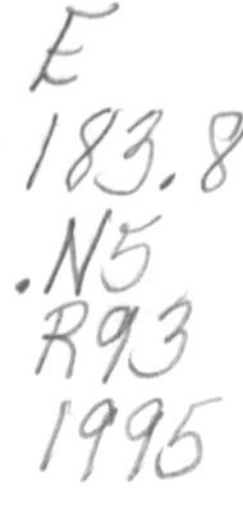



---

First published in the United States of America 1995 by
**ST. MARTIN'S PRESS, INC.,**
Scholarly and Reference Division,
175 Fifth Avenue,
New York, N.Y. 10010

ISBN 0–312–12821–5

Library of Congress Cataloging-in-Publication Data
Ryan, David, 1965–
US–Sandinista diplomatic relations : voice of intolerance / David Ryan.
p. cm.
includes bibliographical references and index.
ISBN 0–312–12821–5 (cloth)
1. United States—Foreign relations—Nicaragua. 2. Nicaragua–Foreign relations—United States. 3. Frente Sandinista de Liberación Nacional. I. Title.
E183.8.N5R93 1995
327.7307285—dc20 95–14923
CIP

---



10 9 8 7 6 5 4 3 2 1
04 03 02 01 00 99 98 97 96 95

Printed and bound in Great Britain by
Antony Rowe Ltd, Chippenham, Wiltshire

For Carole and Daniel Norman-Ryan

# Contents

*Preface* viii

*Acknowledgements* x

*List of Abbreviations* xii

Introduction 1

1 Diplomacy and Counterrevolution 1981–1982 13

2 Contadora: Latin America Repudiates Washington 1983 36

3 Manzanillo and Contadora 1984 60

4 Undermining Democracy: Elections 1984 88

5 Narrowing the Focus: Contadora and Esquipulas 1986 107

6 The Arias Plan 1987–1988 128

7 Bush and the Sandinistas 1989 148

8 The 1990 Elections and Democracy 170

Conclusion 189

*Notes and References* 197

*Selected Bibliography* 254

*Index* 266

# Preface

Throughout the 1980s there were numerous pleas for peace in Central America and more pertinently for this study in Nicaragua. The revolution which brought the Sandinistas to power in 1979 was popular and pluralistic but was undermined slowly through a combination of low-intensity warfare, a possible threat of more direct action, and diplomatic processes that both facilitated the funding of the conflict and its limitation; Washington needed diplomacy to demonstrate Sandinista intransigence, the Sandinistas needed it to prevent direct US action. After a decade of diplomacy: bilateral, regional, and isthmian, a formula for accommodation between Washington and the Sandinistas was not concluded, though several viable plans were on offer. The impasse to the normalization of relations resulted from a challenge to the desire of the United States to exert hegemonic control over the region which, during the period under consideration, was often referred to disparagingly as the US 'backyard'.

The US intolerance of the Sandinista regime stemmed from the perceptions of the Reagan administration which interpreted events through a globalist perspective divorced from the motives of the revolution to provide a better life for Nicaraguans. It was not only the redistributive aspects of the Sandinista revolution, which Washington labeled Marxist, but Nicaraguan nationalism and anti-imperialism which challenged the 'traditional' bilateral relationship and systemic economic patterns. In the initial stages of the revolutionary years the Sandinistas provided a 'threat' of a 'good example' for others to follow, but the arguments offered that they posed a security threat to either the United States or its isthmian neighbours were ludicrous during the 1980s. The diplomatic process was, however, steeped in such obfuscatory rhetoric that it made US compromise more difficult. Public diplomacy on the ideological nature of the 'communist' challenge was aimed at convincing the doubtful US public and Congress that the covert war was needed to contain the Sandinistas. Reagan's doctrine, however, was more concerned with rolling back 'communism' and promoting an exclusive conception of democracy for the Third World; though this had little relation to Nicaragua, which was not communist and was more democratic than its northern neighbours. US diplomacy was conducted within the framework of Reagan's doctrine. Its conduct during negotiations was demonstrative rather than substantive; the point was to block agreement to facilitate the destruction of the Sandinista regime, in the quest to confine 'Marxism' to the 'ash heap of history'. Nicaragua suffered incalculable losses in human lives and much of its infrastructure was destroyed. Without any possibility of prevailing against the United States, it could merely concede issues on the diplomatic level to avert or delay the destruction of the revolution. Despite the faults of the FSLN, their experiment provided a unique combination of mixed systems: state and private; representative and participatory; constitutional and political; governance from above combined with a more inclusive participatory system. Above all it was a Nicaraguan phenomenon. The greatest potential in human development, Isaiah Berlin argues, has come from such experiments in living.

*Kinsale* DAVID RYAN

# Acknowledgements

Specific gratitude for assistance during this study is owed to Professor Dermot Keogh, extensively involved in the earlier stages of research. This study benefited from his insight and restraint. I would also like to thank Professor J. J. Lee, and the Department of Modern History in University College Cork, for providing the opportunity to pursue this work and facilitating the process. Deirdre O'Sullivan and Norma Buckley, in the department, also provided assistance on numerous occasions. Helen Davis in the Boole Library provided invaluable help with computer searches and on reference material. In the latter stages gratitude is extended to De Montfort University, Leicester for providing the time to complete the work. My collegues in History and Media, John Cook, Mark Sandle, Ian Hunter, Chris Goldsmith, and those in 6.2 provided a friendly atmosphere in which to work.

Gathering the information was a difficult and lengthy task. Primarily in this regard I would like to acknowledge the assistance of Peter Kornbluh, James Morrell, Eva Loser, Ben Tonra, Jeff Pyatt, Rob Saute, Karen Rose, Hugh Rojas and Pamela Hussey. A special debt is also owed to the individuals who were generous with their time and their knowledge of the events. They are: Ambassador Bernardo Sepúlveda Amor, Roy Gutman, Victor Hugo Tinoco, and Lawrence Pezzullo. A number of institutions and their anonymous staff provided access to invaluable facilities and information. They were, in Washington, The National Security Archive, The Center for International Policy, The Washington Office on Latin America, the embassies of Nicaragua, Mexico, Costa Rica, El Salvador and Honduras; the Inter-American Dialogue of the Aspen Institute, the Christic Institute, the Library of the Wilson Center, the Library of the School of Advanced International Studies, Johns Hopkins University, CSIS, and the Central American Historical Institute. The US government offices that provided help were the Democratic Policy Committee, the Republican Study Committee, the Arms Control and Foreign Policy Caucus, the House Intelligence Committee, and the Senate Intelligence Committee. The staff of the Georgetown University library were of particular help in finding hearings and reports. In New York, the North American Congress on Latin America permitted me the use of their files. Baroqua College, Brooklyn, provided access to their collection of documents; America's Watch were generous with their assistance. In London it is necessary to thank the Latin American Bureau, the El Salvador and Guatemala Committee on Human Rights, the Catholic Institute for International Relations, the Nicaraguan Embassy, the library staff at the London School of Economics, the staff at the United Nations office in Buckingham Gate, and Amnesty International. I am grateful, too, for the technical assistance of Clare Andrews, Gráinne Twomey and Keith Povey at the publishers.

My family, Carole and Daniel, deserve special thanks, for being tolerant throughout the process. These years could not have been possible without the generous assistance of my parents. My mother, Susan Ryan, has provided constant encouragement; Barbara, Helen, and my father Barry have also supported me through this time. I would also like to thank Paul Emile Cornet for generous hospitality during long stays in the United States.

DAVID RYAN

# List of Abbreviations

| | |
|---|---|
| ARA | Bureau of Inter-American Affairs |
| ARDE | Democratic Revolutionary Alliance |
| ARENA | National Republican Alliance |
| C/CATF | Chief/Central American Task Force |
| CDN | Coordinadora Democratica Nicaragua |
| CIA | Central Intelligence Agency |
| CIAV | International Commission of Support and Verification |
| CIVS | International Commission for Verification and Follow Up |
| CONDECA | Central American Defense Council |
| COPPPAL | Permanent Conference of Political Parties in Latin America |
| DCI | Director of Central Intelligence |
| DIA | Defense Intelligence Agency |
| DRF | Democratic Resistance Force |
| ESF | Economic Support Funds |
| FDN | Nicaraguan Democratic Force |
| FMLN | Farabundo Marti National Liberation Front |
| FSLN | Sandinista National Liberation Front |
| ICJ | International Court of Justice |
| LASA | Latin American Studies Association |
| NSA | National Security Adviser |
| NSC | National Security Council |
| NSDD | National Security Decision Directive |
| NSPG | National Security Planning Group |
| OAS | Organization of American States |
| ONUCA | UN Observer Group in Central America |
| ONUVEN | UN Observer Group for the Verification of Elections in Nicaragua |
| PCN | Nicaraguan Communist Party |
| RIG | Restricted Interagency Group |
| SIG-FP | Senior Interagency Group for Foreign Policy |
| UNO | United Nicaraguan Opposition |
| URNG | Guatemalan National Revolutionary Union |

# Introduction

Four days before the Sandinistas celebrated the first anniversary of their revolution on 19 July 1980, the US Republican Party Platform deplored

> the Marxist Sandinista takeover of Nicaragua and the Marxist attempts to destabilize El Salvador, Guatemala, and Honduras. We do not support United States assistance to any Marxist government in this hemisphere and we oppose the Carter Administration aid program for the government of Nicaragua. *However, we will support the efforts of the Nicaraguan people to establish a free and independent government* [emphasis added].

According to Roy Gutman, Nicaragua was not on the party agenda in early July. This section of the platform was inserted by staff of the Senator for North Carolina, Jesse Helms. Helms had initially provided two sentences, but when the amendment to the platform was turned over to his staff, the final sentence of the paragraph was added. The sentence was later interpreted to include the possibility of removing the Sandinistas from power. This language from the platform adequately represented the thinking of the Republican party, and of the president elected later that year. International conditions were described as 'perilous'; the United States had endured a series of humiliations during the Carter administration, but the Republicans were set to reverse the trend 'by strong Presidential leadership and a consistent, far-sighted foreign policy.' Their aim was to 'practice strength and firmness' to 'guard the peace'. The first challenge was to 'check the Soviet Union's global ambitions'. Specifically, the platform noted 'as the Soviet Union continues in its expansionist course, the potential for dangerous confrontations has increased'. Peaceful negotiations were advocated only if they were pursued from a position of strength.[1]

While the platform may have satisfied Helms, a counsellor to the candidate Ronald Reagan, and later his Attorney General, Ed Meese, entered the caveat: a platform represents the party, whereas, a presidential candidate has his own policies. Reagan had made his approach to regional issues clear during his campaign, 'The Soviet Union underlies all the unrest that is going on. If they weren't engaged in this game of dominoes, there wouldn't be any hot spots in the world.' Historian Walter LaFeber describes his foreign policy as 'simple and direct: it rested entirely on opposing the Soviet Union.' The predominantly globalist perspective of Reagan was constantly exhibited in his rhetoric, dealing with regional issues such as Central America through an east–west prism. The influential Committee of Santa Fe, set out specifics for the inter-American relationship in their report, *A New Inter-American Policy for the Eighties*. The authors of the report, who found employment in the Reagan administration, presented the contemporary world in alarmist terms, arguing 'Containment of the Soviet Union was not enough. Detente is dead. Survival demands a new US foreign policy. America must seize the initiative or perish. For World War III is almost over.' Vital US interests, they claimed, were being threatened by Soviet penetration of Latin America. The Santa Fe document enunciated an argument that would be often repeated by the Reagan administration:

> Cuban aid to left wing movements in Nicaragua, El Salvador and Guatemala have in the last two years turned Central America into an area of great instability. That in turn presents great opportunities for both Cuba and the Soviet Union in Mexico with its oil and Panama with its canal.

The Committee charged the Carter administration with accommodating the Soviet Union and 'their Hispanic–American puppets . . .'. Hence it urged the United States to re-proclaim 'the Monroe Doctrine . . . aiding independent nations to survive subversion'.[2]

The Kirkpatrick distinction, in her article 'Dictatorships and Double Standards' in *Commentary*, between authoritarian governments friendly to, and totalitarian governments opposed to, the United States, provided the rationale for the Reagan administration in dealing with Third World countries. LaFeber, however, points out that had the authoritarians been as 'beneficent and flexible' as claimed, 'the professional elite and the Catholic Church . . . would not have become radicalized. Authoritarians had exploited and divided their societies until revolution became the last hope of the masses and the middle class'.[3]

In Nicaragua the revolution of July 1979, described by Christopher Hitchens as conducted by a broad 'coalition of revulsion' against Somoza, resulted in his departure from Managua two days before the Sandinistas entered the city, ending forty three years of family rule. While the Sandinista National Liberation Front (FSLN), had been operating since the early 1960s, Anastasio Somoza had for the most part enjoyed the support of the United States. The coincidence of the efforts of the Sandinistas, the larger reaction against Somoza, and an administration in Washington that terminated military aid to the regime, led to its collapse in July 1979. The revolution was a 'spontaneous upheaval' resulting from the deterioration of living standards which became especially acute since 1977, though part of a longer trend. The brutal suppression initiated by the Somoza government gave the Sandinistas a 'self directing mass base everywhere in the nation'.[4]

Though the Carter administration tried to prevent the Sandinistas from gaining power, it realized Somoza had to be replaced, but wanted to maintain the system with a government favourable to the United States. The Carter administration response was based on the premise, assumed through most of the twentieth century, that the United States had the right to intervene and control revolutionary change in Central America. The most noteworthy historical statement on this matter was issued in 1904 as President Roosevelt's corollary to the 1823 Monroe doctrine. Aimed at maintaining the prevalent order, Roosevelt declared:

> We would interfere with [Latin America] only in the last resort, and then only if it became evident that their inability or unwillingness to do justice at home and abroad had violated the rights of the United States or had invited foreign aggression to the detriment of the entire body of American nations.

By 'justice', Roosevelt did not mean a social or distributive justice, but rather one that lay in the 'efficient' use of the materials within the region. He declared the interests of the United States were 'in reality identical' to those of Latin America, implying, the extraction of wealth for the prosperity of the few was central to the order of the day. 'They have great riches', Roosevelt informed Congress,

> and if within their borders the reign of law and justice obtains, prosperity is sure to come with them. While they thus obey the primary laws of civilized society they may rest assured that they will be treated by us in a spirit of cordial and helpful sympathy.[5]

In Nicaragua it was soon established that the Sandinistas (FSLN) intended to rule the country, and on 20 July 1979, they set up a provisional government. It set about transforming itself into a vanguard movement. The Carter administration sought aid for the new regime to bolster the position of the private sector against the Sandinistas, and to ensure continued Nicaraguan participation in the international economy. Robert Pastor, Carter's director for Latin American and Caribbean Affairs on the National Security Council outlined three US objectives toward Nicaragua. Washington wanted to maintain political pluralism, a vigorous private sector, and bring about an electoral system; to deny the Sandinistas an enemy, precluding them from obtaining Soviet and Cuban military aid; and to ensure a Sandinista understanding that good relations with the

United States were contingent on confining the revolution within their borders. The premise that the United States had the right to 'manage', compromised their search for self determination.[6]

The Government of National Reconstruction enjoyed broad support, and according to historian James Dunkerley, there was no struggle immediately following the insurrection to exclude individuals from, or to move rapidly to, a 'fully socialist' programme. However, over the next fifteen months the FSLN outmanoeuvred the business leaders, and, by late 1980, had in political terms strengthened their position. Alfonso Robelo, a future leader of the counterrevolutionaries (contras), and Violetta Chamorro de Barrios resigned from the junta due to the increased Sandinista power. Experienced US diplomats related the uncertainty to congressional committees in Washington. They were certain the revolution was not a monolithic socialist experiment. Carter's Assistant Secretary for Inter-American Affairs, Viron Vaky argued that the situation was

> open, confused, [and] fluid . . . A number of different currents are coursing through the place. There are Marxists there. As I indicated, it is not distinguishably Marxist in orientation, but Marxist figures are present in key positions . . . no ideological current predominates in the actual policy implementation at this time.

In addition, Ambassador to Managua, Lawrence Pezzullo added:

> They are confronted with so many basic problems to just survive that those problems dominate them. When you have one million people and you have unemployment running nearly 30 to 40 percent and you have petitioners outside of every Government office, ideology does not carry very far. So they are forced by reality into making pragmatic choices.

Pezzullo later elaborated in the hearing:

> It is very much a Nicaraguan phenomenon. There is no question about that. Sandinismo, whatever its opportunities ought to be, is a Nicaraguan, home-grown movement. Sandino predates Castro . . . There is no reason to believe they are going to go out and borrow from elsewhere when they really have something at home.[7]

During this period it is important to note, 'the FSLN was moving most concertedly against the far left, which . . . was suppressed earlier and more decisively than the right.' Both Cuba and the Soviet Union kept some distance from the Sandinistas, and urged them to maintain a mixed economy. The Carter administration initially tried to mediate between Somoza and the 'moderate' opposition to minimize the FSLN influence, but it ultimately shifted its attitude to one of 'cautious cordiality' to the new government. The Sandinistas could not rid themselves of the latent mistrust of the United States with the history of US intervention in Nicaragua and Washington was preoccupied with the Marxist element of the revolution. Yet the interests of both countries lay in the foundation of good relations. Nicaragua needed the foreign assistance to rebuild the economy; while Washington, though they had lost control of the insurrection, did not want to 'lose' Nicaragua. Policy makers were conscious of not repeating the events of 1959 and 1960: 'when US hostility drove the Cuban revolution into the arms of the Soviet Union.' Vaky explained:

> it is essential to supply aid to keep the monetary/economic system viable and enmeshed in the international economy, and to support the private sector. Failure to do so would leave the private sector abandoned and unable to compete with the currently stronger Sandinista structure.

To that end, the Carter administration requested $75 million for emergency economic aid to Nicaragua, though the request was postponed by opponents of the aid on the floor of the House of Representatives. They were concerned about aiding a 'pro-Cuban Marxist-dominated government'. The delay inhibited Carter's leverage in pursuing a relatively harmonious relationship. The aid was eventually signed into law seven months after it was requested, with several restrictions attached. Sixty percent had to go to the private sector, and could not go to projects involving Cuban personnel. This ensured that US aid would not be used for 'schools, the literacy campaign, health programs, or other reform measures for which Nicaragua' would likely turn to Cuban personnel for advice and support following their reforms in these areas. In addition, Carter had to make a presidential determination that the 'Government of Nicaragua has not cooperated with or harbors any international terrorist organization or is aiding, abetting, or supporting acts of violence or terrorism in other countries', which intended to 'contain' insurrection in other isthmian countries. Despite evidence from the 'intelligence community' that there were some weapons going to El Salvador, President Carter made the certification required of him by Public Law 96–304. A month later, as the evidence became more clear, the Carter administration froze the remaining $15 million, as the Salvadoran insurgents increased their efforts to overthrow the government in San Salvador.[8] By this time Ronald Reagan had been elected to the Presidency. His approach to the situation contrasted that of the Carter administration.

An assumption of international relations, that 'beliefs drive [and] facts only reward or punish', is central to understanding the change of attitude with the change of administration in Washington. Most succinctly put, Reagan believed the revolution was part of a 'Soviet–Cuban geostrategic thrust requiring a primarily military response. Whereas Carter sought stability through progress, Reagan focused on the maintenance of order.' The maintenance of national security in terms of real interests in Latin America included the need to maintain access to strategic raw materials, venues for military bases, regional military support and the preservation of sea lines of communication. While it is assumed in Washington that political instability threatens these interests, Lars Schoultz identifies two belief systems about the causes of instability: those who see instability deriving from poverty and inequality, and those who find the cause of instability in communism. In discussing these two causes of instability, Schoultz is mindful of the caveat provided by Lawrence Whitehead that 'perceptions in Washington of the Central American situation are what shape America's isthmian policies, and those perceptions have a surprisingly loose relationship to local realities'.[9]

Schoultz argues that reforms that are redistributive, aimed at reducing deprivation and injustice, are recognized in Washington as revolutionary; the ideological content of the reform movement is often of little consequence, except in so far as it can be used to shape US policy. Policy makers, though, have been divided on whether poverty or communism is to blame for the instability in the region. Furthermore, an additional division arose from the late 1970s onward, on whether the instability in the region was a threat to US security.[10]

The most credible evidence and arguments suggest the Nicaraguan revolution resulted from socio-economic inequality, not the exported Soviet revolution Reagan constantly referred to. In Nicaragua, Booth and Walker identify the disparity in the distribution of wealth, despite the 'impressive growth, policies of the [Somoza] government'. Real wages declined throughout the 1970s resulting in a drastic fall in purchasing power by 1979. Thus, 'employed, wage-earning Nicaraguans suffered a palpable drop in their ability to feed and shelter their families'. Coupled with this, several groups increased their popular mobilization during this period, and the FSLN, 'the only surviving rebel group of some twenty guerilla bands that had appeared between 1959 and 1962', expanded its links to other social movements and university students. The extreme repression of the Somoza government and the National Guard during this period 'drove thousands . . . to join the FSLN'.[11]

Communist parties had a negligible effect in Central America. While revolutionary groups may have accepted Marxist and Leninist tools of analysis, they did not necessarily pursue a Communist agenda, or serve

Moscow. Traditionally, official Communist Parties in the region have 'fared poorly' due to Soviet inflexibility on the pursuit of national solutions to their problems. Earlier, Moscow did not consider Latin America 'ripe' for revolution, through a doctrinal interpretation of Marxist history, and insisted Communist Parties find accommodation with local dictators. Thus Fidel Castro, frustrated with the Cuban Communist Party which under orders coexisted with Fulgencio Batista, fermented a broad popular revolution against the dictatorship. Similarly, in Nicaragua, the founders of the FSLN 'broke away from the pro-Soviet Nicaraguan Socialist Party precisely because the latter offered no national solutions to Nicaragua's problems.' At their strongest, Booth and Walker summarize, the Communist Parties 'remained weak, conservative, and generally unpopular'. The popular fronts that emerged in Nicaragua, El Salvador, and Guatemala, the Sandinista National Liberation Front (FSLN), the Farabundo Marti National Liberation Front (FMLN), and the Guatemalan National Revolutionary Union (URNG), respectively, were dominated by Marxist–Leninist leaders, who employed 'socialism's emphasis on distributive justice' to counter the injustices of their societies, but they were not subsumed in the Soviet system. Military and economic aid has been accepted from both Cuba and the Soviet Union, but also from any country that would provide aid, including several US NATO allies, and the limited provisions of the Carter administration. Nicaragua maintained a mixed economy and political pluralism.

The influence of Communism in the western hemisphere was often exaggerated given the decades of acute cultural animosity that had to some extent become institutionalized in Washington. Official Communist parties have been weak, and Marxist–Leninist movements have not prospered in the Central American countries such as Honduras and Costa Rica, where the regimes have not, historically, been excessively repressive.[12]

The US response or reaction to revolution in the western hemisphere has been fairly consistent, though some accommodation has been found when the revolutionary governments compromise on Washington's terms. An historical survey conducted by Cole Blasier on US responses to revolutionary change in Latin America during the twentieth century, draws conclusions relevant to the Nicaraguan experience. Two responses are identified. The Mexican and Bolivian revolutions found accommodation with the United States, while Guatemala and Cuba did not. Blasier explains:

> Compromises the Mexicans and Bolivians made to insure friendly relations with the United States and to secure U.S. economic assistance served to check radical elements within the two revolutionary parties,

while U.S. political, economic, and military support strengthened the hand of the moderates.

Suppressive policies toward Guatemala and Cuba tended to polarize these societies and radicalize opposition groups.

Initial accommodation by the Carter administration of the Sandinista regime, in providing economic assistance, and maintaining economic relations, gave Washington some leverage or influence over the FSLN. US ambassador to Nicaragua, Lawrence Pezzullo, used these contacts to curtail the more 'adventuresome' aspects of the new regime and their material support for the Salvadoran guerillas. The Reagan administration cut off the remaining economic aid, curtailed and eventually embargoed trade with Nicaragua, losing a vital component of US influence. 'The termination of aid,' Pezzullo argued, 'clearly signalled a tougher, more aggressive US policy stance . . . and made diplomatic accommodation less likely.' The tools used to modify the Mexican and Bolivian revolutions, economic incentives, were discarded. The tools used to remove the Guatemalan revolution and attempt to oust Castro, economic isolation and counter-revolutionary forces, were adopted in early 1981. Congressional opponents to the administration policy pointed out that this approach strengthened the position of the Sandinistas, as the Assistant Secretary of State for Inter-American Affairs in the Carter administration warned that:

> The Course of the Nicaraguan revolution will . . . depend in no small measure on how the U.S. perceives it and relates to it . . . We might write it off as already radicalized and beyond redemption, but that would surely drive the revolution into deeper radicalization.[13]

Carter's policy was to avoid these consequences.

The appointments by Reagan to the key positions concerned with Central America are indicative of the desire to minimize debate in the administration and to avoid complex policy analysis by removing the Foreign Service experts that had served Carter and previous administrations. Raymond Bonner describes the process as one of 'the most thorough purges in State Department history.' Schoultz, argues such terms are too strong to capture the accuracy of the process, but adds that an 'attempt was clearly made to simplify policy making by eliminating divergent policy perspectives'. The position of Assistant Secretary of State for Inter-American Affairs was filled by Thomas Ostrom Enders. He was the first 'in several decades without any prior experience in the region'. He had previously served in South East Asia, in Cambodia, where he came to the attention of Henry Kissinger, who promoted him to the position of Assistant

Secretary of State for Economic and Business Affairs. Enders had similarly impressed Alexander Haig, Reagan's first Secretary of State, who tasked him with stopping communism in Central America. The job of assistant secretary for Human Rights and Humanitarian Affairs went to Elliot Abrams after Reagan's first nominee was rejected. Abrams muted public criticism of right-wing dictatorships such as the Philippines, South Korea and Taiwan. He had briefly served Jeane Kirkpatrick at the United Nations, and eventually filled the position of the Assistant Secretary for Inter-American Affairs in 1985, after Langhorne Motley who replaced Enders in 1983 resigned. At the ambassadorial level Robert White was 'retired' by Haig. He had served each US president since Eisenhower, and was replaced in El Salvador by Deane R. Hinton who had four years experience in Latin America. In Honduras, Jack R. Binns was replaced by John D. Negroponte who had also come to the attention of Kissinger in Asia; he had one year experience in Ecuador. In Nicaragua, Lawrence Pezzullo kept his post on till August 1981. He was replaced by Anthony E. Quainton who had no Latin American experience, and did not speak Spanish. An area of policy in which disagreements were so profound required the Reagan administration, in Schoultz's view, 'to conduct something resembling a purge in order to make effective policy'. Personnel divisions, still, did not end there. Those in position within the various offices dealing with policy began forming alliances and distinctions within the conservative staff. The bureaucratic factions were split into 'hardline' conservatives and 'softline' conservatives. The effect of 'the skirmishes', Schoultz notes, changed the policy debate:

> The original question was: Is the instability in Central America caused by poverty or by Communist adventurism? Over time the question became: How much Communist adventurism exists? Poverty became irrelevant.[14]

While the revolutionary process in Nicaragua cannot be understood without reference to the extreme poverty and inequality, the Reagan administration tried to do just that. Local realities were subordinated to global ideas. While the Reagan administration argued that 'communists' exploited poverty, critics pointed out that there would be no revolution if poverty did not exist. Though economic aid was increased in numerical terms, it was reduced significantly as a percentage of the total aid to the region; military aid was increased at a disproportionate rate. US aid to Central America is broken into three major categories: military, Economic Support Fund (ESF), and economic. Between the years 1946 to 1980, military aid accounted for an average of 7.7% of total aid. During the

Reagan years military aid increased from 15.4% to 35.8% in 1984, dropping back to 21.1% in 1987. The average for the period was 23.4%, an increase of close to 200%. The rate of increase in Economic Support Funds was also drastic. Between 1946 and 1980 ESF allocations accounted for 3% of total aid. Under Reagan, the average was 43.8%. ESF aid is a combined assortment of various types of aid the United States furnishes, to support '*economic, political, and security policy* goals of the US' [emphasis added]. The Senate Democratic Policy Committee pointed out that,

> since 1951, ESF-type assistance has been used largely to support countries at war or under threat of war . . . it has helped to underwrite the costs of rebuilding Western European military capabilities, contributed in a large way to the war in Vietnam, helped the fight against communism in East Asia, and supported peace efforts in the Middle East. Under the Reagan Administration, it has been a significant component in aid to Central America.

With the significant increases in these two components of aid, the third component, purely economic aid, suffered. Between 1946 and 1980, economic aid averaged 89.3% of total aid to the region, under Carter it maintained this average, but under Reagan it began at 49.5% and dropped to 32.6%, averaging 32.8% for the years 1981 to 1987. The Congressional Budget Office estimated that the Reagan administration reduced spending on non-military programmes by $176 billion between 1982 and 1985.[15]

The emphasis on the military approach to the region was justified by the Reagan administration to counter the growing Soviet presence, and the attempts by the Sandinistas to export their revolution. As pointed out by Lars Schoultz, this had the effect of changing the terms of the debate on US policy towards Central America. Though the policy was, during the first Reagan administration, couched in terms of containing the revolution, during the initial months of Reagan's second term in office, the president made it clear he intended to change the 'structure' of the Sandinista government. A key member of the National Security Advisor's staff, Oliver North, opined that the 'resistance could be in Managua by the end of 1985'. The counterrevolutionary forces, however, had made it clear in 1981 that they intended to remove from power, and not simply contain, the Sandinistas.[16]

By 1985, the Reagan Doctrine had been enunciated. The matter of the doctrine was to 'roll back communism in the Third World' and support a conception of democracy to counter these forces. By 1986 the administration was more or less openly conducting 'covert' wars against the regimes in Nicaragua, Angola, Cambodia, and most forcefully, Afghanistan. The administration's imperative of containing the Sandinistas, presupposed a coordinated revolutionary agenda through out the isthmus. The object of containment was 'not to lose any additional countries to communism', rollback implied reversing the revolution in Nicaragua. William LeoGrande states that the policy makers in Washington, were divided on whether to contain the 'communists' in Managua, or remove them from power.[17]

The specific object of this book is to analyze the diplomatic relations conducted by the United States and the Sandinistas. The struggle over the formulation of policy toward the Sandinista revolution and the responses to the nationalist left regime provide a background to facilitate this objective. Accountability for the failure of the diplomatic processes to find accommodation must examine the role of diplomacy and negotiations in their interstate relationship, but also in the institutional structures of Washington. A negotiated agreement would have served both nations, but may not have served the particular interests of the Reagan administration; a credible, but failed negotiating process served their goals within the Reagan doctrine. His administration was bent on removing the Sandinistas from power, though they were constrained by popular opinion and the political inability to use direct US force in a protracted conflict. A 1987 study concluded:

> During Reagan's first year in office, opinion formed in opposition to the administration's policy and despite concerted efforts by the President and his chief foreign policy spokespersons, it has remained deeply critical ever since . . . The public does not believe that U.S. interests at stake in the region are as vital as the administration has portrayed them, and they are fearful that U.S. involvement will lead to 'another Vietnam'.

The policies were politically counter-productive and exacerbated regional tensions and polarities during a decade that was devastating in terms of lives lost, physical and psychological injuries sustained, and the opportunities forgone in social and economic development. The death toll from conflict was horrendous, but thousands of civilians were also murdered by some regional 'government security forces and associated "death squads" '. In El Salvador the 1993 report of the United Nations sponsored Truth Commission, *From Madness to Hope* blames the army for most of the atrocities committed during the period, while Washington remained a key ally.[18]

The International Court of Justice ruled in 1986 that several actions conducted in and against Nicaragua were in violation of international law. Multilateral diplomatic efforts were initiated to ease the tense bilateral relationship between the United States and Nicaragua. The aim of the

Contadora group was to avert war and further regional crisis, preserving the minimum conditions necessary to promote economic development.

It is important to understand the role of the administration in persistently seeking aid for the contras; and to understand the relation of this issue in both the multilateral and bilateral negotiations. The insistence by Washington to support the contras was a vital component in the diplomatic processes that were conducted during the decade. Finally, an important factor in comprehending the diplomatic activities were the divisions among the staff of President Reagan. Washington intended to remove the Sandinistas from power. It is, therefore, vital to understand the role of negotiations in the attempts to implement the Reagan Doctrine. Negotiations were used to demonstrate to Congress that the administration had, indeed, tried to seek peaceful solutions to the differences between the two governments, and that these had failed. If, however, the purpose was to avoid accommodation of the Sandinista revolution within the western hemisphere, the failure of the process was intended. Certain staff members who sought only to contain the revolution in Nicaragua were not given enough authority and were manoeuvred out of their posts; they were constrained by the latitude within which they could operate. The power struggles between staff members, and between the branches of government, coupled with the lax managerial style of the president, impeded the clear formulation of a coherent policy toward the Sandinista regime.[19] Washington's refusal to demobilize the contras blocked the security agreements under Contadora, and caused half of the Central American Peace Plan to fail.

The analysis of negotiations between the United States and Nicaragua is one of misunderstanding, division, and intolerance, dominated by beliefs that did not accord with the reality of the western hemisphere. Compromise, a necessary tool of diplomacy, was constantly frustrated by voices representing the US desire for hegemony. The Sandinistas did not intend to compromise their sovereignty.

# 1 Diplomacy and Counterrevolution 1981–1982

## ARMS TRANSFER TO EL SALVADOR

After the first direct talks in August 1981 US Assistant Secretary for Inter-American Affairs, Thomas Enders, stated in his first letter to the Coordinator of the Nicaraguan junta, Daniel Ortega:

> the continued use of Nicaraguan territory to support and funnel arms to insurgent movements in the area would pose an insurmountable barrier to the development of normal relations between us. Unless this support is ended now, I can see no way that our proposed dialogue can bear fruit. A halt to the use of Nicaraguan territory for these purposes is, in fact, the sine qua non of a normal relationship.

The impasse to substantial negotiations was set early. Alarmist rhetoric by Reagan administration officials on communism reaching the Rio Grande and California set the tone of subsequent public diplomacy. Central America was defined as the testing ground for the administration, where 'the line' would be drawn against the advance of communism. Cuba was the source of the troubles in Central America and the Soviet Union the 'banker' of their operations. Secretary of State Alexander Haig talked of 'going to the source' to solve the problem of communist intervention.[1]

Within two days of Reagan's inauguration, the United States suspended payment of Economic Support Funds to Nicaragua citing a continued flow of arms to El Salvador. Haig told Ambassador Rita Delia Casco the United States would not just cut off economic aid, but was willing 'to do other things as well'. While the move obviously hurt Nicaragua, their Agricultural Minister, Jamie Wheelock, pointed out that sovereignty was the most important consideration of the revolution, and that the economic considerations were not as important, hence the aggressive act would be resisted. A member of the Nicaraguan junta and later a contra leader, Arturo Cruz, predicted that the perceived aggression would radicalize the revolution.[2]

For US policy makers the issue was a catalyst to further division. US Ambassador to Nicaragua, Lawrence Pezzullo, described as the driving force behind Carter's $158 million aid package, viewed economic aid as an indispensable tool of diplomacy. 'The cut off of aid,' he later pointed out, 'naturally diminished our diplomatic leverage.' It could have maintained the pluralistic dimension of the Sandinista revolution, providing enough incentive to avoid a Cuban type dependency on the Soviet Union.[3] By and large his advice was ignored in Washington.

Europe and Latin American governments did not share Reagan's view of Nicaragua's revolution which was perceived as a problem in Washington who saw a need to 'develop a more realistic appreciation of the situation in Central America'. The State Department put out a White Paper on 23 February 1981 titled 'Communist Interference in El Salvador', based on documents professedly captured from Salvadoran guerrillas, it purported to show:

> Definitive evidence of a clandestine military support given by the Soviet Union, Cuba, and their communist allies to Marxist–Leninist guerillas now fighting to overthrow the established Government of El Salvador.

Though Assistant Secretary of State Bushnell acknowledged evidence suggested that Nicaraguan arms to the FMLN had stopped in the last 'couple of weeks', the use of their territory for such purposes must stop to have a relationship with the United States. Though the White Paper was subsequently discredited, at the time US intelligence did not have evidence of the alleged flow of weapons. Former US ambassador to El Salvador Robert White pointed out the most important source of weapons for the Salvadoran guerrillas was the international black market centred in the United States, and alleged that elements of the Salvadoran military sold weapons to the guerrillas 'even before they got out of their crates'.[4]

Pezzullo held ten meetings with the Sandinistas between January and March 1981 to impress the administration's 'mind set.' Pezzullo was armed with

> an intelligence windfall [that] indicated clearly that the Sandinistas had consorted with the FMLN in passing arms through Nicaragua to El Salvador . . . While the Sandinistas held to the fiction that they were not involved in arms trafficking, our independent reporting indicated they were closing off the channels and telling the FMLN that it was due to U.S. pressure. It was clear that my message that a good relationship with the United States was vital to their security was getting through.

Pezzullo was summoned to Washington before the release of the White Paper where he indicated that the diplomatic pressure was working, the transhipments had 'been substantially reduced.' But his diplomacy was ignored. Pezzullo suspected that Reagan, Haig and Enders ignored the real evidence because they had little faith in Sandinista actions or words and they were being persuaded by the advocates of a 'covert, destabilization effort.' US intelligence nevertheless indicated that the transhipment of arms had ceased. Former US intelligence analyst, David McMichael, later testified to the International Court of Justice that there was no detection of arms shipments during the period of his employment at the Central Intelligence Agency. Though he did not start work till March 1981 he had reviewed previous material, and asserted there was evidence for such activities in late 1980 and 'very early 1981'. McMichael also testified that the existing evidence did not establish that the Sandinista Government was responsible for the arms traffic. The Court ruling of 1986 established:

> an intermittent flow of arms was routed via the territory of Nicaragua . . . the evidence is insufficient to satisfy the court that, since the early months of 1981, assistance has continued to reach the Salvadoran armed opposition from the territory of Nicaragua on any significant scale, or that the Government of Nicaragua was responsible for any flow of arms at either period.[5]

The exaggeration of the US case was predominantly for domestic public consumption and for regional allies. Pezzullo, White, and the head of the US interests section in Cuba, Wayne Smith, all rejected the administration claims. Support for the allegation began to erode when members of the House Foreign Operations Appropriations Subcommittee declared themselves 'wary' of Reagan's policy after listening to Robert White's testimony. Haig's rhetoric was similarly disaffecting the public, prompting Chief of Staff, James Baker, to insist that it stop in favour of a low key approach to the issues. Nevertheless, Haig publicly asserted that the Sandinistas were merely looking for new routes to infiltrate El Salvador, and to stop these activities he stated 'I would intervene if necessary'. Pezzullo argued the administration could have dealt with such matters 'diplomatically if we had chosen to pursue that path'. Haig had established from the Soviet ambassador to Washington, Anatoly Dobrynin, that Moscow was not interested in the Western Hemisphere, and that matters lay between the United States and Cuba, which allowed for a quick solution through 'the unequivocal application of pressure' while Reagan 'still enjoyed the freedom of action he had won at the polls'. Despite administration rhetoric, Haig subsequently acknowledged that it was not an East West global problem. While Smith and Pezzullo drew the conclusion, that negotiations offered the best means to achieve their aims, 'Haig concluded the exact opposite'. The United States 'had a free hand to resolve the problem through *military* means, without fear of Soviet retaliation' [emphasis in original].[6]

By this time the CIA had sent a covert action proposal to the State Department to 'counter Cuban subversion in Central America.' The finding signed by Reagan on 9 March invoking the national security of the United States intended to:

> Provide all forms of training, equipment and related assistance to cooperating governments throughout Central America in order to counter foreign sponsored subversion and terrorism. [Excised] encourage and influence foreign governments around the world to support all the above objectives.[7]

El Salvador received military aid to improve their ability to interdict the alleged weapons despite section 502 (b) of the Foreign Assistance Act of 1961 prohibiting security assistance to countries engaged in violating human rights.

Economic aid to Nicaragua was suspended on 1 April despite a State Department acknowledgment that Nicaragua's response had been positive, and there had been 'no hard evidence of arms movements through Nicaragua during the past few weeks'. *The New York Times* cited an official spokesperson who remained 'concerned . . . that some arms traffic may be continuing and that other support very probably continues'. The messages from Washington were confusing. The Nicaraguan junta released a communique describing the aid cut off as:

> A concrete display of an aggressive will against Nicaragua on the part of those sectors within the present U.S. administration which are radically hostile to our revolution and who seek, through this type of act, to impose their hegemonic interests on our country. . . . An alleged traffic of arms from Nicaragua to El Salvador is employed as a pretext to justify this aggression. Such a falsity has been rejected energetically by our government on each occasion it has been conjured.

Pezzullo agreed with this assessment. 'The termination of aid', he later wrote 'clearly signalled a tougher, more aggressive US policy stance and made a diplomatic solution less likely.' The confusion and division was related to the Senate Committee on Foreign Relations by Robert White who argued that Central Americans had the impression that Washington intended to destabilize Nicaragua, and administration division created confusion; the most important thing in foreign policy, he testified, was 'to speak with one voice'.[8]

Pezzullo believed the proposal to terminate the aid came from National

Security Advisor, Richard Allen. Enders, new in the job, 'may have not seen the significance of conceding on this crucial issue,' though Pezzullo emphasized the point to him. Maintaining some leverage was all-important for a diplomatic solution. Historically, Pezzullo points out,

> Central Americans have had notoriously permeable borders through the years and there was no reason to believe that conditions would change at a time when a revolutionary regime sat cheek to jowl with a revolutionary guerilla movement. The real issue was the flow of a *substantial* amount of arms and the evidence was never there to make that case. Further, I was convinced that we could, and did, temper the flow by pressing the Sandinistas diplomatically.[9]

## THE SANDINISTA MILITARY BUILDUP

US tolerance of Nicaraguan exile camps in Florida seemed to confirm a destabilization programme. The subsequent Sandinistas military buildup was used in the diplomatic process as further evidence of aggressive intentions. *The New York Times* reported that the Florida camps held six hundred exiles dominated by former Somoza Guardsmen and were determined to liberate Sandinista Nicaragua. Nicaragua's Foreign Minister, Miguel D'Escoto, lodged a complaint on the camps and congressional representative, Gerry Studds, requested a 'categoric assurance' that the US government was not cooperating with these groups, but both received a similar reply that investigations were being conducted. By this time the media were reporting that the exiles in the camps planned to invade Nicaragua. The Nicaraguan Democratic Union had requested assistance from President-elect Reagan in December 1980 to support an invasion but had not received a reply. Their letter went on to state that:

> It is logical to suppose that the armed forces of the Central American countries would have a favorable attitude towards the liberation movement of Nicaragua and would give it their utmost support.

Another letter drafted on 6 January from Richard Allen, on behalf of Reagan, stated that the relevant 'policy people' would be 'made aware of your ideas and suggestions in this area'.[10]

Nicaragua's armed forces had grown to 35 000 people, large enough to hold off US forces till public opinion was mobilized against an intervention. The growth responded to the greater cohesion among the other Central American armies. Honduran forces concentrated on Nicaragua, not their traditional enemy El Salvador. Nicaraguan troops were mobilized in response to the increasing incursions into its territory by exile groups. In a confidential memorandum the new designated Assistant Secretary for Inter-American Affairs, Thomas Enders, wrote:

> Incidences in the past months [have] resulted from armed incursions from Nicaragua by ex-Somocista guardsmen . . . Nicaragua's nervousness is stimulated by the raids by Honduran based exiles who receive support from certain . . . military sources.

Pointedly, the Nicaraguan and Honduran governments met in El Guasaule and agreed the border clashes had not been intended by either government.[11]

While Arturo Cruz, the new Nicaraguan Ambassador to Washington, pointed out the camps necessitated the Sandinista build-up, Nicaragua's economy was also hindered by the need to remain in a 'defensive military posture'. It would be a mistake, Cruz suggested, to

> do something rash. To make a decision without a reasonable dialogue would be regrettable, even for future generations. I'm really concerned that this administration might give the 'go' to a policy of total isolation or even something worse.[12]

## THE AUGUST 1981 TALKS

Negotiations were vital to Nicaragua and they had requested them first. Enders wanted to prevent the covert option through diplomacy and, according to Roy Gutman, he made a deal with the influential Congressman Jesse Helms in which he would have six months to negotiate with the Sandinistas after which, he conceded 'we'll do whatever you want'. Helms gave him a year.[13] But Enders had not accounted for the opposition from within the executive branch which reduced his latitude to negotiate.

Though Enders acknowledged the revolution was 'irreversible', and a 'necessary fact', his belligerent tone in Managua did not encourage compromise. An exchange between Enders and Bayardo Arce demonstrated the distrust between the participants. Enders warned: 'You can do your thing, but do it within your borders, or else we're going to hurt you.' Arce replied, 'All right come on in, we'll meet you man to man. You will kill us but you will pay for it. You will have to kill us all to do it.' Enders demanded a halt to the alleged arms flow which the United Stated would monitor. Daniel Ortega explained their sympathy with the Salvadoran people, though confirmed that the Junta and the National Directorate had already decided against arms support. Ortega requested US intelligence to identify the substance of the allegations, but Enders refused, stating the US intelligence sources would be compromised.[14] In fact US intelligence indicated no arms were going into El Salvador via the territory of Nicaragua.

Enders' concession that the Sandinistas could pursue their policies within their borders invited criticism from other US officials. Enders was criticized for not stressing the Sandinista military buildup or the process of democratization; administration hardliners considered Nicaragua's internal affairs problematic. Constantine Menges later accused him and the State Department of pursuing its own agenda, 'without interagency agreement', and without stressing the Sandinista democratic commitments made to the Organization of American States in 1979. According to Menges, Enders told him to get serious, 'there is no chance for democracy in Nicaragua.' While Enders offered the possibility of accommodation between Washington and Managua he told the Sandinistas they may be 'too far advanced on the wrong road.' He offered three incentives for improved relations: the United States would not use the threat of force; the administration would consider the exiles training camps; and aid may be resumed. These were just incentives, not firm commitments, and the Sandinistas could not guarantee Enders spoke for the government of the United States. Written proposals or agreements were not reached or presented at these talks, though Bob Woodward points out that Enders cabled Haig saying an accord could be reached. Haig replied, 'I'll believe it when I see it, and meanwhile lets not hold up on the other plans.' After the talks D'Escoto reiterated Nicaragua's desire to improve relations:

> We have made it a priority to make every effort to reach an understanding, a modus vivendi, with the United States. We don't expect the Reagan administration to like our revolution, but at least to accept it as an irreversible reality and to respect it. We want a new relationship of dignity and respect and not one of docility and servility.

The existence of dialogue in itself was beneficial. Pezzullo even believed there was a possibility for agreement, but 'the hardliners in Washington thwarted Enders', and Managua was 'bereft of statesmen'.[15]

## CLARIFYING THE TALKS

As previously arranged, Lawrence Pezzullo resigned on 18 August 1981. The failure to replace him for seven months suggested Washington was not interested in a dialogue. Enders' first letter to Ortega was delivered among the growing tensions between the two countries. On 31 August 1981, he wrote that the 'demonstration of good will' could possibly bring 'peace to Central America.' A series of illustrative drafts for the normalization of relations, 'will leave Nicaragua strong and secure, they will serve to reinforce the countries national independence.' The first draft arrived a week later on 8 September, indicating a move against the exile camps, which Nicaragua did not consider a concession as US law required such action irrespective of Sandinista behaviour. Denigrating any sense of confidence, a formal note was attached to the draft cancelling the remaining $7 million aid.[16]

A second draft arrived on 16 September proposing a commitment, in accordance with the United Nations, Organization of American States, and the Inter-American Treaty of Reciprocal Assistance, to settle disputes by 'peaceful means'; the condemnation of the threat or use of force; and a commitment to refrain from assisting armed activities originating in either country. Two days later US military manoeuvres for early October were announced. Notwithstanding Enders' second draft, D'Escoto informed Haig and the UN Security Council that the military exercises caused Nicaragua serious concern and that they would have to adopt a state of alert to defend their freedom.[17]

Enders replied on behalf of Haig that the exercises were routine, and did not threaten Nicaragua. The lack of coordination and the conflicting moves by the administration severely harmed the diplomatic process. Official communication was discontinued. Enders' deputy Craig Johnstone, had drafted a proposal addressing Nicaragua's arms buildup, in which he demanded that Soviet tanks be re-crated and sent back. According to Roy Gutman the draft was presented to Nicaragua's ambassador in Washington, Arturo Cruz, who later explained:

> I was flabbergasted. If that was my reaction as a moderate, think of what the reaction would have been in Managua. I told them, this sounds like the conditions of a victorious power.

Johnstone later told Cruz to forget the draft. Curiously, Cruz never presented it to his superiors in Managua.[18]

The following day US Deputy Representative to the United Nations Adelman charged that US efforts at seeking a dialogue had only been met with rhetoric and distortion. 'The fact is', he imputed:

> Nicaragua is helping subvert its neighbours, while building a force which can generate an even more fundamental threat.... Unlike other major

> powers, the United States has never had any imperialist designs or become a colonial power in Central America.

To Nicaraguans these statements represented a fundamental distortion of US history in the isthmus. Their revolution had been named after Agusto Sandino who fought US occupation of Nicaragua earlier in the century.[19]

## BEGINNING DIRECT COVERT ACTION

Inter-departmental disputes resulted in public confusion on the administration's military intentions; these were finally placated by a presidential statement which asserted there were 'no plans' to introduce 'Americans in combat,' but he also asserted, contrary to the evidence, that they opposed the 'exported revolution' coming from the Soviets and Cubans. While use of US combat troops was officially dismissed, Haig refused to assure the House Foreign Affairs Committee that the United States would not destabilize Nicaragua. After an exchange in the committee with Haig, Michael Barnes concluded, 'If I were a Nicaraguan, I'd be building a bomb shelter this afternoon.'[20] Over the next week, seven Latin American countries expressed their concern of an imminent US intervention. Thus the earlier effort to gain regional support had deteriorated.

The National Security Council met on 16 November 1981, to approve a covert action programme against Nicaragua. A week later the National Security Decision Directive (NSDD) 17 authorized the CIA to work with foreign 'governments as appropriate'; to conduct operations against the Cuban presence; to create a force of 500 people, which were to join 1 000 Argentines already in the area. A supporting document claimed it might be necessary to use US personnel to create a proper support base. Bob Woodward points out that further division was created in the CIA around this proposal. Robert Inman, Deputy Director of Central Intelligence, argued that the covert operation should start after diplomatic negotiations had failed. Enders, who made the original presentation, countered that negotiations must be restored to prevent the use of the US military; covert action should not overthrow the Sandinistas but, 'harass the government, waste it'.[21]

A further covert action finding was signed by Reagan on 1 December, relating to the 'National Security of the United States', to 'support and conduct [excised] paramilitary operations against [excised] Nicaragua'. Congressional Committees investigating the Iran–Contra Affair concluded that this 'purpose' conflicted with the official explanation given, that the operation was designed to interdict arms to the FMLN. A finding signed for one purpose and used for another makes the notification of congress a meaningless process; 'a Finding becomes a blank check for the intelligence agency and defeats the notion of Presidential accountability under the Hughes Ryan law.' It ceases at this point, they concluded, to be a 'self-limiting document.' Apart from these legislative complaints, Theodore Draper also points out that this was the third document which authorized CIA activities in Central America during 1981. In March, the anti-Sandinista programme became a more general Central American operation; the November decision (NSDD 17), provided support to the contras; the effect of the December finding was to cover 'up this decision by stating that the US aim was merely to interdict the flow of arms from Nicaragua to El Salvador'.[22]

Basic questions had not been addressed. Robert McFarlane later asserted that there was 'no framework in which to analyze' the December CIA proposal for covert action, and noted that covert activity was not an adequate tool to deal with the threat the administration portrayed. Furthermore, Congress regarded covert action as 'an adjunct of policy, not as its foundation, and surely not a vehicle for waging war with a Soviet proxy'. He argued the administration was not forced to think systematicaly about 'the fatal risks they were running'.[23]

While there were no proposals presented at the talks in Managua during August, and the exchange of diplomatic letters could not establish a mutually agreed basis for further negotiation, they did, however, provide some evidence for congressional and public consumption that diplomacy had been tried. Managua accurately perceived that they would have to alter their revolution to negotiate a peaceful relationship with Washington. Daniel Ortega told the State Legislative Council that they had left 'the door open to understanding', but: 'We do not accept the door that the Americans are opening for us because [it] is too small . . . so small that in order to pass through it, we would have to do it on our knees and we are not going to do that.' The Sandinistas did, nevertheless, initiate a strategy of concessions during exchanges, to maintain the momentum of diplomacy. The failure of all diplomatic processes would have been detrimental to the security of Nicaragua. In Washington appearance was all important; Enders testified to Congress that 'diplomatic means to achieve a rapprochement' had been tried, but little progress was made.[24] Enders position had changed since August due to pressure from within the administration, and the democratization of Nicaragua became the focus of US diplomacy.

## LOW LEVEL DIPLOMACY

The appointment of Anthony Quainton in March 1982 was one of a number of significant changes in the personnel involved in foreign policy generally, and Central America specifically. On 4 January, William Clark, an associate of the President, moved from the position of Haig's deputy to replace Richard Allen as National Security Advisor. In his new position he rivaled Haig in the formation of policy, and power shifted away from the State Department. With an expanded role for the NSA, Clark had a direct reporting relationship with Reagan. These staff changes indicated that Enders' limited search for a diplomatic solution was further denigrated in pursuit of a more forceful policy.[25]

Given the absence of proof for the official contra rationale of interdiction D'Escoto charged that the sustained allegations were not only a 'deliberate lie', to justify the 'involvement in the war in El Salvador', but also that the United States did not want to resolve the issue, to sustain its accusations of the continued arms flow. D'Escoto could not assert arms were not going to El Salvador, but confirmed the Nicaraguan government was not providing 'this service to the guerillas'. Reagan's Ambassador to the United Nations, Jeane Kirkpatrick, referred to D'Escoto's charge as 'false and absurd', asserting they had intelligence that showed, 'categorically that arms pass through Nicaragua on their way to Salvador regularly'. She remarked the United States could not say how much the Sandinistas knew about occurrences on its territory, but asserted the flow was 'large and beyond reasonable doubt' and that Nicaragua's sympathy for the Salvadorans was a 'matter of public record'. US allies in Europe and Latin America, or congressional representatives who had asked for proof were mainly directed to the discredited White Paper of February 1981, D'Escoto charged. Kirkpatrick asserted US policies were widely supported by these governments, but they kept trading with Nicaragua, did not share Washington's concern of the Sandinistas, and France previously recognized the FMLN as a legitimate political force in El Salvador.[26]

The first significant contra action took place in mid-March 1982. Edgar Chamorro, who later joined the Nicaraguan Democratic Force (FDN), recounted:

> The first military successes of the organization came in March 1982, when CIA trained saboteurs blew up two vital bridges in northern Nicaragua . . . 1982 was a year of transition for the FDN. From a collection of small, disorganized and ineffectual bands of ex-National Guardsmen,

> the FDN grew into a well organized, well armed, well equipped and well trained fighting force of approximately 4 000 men capable of inflicting great harm on Nicaragua. This was due entirely to the CIA, which organized, armed, equipped, trained and supplied us.[27]

Interdiction was of minimal significance, a National Security Council document from that time stated that 'we have a vital interest in not allowing the proliferation of Cuba-model states.' The objective in the short run was to 'eliminate Cuban/Soviet influence in the region', with the long run aim of building 'politically stable governments able to withstand such influences'. The document noted in addition:

> the Sandinistas are under increased pressure as a result of our covert efforts and because of the poor state of their economy. For the first time the Sandinistas have cause to doubt whether they can export subversion with impunity.[28]

The timing of the first diplomatic initiative for 1982 is important, casting doubt on the reasons for the covert action. The argument that it was needed to pressurize the Sandinistas to negotiate was belied by the fact that the bridges were blown up three weeks after a Sandinista peace proposal was presented on 24 February. The covert action undertaken was not part of any diplomatic initiative.

On 19 and 20 February, Nicaragua hosted a meeting of the Permanent Conference of Political Parties in Latin America (COPPPAL), which acknowledged the Sandinista peace proposal and emphasized the socio-economic roots of the current crisis. They argued the Sandinistas had maintained the principles of non-alignment and political pluralism, and rebuked the formation of the US supported Central American Democratic Community a month earlier, declaring:

> There do not exist universally valid formulas for building democratic societies. Each country's efforts to find its own path towards justice and liberty according to its particular historic experience and social reality must be respected.[29]

The Central American Democratic Community was formed on 19 January 1982, made up of Costa Rica, El Salvador, Honduras, Colombia, Venezuela and the United States; Guatemala joined later. Nicaragua, Panama, and Belize were excluded. They aimed to promote democratic values and representative democracy; to respect human rights and condemn terrorism; and to eliminate the causes of underdevelopment and exploitation. They declared Central America 'a region of peace', condemning 'any kind of interference in the internal affairs' of these countries, and argued the arms race detracted from the regional economic development.[30]

Shortly after the COPPPAL meeting, the Coordinator of the Nicaraguan Junta, Daniel Ortega, publicized their peace proposal, which primarily addressed their security concerns: they would remain non-aligned; sought 'non-aggression and mutual security agreements' with their neighbours; and called for joint patrols of their frontiers with both Honduras and Costa Rica to prevent activities by 'elements disaffected towards any of the three Governments'. It offered to open talks on any subject with the United States and, importantly, it outlined its needs, aspirations, and propositions in point five:

> On the basis of the fullest respect for the national sovereignty of Nicaragua, non-interference in its internal affairs, non-encouragement from outside of counterrevolutionary activities, non-aggression in the economic field, respect for the right to receive international cooperation and to aspire to a just international economic order – in short, in circumstances which do not compel it to take strict measures for defense and survival – Nicaragua remains disposed to build on its revolution and its progress, within the framework of a mixed economy, pluralism and non-alignment, and to hold democratic elections not later than 1985.[31]

Following Ortega's presentation, Mexican President, José López Portillo, immediately supported Nicaragua urging it to stay on the path it had chosen. He did not defend a particular ideology but the principle of self determination. 'The winds which blow over the region,' he assured the United States:

> do not represent an intolerable danger for the basic interests and the national security of the United States but rather, on the other hand, the risk of historical condemnation for violent trampling on the rights of peoples which without a doubt the United States would claim for themselves, the rights to self determination in independence, dignity and the exercise of its sovereignty . . . the United States must discard any threat or use of force directed against Nicaragua. It is dangerous, unworthy, and unnecessary.

The Nicaraguan 'path' had been outlined by the Sandinistas to the Organization of American States (OAS) in July 1979 in which they pledged to hold the first free elections *this century*. Reagan, however, misinformed the OAS that the Sandinistas had broken their promises, by postponing the elections till 1985.[32]

Democratization, political pluralism, the internal affairs of Nicaragua increasingly emerged as issues around which proposals were formed, though technically they remained the sovereign preserve of Nicaragua. Ironically, the future Central American agreement in 1987 partly found success by first concentrating on the internal situation of Nicaragua. The security issues on military levels, the contras in Honduras, the FMLN in El Salvador, and the relationship of the United States and Nicaragua to these groups respectively were never resolved around the negotiating table while the Sandinistas remained in power. Despite the constant rhetorical references to the Soviet threat, security issues progressively lost ground to internal affairs.

## THE QUAINTON PROPOSALS

Domestic and regional pressure to negotiate began in late February 1982 when 106 members of Congress urged Reagan to accept the Mexican initiative. Fidel Castro indicated Cuban support for the Mexican initiative, if the United States committed itself 'not to invade its neighbours'. On 8 April the State Department summarized eight points Ambassador Quainton had orally presented to Managua the day before, a formal paper was not left with the Sandinistas, though they received one six weeks after they requested it. The proposals were regarded as an expansion of Enders' 1981 talks and retained the precondition that had blocked substantial progress to date. Now, however, Haig told Congress that the administration had 'unchallengable' proof of 'Nicaraguan involvement in El Salvador and Cuban involvement in the command and control of the operations in El Salvador.' His statements were buttressed by the chairman of the Senate Intelligence Committee, Barry Goldwater, who indicated an intelligence review 'left no doubt that there is active involvement by Sandinista government officials in support of the Salvadoran guerilla movement'. And two days later the Chairman of the House Permanent Select Committee on Intelligence, Edward Boland, made similar claims. Haig used these statements after he met Mexico's Foreign Minister Jorge Castañeda on 6 March, to indicate the inadequacies of the Mexican peace proposal because it 'did not address in specific terms Nicaraguan involvement in El Salvador which we feel is an essential and primary aspect of a negotiated solution'.[33]

Furthermore, an NSC summary paper, 'US Policy in Central America and Cuba through F. Y. [fiscal year] '84', asserted 'Cuba and Nicaragua retain the ability to continue or even increase their support for insurgencies and terrorist groups, particularly in Honduras and Costa Rica, where their activities are increasing.' It also noted there had been 'increasing effectiveness of the arms interdiction effort but substantial arms continue to get through'. Yet in May 1982 the CIA admitted to Congress that not a single cache of arms had been interdicted; Ambassador Hinton asked about this by the Senate Foreign Relations Committee a year later replied, 'not a pistola' had been captured. Cuba assured Wayne Smith arms were not being sent to Nicaragua. He pressed the State Department several times for contradictory evidence, and after prevarication finally received a cable from Washington indicating it had no hard evidence of the continued movement of arms.[34]

The indispensable condition for negotiations was largely fictitious, and therefore precluded any progress Nicaragua could demonstrate to eliminate the problem. The attempts by Nicaragua to come to terms with this – Borge indicated the CIA should simply show Nicaragua where the weapons were; Ramirez called for joint border patrols – were not responded to. After all, according to the imposed logic, these issues could not be considered till the problem was solved. While Nicaragua provided other support to the FMLN, the demand that they act unilaterally on this insubstantial allegation to gain access to the US negotiating table precluded accommodation while maintaining the appearance of diplomatic activity.

## THE MILITARIZATION OF CENTRAL AMERICA

Central America was dramatically militarized during the 1980s with increased supplies from both superpowers. Quainton's fourth point dealt with the problem, calling for an arms limitation and a 'regional ban on the importation of heavy *offensive* weapons' [emphasis added].[35] While this was a proposal, negotiation on it did not take place because of the precondition to talks set in Washington. It was dealt with, instead, in a variety of public and private venues, often misleading, and obfuscating the issues involved.

On 8 March DCI Casey asserted that the Soviet Union had been violating the Kennedy–Khrushchev agreement of 1963 for the past twenty years by the importation of offensive weapons by Cuba. The next day officials from the CIA and the Defense Intelligence Agency (DIA) gave a public presentation at the State Department on Nicaragua's military buildup. The presentation was introduced by the Deputy Director of Central Intelligence, Bobby Inman, and the technical information was presented by the Deputy Director for Intelligence and External Affairs for the DIA, John Hughes. Hughes had twenty years earlier presented a similar briefing at the beginning of the Cuban missile crisis. The intention was to review Cuban and 'other Communist nations' efforts to provide modern equipment to the Sandinista army. Specifically he stated that the 'combined military force is now the largest in Central America and totals up to 70 000 men'; and that the 'Sandinistas are achieving military force levels and capabilities that are in excess of those normally required purely for defensive purposes.' The assumption that Nicaragua would automatically use their weapons for offensive purposes was misleading. Political scientist, Kenneth Sharpe, pointed out that 'in the light of recent history – CIA backed invasions of Guatemala and Cuba by exiles – the Nicaraguans are rational in strengthening their military.' Further, he argued Soviet weapons as opposed to Soviet bases in Nicaragua were not a security threat to the United States.[36]

Hughes' presentation ignored these questions, leaving the impression of a US containment of an aggressive power. The presentation did not deal with the rapid build-up in other regional countries financed and supplied by Washington. There had been a 'sharp change from traditional composition of US aid to the region.' A congressional research body found that:

> Between 1946 and 1980, only 7.7 percent of U.S. aid was for military assistance. In FY [fiscal year] 1979 and 1980, the last two years of the Carter Administration, military aid to Central America was more or less consistent with this historical level: 2.2 percent in FY 1979 and 5.2 percent in FY 1980. In 1981, the first year of the Reagan administration, the proportion of military assistance rose to 15.4 percent of total aid, and in FY 1982 continued upward to 25.5 percent.

In concrete terms military aid to Central America from the United States jumped from $2.3 million in 1979 to $115.4 million in 1982. The main recipients of this aid were El Salvador ($82 million), Honduras ($31.3 million), and Costa Rica ($2.1 million). Thus even administration figures for Nicaragua's military buildup were marginally less than El Salvador's, and even the Kissinger Commission acknowledged the first delivery of 'sophisticated Soviet electronic gear' took place in December 1982, a year after covert activities started. The presentation ignored Managua's agreement with France for $16 million in arms. In addition, while the Hughes briefing put Nicaragua's armed forces 70 000, the International Institute for Strategic Studies put the figure at 21 500; with El Salvador's at 16 000 and Honduras' at 11 700.[37]

The amount of weaponry, as presented by Hughes, or the increases in weaponry, as presented here, obscure their nature and therefore their use. In September 1982 a retired marine Lieutenant-Colonel, John Buchanan, referring specifically to the 9 March briefing, testified to Congress that his intelligence gathering ability was not as extensive as high US officials, 'but I do have enough military training and knowledge to see that a smoke screen is being laid.' Soviet weapons supplied to Nicaragua were wholly inadequate for regional offensive operations. Soviet T–55 tanks would be severely constrained by the terrain between Nicaragua and its neighbours. Buchanan suggested:

> One can only conclude that the Reagan administration is distorting the facts in order to justify covert operations aimed at overthrowing the Sandinistas and an unprecedented military buildup in Honduras.

The following day the Permanent Select Committee on Intelligence released a report which acknowledged the result of the briefing in March 'conveyed an implicit judgement about Nicaragua's objectives not entirely consistent with DIA's reasoned judgement, [which] detracted from its informative value.' The report conceded the briefing emphasized the 'capability to launch offensive operations', and the 'analytic judgements about Nicaragua's intentions were quite distinct from those that appeared implicit in the briefing on the build-up.' The photographs used at the briefing prompted Daniel Ortega to denounce the violations of Nicaragua's air space by the United States. 'Nicaragua' Ortega told the United Nations:

> rejects the attempt by the United States to impose humiliating restrictions on its inescapable prerogatives with respect to national defense . . . We feel that we are all obliged to find a solution to the problems facing the region through negotiated, political means, and to never consider the possibility of negotiations to have been exhausted. We think that all efforts must be directed towards finding responses that are congruent with reality, that allow us to begin negotiations right away, discarding preconditions of any kind.[38]

In December 1981 Wayne Smith was informed by Cuban senior foreign policy adviser Carlos Martinez Salsamendi, that they had suspended all shipments of equipment to Nicaragua in the hope of improving the prospects for negotiations. 'Don't misunderstand me', Martinez told Smith, Cuba reserved the right to supply Nicaragua but hoped the suspension would create a positive momentum. Smith reported the information directly to Haig. The subsequent administration acknowledgment to Smith that it had no hard evidence of Cuban shipments of arms to Central America, demonstrated their contempt for 'objective evidence'. Washington had based its policies on ideological preconceptions divorced from Cuban or Nicaraguan behaviour. Smith argues the administration was not interested in practical solutions but was 'intent on proving an ideological point. That is a dangerous, and usually self-defeating approach in international politics.' The NSC concurrently acknowledged its difficulty of gaining support:

> We continue to have serious difficulties with the U.S. public and Congressional opinion, which jeopardizes our ability to stay the course. International opinion, particularly in Europe and Mexico, continues to work against our policies.

It advocated the adoption of a 'more active diplomatic campaign to turn around Mexico and Social Democrats in Europe.' The United States must not allow 'the proliferation of Cuba-model states which would provide platforms for subversion, compromise vital sea lanes and pose a direct military threat at or near our borders.' The Soviet Union had little interest in adopting a belligerent position in Central America. It did not seek bases in Nicaragua. As the Reagan administration made life increasingly costly for the Sandinistas, Brezhnev's policy makers 'were confined to the efforts to consolidate another anti-US regime in the Western Hemisphere', complicating US policy. Vladimir Stanchenko, a foreign policy specialist at the Institute of World Economy and International Relations in Moscow, affirmed there was no thought of obtaining military bases or of attacking sea lanes at the time. In August 1982 the Secretary General of the Soviet Foreign Ministry, Yuri Fokin, stated that they would provide political support, but he asked rhetorically, 'if the Americans invaded Nicaragua, what could we do? . . . Nothing'.[39]

Craig Johnstone, a Foreign Service Official and principal deputy to Enders for Central America, admitted that a Core Group of policy makers in Washington was responsible for coordinating and approving the actions that destroyed the bridges in Nicaragua in March 1982 and the DIA reported that the insurgency had become increasingly more widespread but

> there are no indications that any of these groups pose a serious military threat to the present Sandinista leadership or that there are any serious unification efforts underway . . . Whether it will succeed eventually in *overthrowing the government* will depend largely on successful unification efforts, the extent of popular support received both from within and outside Nicaragua, and the effectiveness of Sandinista counterinsurgency operations [emphasis added].

The first major covert actions drew an immediate response, the Sandinistas declared a state of emergency citing the 'important revelations' of the covert plans reported publicly in Washington. The NSC acknowledged the pressure resulting from the covert actions.[40]

## ADDING THE ISSUE OF DEMOCRACY

Democratization as conceived by Washington provided an additional barrier to negotiations through point eight in the Quainton proposals. Haig attributed the shift in policy to a liaison formed between Enders and Clark while he was preoccupied with the Malvinas/Falklands conflict. It was a controversial issue dealing with the internal elements of another sovereign country. Haig opposed the inclusion of democratization because neither superpower had the right to 'insist on a political formula in any developing country'. The particulars of the point were not spelt out till August, after Haig had resigned. Quainton, too, disagreed with the inclusion of the point, and perhaps for this reason did not leave a copy of the proposal with Julio López Campos, a foreign policy expert for the Sandinista Party, or with Victor Tinoco, the Vice Minister of Foreign Affairs. The State Department version differed from Quainton's original note which was more demanding, stating the holding of elections would be 'essential elements' for future political relations. Implying, perhaps, that normal relations could not be resumed till after the proposed 1985 elections. The demand drew the response. Nicaragua's official reply on 7 May 1982 stated:

> We regard the inclusion of point eight as an inexcusable position of interference in matters which are of Nicaragua's sole and exclusive competence; it relates to aspects of sovereign decision making in exercise of our right to self determination, such as our right to develop our Revolution in a fully independent manner within whatever economic–social order we consider most appropriate and such as our equally sovereign decision to hold elections on the date already announced on several occasion.[41]

The elections for the Constituent Assembly in El Salvador followed shortly after Nicaragua imposed a state of emergency. The apparent contrast in government direction provided additional material for Washington's public diplomacy campaign. The Nicaraguan internal opposition did not have to operate under life threatening circumstances. By contrast, in the preceding two years, seven hundred Christian Democratic Party workers had been killed in El Salvador. A 1984 report commissioned by the Department of State confirmed that 'with the exception of Britain all allied NATO governments dis-associated themselves from the "fraud" of El Salvador's 1982 elections.' Even Britain's official observers took exception to the US role. Lord Chitnis of the Parliamentary Human Rights Group characterized the process as 'reform plus repression – designed to win international support and keep open the vital lifeline of military and economic aid from the United States.' He concluded in his report:

> that the election in El Salvador was so fundamentally flawed as to be invalid for the following reasons: Limited choice . . . First there was a refusal of all parties to the left of the Christian Democrats to participate in the election, on the understandable grounds that had they done so they would have been butchered . . . Second, and more important, the electorate was given no choice on the question most of them cared about – how to end the war and murderous violence. Every party which stood favoured the military prosecution and even intensification of the war. None openly favoured a negotiated settlement . . . It is clear to me that the result of this strange, *foreign-inspired* election cannot be said to represent what in normal circumstances would be a free and unfettered choice of the people of El Salvador about their future [emphasis added].

Enders, however, characterized the Christian Democrats as a 'center left' party giving legitimacy to the range of choice Salvadorans had in the election. While the election, he conceded, was not 'violence free', it was not 'meaningfully influenced by the use of force'. He claimed that political violence had declined in El Salvador, from 600 to 2 000 a month to 300 to 500 a month, depending on which figures were used. So, logically, his statement is true, though these lower numbers still represent an abysmal record of human rights abuse. While human rights were abused in Nicaragua, such killing did not occur. Yet, Enders warned, the Sandinistas were creating a new 'dictatorship based once again on a privileged and militarized caste', the government was 'beginning to make war on its own people'.[42]

## ATTEMPTS AT CONVENING NEGOTIATIONS

Early in March Junta member Sergio Ramirez vehemently denied the problems of the region were a result of the superpower conflict, maintaining such notions ignored 'the long history of poverty and injustice, of exploitation and plunder, that has lead our peoples to rebel'; but Nicaragua was still ready to begin negotiations on any issue concerning both governments. Discussions began two days later, when Haig met Mexico's Foreign Minister Jorge Castañeda de la Rosa, at the United Nations in New York, though at this point Haig was isolated. A CIA employee, and later member of the NSC, Constantine Menges, described the talks as the 'second attempted State Department end run on Central America.' He stated

Enders had persuaded Haig to hold two meetings with Mexico's 'pro-Sandinista' Foreign Minister, but the 'panic' was 'halted' when Clark told Haig about the impact the meetings would have.[43]

Further secret meetings were held between Vernon Walters and Fidel Castro. Cuba had earlier indicated its disposition to negotiations, but the talks with Cuba bore no fruit. Wayne Smith, in Cuba at the time, maintained that Walters visit was a 'charade aimed at giving the impression of a willingness to talk where in fact no such willingness existed.' Smith was told by Cuban Vice President Rodriguez of his country's desire for a solution to the regional crisis addressing mutual security concerns through a process of mutual respect. If the intention of the talks with Cuba was to leave a paper trail to show Congress that the administration had tried to negotiate, the methods for doing so were inept. Haig indicated that at a time of crisis, contact and discussion became more important, but while arguing Central America was 'a global, a regional, and a local problem' it did not follow that the Soviets or the Cubans should' be invited to the negotiating table'. *The New York Times* reported that Cuba wanted wide ranging talks on the region, but would not withdraw support for the Salvadoran guerrillas as a precondition. As a gesture of good will it had stopped shipping arms to El Salvador for the past fourteen months. This message from Castro to Walters was passed through the Mexican Foreign Minister, Castañeda, who thought Nicaragua and Washington should not have 'great difficulty in reaching an arrangement'. He also pointed out while US interests were best served by diplomacy, they had not discounted 'the possibility that it is keeping other options open, other irons in the fire'. Haig characterized Castañeda's optimism as a subjective judgement on his part.[44] Preconditions, by their nature limit the prospect for negotiation; they demand something of one participant before they are dealt with at the table; such demands do not adhere to the principle of mutual respect between the negotiators. To maintain dignity, Cuba could not see why they should stop arming Salvadoran insurgents when the United States was arming the contras.

## THE OTHER IRONS IN THE FIRE

Daniel Ortega told the UN Security Council Nicaragua did not pose a threat to the national security of the United States, but covert action against them forced them to convene the UN meeting. If the peace efforts failed Ortega stated, they would 'fight to the last drop of blood', to safeguard their sovereignty, but it was imperative to 'find a solution' and begin negotiations 'discarding preconditions of any kind'.[45]

The US precondition was insurmountable because the subject of it did not exist in significant quantities; there was no proof of Sandinista involvement in these activities. The National Security Council summary paper made clear the intention to co-opt 'cut-and-run negotiation strategies by demonstrating a reasonable but firm approach to negotiations and *compromise on our terms*' [emphasis added]. As far as the policy implications of talks were concerned, the US must 'step up efforts to co-opt the negotiations issue to avoid Congressionally mandated negotiations, which would work against our interests'.[46]

## THE DIPLOMACY OF EVADING NEGOTIATION

Nicaragua's Ambassador to the United States met Enders at the State Department to present a formal response to Quainton's proposals. A thirteen point counter proposal was also submitted indicating a willingness to sign a non-aggression pact with its neighbours. Washington would have to stop providing financial support to the contras and explicitly promise not to invade Nicaragua. Haig and Enders, preoccupied with their 'shuttle diplomacy' on the Malvinas/Falklands conflict, did not give serious thought to the proposals, prompting Borge's accusations of 'dilatory tactics in the negotiations'. Quainton then delivered a message to the Sandinistas insisting that any dialogue would have to be strictly bilateral, despite an earlier offer at the UN that talks could be held at all levels. Nicaragua wanted to hold them at the level of Secretary of State or Assistant Secretary of State, while the United States wanted discussions to take place at ambassadorial level. The US objection and objectives were put forward in a 1985 report:

> Nicaragua responded by taking refuge in procedure, demanding that the talks take place at a higher level and that the Mexican government be drawn into the dialogue but avoiding any comment on the substance of the proposals . . . At the same time, the Sandinistas repeated rejection of the U.S. diplomatic efforts led to concern by the United States that *a policy confined to diplomatic representations could not be effective in modifying Nicaraguan behaviour and forced consideration of alternative means of achieving that objective* [emphasis added].[47]

Despite the allegations of this report, Nicaragua had responded to the eight US points on 7 May; each point was considered. It rejected the precondition, questioning US intentions on effective negotiations. Central

America would welcome a formal US commitment to 'adopt a new conduct that would overcome its historical practice of intervention in our countries.' The paper noted Nicaragua would not hesitate to sign a declaration of non-intervention.[48]

The US precondition and the Sandinista rejection of it remained in place. Castañeda sounded the end of his participation: 'we contributed in a modest way, but we can't do more than that. Perhaps in the future something more can be done.' US officials explained they

> were cool to the [Mexican] initiative from the beginning, but we were effectively ambushed by Congress and public opinion. We had to agree to negotiate or appear unreasonable.[49]

In mid-April, Eden Pastora, a disenchanted Sandinista leader who resigned in July 1981, turned up in Costa Rica claiming to be the 'watchful eye' of the revolution. His presence to the south of Nicaragua created a logical problem with regard to the US finding of December 1981 authorizing the 'interdiction' efforts. William Casey requested that a new finding be dealt with at a meeting on 13 July 1982. The purpose of the new finding would be to

> Support and conduct [excised] covert activities, including paramilitary activities, designed to [excised] to facilitate the efforts by democratic Nicaraguan leaders to restore the original principles of political pluralism, non-alignment, a mixed economy and free elections to the Nicaraguan revolution.

(The Iran–Contra Report quotes a section of the purpose of this finding as 'effect changes in Nicaraguan government policies'.) Ultimately, the finding was not approved, leaving the interdiction rationale in place. The State Department increasingly lost control of the Central American policy; and with it the possibility for bilateral negotiations were diminished. By 25 June 1982 Haig had resigned and was replaced by George Shultz.[50]

# 2 Contadora: Latin America Repudiates Washington 1983

Towards late 1982 the increased cohesion amongst regional Latin American governments and the growing congressional wariness of the covert activities reduced the administration's capacity to pursue its agenda. Though not totally cohesive, members of both groups moved towards curtailing contra funds against the thrust of the administration and the Central American governments provided with inducements to support the programme. The competing fora for dialogue and policy decisions became contentious diplomatic issues. As earlier surmised by Foreign Minister Jorge Castañeda, Mexico again offered a new search for peace. A joint letter from President José López Portillo and his Venezuelan counterpart, Luis Herrera Campíns, in September described to Reagan the grave situation between Nicaragua and Honduras, exacerbating the economic difficulties of these countries. Though they claimed to share a common objective with Washington to attain international peace and economic development in an 'environment of freedom', their contribution would pursue different methods to those of the United States. The US response in an undated letter from Reagan to López Portillo sometime between 21 September and 4 October, welcomed the initiative, and set out four goals to be addressed in the regional context. Primarily, 'democratic pluralism within each nation that includes free and fair elections,' had to be achieved; support for 'terrorist and insurgent' groups had to stop; a verifiable agreement banning importation of heavy weapons had to be reached; and foreign 'security and military advisors' had to be limited. With remarkable duplicity he wrote: 'as long as nations continue to interfere in the affairs of their neighbours and to promote destabilization and terrorism, there can be no peace in Central America.' The multiple references to 'democratic' governments in this letter referred to the Central American countries that had recently held elections. The essence of the message created its own impasse: negotiations had to be 'within a regional context', but Nicaragua and Guatemala did not qualify as democratic by US criteria, and were not invited to the San José meeting in early October. Hence such negotiations could only produce partial objectives. Mexico did not attend for this reason, and Venezuela sent a message instead of a delegation, because of its earlier joint effort with Mexico.[1] Nicaragua was practically eliminated from the process.

The San José peace initiative coincided with further administration attempts to procure contra funding. Ambassador Langhorne Motley at ARA [Bureau of Inter-American Affairs] encouraged the use of public diplomacy as an 'essential element in the conduct of foreign affairs', designed to influence the media, Congress, and hence the agenda of the negotiations. The focus on convening and gathering at the meeting provided evidence of negotiations for congressional consideration. Perhaps for this reason the reply to the Mexican–Venezuelan initiative was not sent till a few days before the meeting, mitigating the impact of any substantial proposals. Nicaragua's verbal and written response denied the regional crisis resulted from their military build-up, asserting they would not initiate any conflict, their sole interest was to 'defend itself in the event that the numerous threats of an armed attack against our country are carried out'.[2]

The San José Conference, known also as the Forum for Peace, produced the 'Declaration on Democracy in Central America,' on 4 October 1982, without Nicaragua's participation. Of the ten primary points made, democracy appeared in five. The declared faith in representative democracy implicitly seemed to discredit efforts of a more participatory variety. The governments urged a respect for non-intervention in the affairs of states, and principally had to:

> Prevent the use of their territories for the support, supply, training, or command of terrorist or subversive elements in other states, end all traffic in arms and supplies, and refrain from providing any direct or indirect assistance to terrorist, subversive, or other activities aimed at the violent overthrow of the governments of other states.[3]

But the contra forces were not dealt with as Mexico and Venezuela had urged; Honduras was not pressurized to expel them, nor Washington to stop financing them. The exclusion of the contra issues implied they were not terrorists or subversives and lent them greater legitimacy.

As Reagan met with Mexican President-elect, Miguel de la Madrid, in Washington on 6 October 106 Congressmen urged a positive response to the Mexican–Venezuelan initiative. Their letter implicitly rebuked US policy by omitting mention of the Forum for Peace, but emphasizing the critical timing of the Mexican–Venezuelan initiative. The congressmen noted 'avenues for political dialogue' remained open to ameliorate the tension and reduce the border clashes that brought 'Central America perilously close to a region wide conflagration.' Reagan quickly described the Mexican–Venezuelan initiative as 'very constructive', but indicated his preference

to negotiate under the Forum for Peace. So imminent talks with Nicaragua were precluded as US officials pointed out that they saw little hope of achieving peace. They would, however, go through the motions anyway: 'if the peace initiatives don't work, it leaves Nicaragua isolated by the other countries as the aggrieved parties.' At this time the *Miami Herald* cited General Wallace Nutting, head of the US Southern Command in Panama on the prospect of 'a reversal of the situation in Nicaragua'.[4]

## THE BOLAND LIMITATIONS

The public profile of the covert war increased dramatically and shattered the contra rationale of interdiction when the 8 November 1982 issue of *Newsweek* reported on the 'larger plan to undermine the Sandinista government.' The CIA approached Edgar Chamorro to join the political directorate of the FDN. He was told the president wanted 'to get rid of the Sandinistas'; the United States was fully prepared to back the FDN and that 'by the end of 1983, we would be marching into Managua to take over the Nicaraguan Government.' With congressional moves to prohibit the overthrow of the Sandinistas the CIA told Chamorro that 'the creation of a political directorate composed of prominent, respectable civilians might persuade the Congress not to enact such legislation.' But as the FDN held their first press conference in Miami, Congressman Tom Harkin proposed that no funds provided in this Act:

> may be used by the Central Intelligence Agency or the Department of Defense to furnish military equipment, military training or advice, or other support for military activities, to any group or individual, not part of a country's armed forces, for the purpose of assisting that group or individual in carrying out military activities in or against Nicaragua.

Harkin pointed out that it would appear hypocritical if the US was accusing the Sandinistas of exporting subversion and terrorism, 'if the United States is engaged in much the same type of activity'. Edward Boland, Chairman of the House Intelligence Committee, provided a compromise amendment that limited funds 'for the purpose of overthrowing the government of Nicaragua or provoking a military exchange between Nicaragua and Honduras.' The more comprehensive Harkin amendment would have prohibited military activity in or against Nicaragua, but Boland's amendment was more limited. Harkin again tried to prohibit aid to groups known to 'have the intent of overthrowing the government of Nicaragua,' but this amendment was also defeated. The Harkin prohibitions would have benefited the diplomatic process by aiding regional demilitarization. The adopted Boland amendment (411–0) was in effect a compromise not liked by the White House, but 'agreeable to them'. It was attached to the Defense Appropriations Act for fiscal year 1983 and became law on 21 December 1982. It remained in place till October 1983.[5]

The *Iran–Contra Report* later explained that the administration held that as long as the United States was not seeking to overthrow the Sandinistas, the contra intention was irrelevant; this stance was justified because the second Harkin amendment, on contra intentions, was defeated. The report concluded that 'the administration's willingness, indeed eagerness, to exploit ambiguities in Boland I, presaged its attitude toward the later Congressional efforts to limit Administration support for the contras'.[6]

The CIA told Edgar Chamorro and the FDN to change their stance after the Boland amendment had passed; they had to publicly emphasize their interdiction role. But Chamorro recounts:

> our goal, and that of the CIA as well (as we were repeatedly assured in private), was to overthrow the Government of Nicaragua, and to replace the Sandinistas as a government. It was never our objective to stop the supposed flow of arms, of which we never saw any evidence in the first place. The public statements by United States Government officials about the arms flow, we were told by the CIA agents with whom we worked, were necessary to maintain the support of the Congress and should not be taken seriously by us.

Boland assumed the administration would act in accordance with the thrust of the amendment, not on the narrow legal definition pivoting around the word 'purpose'. He did not see how the administration would justify any other interpretation.[7]

## CONTADORA

The four regional countries meeting on the island of Contadora, off the coast of Panama, addressed the problems within and among the Central American republics. The San José proposals, mainly focused on internal affairs were combined with the Mexican–Venezuelan initiative on security among countries. While the power within this new forum was being defined, states searched for leverage. Nicaragua initially preferred bilateral formulae with its neighbours and with the United States, and Washington, excluded from the process, wanted to maintain influence in the new framework of negotiations; if a peace that guaranteed Sandinista security was on the agenda, it either had to be co-opted or marginalised. The administration was divided on the role of negotiations but they were mandated by congressional pressure. Enders saw the covert policies as a means to induce the Sandinistas to, and as extra leverage at, the negotiating table, but hardliners within the administration were not interested in a formula leaving the Sandinistas in power; they moved to isolate Enders.

The four foreign ministers of Mexico, Colombia, Venezuela, and Panama, met on Contadora in early January 1983 stressing the urgent need to 'intensify the dialogue' to confront 'the political, economic and social problems which are jeopardizing the peace, democracy, stability and development of the peoples of the continent.' They conveyed concern about 'direct or indirect foreign interference' and recommended removing the east-west interpretation of events to reduce tensions. The importance of negotiations was highlighted as they urged states 'to refrain from actions which might aggravate the situation and pose the danger of a broader conflict extending throughout the region'. The socio-economic roots of revolution were emphasized as they stressed the need 'to reorder the international economic system' to avoid the systemic distortions that produced imbalances in developing countries. These larger issues did not find their way into the substance of future draft proposals. Significantly, the United States was not included in the process. The State Department reported it was approached privately to 'request its understanding' that the exclusion was to 'allay expressed Sandinista concerns that a multilateral effort involving the United States would be unfairly weighted against Nicaragua.' The Sandinistas were aware of the attempts to isolate Nicaragua. The public diplomacy campaign facilitated the plans to destabilize and 'create suitable conditions for military aggression' despite Nicaragua's offers to negotiations 'without any strings attached'. The San José process was seen to be part of the larger process of the US 'worldwide slander campaign, trying to isolate Nicaragua politically and economically.' By January 1983 four committees had been set up by National Security Decision Directive 77 to manage 'public diplomacy'.[8]

Under instructions (from the CIA station chief, Joseph Fernandez) the FDN released a 'peace initiative' on 13 January 1983 to divert attention from Contadora and to demonstrate their apparent willingness to negotiate. It 'essentially demanded the surrender of the Sandinista government'. The FDN agreed to halt its 'defensive paramilitary actions' if the Sandinistas complied with twelve conditions, unacceptable to a government under attack, three of which demanded the substitution of the Sandinista army, a reduction of their weapons, and elections before September 1983. The inevitable '*rejection* ... was what we *wanted*' [emphasis in original], to blame the Sandinistas with intransigence. Chamorro later explained the motive:

> The CIA gave top priority to these 'diplomatic' moves, which were nothing more than an attempt to neutralize the Contadora proposal. Ours was an unacceptable, shabby proposal a parallel document without substance whose purpose was to confuse the public.[9]

## PUBLIC DIPLOMACY

The efforts at public diplomacy reached an initial crescendo in March and April 1983 when high level personnel from the State Department and the White House presented their case to a number of fora including congressional hearings. The effort climaxed with the Reagan speech to a joint session of Congress. The atmosphere induced by these presentations was in the main confrontational. Enders and Shultz outlined their objectives, to promote and protect democracy; to provide economic assistance; to train the Salvadoran military; to offer hope; to deter the Soviets and Cubans from introducing forces in Nicaragua; and to 'foster peaceful solutions in Central America'. Enders saw some merit in removing the conflict from an 'east-west competition' by removing '*all foreign troops and military advisers*' [emphasis added], and defusing tensions through verifiable agreements, but refused to support '"negotiations" designed to divide up power among armed groups on the basis of bullets instead of ballots'.[10]

Congressional members questioned the rhetorical excesses of administration statements, specifically referred to by Senator John Glenn as an 'orchestrated chorus of voices', suggesting that the Salvadoran government would imminently fall if aid to their military was not approved. Senator Kassebaum asked 'what has brought us to that sort of rhetoric?' and Senator Dodd explained that public diplomacy had a self-fulfilling objective: 'sometimes when we say something often enough, whether or not it is entirely accurate, it has a way of gaining a certain amount of credibility on its own simply because it is mentioned enough.' Dodd suggested the bulk of FMLN supplies were captured from the Salvadoran military. Fred Ikle of the Defense Department denied this, stating the bulk came from Nicaragua. In the UN Security Council Jeane Kirkpatrick attacked the Sandinistas alleging the continued violation of Honduran sovereignty 'so repeatedly . . . that it is literally the case that one loses count of the instances'.[11] But she did not account for the contra failure to interdict one shipment of this allegedly continuous supply. Had there been some fire beneath this smoke, a demonstration of evidence would have been appropriate and enhanced executive credibility.

The Soviets sought and received assurances from Kirkpatrick that the United States did not have plans to invade Nicaragua, though the *Miami Herald* reported that a list of diplomatic and military options had been drawn up. Unnamed high level officials, considered options in response to a 'crisis in Nicaragua that could involve a Cuban missile-style confrontation'. Among the options were open support for the contras and selective air strikes against Soviet or Cuban targets if Nicaragua acquired jets.[12]

Reagan's speech to the joint session of Congress on 27 April 1983 marked an initial peak to the public diplomacy, dramatically increasing the stakes of the domestic debate. While other joint sessions had been called to resolve a crisis, Reagan stated he sought to prevent one. He held that the credibility of the United States, the cohesion of their alliances, such as NATO, and the safety of 'our homeland' were involved. 'Violence', Reagan charged, 'has been Nicaragua's most important export.' The United States did not seek to overthrow the Sandinistas, but to see they did not 'infect' other Central American nations 'through the export of subversion and violence'. The Sandinistas posed a challenge to 'freedom and security in our hemisphere'. The burden was placed on congress:

> I do not believe that a majority of the Congress or the country is prepared to stand by passively while the people of Central America are delivered to totalitarianism, and we ourselves are left vulnerable to new dangers . . . Now, before I go any further, let me say to those who invoke the memory of Vietnam: There is no thought of sending American combat troops to Central America.

The United States had to act within the relatively new constraints of the 'Vietnam syndrome', they could no longer give open ended commitments such as Kennedy's pledge to 'pay any price' or 'bear any burden' to 'assure the survival and success of liberty'. Hence low intensity conflict through proxy forces was adopted. But according to the speech, the stakes were high. References to another missile crisis and by reflecting on Truman's Doctrine Reagan universalized the alleged threat, making it a political liability for congressional rejection of his thesis. The request for $600 million for fiscal year 1984 was intended to reflect the importance of US policies, the rejection of which would be seen as appeasing the Soviets. Reagan concluded:

> The national security of all the Americas is at stake in Central America. If we cannot defend ourselves there, we cannot expect to prevail elsewhere.

> Our credibility would collapse, our alliances would crumble . . . We have a vital interest, a moral duty, and a solemn responsibility. *This is not a partisan issue* [emphasis added].[13]

The Democratic response, by Senator Dodd, simply did not agree, 'tonight the President may have brought people to their feet, but I do not think he brought them to their senses.' An alternative policy would also oppose Marxist states in Central America, and prevent Soviet bases in the region, but Dodd rejected the contention that revolution was caused by Soviet manipulation:

> If Central America were not racked with poverty, there would be no revolution. If Central America were not racked with hunger, there would be no revolution. If Central America were not racked with injustices, there would be no revolution. In short, there would be nothing for the Soviets to exploit. But unless those oppressive conditions change, that region will continue to seethe with revolution – with or without the Soviets.

Echoing President Kennedy, Dodd proclaimed 'we must make violent revolution preventable by making peaceful revolution possible'.[14]

## CONGRESS QUESTIONS EXECUTIVE INTENTIONS

The first major debate on the interpretation and intention of the Boland amendment ensued when *The New York Times* reported the contras had predicted the fall of the 'Marxist dictatorship' in six months revealing the discrepancy in their ostensible and actual motives. The legality of the administration's support of the contras pivoted around the different meanings of 'purpose' and 'intent'. The 'purpose' of the US agencies supplying the assistance was not to overthrow the Sandinistas, even if this was the 'purpose' of the recipients. The Chairman of the House Foreign Affairs Subcommittee on Western Hemisphere Affairs, Michael Barnes, argued that 'not a jury in the country would accept this, and the House will not accept it'. The chairmen of the Intelligence Committees could not agree on the issue. Senator Barry Goldwater was satisfied, having received confirmation from DCI Casey, that 'the [CIA] is not violating the letter or the spirit of the Boland amendment'. But Boland disagreed, based on 'strong' evidence he thought there had been 'an apparent violation of the law' because the operation had gone 'beyond merely stopping the infiltration of arms and equipment into El Salvador. Nevertheless Reagan asserted his administration's compliance with the law.[15]

The White House wanted 'prompt' approval of funds to pursue their aims. To compromise with congress, 'verifiable and reciprocal' negotiations had to be supported. Thirty million dollars was approved by the House Foreign Operations Appropriations Subcommittee, chaired by Clarence D. Long, after the appointment of a special envoy for Central America was agreed on. Richard Stone, a former Democratic Senator for Florida was named ambassador at large on 28 April. Initially the administration opposed the appointment, according to an aide to Long, because it may give rise to 'inflated expectations' of a negotiated solution. Further disagreement between Long and Secretary of State, George Shultz ensued on whether Stone should concentrate on lobbying Congress or pursuing peace in Central America. Shultz wrote to Long on 26 April suggesting Stone would seek funds for the Salvadoran military as 'essential to provide the shield we need to succeed in our broader efforts . . . to make possible a longer term and more meaningful peace in Central America'. Stone maintained funding difficulties were encountered because many congressmen did not know the facts, the priorities, the emphasis, and the nuances of the policy. He was well placed to inform them given his previous responsibility as chairman for the inter-agency 'public diplomacy strategy concerning Central America'.[16]

By mid-May the House Intelligence Committee clearly dissatisfied with the covert operation reported there had been no 'diminishment in arms flow to the Salvadoran guerillas' in the past eighteen months. The committee was not willing to assure the House that the programme did 'not have the purpose to overthrow the government of Nicaragua'. And further the programme had not induced a change in Sandinista policies. Overall, the operation was ineffective, unnecessary and counterproductive. The Senate Intelligence Committee, chaired by Barry Goldwater, supported the administration. By this time the Sandinistas were also fighting the Democratic Revolutionary Alliance (ARDE), headed by Eden Pastora on the Costa Rican border. Geographically these forces could not be involved in interdiction, leaving the argument in shreds. By 6 May, when William Casey appeared before the Senate Intelligence Committee, the members agreed that the purpose had moved beyond interdiction. Casey conceded the finding needed to be 'recrafted . . . Goldwater suggested a new finding, one that laid out a new purpose – pressure, democratization, efforts to force the Sandinistas to negotiate.' The administration would 'articulate its goals more exactly'.[17] A new finding was signed in September 1983.

## INITIAL MOVEMENT BY CONTADORA

Mexico's Foreign Minister, Bernardo Sepúlveda Amor, was optimistic about a negotiated solution because Contadora 'found much sympathy both from Commander Daniel Ortega and President Monge'. As Shultz prepared to visit Mexico media reports suggested the two governments were on a collision course over the question of negotiations. Shultz tried to take wind out of the Contadora sails stating 'I don't know of any new initiative that might be talked about, but we're certainly going to discuss these issues.' Following his visit Contadora indicated that there was indeed a new initiative which formed the outline of their future documents, based on resolving,

> the arms race, arms control and reduction, the transfer of armaments, the presence of military advisers and other forms of outside military assistance, actions aimed at destabilizing the internal order of other countries, threats and verbal aggression, warlike incidents and frontier tensions, the violation of human rights and individual and social guarantees, and the grave economic and social problems which are at the heart of the region's present crisis.[18]

Despite these moves, unnamed officials in the Reagan administration charged that Nicaragua was considering the placement of Soviet missiles on its territory. Daniel Ortega felt compelled to clarify 'that the installation of Soviet missiles in Nicaragua has arisen only in the mind of the United States Administration.' Nicaragua would not become 'anybody's military base.' Military cooperation had been requested from a number of countries including the United States 'which turned us down from the outset'. As a sovereign country they requested 'cooperation from any government that sees fit to provide it, no matter what its political, economic of [sic] social system may be.' The interdiction of Libyan planes bound for Nicaragua produced mainly defensive equipment, and 'the limited amounts of truly modern equipment acquired by the Sandinistas . . . came from Western Europe.' Cumulative Soviet transfers to Nicaragua between 1981 and 1985 was equal to the cumulative US military transfers to El Salvador between these dates. This does not account for transfers from other countries. A larger proportion of Nicaragua's weapons came from non-Soviet sources. 'All too many US claims proved open to question' noted Carl Jacobsen in a report commissioned by the State Department. The imposition of security limits would have affected other Central American countries more broadly.[19]

## ENDERS REASSIGNED

The process of Enders' removal, and the reasons for it, exemplify the issues that mitigated the chances of a negotiated solution. The evident administration infighting reflected on the decision-making processes, and the timing of decisions adversely affected diplomatic initiatives. Enders, aware of these problems, saw that there was no structure to deal with the issues. He thought he could control policy through the interagency core group system. A critic of Enders' management style, Constantine Menges, charged that he tried to use the process to exclude other departments: 'his method was to have the formal interagency meetings cover only routine issues and leave policy questions for "informal discussions" by his personal invitation only.' Menges saw Enders as having full control over Latin American issues as Shultz's sole advisor on the area. Lawrence Eagleburger, an aide to Shultz, would be used to 'outmaneuver' other State Department officials, and after Clark moved McFarlane to the NSC, Enders had another 'ally' in the Council. Menges thought Enders was trying to exclude Reagan appointees and other 'senior Defense officials' from the 'interagency' meetings. The NSC staff could then avoid alerting' Clark or the president to the full implications of new State Department initiatives'. The controversy surrounding Enders' 'two-track' initiative prompted his removal.[20]

The 'two track' option was a combination of the use of force and diplomacy to contain the Sandinistas in Nicaragua and exclude other powers from the region. Enders did not want to abandon negotiations as the only possible means of attaining a peaceful settlement. He advocated continued contra support to pressure the Sandinistas to negotiate, and continued support for San Salvador while it pursued negotiations with the FMLN. Enders realized Congress wanted 'to exhaust such opportunities as there may be to reach a responsible solution through negotiation', hence the broad policy outlines would meet congressional constraints. But Enders's security provisions divorced from the globalist perspective met resistance in the White House in early 1983. Menges told Casey the State Department had new proposals and within hours Casey had a copy of the 'two-track' memo. Menges described it as a joint attempt with Mexico to 'Latinize' the conflict. Mexico's policies were considered to be at complete odds with those of the administration: abandoning the quest for democracy in Nicaragua, allowing the FMLN to share power in El Salvador, and opposed to contra aid.[21]

The Contadora initiative had emerged from the perception that the solution to the conflict had to be 'Latinized'. Enders had been a prime force behind the San Jose initiative in late 1982. When the Honduran Foreign Minister, Paz Barnica, asked Sandinista Deputy Foreign Minister, Victor Tinoco, why Nicaragua had not attended? Tinoco replied, 'We are not going to participate in any group in which the United States is participating.' Paz Barnica then approached foreign ministers from Mexico, Venezuela, and Colombia to suggest a Latin effort at finding a solution. Enders, too, saw merit in the idea of excluding extra-regional powers from the area. Enders had explained to Senator Zorinski: 'I think it is a good idea. I think we should see them get on with it, and maybe the Central Americans can make some progress with their own problems themselves.' Other influential officials were not receptive to the prospect of extricating the United States from Central America. Clark reportedly felt Enders was trying to produce a breakthrough with the 'two track' policy that was not consistent with administration policy; the United States would not withdraw support from its allies in the region. Clark presented the memorandum and his case to Reagan. Bob Woodward states Enders was accused of defeatism and Clark also 'made it clear that not only did he himself have a distaste for negotiations, but he was not sure the White House wanted the centrist congressional support.' The patriotism of those who wanted to pursue dialogue was questioned. Frank McNeil, then Ambassador to Costa Rica, explained, the 'right' charged Enders 'with pursuing containment, of a willingness to settle for less than the destruction of Nicaragua.' Enders later reflected that the prevailing atmosphere was one 'in which it was clear that the president wanted action, but did not have a precise action plan to propose'.[22]

The authors of the 'two-track' policy paper did not expect a peace settlement in the short run, but Frank McNeil, a contributor to the paper, thought it more likely now than during the August 1981 talks in Managua; the regional process made more sense than a bilateral one. Deane Hinton, Enders and McNeil were relieved '[i]n the shootout over the two track policy'.[23] Towards the end of May Enders became the ambassador to Spain, his policies became the basis for Shultz's understanding, and ironically the basis for the administration's future finding on Central America.

To clarify matters, after a White House meeting on 25 May 1983, Shultz wrote a memorandum to the President outlining his understanding of the management of the Central American strategy. Reagan's reply, drafted by Clark, demonstrates the continued misunderstanding among top level policy makers. Shultz understanding of what exactly US policy was is worth examination because it places negotiations within the overall strategy. Shultz wrote:

> we need an effective shield to protect the Salvadoran democracy against the efforts of the rebels to destroy the government and the economy. We have to safeguard not only El Salvador but also the other Central American countries against the Nicaraguan *virus*. At the same time we have to win the struggle in our own country to help the American people understand the Soviet–Cuban–Nicaraguan threat to the whole region. And we have to obtain the support of the Congress . . . we must maintain pressure on the Nicaraguans to cease and desist from exporting their revolution to neighbouring countries.
>
> Though we must continue to strengthen the shield against the Salvadoran rebels and keep the pressure on Nicaragua, *we cannot expect a military solution*, at least in the next several years. In all likelihood *the only way in which we can reestablish a peaceful Central America, free from foreign incursions into democratic countries, is by regional negotiations leading to a reciprocal and verifiable agreement* in which the Nicaraguans come to terms with the need for them to mind their own business. At the same time, in forcing Nicaragua to the negotiating table, we must not sell out the Nicaraguan patriots who wish their government to live up to the promises of free elections and a pluralistic society made when the Sandinistas came to power . . .
>
> Negotiations with either the Nicaraguans or the Salvadoran rebels will not be easy, because we will be dealing with people we don't like and don't trust. Moreover, we will not be able to achieve success unless we can show the Nicaraguans that they cannot defeat the anti-Sandinista forces in Nicaragua . . . Finally, in bringing about a reciprocal and verifiable agreement, we have to be willing and able to deal effectively with major governments like Mexico [emphasis added].

While regional negotiations were provisionally endorsed, continued support for the contras went against their thrust. The management situation, Shultz said, was 'a mess' that 'would not work even if the problems were simple'.[24]

## THE FRAMEWORK FOR NEGOTIATIONS

Diplomatic tension between Nicaragua and the United States increased in early June when both countries engaged in an exchange of expelling diplomats. The *Washington Post* described the relations as at the lowest point since the Sandinistas came to power in 1979. The three US diplomats expelled were charged with an attempt to kill Miguel D'Escoto, which was rejected by Washington; twenty-one Nicaraguan consular officials were expelled and closing six consulates, though embassies remained open and diplomatic relations were not severed.[25]

Stone's appointment coincided with Enders' departure and replacement by L. Anthony Motley. The two new figures soon became antagonists in a bid to control diplomacy. Washington had to use Stone's appointment for congressional purposes and Nicaragua needed to maintain any negotiations to ward off additional contra funds or other action. During Stone's thirteen day visit to the region, in Nicaragua he suggested talks with the contras should begin; which had been repeatedly rejected because the Sandinistas sought a dialogue with their opponents' paymasters and advisers in Washington. But Stone maintained discussions should remain at the regional level. The Sandinista Foreign Ministry released a statement denigrating the discussions held days earlier, to quell any benefit Stone's trip would gain the administration with Congress. Nicaragua had not found:

> a basis for believing in the usefulness of Mr. Stone's trip, which supposedly was made to find a solution to the regional crisis through dialogue. On the contrary, this trip seemed more to be part of the propaganda campaign aimed at strengthening the policy that proposes aggression and war in Central America.

The statement asserted that Stone did not see the need for bilateral talks because the 'United States does not feel threatened by Nicaragua'. But Nicaragua did feel threatened by the United States and the Foreign Ministry argued the 'aggressive policy constitutes a fundamental aspect of the Central American crisis'.[26] Herein lay another impasse. As the Sandinistas had refused to hold talks with the contras, Washington continued to insist on them. This remained effective for almost five years, till in 1988 the Sandinistas agreed to such talks.

Despite the 7 June approval by the House Foreign Affairs Committee of a bill (HR 2760) that would have cut aid to the contras, the threat against Nicaragua escalated when William Casey requested and obtained more funds for the covert programme. Precautions had been taken after the House Intelligence Committee indicated no funds would be available if the aim was to assist the contras in deposing the Sandinistas. Congress still needed further persuasion hence the office of Public Diplomacy for Latin America and the Caribbean was set up in the State Department, headed by Otto Reich. Simultaneously, the CIA tried to induce support from the Defense Department and on 12 July Reagan directed it to 'provide maximum possible assistance to the Director of Central Intelligence in improving support to the Nicaraguan resistance.' The *Iran–Contra Report* noted 'equipment then could be stockpiled by the CIA and provided to the contras if the need arose'.[27] Should aid be totally cut off, the contras would have some leeway.

The administration was divided over the tactical plans should Congress terminate aid. An NSC official, Walter Raymond, reduced the issue, for Clark, to either accepting a compromise position or to 'stonewall the whole thing'. A compromise was urged 'to get bipartisan support for this action',

> The key points if we were to arrive at a compromise would be House support for our program as long as it is not for the overthrow of the Sandinistas and until the Sandinistas stop intervening in neighbouring countries. That is not a bad position to be in at this juncture.

Raymond noted that members of Congress had negotiated with the administration 'in good faith' and that if they tried to defeat the Boland–Zablocki bill, it would have negative repercussions on congressional relations. Raymond understood from McFarlane that Jim Wright would not reduce Congressional pressure on this point. Others in the NSC structure, including Oliver North advised against any delayed request because 'those against will continue against'. They believed it was 'important as a signal of strength and purpose that we let the opposition on the Hill know that we believe in and intend to continue to pursue this program until such time as the full Congress successfully votes to stop it'.[28]

By July the administration had increased its military pressure and Nicaragua continued its military buildup. The Sandinistas had received 'serious warning' on Washington's intentions from the presidents of France and Spain; Moscow had also indicated they regarded the situation as 'very worrying'. Contadora's declaration from Cancun, Mexico, on 17 July 1983, was born in part because of 'the increasing conflict' and the potential for more general hostilities. They called for an adherence to international law and within the region proposed a series of security measures to begin negotiations on. Mexico's Foreign Minister, Bernardo Sepúlveda, cautioned against expectations 'spectacular solutions,' but noted the situation required 'an investment of very considerable diplomatic work . . . that bears fruit only in the medium term'. Reagan and Castro were asked to support their efforts.[29]

On the fourth anniversary of the revolution Nicaragua accepted the multilateral forum to 'end excuses' to facilitate the 'foundations for peace'. Consequently the Sandinistas conceded to a US demand that negotiations take place at the regional level and put forward a proposal 'in spite of our absolute conviction that the greatest threat to peace in the region demands bilateral solutions'. The proposal addressed key Contadora concerns but also reflected the increasing pressure on Nicaragua. Heeding the European presidential warning Managua placed the onus on Washington to respond diplomatically before reverting to other methods. The US response was unusually swift. Reagan welcomed any 'verifiable proposal' to decrease tensions, described Ortega's move as a 'positive step' because it acknowledged 'the regional nature of the problem. Sepúlveda, described Nicaragua's proposal as 'a step forward in the process toward peace' and *The New York Times* editorialized under the title 'A Peace Scare From Managua':

> The greatest awkwardness concerns military intervention. Mr. Reagan has had trouble proving any significant Nicaraguan role in El Salvador. Yet America's support of rebels in Nicaragua is now blatant.

As Contadora stepped up its diplomacy US military manoeuvres were announced. Intended or not, they dramatically increased the regional tension. On 28 July, Clark wrote a memorandum to most cabinet members and chief military advisers indicating the presidential approval of National Security Decision Directive (NSDD) 100 on 'enhanced US military activity and assistance in the Central American region.' NSDD–100 invoked the 'consolidation of a Marxist–Leninist regime in Nicaragua,' and stated:

> Our ability to support democratic states in the region, and those on the path to democracy, must be visibly demonstrated by our military forces . . . Adequate U.S. support must also be provided to the democratic resistance forces within Nicaragua in an effort to ensure that Nicaragua ceases to be a Soviet/Cuban base and that the government adheres to the principles that it agreed to in July 1979.

US support for Contadora was beneficial to the legislative strategy, but if this group arrived at a solution, the US presence in the region would be curtailed and all governments would remain in power. A further legislative strategy centred around the creation of the Bipartisan Commission to find solutions to the crisis. The appointment of Kissinger to head the group was criticized due to his preference of viewing Third World problems as a part of the East–West conflict, a view shared by the administration and opposed by Contadora. *The New York Times* cited unnamed Latin officials and western diplomats who suggested the US aim was not just peace, but 'peace with a defeated Nicaragua'. After Congress held closed discussions on the covert operations, representative Bill Alexander emerged to state:

> Without revealing classified information, I can say that the covert action hasn't worked. [He remained convinced the administration] has a hidden

agenda undisclosed to Congress and the American people, and while talking about peace in the region it is seeking a military victory.[30]

The House Bill HR 2760 which cut off aid to the contras on 28 July 1983 went through several amendments before a final version came to a vote. Largely along partisan lines, the bill was passed 228 to 195. The final version included an amendment by the Majority Leader, Jim Wright, which inserted a finding by Congress that stated, if the United States attempted to oust a government in Central America, it would be a violation of international law, as well as the United Nations Charter, and that of the OAS. Contadora agreed to continue discussions in August, despite the Panamanian Foreign Minister's assessment that time was running out for a negotiated solution. D'Escoto described the process as negotiating with 'a gun at our heads' due to the US military manoeuvres.[31]

## CONTADORA DEFINES ITS OBJECTIVES

Speaking for the four Central American countries, Honduras attempted to define their position on Cancun, and present an alternative working document, suggesting the isthmian protagonists should take primary responsibility for finding agreement. Any solution had to account for all interests of all countries, 'not the isolated interest of any particular country.' Though there was, for tactical reasons, a preference to deal with the problems of the other countries first. Contadora wanted to force each country to address its own conditions as well. Paz Barnica pointed out that D'Escoto had accused other countries of only paying 'lip service' to the Cancun declaration, which was specifically denied. Regional ministers did not want to leave the search for solution to the Central Americans and Contadora stepped up its activities during the summer of 1983. The isthmian governments were too close to Washington, and tensions increased when the FDN criticized the House cut in aid, suggesting that if they could not do the job, the United States would 'eventually have to get involved in the fighting . . . from the cost efficiency point of view, it is better for [it] to fight now.' During this period FDN attacks from Honduras increased, and Nicaragua's interior Minister, Tomás Borge stated they would not negotiate on the size of their armed forces. To do so under prevailing conditions would amount to capitulation, so arming the population was seen as a means to ensure Sandinista survival. Other Central American governments did not have confidence of such popular support. While Nicaragua's population was armed to resist attacks Borge maintained the chances of an invasion were reduced, because of US public opposition to the prospect. But in Washington ambassador at large, Vernon Walters, delivered a speech to the Central American outreach group, made up of private individuals who supported, and participated in, the broader policy debates. The Brezhnev doctrine guaranteed the achievements of socialism, and stated that the Red army reserved the right to intervene to protect these gains. 'I am not sure that we shouldn't have a doctrine that guarantees the achievements of democracy. We apparently let the Monroe Doctrine fall into . . . desuetude', Walters maintained. The credibility of US support for democracy was inconsistent due to its support of strong regional dictatorships.[32]

New initiatives were added to the Nicaraguan and Central American proposals at the seventh Contadora meeting of 7 to 9 September. The Document of Objectives agreed on by all governments sought to formalize commitments as soon as possible. It covered all the security, economic, and social concerns and included a call for 'national reconciliation in those cases in which deep divisions have been caused within society'. Contadora's credibility was enhanced with the twenty-one points accepted as the formula for negotiations. Four main areas were covered: demilitarization, nonintervention, self-determination, and democratization. The document was endorsed by extra-regional protagonists including the United States, Cuba, and the Soviet Union. Washington saw no contradiction in their endorsement and their continued covert activity. The specifics of the document would have addressed Washington's concerns in Nicaragua: Soviet bases would be precluded from the area; substantial arms traffic had to stop; military levels balanced; irregular forces expelled from any signatures territory; civil and economic rights would have to be guaranteed; and a process of democratization and elections would have to be implemented. The conditions, though, would have undermined administration goals in other isthmian countries: it would have to disband its bases in El Salvador and Honduras; cease sending arms to the Salvadoran government; and cease its support for the contras. Nicaragua would have to expel the command and control centres of the FMLN, Honduras would have to expel the contras. The FMLN controlled a significant portion of El Salvador while the contras did not consistently control any portion of Nicaragua. A mostly censored memorandum from Shultz to Reagan noted, US objectives: 'will require sustained US efforts for some years. Any negotiated regional agreement could of necessity be only *part of a process* involving the continuing application of US resolve and resources over time' [emphasis added]. The Reagan administration had committed itself not to abandon the contras, and stymied security negotiations in Contadora. Under 'US Strategy' Shultz suggested: 'if we can continue to fund the contras (or, if necessary, alternative benefactors are found), negotiations can proceed at a measured pace with the US in the background'.[33] The ostensible search for negotiations, though they were blocking the only forum that was searching for a solution became the foundation for the September 1983 finding to justify contra support to Congress.

Significant covert activity usually accompanied any significant diplomatic move. The day before the Document of Objectives was signed, the FDN and CIA 'assets' blew up the underwater facilities at Puerto Sandino where oil was unloaded for Managua. Clarridge considered several alternatives, but decided on the operation that occurred during the time span of the Contadora meeting. Chamorro recounts:

> the CIA blew up the pipeline at Puerto Sandino, just as Clarridge had advised us it would. The actual operatives were Agency employees of Hispanic decent, referred to within the Agency as 'Unilaterally Controlled Latino Assets' or UCLAs. These UCLAs, specially trained underwater demolitions experts, were despatched from a CIA 'mother ship' that took them to within striking distance of their target. Although the FDN had nothing whatsoever to do with this operation, we were instructed by the CIA to publicly claim responsibility in order to cover the CIA's involvement. We did.[34]

## THE NEW FINDING

While a CIA National Intelligence Estimate submitted to Congressional committees concluded 'there are no circumstances under which a force of US-backed rebels can achieve a military or political victory over the leftist Sandinista government' Washington was not deterred from pursuing contra aid. The new finding, approved by Reagan, proposed to provide,

> support, equipment and training assistance to Nicaraguan paramilitary resistance groups as a means to induce the Sandinistas and Cubans and their allies to cease their support for insurgencies in the region; to hamper Cuban/Nicaraguan arms trafficking; to divert Nicaragua's resources and energies from support to Central American guerilla movements; and *to bring the Sandinistas into meaningful negotiations and constructive, verifiable agreement with their neighbours on peace in the region* [emphasis added] . . . encourage regional cooperation and coordination in pursuit of program objectives.

Washington wanted negotiations around the 'original promises' of the revolution which were consistently misrepresented. Foremost was the Sandinistas' commitment to hold the first free elections this century. This was the only specification of a time frame, and the International Court of Justice pointed out that in these promises they could find no 'legal undertaking' on behalf of the Sandinistas. 'The resolution of 23 June 1979 also declares that the solution of their problems is a matter "exclusively" for the Nicaraguan people.'[35]

The finding moved from the specific aim of interdicting arms to broad purposes of putting pressure on the Sandinistas. Robert Pastor, President Carter's regional NSC adviser, pointed out that the new finding was an 'open ended' commitment, which pursued an 'unobtainable objective'. A contradiction arose owing to congressional insistence that 'a military victory' should be renunciated as a 'bipartisan compromise', yet the administration believed, according to the *Iran–Contra Report* that 'only the prospect of a military defeat would push them toward a negotiating posture'.[36]

## NICARAGUA RESPONDS TO CONTADORA

In late September Nicaragua ratified the Contadora Document of Objectives. Further confusion prevailed in Washington with the resignation of Clark in October 1983. Despite Shultz's backing, James Baker, considered a moderate, did not get the job; it would send the 'wrong' signal to the Soviets! A compromise choice for NSA was made in Robert McFarlane, Clark's deputy. But before departing Clark had moved Constantine Menges from the CIA to the NSC, who on later admission was 'not too happy with McFarlane's appointment'. Roy Gutman, notes that by the end of 1983 Menges had become a strong opponent of negotiating with the Sandinistas.[37]

During the staff changes Motley went to Nicaragua, which was, apart from Stone's July trip, the first visit by a senior policy making official since early 1982. Motley had two hours with Ortega and another two with D'Escoto intending to 'explore precisely what the feelings of the Government' were on the Contadora Objectives. The following day *The New York Times* reported he thought the Sandinistas were serious about the document. Simultaneously Nicaragua released a peace proposal within the Contadora framework. Motley, when asked, stated Washington would abide by the objectives when

> the five countries can arrive at agreement that they are satisfied with among themselves – not only signed a piece of paper, but they're

> comfortable with it – that we've gone a long, long way to satisfying ours which were embodied within those 21.

Any conclusion to the negotiating process was effectively precluded without a commitment to disband the contras. This fundamental contradiction persisted throughout the Sandinista period in power. Despite this logical impasse Nicaragua made further proposals on 15 October 1983, and presented by D'Escoto to Motley five days later in Washington. The premise of the draft documents was that 'Central American countries require, as a prior condition, that their security be guaranteed'. By Nicaragua's own admission:

> These documents, *which cover the issue of security alone*, do not pretend to exhaust all the possible agreements that could emerge from the documents of Contadora. They simply lay the juridical foundation and establish the mechanisms of control to ensure that the States will not be attacked from other states of the Central American region or from outside the region [emphasis added].

All four drafts had to be accepted in order to guarantee security. The first dealt with US–Nicaraguan security; the second between Honduras and Nicaragua; the third, on El Salvador; and the fourth on peace in Central American. Article three of the first draft in effect would have put an end to the contras and support for the FMLN. The State Department characterized the proposals as inadequate because 'the appropriate forum for carrying out negotiations is the Contadora process'. Soon after a *Washington Post* editorial opined that the US response was also 'inadequate'. Washington now had a diplomatic instrument to ensure Nicaragua left its neighbours alone, but they concluded, 'it is no surprise to hear American officials saying in private that Nicaragua is not "hurting enough yet"'.[38]

Washington accused Nicaragua of trying to undercut Contadora 'by pursuing their own agenda in other fora'. After signing the Document of Objectives Nicaragua introduced the issues to the Security Council of the United Nations 'breaking an explicit commitment to the Contadora group that it would not do so'. A 1985 Department of State report indicated that these draft proposals were revealing in that they ignored the issues of national reconciliation, restoring the military balance in the region, and the treatment of foreign military advisors. If the United States had responded to the bilateral draft, it would have been breaking their own long standing demand that negotiations go forward under a regional framework. Washington was adamant that diplomacy had to be multilateral, yet Contadora's 21–22 October meeting believed the process could reach conclusion and urged 'Central American countries to expedite and increase their efforts toward that end, and we also urge those states with interests in and ties to the region to cooperate in the achievement of our objective of peace'.[39]

Sufficiently distant from the atmosphere created when the Soviets shot down Korean Airline flight 007, Congress moved again to cut aid to the contras. Boland accused the administration of waging war in Nicaragua, contending that: 'Military victory is the Administration's bottom line'. The House voted along much the same lines as the July vote; 227 voted to end aid, 194 voted to continue it. Days later the United States invaded the island of Grenada and overthrew the leftist government of Bernard Coard who had recently deposed the New Jewel movement led by Maurice Bishop. The invasion was regarded as a test run in Nicaragua. With the situation deteriorating, Daniel Ortega visited Mexican president de la Madrid to initiate further diplomatic contact. That same day, 10 November, Ortega and Stone flew back to Managua to hold further talks, as it was widely believed time was short for a diplomatic solution. The process might not be fruitful, Mexican officials surmised, because Nicaragua was the only country to present new proposals.[40]

Concurrently the UN General Assembly passed a resolution calling for the cooperation of all countries with Contadora. The resolution noted the 'military presence of countries from outside the region, the carrying out of overt and covert actions . . . which have served to heighten tensions.' It condemned such acts of aggression; 'especially serious' were the 'attacks'

> launched from outside Nicaragua against that country's strategic installations, such as airports and seaports, energy storage facilities and other targets whose destruction seriously affects the country's economic life and endangers densely populated areas.

It also condemned the loss of life and destruction in El Salvador and Honduras, but it is notable that the resolution did not state that these originated from outside those countries.[41]

The following day the administration and Congress reached a compromise of $24 million as a limit on contra spending for fiscal year 1984. At their rate of expenditure the money was expected to run out in June 1984, at which point Congress would be given another opportunity to consider the programme. The compromise intended to promote the atmosphere for dialogue, still within days the administration denied Borge a visa to the United States to hold talks with officials, congressional members and the public. Borge earlier explained the battle for Central America was to be fought in the United States through the mobilization of public opinion, but his access was denied. Senator Daniel Patrick Moynihan, influential in working out the compromise funding, stated that 'a willingness to talk was implicit in the commitments given to intelligence committees. But this situation has some of us feeling that maybe we were euchred.' Deception was indeed involved.[42]

By December the Sandinistas had offered concessions which were rejected by Washington, though they were specifically noted by the Secretary General of the United Nations, Javier Pérez de Cuéllar. Late in November 1 200 Cubans, mostly teachers and agricultural workers, and 2 000 Salvadorans left Nicaragua. The Sandinistas announced that a further 1 000 Cubans, including military personnel would leave soon, to test US willingness to negotiate. The Secretary of State's office declared they were 'not open to accepting symbolic actions'. The Secretary General's report of December 1983 noted a

> perceptible movement in the position of the Government of Nicaragua, consisting mainly in the submission of proposals within the framework of the efforts of the Contadora Group and in the measures which, notwithstanding their domestic nature, take cognizance of certain requirements of the other countries of the region.[43]

In January 1984 Contadora 'laid down some specific measures for the implementation' of their objectives, tightening the intentions and agenda in their new document: 'Norms for the Implementation of the Commitments of the Document of Objectives'. Washington, however, continued their attempts to isolate and hurt Nicaragua. On his return from a trip to Europe, Richard Stone reported to Shultz, 'We clearly have made some progress in moving the Europeans toward our position on Nicaragua. We made some progress on targeting economic assistance away from Nicaragua and toward El Salvador.' Further efforts to damage the economic structure and possibly halt shipping to Nicaragua came in 1984 when Edgar Chamorro was woken on 5 January and handed a press release by a CIA agent. 'I was surprised to read', he later recounted: 'the F.D.N. – were taking credit for having mined several Nicaraguan harbors. The truth is that we played no role in the mining of the harbors.'[44]

On the diplomatic level Motley accused the Sandinistas of deception, arguing that 'In the guise of "negotiating", Nicaragua was *rejecting* accommodation' [emphasis in original]. The National Bipartisan Commission on Central America delivered its report in mid-January intending to find policies acceptable to both political parties. Michael Barnes, a counsellor to the commission, stated, 'the central thrust of this report is to recommend military solutions for the region and to deny the viability of political ones'. Colombian Foreign Minister Lloreda Caicedo, pointed out:

> the United States has not discarded a possible military solution, and the Group insists that any military solution must be discarded, not only by the United States but by the USSR and Cuba. There is a difference in this regard.[45]

A number of bureaucratic manoeuvres took place to remove Stone, later described by Otto Reich as 'unique in the annals of bureaucratic back-stabbing'.[46] While his removal lowered hope for a negotiated solution, the process was important during the election campaigns of 1984.

# 3 Manzanillo and Contadora 1984

A Contadora agreement would have isolated the Soviet presence from the region and brought 'in the plural forces of Western Europe, Japan, and the multilateral organizations', thereby reducing US hegemony, as the Mexican novelist Carlos Fuentes informed the Kissinger Commission. Washington, however, actively pressured European governments, notably the French, and used its influence in multilateral lending organizations to block loans or aid, isolating Nicaragua and forcing a greater dependency on sources beyond US influence. As Eastern Bloc aid increased, Washington had a self fulfilling argument that the Soviets were indeed increasing their presence in the region. A semblance of moderation was needed to gain congressional support and the findings of the Kissinger Commission were used to this end. Basically, Reagan erroneously informed Congress on 17 February 1984 that Kissinger had reached similar conclusions to those of Contadora; but while Contadora wanted to limit arms to the region, Kissinger advocated an increase. The intention to gain a policy consensus had a limited effect; North noted to McFarlane that Kissinger had 'defended [the contra] program most eloquently' in a private meeting with Speaker of the House, Thomas O'Neill, and Boland, and Kissinger 'believes that with a well led and cooperative effort we can carry the day on this issue'. Kissinger advocated a more active effort at exposing the realities of the region, but allegations on Soviet activity and their actual presence differed considerably.[1]

When the Document of Objectives was transformed into a legal draft for the purposes of signing a treaty, the section on the illegal transfer of weapons was readily acceptable to Nicaragua, perhaps because as Representative Clarence Long, Chairman of the House Appropriations Sub-Committee, concluded that 'we are the principal suppliers' of the rebels. All parties would have to stop the transfer of arms from governments, individuals, regional or extra-regional groups, and stop supporting individuals, groups, irregular forces advocating the overthrow or destabilization of other governments. Researchers at the Stockholm International Peace Research Institute indicated the objections to the security clauses put forward by Costa Rica, El Salvador, and Honduras implying a threat from Nicaragua were 'not convincing'. Nicaragua was hardly in a position to sustain a military action against either of these countries; had they tried, they would have been subject to a retributive collective action under the Rio Treaty involving the United States in a direct response. To some extent the Soviets played a cynical game of bolstering revolutionary movements to force the United States 'to divert both greater attention and resources' to the region. The bottom line however remained that the Sandinistas had to accept responsibility for their own survival and publicly Moscow constantly supported Contadora. Western diplomats argued at the time, that Soviet involvement in Nicaragua was 'cautious', as did Peter Clement, a CIA employee in the Office of Soviet Analysis, 'in reviewing Soviet policy toward Nicaragua since 1979, one is struck by the general caution with which Moscow has proceeded' because Moscow was not willing to tie its prestige to the Sandinistas. Yet sufficient aid had to be provided '. . . to ward off future accusations that she might have betrayed the revolutionary cause'. Carl Jacobsen argued Moscow was unable to control events because of other agencies and governments ignored by Washington:

> The counterweights to Soviet influence are also more far-reaching and varied than sometimes appreciated. Extensive West European presence is often commented on, as is pervasive Church influence. Other actors have also moved in. UN agencies fund a large number of Nicaraguan development projects; Japan's trade with Nicaragua has risen in direct reverse proportion to Washington's economic disentanglement; Algeria picked up the sugar quota that America cancelled; the larger South American states have given Nicaragua significant support; even U.S. and contra-aligned Honduras, El Salvador and Guatemala maintain trade with Managua.[2]

## MINING NICARAGUAN HARBOURS

In late February 1984 Reagan determined a further $14 million for the contra programme was 'essential to continue these activities and prevent a major foreign policy reversal'. His memorandum of 21 February pointed out the legislative strategy for obtaining funds should emphasize a negotiated solution and the importance of the 'resistance program'. In the absence of US proposals, the only significant negotiating process, widely supported, was Contadora which wanted to disband the contras. An FDN proposal of the same day suggested they would suspend their military actions while they searched for peace, but effectively blocked negotiations by demanding 'immediate substitution of the Sandinista regime'. Congress concurrently backed Contadora and called for the 'immediate elimination of illegal arms traffic and *all forms* of support for insurgents' [emphasis added]. It also suggested US regional policy should be conditioned by the degree a government supports Contadora. With the prospect of limited future funds NSA McFarlane pointed out that unless additional funding is found the 'program will have to be drastically curtailed by May or June of this year'. The fiction of a search for a negotiated solution was essential given the Intelligence Authorization Act requested a Presidential report that had to indicate 'steps taken and recommendations for further action to achieve a negotiated settlement in Central America'. Such congressional demands shaped the rhetoric and reasoning of the administration. McFarlane put forward the proposition that:

> Should these efforts have to be terminated for lack of resources, we will have lost our principal instrument for restraining the Sandinistas from exporting their revolution and, in fact, for facilitating a negotiated end to the regional conflict. The international repercussions of this failure in American policy will affect friends and adversaries alike. We must avoid precipitating perceptions of a second 'Bay of Pigs' or creating an environment conducive to the collapse of El Salvador or increasing the threat to Honduras.[3]

Nicaragua initiated a complaint on the violation of its waters and air space before the UN Security Council in early February. Its allegations were subsequently proved largely accurate, most pointedly by NSC operatives Oliver North and Constantine Menges, who wrote in early March 1984 that 'four magnetic mines' had been placed in the harbour of Corinto on 29 February, ARDE, 'in accord with prior arrangements . . . took credit for the operation'. The US intended to 'severely disrupt the flow of shipping essential to Nicaraguan trade during the peak export period.' In another case the objective was to 'further impair the already critical fuel capacity in Nicaragua'. The attempted commercial blockade was in defiance of the rules of international shipping and international law. The Sandinistas assert that confidence in the peace process was undermined by such activities and that until the United States renounced such activities

> we cannot and must not entertain false hopes concerning a political solution, and the Nicaraguan people must continue to prepare to fortify themselves in order to be able to oppose and defeat imperialistic aggressiveness and intervention.[4]

In accordance with congressional requirements the administration's report by Shultz on the 'US Peace Efforts in Central America' laid the blame on the Sandinistas for refusing to negotiate with the contras on their earlier terms. The report suggested the OAS would be helpful in implementing specifics of an agreement but noted such a shift in the negotiating process would be interpreted as a 'vote of no confidence in Contadora that would greatly reduce its effectiveness. Others would see it more simply as a US effort to sabotage the peace process.' To bolster the perception of US activity in the search for peace, Shultz pointed out the prompt appointment of Harry Shlauderman to replace Richard Stone. Credit for success in the peace process should be given to the on going pressure from the neighbouring countries, the United States, unnamed 'international bodies', and the armed Nicaraguan opposition. The 'grudging' participation by the Sandinistas was due to the 'desire not to be blamed for failure'. He held Nicaragua's neighbours and the United States believed the pressure was working;

> and, indeed, has proven to be the only effective inducement to the Sandinistas – we believe that it should only be reduced or removed when Nicaragua undertakes the real changes in its external and internal policies that will contribute to regional peace.

Shultz quoted the report: 'we do not believe it would be wise to dismantle existing incentives and pressures on the Managua regime except in conjunction with demonstrable progress on the negotiating front.' While some change had occurred on Sandinista 'intransigence', no change had occurred in 'their goals of spreading revolution or consolidating their rule'.[5]

Motley set forward the arguments before the Subcommittee on Foreign Operations of the House Committee on Appropriations, highlighting the deteriorating economic situation which provided an opportunity for communist exploitation. The request for economic assistance was couched in the overall support for the peace process which 'if implemented on a verifiable and reciprocal basis, [would] meet our concerns in both Central America as a whole and in Nicaragua.' But any successful agreement could not be sustained in the face of economic collapse, hence any settlement necessitated the approval of aid. An additional requirement outlined by Motley was that the flow of resources should have some consistency:

> Resource predictability would provide the basis of confidence that regional diplomacy needs to channel events toward peaceful solutions, including negotiated solutions wherever possible.
>
> Demonstration by the United States of a long-term commitment through the provision of adequate levels of economic and military assistance and the adoption by Central American governments of

> appropriate economic, political, and social policies/reforms are all essential to an active diplomacy for peace.

Motley held: 'Economies must be protected as well as developed. Governments must be worth defending. Homegrown poverty and Cuban-directed guerilla warfare work in tandem; our policies must address both'.[6]

The Director of Central Intelligence, William Casey, was not relying on congressional favour. Toward the end of March 1984 he wrote to McFarlane on the need to find alternative sources of funding for the contras given congressional unpredictability. While administration policies were presented as an attempt to pressure the Sandinistas towards a negotiated solution, the *Iran–Contra Report* noted a significant departure from these parameters by Oliver North. It established that by March 1984:

> it had become clear that the diplomatic end the Finding described was not what North anticipated or encouraged. In memoranda to McFarlane, he proposed significant military actions against the Sandinistas, the details of which cannot be disclosed for national security reasons.[7]

On 6 April the United States modified their acceptance of the compulsory jurisdiction of the International Court of Justice because Washington could not accept international jurisdiction for isthmian problems. The withdrawal lasted for two years and took effect immediately ostensibly to avoid undermining the Contadora process 'which seeks a negotiated solution to the interrelated political, economic and security problems of Central America'. Nicaragua had called an urgent meeting of the UN Security Council in late March which on 4 April produced a draft resolution in opposition to US arguments. It urged states of the region, and 'other States' to 'refrain from continuing or initiating military operations with the objective of exercising political pressures which would aggravate the situation in the region and hinder the negotiation efforts by the Contadora Group'. The resolution called for an immediate end to mining Nicaraguan ports resulting in the loss of life; it reaffirmed Nicaragua's right to live in peace and security; and, it called 'on all States to refrain from carrying out, supporting or promoting any type of military action against any State of the region as well as any other action that hinders the peace objectives of the Contadora Group'. The United States vetoed the resolution, Britain abstained, the other thirteen members of the Security Council voted in favour of it.[8]

Mexico and Panama and the French in a letter to Colombian President Betancur protested the mining. The French expressed the extreme worry

of both Foreign Minister Claude Cheysson and P
demning the resulting deprivation of vital huma
pertinently they considered the mining a 'direct
Group' and offered to clear the mines from Nicar
a spokesperson for the State Department accused the
of 'helping export revolution', and stated that 'doubts still exist
nature of French aid to Nicaragua'.[9]

*The New York Times* revealed the administration had also devised contingency plans for the use of US combat troops in the region if current strategies failed. The article alleged that the key strategists were Under Secretary of Defense for Policy, Fred Ikle, his aide, Nestor Sanchez, from the National Security Council, Oliver North and Constantine Menges, and from the US Southern Command, General Paul Gorman. The intention was to use the 'Vietnam syndrome', to send a message to Congress: that if current policies were not supported, US combat troops would be the next step. An ulterior motive was to send leftist forces within and without the hemisphere a message that ultimately they would have to deal with the United States.[10]

The inter-branch acrimony in Washington over the mining largely obscured the issues at the international level. A letter Goldwater wrote to Casey reveals the attention placed on domestic implications rather than the morality or legality of the operation. Goldwater's letter described his mood bluntly: 'It gets down to one, little, simple phrase: I am pissed off!' Primarily because Casey had informed the House committee, but because he had not informed the Senate committee, Goldwater had denied Reagan had approved the mining during the debate on contra aid: 'I found out the next day that the CIA had, with the written approval of the President, engaged in such mining.' Goldwater's exasperation at not being informed culminated in the assertion: '*mine the harbors of Nicaragua? This is an act violating international law. It is an act of war*. For the life of me, I don't see how we are going to explain it' [emphasis added]. Following this the Senate voted 84 to 12 to pass a resolution which stated: 'No funds heretofore or hereafter appropriated in any Act of Congress shall be obligated or expended for the purpose of planning, directing, or supporting the mining of the ports or territorial waters of Nicaragua.'[11]

When Nicaragua brought its case to the International Court of Justice the US response was swift. A statement emphatically denied the existence of plans to use US troops in Central America, and indicated the United States did not intend to 'destabilize or overthrow the Government of Nicaragua'. Larry Speakes, imputed the Sandinistas had gone outside the normal hemispheric fora by 'making propaganda at the United Nations' attempted to sidetrack negotiations by going to the International Court Justice.' In any event, he concluded,

> The real issues are whether we in the United States want to stand by and let a Communist government in Nicaragua export violence and terrorism in this hemisphere and whether we will allow the power of the ballot box to be overcome by the power of the gun.

A verifiable Contadora agreement would have strictly limited the presence of both superpowers. The Deputy Secretary of State, Kenneth Dam, argued Nicaragua was 'forum shopping', a tactic familiar to all lawyers. But US isolation was becoming more acute, Richard Falk, Professor of International Law at Princeton, pointed out that Latin American diplomats made 'no secret of their conviction that the major obstacle to a peaceful settlement is to be found in the Reagan White House'. Polls also indicated only a third of the American people supported Reagan's policies in Central America, with over half polled believing that the policies may lead to war and sixty-seven per cent disapproved of the mining operation.[12]

The covert funding efforts from third governments were impeded by the apparent opposition. The potential involvement of South Africa produced some wariness of their offer of assistance. A heavily censored CIA cable indicated:

> DDCI [Deputy Director of Central Intelligence] advises that there are some second thoughts around town as to the wisdom of involving [deleted] in already complicated Central American equation. Request you hold off on this aspect of your discussions until we can get definitive word to you.

In early May another cable regretted: 'Current furor here over the Nicaraguan project urges that we postpone taking [deleted] up on their offer of assistance'.[13]

By mid-May the International Court of Justice ordered the United States to 'cease and refrain from any action restricting, blocking or endangering access to or from Nicaraguan ports, and in particular, the laying of mines.' Two years later the Court found against the United States on three counts 'in breach of its obligations under customary international law'.[14]

## THE INTELLIGENCE COMMITTEES

The only covert operation the Boland Committee in the House opposed was the Nicaraguan programme, normally it approved the proposed covert operations. The committee acted only when events forced them. The original Boland amendment was passed unanimously indicating compromise with the executive branch. In 1983, when the (whole) House voted to cut funds from the programme in Nicaragua, Boland 'judiciously, act[ed] to terminate aid to Nicaragua only when it was obvious that the will of the House was being flouted.' The impression that congressional committees were opposed to the administration is somewhat a misnomer. The operations in Afghanistan were supported because congressional committees were involved in the non-contentious use of US power. There was no breach of security and Senators Paul Tsongas and Malcolm Wallop took the initiative in October 1984, arguing in language echoing a sentence from the Kissinger Commission report, 'It would be indefensible to provide the freedom fighters with only enough aid to fight and die, but not enough to advance their cause of freedom,' sponsored a successful resolution to expand the programme.[15] The Nicaraguan programme dwarfed in size compared to the Afghan operation, but the administration had challenged traditional congressional powers.

## BILATERAL AND MULTILATERAL DIPLOMACY

The Reagan administration was under considerable pressure to demonstrate a willingness to pursue a negotiated solution in Central America. Specifically, Congress expressed support for the Contadora initiative through House Concurrent Resolution 261, which it passed on 1 May 1984. In early May the former President of Venezuela and the then current vice president of the Socialist International, Carlos Andréz Pérez, indicated Washington was the main stumbling block to Contadora. He charged State Department officials 'speak of support . . . but when we dig a little deeper, we find that they do not really believe in Contadora.' Washington maintained its usual position. Secretary of State for Inter-American Affairs, Langhorne Motley, reaffirmed

> a combination of pressure and inducements is essential. The need for pressures arises from one fundamental reality: the need to convince the Sandinistas of the unworkability of their starting assumption that their Cuban/Soviet ties would enable them to assault their people and their neighbours with impunity.

There was no evidence of a Sandinista threat to its neighbours outside the ideological conception that all 'Marxist' states were expansionist and aggressive. The International Court of Justice took a different view ruling in 1986 that,

> the Court does not believe that the concept of 'armed attack' includes not only acts by armed bands where such acts occur on a significant scale but also assistance to rebels in the form of the provision of weapons or logistical or other support.

The judgement stated further, such support could be regarded as intervention, and the state which is the victim of the armed attack must declare this view; customary international law does not permit another state to exercise the right to collective self-defense based on 'its own assessment of the situation'. While El Salvador had declared itself a victim of armed attack, the Court noted, it had not done so till some three years after the United States had implemented its response to Nicaragua. A legal US response necessitated proof of a Nicaraguan attack on any of the Central American states. On El Salvador the Court found that assistance to the FMLN was not

> on a scale of any significance, since the early months of 1981, or that the Government of Nicaragua was responsible for any flow of arms at either period. Even assuming that the supply of arms to the opposition in El Salvador could be treated as imputable to the Government of Nicaragua, to justify invocation of the right of collective self-defense in customary international law, it would have to be equated with an armed attack by Nicaragua on El Salvador the Court is unable to consider that, in customary international law, the provision of arms to the opposition of another State constitutes an armed attack on that State. Even at the time when the arms flow was at its peak, and again assuming the participation of the Nicaraguan Government, that would not constitute such armed attack.

The Court concluded the US arguments on self-defence could not be upheld.[16]

In mid-May the Mexican President Miguel de la Madrid, on a visit to Washington, warned on arrival at the White House:

> Peace has been disrupted in Central America and the risk of a generalized war, the scope and duration of which no one can foresee, is growing. Every country on the continent must do its utmost to restore peace and avoid war by respecting and upholding the sovereignty of its people to decide their own destiny and by rejecting interventionist solutions of any kind.

In response Reagan stated that the differences with Mexico over Central America were 'not on goals or principles. [But] on the means by which to achieve our goals.' Their ideas on the principle of non-intervention diverged sharply, but Reagan nevertheless praised the efforts of Contadora but stated the problems of Central America were too close to ignore. However, Reagan asserted the United States would 'go the extra mile to find peaceful solutions and to protect democracy and independence in the hemisphere.' The extra mile, however, did not involve compromise. The United States attempted to shape the peace along their lines. According to the *Miami Herald* a National Security Decision Document, signed by Reagan in February 1984 suggested a willingness to apply pressure on Mexico. The relevant paragraph authorized officials to 'intensify . . . diplomatic efforts with the Mexican Government to reduce its material and diplomatic support for the Communist guerrillas [in El Salvador] and its economic and diplomatic support for the Nicaraguan government.' While pressure had to be used in the context of US bilateral interests some officials proposed economic sanctions if Mexico failed to comply with their intentions; ultimately it was decided to confine US actions to the diplomatic level. The *Miami Herald* cited US officials as indicating the moves in 1984 by Mexico to upgrade its relations with El Salvador as indicative of their response.[17]

On 18 May 1984, immediately after de la Madrid's warning, the US National Security Council prepared their response and their strategy for obtaining further supplemental funds for fiscal year 1984. A memorandum from NSA McFarlane to Reagan, drafted by Oliver North, pointed out the deadlock in the appropriations systems in the House and Senate. Congressional supporters of the administration argued an 'orchestrated presentation in a closed session' was necessary; and 'a concerted lobbying effort' would be required to convince the undecided. The Nicaraguan programme should be framed as a 'watershed' issue that may prohibit funding of other 'anti-communist democratic resistance groups'. McFarlane concluded: 'we *must* portray this vote as an issue of long term significance which will affect future Administrations, whether they be Democratic or Republican' [emphasis in original]. Reagan's subsequent memorandum exhorted recipients to

> frame our approach on the strategic importance of Central America to our own national security. It should be stressed that continuing the Nicaraguan program is critical not only to the future of Central America but to our world wide credibility. Measures should be taken to cause a closed briefing for the entire House of Representatives so that there can

> be no doubt that 'terminating' this program would have disastrous results for the United States.[18]

## BILATERAL TALKS AT MANZANILLO, MEXICO

The United States changed tactics as a direct result of de la Madrid's visit. After over two years of insisting that the appropriate forum for negotiations was multilateral, the State Department entered bilateral negotiations with the Sandinistas. In a number of conversations with Reagan and Shultz, Mexico emphasized the need for direct bilateral communication between Washington and Managua in addition to Contadora's arrangements. Shultz told Sepúlveda that Reagan would have to be consulted on the possibility and later Ambassador Shlauderman told him Shultz had obtained presidential authorization to start negotiations. Yet, the commitment to negotiations was strongly opposed by other senior and influential US officials. Sepúlveda was aware of the divisions which created problems for Shultz's approach. Because of the

> different decisions on the part of different interest groups, different personalities in the National Security Council and that meant a constant horse trading, a constant negotiation and not always did they reach a clear cut decision in favour of negotiations in the Central American process.[19]

The talks still benefited the administration's legislative strategy as Shultz could announce in Managua on 1 June 1984: 'President Reagan sent me to Central America on a mission of peace.' His meeting with Contadora leaders determined their effort was the most efficacious method to resolve the regional issues, but the US position was reiterated and Harry Shlauderman was designated to continue discussions for the United States. The two-and-a-half-hour talks with Daniel Ortega were the first high level discussions since Enders' informal talks in August 1981. Nicaragua's Foreign Minister, D'Escoto, stated that he could not help but think that these actions were being undertaken 'to put a little bit of makeup on the face of the Reagan administration.' D'Escoto questioned the timing but stated:

> We are willing to give it a chance . . . Is it a publicity stunt? Is it because of the fact that the Reagan administration realizes that its image has been quite damaged by this warlike attitude, because of this flagrant violation of all principles of international law.

Still Managua named its Deputy Foreign Minister, Victor Hugo Tinoco, as its representative at the talks. Managua's flexibility was noted because the official communique ruled out 'internal affairs or any other matter concerning sovereignty or self determination' but US security concerns could be guaranteed through treaties. Nicaragua indicated its 'hopes that the visit of Mr. Shultz constitutes a serious step that effectively will be the start of a process of seeking political solutions to the problems.' The good will, however, had to be backed up by movement towards ending the covert war.[20]

The Mexican Foreign Minister indicated a number of measures could be taken to eliminate the security risks in Central America. Decisions on internal matters such as democratization would have to be taken immediately, but their effects would not be seen for some time, whereas outcomes of security decisions could be seen immediately. The Contadora forum was a more appropriate place for decisions on internal matters such as democratization, as Nicaragua and other participants could agree specific limitations to their sovereignty through entry into a treaty. But immediate movement on security was not a US intention within the Contadora framework. Shultz affirmed on 3 June 1984, that the administration would pursue its quest for $21 million in supplemental aid for the contras. There was a general attempt, though, to play down the significance of the meeting to prevent 'any great enthusiasm' or hope for the process. In spite of these apparently placatory moves, the House of Representatives refused the requested additional funding, and in late June, despite Senator Dodd's initial estimation that the Shultz trip would 'add to the administration's credibility and enhance its margin of victory', the Senate also voted to delete its amendment to the Agricultural Bill that would have allocated the $21 million to the contras.[21]

As Shlauderman and Tinoco commenced their meeting in the Mexican resort of Manzanillo, the National Security Planning Group were meeting in Washington to discuss their negotiating strategy. McFarlane summarized the recent congressional position and indicated the key question on negotiations concerned the prospect for talks with Nicaragua, and whether they wanted a reasonable agreement.

> Based on the answer to that question – how do we keep the friendly Central American governments together and focused on a multilateral, comprehensive, and verifiable treaty? What can we do to reinforce the confidence of the Central American and regional countries in the US in the light of questions about continuing congressional support for the anti-Sandinista program?

Shultz argued the administration would not have achieved the deployment of Pershing missiles in Europe 'had it not been seen that we had a credible, vigorous negotiation going on.' The United States had made credible proposals which were rejected by the Soviet Union. 'This is useful,' Shultz noted, 'because it shows who is at fault for the lack of progress.' Negotiations were 'essential . . . or else our support on the Hill goes down'. Hence,

> it is not a question of making a prediction about the outcome of the negotiations, rather it is important that we don't get sucked into something bad as it is essential to our strategy to key everything we do to support for the Contadora regional processes as I shall call it.

Congress had not approved administration requests and while congressional members were out of Washington for the following three weeks 'therefore, anything credible going on the negotiating track can only help us'. Shultz noted a shift in Mexican attitudes and indicated there was some impatience with the Nicaraguan negotiating posture. The other Central American countries were worried about the bilateral talks but 'these concerns can be assuaged' through close consultation; Honduras, for instance, was worried about the decline in the US military presence. Shlauderman was instructed 'only to talk about modalities and procedure – not to table anything' in Mexico, 'but to continue these negotiations, we must have content', Shultz added, concluding:

> Ambassador Shlauderman has a tableau of these four steps with blanks where any numbers are involved. From the standpoint of negotiations, we need to get the word to go ahead, or we need to decide on some other approach. *Then, we will subvert the whole thing and it will have to abort. I have to get word to Shlauderman* [emphasis added].[22]

Following Shultz, Casey summarized the developments of the covert operations. He requested a decision on the authorization for the FDN to obtain funds from third parties but did not mention the Saudi Arabian money already contributed to the contras. Weinberger recommended that the administration hold Congress accountable for not providing the funds to 'protect democracy' and 'take the offensive against the Democrats in Congress'.

Funding remained the key problem. Reagan's first statement during the meeting highlighted this, and his perception of the current impasse:

> It all hangs on support for the anti-Sandinistas. How can we get that support in the Congress? We have to be more active. With respect to

> your differences on negotiating, our participation is important from that standpoint, to get support from Congress.

He generally observed:

> If we are just talking about negotiations with Nicaragua, that is so far-fetched to imagine that a communist government like that would make any reasonable deal with us, but if it is to get Congress to support the anti-Sandinistas, then that can be helpful.[23]

Shultz noted Contadora support for the bilateral negotiations but wondered how Washington could conduct the talks to leave the perception that it was aiding the multilateral process. Shultz conceded that 'if people here are so reluctant, then we can go back and try to abort this whole thing'. The chances, he stressed, of a positive negotiation with Nicaragua were 'two-in-ten, but if it doesn't succeed, it needs to be clear where the responsibility is, and that we have tried to help our Contadora friends obtain a positive outcome.' Finally, McFarlane concluded, 'Marxist–Leninist regimes historically do not negotiate in order to make reasonable concessions . . . For them negotiations are tactical exercises to split up their opponents and to obtain their goal'.[24]

The State Department did not intend to negotiate a separate bilateral treaty, but Shultz pointed out Contadora was 'delighted with our initiative' and he had spent time discussing the matter with the House speaker Tip O'Neill. Reagan's position was that the Central American countries must be supported and assured of the US commitment to them. He recommended persisting in the talks, because, 'to back away from talks will also look like a defeat', but he could not imagine that Nicaragua would offer anything reasonable in a bilateral treaty.[25]

The decision document resulting from the meeting instructed Shultz to continue the talks with Nicaragua, based on NSDD 124 seeking the four administration goals: democratization, an end to export of subversion, removal of Soviet/Cuban personnel, and a reduction of Nicaraguan forces. Again in opposition to the thrust of Contadora the Secretary of Defense was instructed to provide plans for increasing the military activities in the region.[26]

At this point interdiction or the export of subversion was totally fallacious given the congressional awareness that a new radar system and patrol boats in the Gulf of Fonseca had found nothing and the overland operation interdicted an empty truck. Representative Gejdenson observed:

> it seems to me for all the effort we have placed on interdiction, there is not much evidence of a big flow.

> It seems to me that if the flow of arms to El Salvador was as great as the administration suggests, with a serious effort to monitor the border you would have stumbled on more weapons than we have interdicted. I think we have to take a look at what is happening with the equipment and arms to El Salvador once we ship it.

The contras were assured of US support and Edgar Chamorro testified, he was told

> the United States Government would find a way to continue its support . . . Mr. Lehman assured us that President Reagan remained committed to removing the Sandinistas from power. He told us that President Reagan was unable at that time to publicly express the full extent of his commitment to us because of the upcoming presidential elections in the United States. But, Mr. Lehman told us, as soon as the elections were over, President Reagan would publicly endorse our effort to remove the Sandinistas from power and see to it that we received all the support that was necessary for that purpose.

Prior to the fourth session at Manzanillo Nicaragua refuted US claims on the their continued export of revolution and proposed joint border patrols with Honduras, aided by US intelligence to 'contain the trafficking of arms and men from Nicaraguan territory to El Salvador as well as from Honduran territory into Nicaragua'.[27]

Nicaragua scheduled its elections for 4 November 1984, just two days before the US election; it would bestow greater legitimacy on their regime and enhance their position in Contadora. The Sandinistas had to ensure the domestic opposition participated to enhance their democratic credentials. In early August opposition parties stated they would only participate in the elections if the Sandinistas reinstated the *habeas corpus* and the press restrictions were liberalized. As far as Washington was concerned the participation of contra representatives became an important test of Sandinista tolerance and pluralism, even though these groups remained armed. Arturo J. Cruz Sr., the former Nicaraguan ambassador to Washington, flew into Managua as the presidential representative for the opposition coalition. He announced he was pulling out of the race after forty-eight hours in Nicaragua, contending the Sandinistas had not met his demands. Cruz failed to register his candidacy because the Coordinadora Democratica's (CDN) demand that the Sandinistas begin direct talks with the contras was rejected. Cruz argued that the elections were entirely for 'outside consumption' and to 'appease international opinion'; without CDN participation the process was denied the 'largest of the democratic forces' and could not be considered legitimate. And without 'free' elections the contras would always be justified in their war against the Sandinista regime.[28]

The fourth round of Manzanillo negotiations took place in the wake of yet another move by Congress to terminate contra funding. The House of Representatives passed Resolution 5399 on the Intelligence Authorization Bill prohibiting the use of funds for covert activities in Nicaragua. The vote, 294 to 118 was the fourth time in fourteen months the House voted against supporting the contras. The meeting was marred by revelations on attempts to assassinate Sandinista leaders derived from the CIA-authored manual *Psychological Operations in Guerilla Warfare* which was circulating among contra groups. A section of the manual advocated the possibility 'to neutralize carefully selected and planned targets, such as court judges, *mesta* judges, police and State Security officials, CDS chiefs, etc.' Despite acrimonious exchanges the talks were characterized by the Sandinistas as fluid and substantive. Daniel Ortega pointed out the process could 'establish firm bases that could lead to a political, negotiated solution that gives a measure of mutual security to the United States and Nicaragua'.[29] Shlauderman orally presented the US position during the session. The text of the proposal was delivered to the Sandinistas weeks later at their fifth session in early September. The proposal was divided into six sections on: advisers, support of insurgencies, levels of arms and forces, democracy, economic cooperation, and verification. Each of these was divided into three stages of 30, 60, and 90 days. Some actions would have to take place on all sections within each time period.

On the security issues, the first three sections of the proposal, stated that in the first 30 days Nicaragua would have to withdraw a third of the Cuban and Soviet personnel. In return the United States and the other Central American countries would take the Nicaraguan actions into consideration. Nicaragua would have to close FMLN command and communications centers but the contras would merely agree not to mine or attack the harbours or petrol tanks; their normal destructive activities were permitted. All countries would agree to not introduce offensive weapons and begin negotiations on arms inventories. The United States would still be allowed to hold naval exercises in he area, albeit with prior notification and with some unspecified foreign observers present.

At the end of 60 days, Nicaragua would have to expel another third of its foreign advisers while the United States continued to take these moves into consideration. FMLN training centers would be closed down, contra camps could remain with a ceasefire arranged with the Sandinistas. There was no reciprocal obligation at this stage on Honduras to close down FDN camps, or on Costa Rica to close ARDE camps. After 90 days, all Soviet and Cuban personnel would be withdrawn, but the United States would still be taking these changes into consideration. All Salvadoran guerrillas would have to leave Nicaragua, and all contras would have to leave Honduras and Costa Rica, their external logistics and support would cease while they were re-incorporated into their respective political systems. The section on democracy provided a schedule for this re-incorporation of insurgent forces. Nicaragua was obliged to invite all tendencies to run in elections, restore political rights, and guarantee equal access to the media. El Salvador had to invite the opposition to run in the March 1985 elections, offering them security guarantees. There were no similar requirements for Guatemala or Honduras. The symmetry imposed in the system between the contras and the FMLN was a misrepresentation of their composition. The bulk of the FMLN operated and occupied large sections of El Salvador while ARDE or the FDN operated from outside Nicaragua. Incorporating the contras into the Nicaraguan political system would have been an implicit Sandinista concession. The structure of the proposal inaccurately implied the FMLN were controlled by the Sandinistas or Cubans. Though contra strategy was largely directed by Washington, the Sandinistas did not control the activities of the FMLN. FDN leader Edgar Chamorro later confirmed:

> I joined on the understanding that the United States Government would supply us the means necessary to defeat the Sandinistas and replace them as a government, but I believed that we would be our own masters. I turned out to be mistaken. The FDN turned out to be an instrument of the United States Government and, specifically, of the CIA. It was created by the CIA, it was supplied, equipped, armed and trained by the CIA and its activities – both political and military – were directed and controlled by the CIA . . . It could not exist without the support and direction of the United States Government.

The State Department laid out its intention in a 1985 report *Revolution Beyond Our Borders*: on Manzanillo 'the United States entered the discussions prepared to reach bilateral understandings that, channeled into the multilateral process, would facilitate conclusion of a comprehensive Contadora regional agreement.' But the proposal mandated Nicaragua to fulfil requirements beyond their control.[30]

The talks were described by Mexican Foreign Ministry spokesman, Augustin Gutierrez, as focusing on 'substantive issues'. Further, these bilateral talks provided proof that the Mexicans had not distanced themselves from Nicaragua. The allegations that Mexico had become disillusioned by the Sandinistas and that they saw some benefit resulting from the US application of pressure on the Sandinistas was emphatically denied by Sepúlveda.[31]

On contra funding the administration was considering whether it should compromise with congress openly or continue solicitation of third party funds. The office of the General Counsel was consulted on the latter alternative, and indicated on 23 August 1984 that 'the Agency' [CIA] was permitted to request that third countries continue the programme at their own expense but US funds could not be used to reimburse any state at some future date. The counsel wrote:

> On its face and by its very title, the House version operates as a *total prohibition* on the use of any funds by U.S. intelligence elements during FY 85 for direct or indirect support of military or paramilitary operations in Nicaragua by anyone. This language effectively blocks all direct U.S. activities in Nicaragua and precludes U.S. financial support for the Contras during FY 85 by any means [emphasis added].

A loophole or 'grey zone' was identified which was already in operation under certain NSC officials. Legal counsel wrote that the prohibition was on 'funding not discussions'. As long as Washington made no reciprocal commitments it was interpreted to comply with the law:

> If, however, the third country expected repayment from the U.S., such assistance would be forbidden. If such a country provided aid with the understanding that the U.S. would provide an equal amount for one of their programs, the Agency would be in violation of both the letter and the spirit of Section 107 and would be open to charges of deliberate circumvention of the law.[32]

## THE FIRST CONTADORA ACT

Significant diplomatic events took place in the two months prior to the November elections. The US proposals at Manzanillo were tabled at the fifth session on 5 and 6 September 1984 and Contadora submitted their revised draft agreement on 7 September. Nicaragua's response to both of these documents met with US disfavor; it rejected the US proposal and accepted Contadora. The Contadora group had met the Central American leaders on 9 June 1984 and submitted its first draft treaty – the Contadora Act for Peace and Cooperation in Central America. The five isthmian and four regional countries revised the act over the next three months and presented it to the Central American governments on 7 September for relevant 'improvements', and signature 'in the not too distant future'. This draft resulted from what Contadora described as an

> intense process of consultations and a broad exchange of views with all the Central American Governments, which provided the Contadora Group with valuable ideas for revising and enhancing the Act and *for facilitating a consensus* that would be reflected in legal commitments undertaken by *all parties* [emphasis added].

The group specifically noted 'negotiating implies yielding some ground in order to secure the ultimate objective which is considered essential.' The Central American participants had provided ideas that facilitated consensus and the initial reaction from Shultz was positive. He called the treaty an 'important step forward' and favourably mentioned the conditional acceptance of the four Central American countries on the day the document was released. The negative reaction came from Managua. Foreign Minister D'Escoto argued that as long as Nicaragua was 'being attacked . . . it is totally inconceivable, unacceptable, that we should be asked to disarm.' The problem was one of timing. Would the Nicaraguan government be expected to disarm before the contras were demobilized? Sepúlveda stated that while some 'fine-tuning' was necessary for completion, this current document was a 'considerably more precise version' of the June document already approved in principle. Shultz, however, noted reservations about the Act in a letter to the European Community foreign ministers. The agreement was considered important and Nicaragua was blamed for their reservations. Shultz wrote:

> from our perspective this document presents many positive elements but lacks specificity in some aspects, particularly with respect for verification and enforcement of the commitments undertaken. We also identify a serious deficiency in the deferral of negotiations of reductions in arms and troop levels and withdrawal of foreign military and security advisers until after the conclusion of the basic agreement . . . Nevertheless, we consider the Contadora draft an important step forward, as do the governments of El Salvador, Honduras, Guatemala and Costa Rica. They tell us they are firmly committed to negotiations based on the current draft that would lead to a comprehensive agreement. Nicaragua, on the other hand, has rejected key elements of the draft, including those dealing with binding obligations to internal democratization and to reductions in arms and troop levels.[33]

Menges in the NSC saw a need to 'counter the active pro-Sandinista diplomacy of the Mexican government' which was trying to guarantee

Sandinista power through diplomatic methods leaving El Salvador and Honduras isolated in the region, by 'the political front of the communist war for control of Central America.' Washington had to rally the three other Contadora countries in support of the four 'friendly' isthmian governments. In early September Menges travelled to Europe to brief EC foreign ministers on Central America, but their first draft declaration was considered 'very adverse'. It failed to support 'the region's genuine democrats', and failed to 'condemn the aggression of communist Nicaragua'. While Menges was in Europe, Contadora released its 7 September draft and, according to Menges, Shlauderman left a copy of the US formula at the Manzanillo meeting contrary to Reagan's written instructions. Menges urged Europeans not to endorse the Contadora draft.[34]

President Duarte indicated he was ready to sign the document before November 1984, and Foreign Minister Carlos Guttiérez of Costa Rica stated his country had decided to sign the text because it had considered all their earlier objections. According to the US ambassador, Curtin Winsor, the Costa Ricans believed they could sign the treaty because no 'communist' government would sign a document involving multilateral verification; Nicaragua would inevitably back away from the Act. On 19 September Honduras indicated some further revisions were needed, except two days later Daniel Ortega sent a message to Contadora accepting 'in its totality, immediately and without modifications, the revised proposal submitted on September 7'. The following day, after visiting three Contadora countries, President Duarte of El Salvador stated: 'Let us do something. Let us sign the document' and promised to send the 55 US military advisors back home. By accepting the Act Nicaragua had to expel all Soviet bloc advisors, estimated by the State Department at 3 500. Imports of all Soviet weaponry would have to be cut off; Nicaragua's army would have to be reduced; all aid to Salvadoran guerrillas would have to be halted; dialogue with the internal opposition would have to be conducted; and verification commissioners would be allowed to inspect the implementation of all of these commitments. James Dunkerley argues that the corresponding reductions required of the other Central American nations, especially El Salvador, 'represented a far greater threat to Washington's strategy in terms of both formal military aid and support for the Contra'.[35]

Nicaragua required signature by Washington on an additional protocol prohibiting further contra aid. Tinoco indicated Nicaragua had the impression it would be difficult for the United States to sign the agreement. With El Salvador and Costa Rica tentatively committed, and Nicaragua firmly committed, Washington started to find substantial faults with the treaty. The Sandinistas were accused of conducting a 'public relations coup' and

State Department spokesman, Alan Romberg argued: 'Nicaragua is clearly seeking to close off debate on those provisions of the latest draft concerning the size of military forces and procedures for verification and control.' Washington disliked the protocol requiring US signature because it would have required both superpowers to formally agree not to interfere with the implementation of the treaty. The very signature of the Soviet Union or Cuba on a protocol, admitted a political role of these powers in the isthmus; hence the signatures themselves were unacceptable. Though the administration thought Soviet and Cuban involvement extensive any joint signatures would imply an equal right of both powers to involvement in the western hemisphere, traditionally regarded by US policy makers as their sphere of influence. The Sandinistas had accepted the Contadora Act over the bilateral proposals because the latter was intended solely to facilitate signature of the former, and from Nicaragua's point of view Contadora gave the Sandinistas more security than Manzanillo currently offered.[36]

With the unexpected Sandinista acceptance, Washington made their substantive objections and moved to reverse the verbal acceptances of their regional allies. The National Security Council took the lead in this effort. A letter drafted by the NSC from Reagan to his counterparts in Central America was cleared by the departments of State, Defense and the CIA, stating the 7 September 1984 Act did not meet the criteria for a 'genuine political settlement'. Menges reminded McFarlane of the urgency to deliver the letter to prevent the EC foreign ministers endorsing the Act, and to avert Central American acceptance of the Act. Menges noted that shortly after this, 'the four Central American presidents . . . issued statements *rejecting* the September 7, 1984 draft treaty' [emphasis in original]. Statements by the foreign ministers of El Salvador and Honduras reflected aspects of Reagan's letter. Changes unacceptable to the Sandinistas, though acquiesced in by Sepúlveda, and the Central American presidents scheduled their meeting to formulate a counterdraft for 19 October 1984.[37]

Sepúlveda later recalled the original draft was also blocked from becoming an official Security Council document:

> Certainly there were two instances in which it was very clear that the U.S. was blocking Contadora at the level of the Security Council. One was related to the submission of the first draft of the Contadora Act to the UN, and at that time what we wanted was to make certain that such a draft would be accepted by the five Central American governments. Much to the surprise of the U.S. government Nicaragua publicly declared that it was ready to accept that international treaty. And at first the other four Central American countries said they were ready to

accept it, and that was basically because they had participated in the negotiations and they did see that the draft treaty reflected their basic concerns . . . because of very strong pressure on the part of the U.S. government and at that time by Jeane Kirkpatrick herself, because we were together at the UN, all the foreign ministers . . . because of the pressure exerted there in New York, the . . . three . . . decided to ask for a review of that draft of the Contadora Act. And certainly Ambassador Kirkpatrick played a very relevant role in convincing these three countries to change their position.[38]

The EC delegation at the end of September produced a declaration that tried to satisfy both positions on the 7 September Act. In the final analysis, it endorsed further negotiations which was favourable to Washington and the amended positions of the four Central American countries. Most significantly:

> They noted with satisfaction the progress achieved so far toward such a solution, and that the revised draft Contadora Act for Peace and Co-operation in Central America is a fundamental stage in the negotiating process for the attainment of peace in the region.

Apart from the political endorsement of the Act, the United States did not want the EC to aid Nicaragua in any way. Economic isolation was a key part of the overall strategy. Shultz wrote to the EC foreign ministers early in September strongly urging that any 'region to region assistance does not lead to increased economic aid or any political support for the Sandinistas'.[39]

In Washington the National Security Council had triumphed in getting their position to the fore. A background paper in late October noted, 'we have trumped the latest Nicaraguan/Mexican efforts to rush signature of an unsatisfactory Contadora agreement and the initiative is now with the Core Four.' The document also stated:

> The Administration is on record in opposition to signing a Protocol, both in principal [sic] and specifically in the case of Contadora. We have attempted to prevent adoption of a Protocol that would be open to Cuban, Soviet, or other unwelcome signatories.

Yet Contadora knew the extra-regional powers would have to agree and abide by the treaty to guarantee Central American security. Sepúlveda stated later:

> It was essential to make certain that the U.S. was committed to the Contadora arrangement; it was essential to make certain that Cuba fully understood the nature of the process and made an important political

> contribution for the implementation of the treaty; that the Soviet Union was ready to accept the terms of the Contadora process and also to endorse and implement the results . . . We did realize that it was not enough to have the agreement of the five Central American countries, the other three countries, the U.S., the Soviet Union, and Cuba had to make an important political contribution.[40]

The United States used the outcome of the diplomatic activities of late September to bolster its case at the International Court of Justice. The US legal representative at the Hague argued Nicaragua portrayed Washington as the major obstacle to Contadora. The Court was specifically referred to the EC declaration describing the Act as a 'stage' in the negotiating process;

> *Nicaragua alone* wishes to stop the Contadora negotiating process at the stage of an intermediate draft agreement. Under these circumstances, Nicaragua cannot plausibly contend that it is the United States that is blocking progress in the negotiations [emphasis in original].

Isthmian countries argue the Court was only dealing with an isolated issue in the overall political context and suggested there was unanimous agreement that the Court's entertainment of Nicaragua's claims 'seriously risks undermining the possibilities for Contadora's achievement of peace in Central America.' Ironically, he United States noted

> Complex multilateral negotiations require a delicate balance of concessions and compromises. If, in the midst of such negotiations, one party achieves some or all of its negotiating objectives elsewhere, the balance of concessions and compromises may be irretrievably upset.

The International Court of Justice later ruled that the United States 'violated a number of principles of customary international law.' Apart from these there was the further principle to 'seek a solution by peaceful means.' It noted Article 33 of the UN Charter and stated the Contadora process corresponded 'closely to the spirit of the principle which the Court has . . . recalled' and was considered a 'unique contribution' to regional peace. Sepúlveda pointed out a coincidence between Contadora meetings and covert activity, specifically the

> shelling of the City of Managua, the attack on Puerto Corinto, the attack on Puerto Sandino, or border incidents [led the Contadora countries] to believe that there is a connection between our meetings and the desire to disrupt them with actions of this sort.

The Chairman of the House Foreign Affairs Subcommittee on Western Hemisphere Affairs, Michael Barnes opined in early October that US objections to the treaty 'reinforce my belief that it never had any real interest in a negotiated settlement.' There were capable diplomats in the region and it was 'unseemly for us to be telling the countries of Central America why they should reject this treaty'.[41]

The idea for the bilateral Manzanillo talks was described as a 'coup within the administration'. Casey, Weinberger, and Kirkpatrick were informed orally without deliberate briefing papers. Casey was informed by Motley that they were going to try a publicity stunt. The talks would focus on form rather than substance with the aim of appeasing Congress. North, Menges and Ikle were not informed of the Shultz visit to Managua before it took place. Though both governments agreed not to disclose information to the media to avert a public relations exercise, Ortega broke the agreement in October 1984 at the Untied Nations. He described the US proposal that Shlauderman left with Tinoco in early September as 'totally irrational' which would, if made public, 'be proof of the lack of responsibility, the lack of sincerity of the United States'. The proposals were designed to 'liquidate' the revolution and step up military intervention.[42]

CIA assistance to the contras had slowed since the summer of 1984 as funds ran out. But since Reagan clearly wanted continued contra support the job fell to the NSC. A National Security Planning Group (NSPG) meeting on 11 September 1984 noted that sophisticated Soviet block arms continued to reach Nicaragua which intimidated the other countries from achieving a multilateral agreement. Any US support for the contras would be 'conducive to restoring influence over resistance activities which has diminished as a consequence of no US funding'. On 19 September 1984 Reagan signed a finding authorizing the activities outlined in a NSDD. The relevant portion of the NSDD remains censored; but the procedures for its implementation reveal that, North told McFarlane: 'the NSDD calls for the CIA to provide assistance to the Nicaraguan Resistance Forces in interdicting Soviet arms bound for the FSLN in Managua'.[43]

The following day a further Boland amendment was enacted by Congress. In the Senate two amendments had been defeated days earlier that would have curtailed contra activity: Senator Daniel Inouye sought to 'wind down' the contra forces by barring further aid to them except for $6 million for resettlement outside Nicaragua and Senator Dodd proposed an amendment to bar the contras using US money to engage in 'terrorist' activities. Intense administration pressure was applied on the Senate to reject these amendments. On 10 October the House approved a conference report on H. J. Res. 648 [House Joint Resolution], which gave the contras

$14 million that could only be released after 28 February 1985. Section 8066(a) prohibited funds to the contras in what became known as the second Boland amendment. The following exchange took place during the debate:

> *Livingston*: Does this prohibition prevent any expenditure of funds, direct or indirect, for arms or weapons or use of force in Nicaragua by the United States?
> *Boland*: If it is directed against the Government of Nicaragua, the answer would be in the affirmative, yes.
> *Livingston*: Are there no exceptions to this prohibition?
> *Boland*: There are no exceptions to the prohibition.

The following day Boland elaborated on the stringency with which the amendment was written, stating that it also prohibited the transfer of equipment acquired at no cost. The provisions intended to allow the President to consider important developments in the five months till the end of February 1985. The developments listed by Boland for consideration were: a proposal for talks to begin between the FMLN and the Government of El Salvador; the results of the bilateral talks between the United States and Nicaragua; a resolution of the Contadora treaty; and the elections in Nicaragua. Boland finally asserted 'the compromise provision clearly ends US support for war in Nicaragua'.[44]

Oliver North and John Poindexter disagreed on the intention of the amendment. They both later testified that the amendment was a prohibition on agencies involved in intelligence matters; the National Security Council was not founded in 1947 with this purpose in mind and was therefore technically not described as an agency engaged in intelligence matters. Hence, under that analysis, the NSC was free to assist the contras. As the CIA was precluded from acting in this area Poindexter described North as the 'switching point that made the whole system work . . . the kingpin to the Central American opposition . . .'. Theodore Draper points out that in theory the NSC is involved in coordinating intelligence not collecting it; in practice what 'counted most was what the NSC staff did, not what it was theoretically supposed to do or not do.' North's activities were so wide and varied, the distinction between collecting and coordinating intelligence, Draper argues 'hardly mattered'. The actual amendment, as approved by President Reagan on 12 October 1984 read as follows:

> During fiscal year 1985, no funds available to the Central Intelligence Agency, the Department of Defense, or *any other agency or entity of the United States involved in intelligence activities* may be obligated or

> expended for the purpose or which would have the effect of supporting, directly or indirectly, military or paramilitary operations in Nicaragua by any nation, group, organization, movement, or individual [emphasis added].[45]

If the administration intended to pursue contra aid after the five month period (covertly procured throughout it), each of the five issues Boland noted for presidential consideration had to be denigrated. Especially, Contadora had to be shown to be ineffective, the bilateral talks inappropriate, and the Nicaraguan elections undemocratic.

## THE TEGUCIGALPA COUNTER DRAFT

During October 1984 Washington sought to shape the outcome of the Contadora process through active engagement with isthmian governments. The most suitable result, apart from Sandinista capitulation, was to ensure the process did not produce results. While Shultz celebrated 'democracy' in Panama, he indicated Washington had put forward general comments on changes needed in Contadora,

> but basically the countries involved in the Contadora process are the ones that are shaping this, so it isn't so much a question of us putting out something and people reacting to it but rather of people discussing together some of their views.

The National Security Council had a rather different interpretation of the US role. A background document recounted under the section on Core Four Position on the Draft Contadora Treaty:

> *We have effectively blocked Contadora group efforts* to impose the second draft of the Revised Contadora Act. Following *intensive U.S. consultations* with El Salvador, Honduras, and Costa Rica, the Central Americans submitted a counterdraft [sic] to the Contadora states on October 20, 1984. It reflects many of our concerns and shifts the focus within Contadora to a document broadly consistent with U.S. interests [emphasis added].[46]

The revisions took place at the invitation of the Honduran government producing a document on 20 October known as the Tegucigalpa draft which differed significantly from the 7 September Act. On arms negotiation, the Department of State later wrote, the key criterion was that no armed institution could have the capability of imposing hegemony on any other country 'considered individually'. Irregular forces, according to the new draft, would have to be relocated outside the area after they had been disarmed; the FMLN would certainly have rejected this, causing the failure of the process. Military exercises would not be proscribed, but subject to 'restriction', giving the advantage to the United States. Military bases were also proscribed by Contadora, but the Tegucigalpa draft left the issue to be negotiated on within 90 days of signature. The issue of the protocol was left for ongoing consideration, and the verification mechanisms were to be given funding before agreement, but the enforcement mechanism was changed from the requirement of a unanimous vote by the five foreign ministers to a decision by consensus. Should a consensus not be reached, rather than referring the matter back to Contadora, it would be taken up by all nine participants leaving the Contadora nations in a minority position.[47]

Guatemala did not send its foreign minister to the meeting in Tegucigalpa. In his place, the Deputy Minister for Foreign Affairs, Mario Marroquin Najera attended. Guatemala though consenting to the communiqué, did not sign it. In Washington, the NSC was aware of the problem. The Council proposed 'US Efforts to Obtain Guatemalan Cooperation in [the] Contadora Process'. The NSC noted

> the uncertain support of Guatemala for the Core Four is a continuing problem. Guatemala's chief security concern is its guerilla insurgency and the sanctuary that it has until recently enjoyed in Mexico. Mexico's removal of the border refugee camps and the need for future cooperation provide a strong incentive pulling Guatemala towards Mexico in Contadora. We have undertaken intensive efforts with Foreign Minister Andrade and Guatemalan Chief of State Mejia on this issue . . . We will continue to exert strong pressure on Guatemala to support the basic Core Four position.

The United States later held that there were no substantial changes made to the 7 September Act by the 20 October revisions. The differences, it argued, lay in the strengthening of the verification procedures. Tom Farer claimed the revised document tended 'strongly to slow and weaken the process of military de-escalation and negotiation'.[48]

The attempt to delay significant advances in the Contadora process beyond the five month period Boland allowed for consideration in his compromise amendment was successful. The NSC noted that the 'regional peace talks, [were] moving in a direction favorable to US interests' though 'Congressional failure to fund the armed opposition is a serious loss.' The document later stated that 'Contadora spokesmen have become notably subdued recently on prospects for an early signing . . . [S]ome now conclude that agreement may not be reached for some months.'[49]

## NICARAGUA'S MANZANILLO PROPOSAL

Nicaragua adopted the Contadora Act of September as its negotiating base with the United States. Tinoco, presented the Nicaraguan position in writing at the seventh Manzanillo session. The proposal basically required simultaneous action on the whole range of issues. Since Nicaragua neither engaged in international exercises nor hosted military bases, the onus was now on the United States. Nicaragua's adoption of Contadora as their negotiating position put the United States in an awkward public position as the State Department had initially considered the Contadora Act a positive document. Washington had initially encouraged others to accept the document including the Sandinistas in the hope that their expected rejection would provide the administration with a propaganda victory.[50]

The United States refused to modify their proposal presented orally to the Sandinistas in August 1984 and the Sandinista proposals were similarly not accepted. Administration officials told *The New York Times* that Shlauderman's latitude was limited by negotiating instructions written in Washington precluding a serious exploration of the resolution of differences: 'No one will tell Shlauderman what the endgame is, what the road map to a final agreement is. The reason is that the Administration doesn't really want a settlement with the Sandinistas.'[51]

# 4 Undermining Democracy: Elections 1984

Democratization had been a contentious diplomatic issue since 1982 when it was injected into the Quainton proposals. The Sandinista policy on elections began before the revolution in a statement sent to the OAS, used repeatedly by Washington to allege revolutionary promises had been broken. Its inclusion as an internal Nicaraguan matter raised questions on state sovereignty and its significance in international law. Its inclusion at the bilateral level was more offensive than its inclusion in the regional process where each country would be expected to make concessions on its sovereignty.

The diplomatic exchanges on the elections related more to Washington's policy requirements than objective analysis, given the US stance was formulated prior to the events, hence conclusions of the international observers could not have considerably affected the diplomatic processes. The word 'democracy' carries considerable 'ideological freight' in the context of Central American diplomacy. Months before the Nicaraguan election Reagan characterized the process as a 'Soviet style sham', whereas the elections in Guatemala in 1985 were described by the State Department as the 'final step in the re-establishment of democracy'. John Booth points out some interpret the 1984 Nicaraguan elections as a consolidation of democracy, while those held in El Salvador (1982, 1984), and Guatemala (1985), were manipulated to allow the United States to send further aid to their militaries, strengthening the anti-democratic elements in those countries. Nicaragua's process of democratization was inhibited by the absence of a consensus manifested in political factions coupled with US efforts to disrupt the electoral process through the proxy war. Peace needed to be achieved for the consolidation of democracy.[1]

Susanne Jonas identified a distinction which sheds light on the process of negotiations and the question of political legitimacy with which the United States viewed the Sandinista government. The contractual legitimacy accredited to the state by maintaining an embassy in Managua is distinct from the views on political legitimacy held by the administration. The proposition distinguishes between representative democracy and 'anti-Communist or counterinsurgent democracy'. In the context of the Reagan Doctrine, 'restoring democracy' implied the 'rollback or elimination' of states labeled 'Communist'. Hence the promotion of instability and physical destruction as part of a process of 'promoting democracy' are only compatible if 'democratic' is equated with 'anti-Communist'. Washington denigrated Sandinista legitimacy which inhibited a serious process of arriving at mutual concessions. Alejandro Bendaña, of the Nicaraguan Foreign Ministry, pointed out:

> Washington simply refused to deal with us seriously. Serious negotiations presume a recognition of the legitimate interests of your opponent, indeed of the legitimacy of the opponent; which explains why the U.S. systematically refused to seriously negotiate with Nicaragua.[2]

The 1984 elections offered a potential for the Sandinistas to gain further legitimacy in the international arena.

## BACKGROUND TO THE ELECTIONS

Just under a month before the FSLN came into power on 19 July 1979 the OAS passed a resolution over the objections of the Nicaraguan representative of the Somoza government. Point four of the resolution stated that Nicaragua should hold 'free elections as soon as possible, that will lead to the establishment of a truly democratic government that guarantees peace, freedom and justice'. A week before seizing power the Sandinistas enunciated their electoral intentions and ratified them in a telegram from Costa Rica; the relevant section read:

> [we] plan to call the *first free elections our country has known in this century*, so that Nicaraguans can elect their representatives to the city councils and to a constituent assembly, and later elect the country's highest authorities [emphasis added].[3]

The precise wording of this communication is important, because it formed the corner stone of the Reagan administration's rhetoric on democratization in Nicaragua. Washington consistently interpreted the content of this message to allege the Sandinistas had not fulfilled their promises on democracy and pluralism.

In 1980 the Sandinistas announced they would hold elections in 1985 and on 21 February 1984 the date was set earlier than anticipated for 4 November 1984. The intention was to have an elected government in place before the anticipated re-election of Reagan on 6 November. There were negotiations between the Sandinistas and the candidate for the *Coordinadora* (CDN) coalition, Arturo Cruz, mediated by the Socialist International through Willy Brandt, to delay the date of the election but ultimately the

Sandinistas retained their schedule. The decision to do so concluded the participation of Cruz and the *Coordinadora*. In Washington, the participation of Cruz was not dependent on the outcome of the Socialist International mediated talks. According to unnamed 'senior administration officials' Cruz was never going fully to participate in the elections. *The New York Times* cited US officials who stated 'the Administration never contemplated letting Cruz stay in the race, because then the Sandinistas could justifiably claim that the elections were legitimate', making US opposition much more difficult. Craig Johnstone, the Deputy Assistant Secretary of State for Central America, denied the contention stating the United States favoured full participation. The administration was divided on the CDN participation resulting in confused US responses. Roy Gutman was informed that the CIA and the White House staff wanted 'to avoid participation' but the State Department debated 'whether to go halfway or not', supporting the Cruz candidacy; Casey and Kirkpatrick in the cabinet, North and Menges in the NSC supported Cruz 'in the expectation that he would not participate in the elections.' The President's indecision on competing strategies allowed the various power centers to pursue their policies 'according to their interpretation of the goals'. The US ambassador to Costa Rica reportedly stated to an assistant to Cruz, Bill Baez, 'There is a division in the government. Some people in the State Department are saying you should participate. I represent the views of the White House. My opinion is that it is not appropriate to go.' Cruz himself told an NBC reporter before leaving for Managua: 'You know I'm really not going to run.' Cruz's withdrawal was then used to question the legitimacy of the process. The Latin American Studies Association (LASA) delegation also found that in the six month period prior to the elections Washington used a combination of diplomatic, economic, and military pressures to systematically

> undermine the Nicaraguan electoral process and to destroy its credibility in the eyes of the world. Within Nicaragua, the behaviour of U.S. diplomats was clearly interventionist. This behaviour included repeated attempts to persuade key opposition party candidates to drop out of the election, and in at least one case, to bribe lower-level party officials to abandon the campaign of their presidential candidate, who insisted on staying in the race.

Furthermore, the administration successfully portrayed Cruz as the only legitimate opposition figure. His participation was presented as a 'litmus test' of free elections. LASA claimed that there was 'never any credible evidence that Cruz . . . had a broad popular following'. A National Security Council document stated under a heading on Public Diplomacy: 'We have succeeded in returning the public and private diplomatic focus back on the Nicaraguan elections as the key stumbling block to prospects for national reconciliation and peace in the region.' The document concluded that the Cruz withdrawal 'left the Sandinistas holding a near worthless hand', they would not have the 'legitimacy they covet'. The *Washington Post* added that the document included a section on a plan to convince the Americans and the world that the elections were a 'sham'.[4]

## THE 1984 ELECTIONS

The 1984 elections were judged by prominent international observers as being predominantly free and fair. LASA found that no major political tendency was denied access to the process; 'the only parties that did not appear on the ballot were absent by their own choice, not because of government exclusion.' The FSLN abused its incumbent position in some ways, but generally, 'the FSLN did little more to take advantage of its incumbency than incumbent parties everywhere (including the United States) routinely do, and considerably *less* than ruling parties in other Latin American countries traditionally have done' [emphasis in original]. By standards in Latin America, LASA stated, the election was 'a model of probity and fairness'.[5]

The British delegation, made up of a member from each of the major political parties, 'were very conscious of the exceptional nature' of the election due to the historical background of over four decades of dictatorship. The elections were described as an 'important step' in the process of transition from dictatorship to the 'institutionalisation of a democratic system of government'. The substantial minority elected to the Assembly made the body 'representative of opinion in Nicaragua, and is further grounds for treating this election as authentic and democratic'. The Socialist International report highlighted the electoral context of war, fear of invasion, poverty, the absence of a democratic tradition, and the focus of world attention. It considered the electoral law satisfactory, noted incidences of harassment of opposition parties, unequal access to radio and television, and some censorship unrelated to the war, which they considered regrettable.[6] While the other reports took account of these issues, they did not deem them sufficient to alter their conclusions, given the historical and political context.

The Sandinistas won 67% of the valid votes, and 63% of the total votes cast. 20.5% of voters chose parties to the right of the Sandinistas; 25% of the electorate abstained; the British delegation noted that considering the normal abstention level in elections throughout the world, the CDN could only credibly claim 'a relatively small proportion of the non-voters as its own supporters.' Given the large minority vote they argued 'the results were an accurate reflection of political loyalties in Nicaragua and a good measure of the popularity of the Sandinistas'.[7]

The Sandinistas met their obligations, as far as the specific wording of their 'promises' to the OAS in 1979, were concerned. The first free and fair elections this century had been conducted. The Reagan administration took a different view, to some extent because the elections and democratization had been a corner stone of their diplomacy for over two years; it was imperative to retain the issue within the negotiating fora. The day after the poll, John Hughes of the State Department was asked a question on the elections to which he immediately responded: 'What election?' Elaborating, he purported the 'Nicaraguan people were not allowed to participate in an election in any real sense of the word.' The process was labelled a 'farce', because without 'meaningful opposition' the situation was unchanged. He described the poll on 4 November 1984 as a 'lost opportunity' for the Sandinistas and the event a 'piece of theater'. Asked how it would affect the bilateral talks between the two countries, Hughes responded Washington had 'pledged ourselves to continue serious talks with the Sandinistas, and those continue to go forward'.[8] The Sandinistas, however, gained further legitimacy making it difficult for the issue to be introduced into the bilateral formulae, without any compromise from Washington.

The administration only considered the issues within the political context of the Cold War and their 'anti-communist' strategies. LASA asked a senior US official why the United States had endorsed the Salvadoran elections in which parties to the left of the Christian Democrats were excluded, while condemning the more inclusive Nicaraguan process? The explanation given was demonstrative of administration thinking on the matter:

> The United States is not obliged to apply the same standard of judgement to a country whose government is avowedly hostile to the U.S. as for a country, like El Salvador, where it is not. These people could bring about a situation in Central America which could pose a threat to U.S. security. That allows us to change our yardstick.

LASA suggested the most plausible explanation for Washington's conduct was the 'deep, ideologically grounded hostility of the Reagan Administration toward the Sandinista government, whose elimination has been the primary objective of US policy'.[9] The elections made little difference to the bilateral negotiations because Washington did not admit the political legitimacy of the Sandinista government.

The campaign and the election results were further obscured by two separate incidences. Prior to the election it was revealed that the CIA had authored a manual on 'psychological operations' which advocated the 'neutralization' of certain Sandinista officials. The word was widely interpreted to indicate assassination, which is both contrary to US law and Reagan's Executive Order 12333 of 1981. Reagan, however, explained the term 'neutralize' as a peaceful means of deposing Nicaraguan officials: 'You just say to the fellow who's sitting there in the office, "You're not in the office anymore."' He described the issue as 'much ado about nothing'. The administration concluded there had been no violations of law, but 'lapses in judgement'. However, investigations conducted by the Congressional Intelligence Committees were more critical of the CIA. Chairman Boland concluded that there was insufficient concern regarding the restrictions on the CIA to aid the contras but stated the violation of his amendment was one of 'negligence, not intent.' The administration indicated it would discipline those involved. FDN leader Edgar Chamorro, involved in translating the manual, was quite categorical in his comments on the portion of the guidebook, stating that it advocated '"explicit and implicit terror" against the civilian population, including assassination of government employees and sympathizers.' He concluded in his affidavit: 'the practices advocated in the manual were employed by FDN troops. Many civilians were killed in cold blood. Many others were tortured, mutilated, raped, robbed or otherwise abused.' The 'atrocities', he stated, 'reflected a consistent pattern of behaviour by our troops'. Following admissions to the press on these matters, Chamorro was reassigned to the FDN office in Miami.[10] Thereafter, he resigned.

The other incident that distracted from the results of the elections was the claim Nicaragua was about to import MiG aircraft. Earlier in the year, Reagan had instructed Shultz in a secret directive to warn the Soviet Union, Cuba, and Nicaragua that the United States would not tolerate the deployment of advanced combat aircraft in Nicaragua; the warning was repeated in early November 1984. Reagan stated that the delivery would indicate that Nicaragua was 'contemplating being a threat to their neighbors'. The State Department indicated the US would regard such an acquisition with 'particular exception' describing their presence as 'particularly destabilizing, and obviously having an offensive reach beyond the boundaries of Nicaragua'. According to the London International Institute for Strategic Studies, in 1984 El Salvador had 59 combat aircraft, Guatemala had 16, Honduras had 30, and Nicaragua had 12. Daniel Ortega argued the intention was to make 'American people forget that Nicaragua had elections and to portray Nicaragua as warlike'. The LASA delegation concurred stating the outcome of the elections were virtually ignored in the United States. Another possible motive behind the unfounded allegations of the MiG delivery was to overcome administration divisions on Nicaraguan policy. The acquisition of advanced combat aircraft would effectively weaken or even silence those in the State Department more favourable to continued negotiations. *The New York Times* was informed by an official on 11 November 1984:

> Some of those who want us to adopt a harder line have long wished that MIG's would be delivered because they know that would tilt the policy in their direction. The arrival of MiG's would break the bureaucratic tie ballgame over Nicaragua. The next best thing to the delivery of MiG's was the possibility that they might arrive any day.[11]

While diplomacy continued there were explicit indications Washington considered the removal of the Sandinistas. Reagan had indicated that there was no desire to send troops to Central America and that there were no plans to do so. The government, however, would continue trying to gain contra funding. Ortega charged Washington with trying to 'liquidate our revolution', which was in fact being considered by the NSC. Oliver North held discussions on the matter on 6 November 1984, after which he wrote to McFarlane that he and FDN leader Calero 'briefly reviewed the prospects for a liberation government in which Cruz and Calero would share authority'.[12]

With the increased tension during November Contadora issued a communiqué explicitly stating that a 'solution based on force or military action was the wrong course to take', and called for a clear expression of the political will to search for a negotiated agreement. They also drew the attention of states with 'links to and interests in the region' for the need of a 'constructive attitude . . . so that the negotiation process could be brought to a speedy conclusion.' Within days the OAS endorsed the Contadora negotiations and called for the 'prompt signature of the Contadora Act'. The resolution referred to the 7 September Act, the Tegucigalpa counter-proposal had not been adopted by Contadora. Contadora wanted a prompt signature because the Central American states had increased their cooperation with Washington on contra operations, and the divisions in the Reagan administration were becoming increasingly public, diminishing the prospect of an unified commitment by the entire government. The divisions were internally acknowledged by the Deputy National Security Advisor, John Poindexter, who tried to formulate a response for

McFarlane. His prescription was likely to exacerbate the discord. He wrote: 'Continue active negotiations but agree on no treaty and agree to work out some way to support the Contras either directly or indirectly. Withhold true objectives from staffs'.[13]

These policy divisions were fermenting conflict amongst contra groups. A meeting between contra leaders, Menges and other NSC staff, concluded it had become obvious the State Department were opposed to a resumption of contra assistance, but Kirkpatrick, Casey and Weinberger would ensure they received support. North stated that Calero was 'distressed and confused . . . he feels that the mixed signals he is receiving portends serious problems within the Administration.' North concluded:

> Calero has too much on his mind to be burdened with our internal differences. It is unfortunate that we now seem to have so many voices speaking for our intentions. Before this goes any further, it would seem appropriate to clarify the roles various people will be playing in the days ahead.

The signals Calero was receiving were indeed mixed, North was actively engaged in the attempts to gain further contra funding or cooperation from third countries, which had prompted the mid November Contadora communique. However, the effective leader of one of the Contadora countries, Manuel Noriega, was also involved in supporting the contras, and North informed McFarlane the People's Republic of China (PRC) were involved in negotiations with Guatemala for the latter to ostensibly purchase weapons. North advised 'that the purchase was not really intended for use by the Guatemalans but rather for the Nicaraguan Resistance Forces'. The transaction ran into difficulty when China discovered that a number of the Guatemalan officers had been trained in Taiwan, thus an 'end-user certificate' indicating Guatemala was not politically appropriate. Chile was then considered. North confirmed, however, that Calero as head of the FDN, 'was willing to commit to a recognition of the PRC once the Resistance Forces had succeeded'. Ultimately China sold the weapons to the contras. The United States disclosed isthmian support at the 1989 North trial:

> Guatemala had provided aircraft and had agreed to facilitate Resistance shipments of munitions and other material. Honduras had permitted the Resistance to operate from within its borders, had repaired Resistance aircraft at cost, had allowed government aircraft to bring in aircraft parts, had permitted the Resistance to borrow ammunition when Resistance stocks were too low, and had provided the Resistance with false

> end-user certificates . . . El Salvadoran military officials continued to allow the use of a military airbase in support of ARDE air operations.[14]

This extensive support betrayed the Contadora objectives signed by all participants in 1983.

The CIA was aware of and facilitated the meetings between the staff of the NSC and foreign officials. CIA director, William Casey, looking for a 'comprehensive' analysis of the situation in Central America that could be supported by 'all elements of the US Government' stated in a memorandum to his deputies, his division and area chiefs, that 'in our backyard we should not . . . discourage support to check Soviet and Cuban expansionism from these and other countries . . .' A week later the Deputy Director for Intelligence, Robert Gates, maintained it was time to 'talk absolutely straight about Nicaragua'. He continued:

> The truth about the matter is that our policy has been to muddle along in Nicaragua with an essentially half-hearted policy substantially because there is no agreement within the Administration or with the Congress on our real objectives. We started out justifying the program on the basis of curtailing the flow of weapons to El Salvador. Laudable though that objective might have been, it was attacking a symptom of a larger problem in Central America and not the problem itself.

He advocated 'a comprehensive campaign openly aimed at . . . ridding the Continent of this regime as our primary objective'. His four-point programme included ending diplomatic relations and recognizing an exiled government; overt military support for the contras; economic sanctions 'including a quarantine'; and 'politically the most difficult of all, the use of air strikes'.[15]

The hostilities and the added tension engendered by the two countries effected the diplomacy at Manzanillo. By mid-December 1984 Nicaraguan officials were questioning the efficacy of the negotiations in conjunction with the covert action. After eight meetings at Manzanillo Nicaraguan officials stated Washington was trying to create the impression of progress to placate domestic criticism of their policies, the talk on the proximity of an accord was 'totally removed from reality' and it was 'clear that the United States doesn't want an agreement with Nicaragua. They are just trying to reinforce the ground work for the one policy that persists in the Administration, a military solution in Central America.' The House Committee on Intelligence also found numerous citations in the CIA manual referring to 'overthrowing the Sandinistas'.[16]

In fact several new options were being developed by Oliver North which were to be simultaneously discussed with Central American and congressional leaders to determine which one was most 'palatable' to them before a final decision was made. To this end, McFarlane travelled to Central America between 17 and 19 January 1985. The specific objectives of the trip were to discuss the regional issues, listed as the militarization of Nicaragua and Soviet assistance; Contadora; Manzanillo, and economic aid. Contra military capabilities had to be assessed, their credibility, and the willingness of regional countries to support them were to be discussed 'directly and privately'. North informed McFarlane:

> Your visit will be reassuring to our friends in the region who perceive indications of a downward trend in our relations during the opening of the second Administration . . . The Hondurans are particularly concerned over what they see as mixed signals regarding our recognition of their vulnerable position on Contadora and our willingness to renew support for the Nicaraguan resistance. Despite our plans to hold the Manzanillo talks temporarily in abeyance, our friends have doubts about our steadfastness in dealing with the Sandinistas.

McFarlane received a private briefing from the CIA's Chief of the Central American Task Force, Alan Fiers, stating that Guatemala would continue to support the resistance if it received a '*quid pro quo* from the United States in the form of foreign assistance funds or credits, diplomatic support or other forms of assistance'.[17]

North suggested several options for consideration in the second term of Reagan's presidency. The options included 'seeking a negotiated solution toward Nicaragua, restoring US government support to the Resistance, or using US military force to overthrow the Sandinista regime.' The second option had several elaborations considered in detail. They included, the continued US solicitation of third country support; the restoration of the original 'CIA managed' programme; a combination of US non-lethal support coupled with lethal support given by third countries; a clarification of congressional attitudes to third country support; 'overt assistance to a new state established by the Resistance'; and the revival of the collective security idea in the form of reconstituting CONDECA, which could divert a section of its finances to the contras. While option E was entirely deleted in the document, the US government, in 1989, identified it as the option of giving overt assistance to a state established by the resistance. Each option is considered for its merits and demerits with regard to the Central American countries, congressional legislation and the amount of US control over the forces. North argued they would have more success if perceptions were changed on the regional threat from the Sandinistas to the Soviets.

He counseled, 'we should move immediately to re-orientate the perceived threat from the Sandinistas to focus on risks posed to US security by the active involvement of the Soviet Union and its surrogates in establishing a client state in Nicaragua.' North advocated option C., the combination of non-lethal US support with lethal support 'provided through third country financial assistance and direct provision of arms and ammunition'. He recommended the requests to Congress should be for a much larger sum reflecting the administration's perceived threat of the Soviet Union in Central America: 'A figure closer to $100M would indicate to the Congress the urgency of the situation and our concerted belief that an adequately funded resistance force could provide sufficient pressure to deter further Soviet/surrogate encroachment in the region.' A request for this amount was put forward and passed by Congress in 1986, but the political climate in Washington during 1985 did not permit such a solicitation. North argued the contra strategy 'must be designed to prevent the consolidation of a Marxist–Leninist FSLN government in Nicaragua' within the constraints of various objections. McFarlane was informed 'one of the most important issues on this trip is to determine what type of support the resistance is most palatable to our friends in the region. Don Fortier is pursuing the same strategy with the leadership in Congress'.[18]

In mid-January 1985, the State Department, the Office of the Secretary of Defense, the CIA, the Joint Chiefs of Staff, and the NSC supported the third variation on the second option: non-lethal US support with third country lethal assistance. Thus the first and third options, a negotiated solution and direct US intervention were not deemed efficacious and were not pursued. This course was decided on despite the Contadora declaration issued days earlier on 9 January 1985, stating political intransigence must not be allowed to impede dialogue and negotiations. They urged the Central American governments to adhere to the 1983 Document of Objectives, and 'refrain from any action which would thwart the ongoing efforts to achieve peace' and called on 'the Governments of the United States and Nicaragua to intensify the talks which they have been holding in Manzanillo, with a view to reaching agreements that will promote the normalization of their relations and regional detente'.[19]

Ortega argued a normalization of relations was essential to Nicaragua, but could only be achieved if the contras were defeated, Washington was persuaded that military options would not solve the regional problems, and US 'neocolonial' attitudes towards Nicaragua were abandoned. Two days later on 18 January 1985, Washington announced it was suspending the bilateral negotiations, accusing Nicaragua of a lack of interest in serious exchanges. The decision was conveyed to the Sandinistas through the US

Ambassador to Managua, Harry E. Bergold, who indicated it would be inappropriate to schedule further discussions. Tinoco only received the news in his attempts to schedule the tenth meeting for 24 to 25 January. Tinoco called the suggestion that Nicaragua was not serious 'absurd', adding that 'the few people in the Reagan Administration who favoured a policy of dialogue have been pushed aside'.[20]

The State Department announcement explained: 'at this time, the Contadora process is about to enter a new phase of negotiations, and we believe it appropriate and possibly helpful to that process to hold off any further Manzanillo meetings while those negotiations are in progress.' A White House official added that there was no point in pursuing the discussions unless the Sandinistas were prepared to make concessions, with the implicit message that contra funds would be pursued to bring about this flexibility: 'To put it simply', the official stated, 'we're not going to get anywhere in negotiations unless the Nicaraguans are scared to death of the rebels'. The official rationale was maintained in a Department of State report of late 1985 which explained that because of Nicaragua's adoption of the 7 September Contadora draft as its negotiating position, the United States had either to accept this or enter into a purely bilateral relationship. 'Neither alternative was acceptable', the United States did not schedule further discussions 'pending demonstration that Nicaragua was prepared to negotiate seriously within the Contadora framework.' Though Nicaragua had accepted the Contadora Act without modification in September 1984, their adoption of this act as their position in the bilateral negotiations could have been negotiated on. Further, Nicaragua had adopted this position in late October 1984, yet over two months elapsed before the termination of the bilateral discussions were announced. Hence, any adverse reaction to the ending of diplomacy would not occur prior to the US November elections. Washington left open the possibility for further discussion at some future date.[21]

The Mexican Foreign Minister, Sepúlveda, later stated the US thought their basic political objectives were not being fulfilled through Manzanillo:

> It was very clear that the two parties were not reaching an agreement on very basic issues and that the U.S. government decided that there was no point in continuing these conversations . . . *In Contadora we thought that bilateral negotiations were essential* and that an agreement by the two parties would contribute very much to facilitating an understanding . . . within the five Central American countries [emphasis added].[22]

Thus US reasoning on the multilateral process conflicted with the architects of Contadora. The US position was untenable, if it had reached agreement with Nicaragua, its isthmian allies would have experienced extreme Contadora pressure to sign the Act, which they verbally acquiesced to before Nicaragua accepted the same Act. The bilateral proposal presented by the United States, orally in August 1984 and in writing in September contained conditions a sovereign government would not accept. On the multilateral level, the US activities in support of the contras, ultimately infringing US law, demonstrated a commitment to an element that in effect guaranteed an impasse in the Contadora process because it insisted on the cessation of support for insurgent movements. Washington continued to rhetorically support Contadora. Simultaneous to its termination of bilateral negotiations, Washington announced its withdrawal from the proceedings at the International Court of Justice (ICJ). It argued the conflict in the region was an 'inherently political problem' not a narrow legal dispute, and therefore inappropriate for judicial resolution. 'The conflict will be solved only by political and diplomatic means – not through a judicial tribunal.' The Court had not intended to resolve the regional problems, its mandate was to examine the specific violations of international law alleged by Nicaragua against the United States, and the Court had recommended the Contadora process for the resolution of the political disputes. Washington argued its provision of a 'security shield' was an inherent 'right of collective self-defense, enshrined in the UN Charter and the Rio treaty', it claimed to be acting in defense of 'vital national security interests' and in 'support of the peace and security of the hemisphere'. Nicaragua had apparently threatened the region through its 'huge buildup of Soviet arms and Cuban advisers, its cross border attacks and promotion of insurgent movements in the area'. The ICJ explained in its 1986 ruling that 'in the case of individual self-defense, the exercise of this right is subject to the State concerned having been the victim of an armed attack'. The United States had not been the victim of an armed attack by the Sandinista regime. As for collective self defense, 'the State which is the victim of an armed attack . . . must form and declare the view that it has been so attacked'. Another State is not permitted to 'exercise the right of collective self-defense on the basis of its own assessment of the situation'.[23] El Salvador had not declared itself the victim of attack until over two years after the United States had mobilized the contra forces.

The administration not only wanted to influence the government, but remove the Sandinistas from power. In a discussion on an intelligence estimate for Nicaragua in late January 1985, North informed Poindexter that 'those knowledgeable of current resistance activities and operations believe that with adequate support the resistance could be in Managua by the end of 1985'. Soon after, the State Department's Bureau of Intelligence and Research reported the Sandinistas intended a major 'sweep' against the contras, though they would not be considerably affected due to their 'improved tactical skills.' With these indications Washington sought to bolster the Honduran government of President Roberto Suazo Córdova through both diplomatic and material support. North wrote a memorandum for McFarlane seeking concurrence for a presidential cable to 'emphasize for President Suazo our support in the event of a Sandinista attack'. McFarlane's memorandum indicated the FDN had mobilized with the last of their rifles and ammunition provided by Honduras to disrupt the attack. Honduran authorities did not perceive the Sandinista concentration of troops as a threat to their forces, McFarlane reported 'no Honduran units have been put on alert or moved to the area and there are indications that the Honduran Government has ordered nearly all of the resistance personnel to vacate their base camps by next week.' McFarlane suggested the cable to Suazo 'could have a stiffening effect on Honduran resolve in the face of the Sandinista offensive'. He ordered his deputy, Poindexter, to chair a crisis pre-planning group to assess US contingency actions. Motley confirmed to Shultz that Tegucigalpa had asked the contras to return to Nicaragua because they were 'evidently anxious to avoid a Nicaraguan cross border attack against such a large FDN concentration on Honduran territory.' The meeting concurred it was necessary to 'encourage the Hondurans to remain firm in their support for the FDN during the coming weeks before Congress votes on US aid.' The steps outlined in this regard included the presidential cable, expedited Defense Department delivery of military supplies, disbursement of Economic Support Funds (ESF), and the Joint Chiefs of Staff were requested to move US naval forces to the Honduran coast. The cable sent to the CIA chief of station in Tegucigalpa, to be delivered to President Suazo by the US ambassador, John Negroponte, stated:

> We have recently been appraised of Sandinista military attacks on the territory of Honduras using material provided by the Soviet Union . . . Should such an attack against your territory occur, please be assured that the United States is fully prepared to meet its responsibilities for collective defense under the OAS Charter and the Rio Treaty . . . We hope and pray that such an attack will not occur and that you and your government will continue to do all [in] your power to support those who struggle for the cause of freedom and democracy.

A presidential letter was also to be sent, 'to provide several enticements to Honduras in exchange for its continued support of the Nicaraguan

Resistance'. These enticements, however, had certain conditions attached which were delivered verbally by 'an emissary'. As a document from the North trial stated, 'The CPPG did not wish to include this detail of the *quid pro quo* arrangement in written correspondence.'[24]

The direct bilateral support given to Honduras by the United States in return for their contra support was not the only impediment to a negotiated outcome. During February 1985 the obstacle to a diplomatic solution was strengthened and the isthmian governments spoke of the end of the regional process. Nicaragua called on the United States to resume bilateral negotiations, reasoning that if talks were not resumed before Congress voted on and approved aid Washington would be less willing to engage in diplomacy. Nicaragua conceded the United States could have a limited military presence in Central America, which departed from its original insistence that all foreign military personnel should be removed from the region. There was further pressure from US allies in Europe to continue bilateral discussions. Spain and West Germany had publicly criticized Washington for their withdrawal from Manzanillo, and Prime Minister Thatcher signalled a departure from Britain's previous position by receiving Nicaraguan Vice President, Sergio Ramirez in London.[25]

The Reagan letter was sent to President Suazo further diminishing the prospects of fulfilling the provisions of the Contadora objectives. It indicated the United States would increase its military support and that military manoeuvres would continue in the area. In delivering the letter, Ambassador Negroponte was instructed to make certain oral points included among others, was that: 'We are working in close harmony on Contadora issues'. Negroponte was also to inform Suazo that the United States was 'mindful' of the desire to portray strong US support for the government, coupled with the 'need not to appear intrusive in your internal affairs during an election year'. Finally, Negroponte was instructed to relate to Suazo that if the contras were severely damaged, it would be 'a tragic blow to the democratic states of Central America and to our joint efforts to achieve a regional settlement and preserve the democratic option in Nicaragua.' The text of the letter was approved by Reagan, as indicated in a memorandum to him from McFarlane. The latter informed the President that Honduras had earlier in 1985 decided to withdraw their support from the contras, but during McFarlane's trip to the region in mid-January, a member of his staff had a meeting with officials 'close to Suazo' resulting in 'the Hondurans reversing their stated intention to withdraw support from the freedom fighters'.[26]

The mid-February meeting of the Contadora group was cancelled due to Costa Rica's withdrawal from the process resulting from a dispute with

Nicaragua on the rights of asylum of one of its citizens in a Nicaraguan gaol. Nicaragua immediately responded calling Costa Rica's withdrawal a 'manoeuver' backed by Washington to force the suspension of the regional meeting. Nicaragua submitted Washington

> not only succeeded in effectively blocking the Contadora process but also completely negated the viability of a process which requires that all the countries involved should be able to take their own decisions on the basis of their national interests, without intervention or diktat from third States.

Nicaragua charged the interventionist policies of the United States 'constituted a blow from which, in our view, the Contadora negotiation process would find it difficult to recover'.[27]

By mid-February 1985 Washington increasingly focused on the internal situation in Nicaragua. A senior administration official held a White House press briefing indicating they were trying to prevent 'the final consolidation' of the Sandinistas 'as a totally Marxist–Leninist society'. The delivery of Soviet weapons to Nicaragua was presented as a direct threat to its neighbours, and 'could even pose a strategic threat to the United States'. The official was further questioned on this point by reporters. When asked if the Sandinistas had anything besides helicopters, the following exchange occurred:

> *Official*: That's about it as far as I have on the list here.
> *Questioner*: Do you really think that poses a threat?
> *Official*: Well, I don't think a helicopter's going to fly up from Managua to –
> *Questioner*: Washington . . . That's why I was wondering why you said it poses a threat –
> *Official*: If these guys continue unabated with the strength they've got, and the willingness of the Soviets to support them, they could certainly leap-frog up the peninsula . . .
> *Questioner*: You're saying prospective strategic threat, rather than one – they don't currently pose a strategic threat to the United States today?

The Official resorted to the fact that the Soviets were supplying Cuba and according to his analysis there was no reason they would not supply the Sandinistas in the same way. The official, however, confirmed that the administration was 'stopping short of saying we're advocating overthrow'. The ostensible reason was to avoid running into legal barriers. The official also confirmed that the United States wanted to see Nicaragua 'lay out . . . principles of pluralistic society', in which free elections would be held, and the opposition would be allowed to 'flourish'.[28]

Days later President Reagan gave his first press conference of the new administration in which he acknowledged the intention to remove the government 'in the sense of its present structure, in which it is a Communist totalitarian state, and it is not a government chosen by the people'. The contras were termed 'freedom fighters', and described as one element of the revolution against Somoza. Asked if he was advocating the overthrow of the present government, Reagan replied: 'Not if the present government would turn around and say, all right, if they'd say, "Uncle. All right, come on back into the revolutionary government, and let's straighten this out and institute the goals".' Immediate diplomatic repercussions resulted. The Nicaraguan Embassy in Washington released a statement accusing the administration of totally misrepresenting conditions in Nicaragua; contra leaders were former members of the National Guard under Somoza, and these elements opposed the revolution. Tinoco wondered 'If Mr. Reagan is saying his goal is to overthrow our government, how can we continue in Contadora to try to solve the problems in the region?' As far as Nicaragua was concerned Contadora was 'dead'. The State Department responded Nicaragua had 'been trying to undermine Contadora all along'.[29] Tentatively at least, two Central American countries had publicly denigrated the Contadora process. Others had undermined it implicitly through their assistance to the United States in ventures contradictory to its principles.

The status of the contras was important insofar as it affected future diplomacy and brought in the demand by the United States that the Sandinistas engage in dialogue with them to solve their internal problems. The Reagan reference to the contras as 'freedom fighters' contradicted Sandinista portrayals of them as terrorists. Reagan explicitly stated the contras were an element of the revolution, but the leadership of the main contra force, the FDN could not accurately be described as such. The Arms Control and Foreign Policy Caucus found in a 1985 report, *Who Are The Contras?* that while the 'foot soldiers' were mainly 'peasants . . . 46 of the 48 positions in the FDN's command structure are held by former Guardsmen'. It found while the civilian directorate had been 'cleansed' to reduce the role of guardsmen and Somoza associates

> the military leadership has not [been] . . . the key military strategist positions, including the Strategic Commander, are held by ex-National Guardsmen; as are *all* of the General Staff; four out of five of the Central Commanders; six out of seven of the Regional Commanders; and probably all 30 task Force Commanders.

Furthermore, controversial leaders such as Ricardo Lau, an ex-National Guardsman, was alleged to have taken less visible positions 'to make the nature of the contra army more acceptable to Congress', due to the reputed 'atrocities' committed while in both the National Guard and the FDN. The report concentrated on the FDN because it received the most support '(if not all) of US funds approved for expenditure', and was described as the only significant contra military force at the time.[30]

Throughout March 1985 the administration engaged in re-supplying the pivotal Central American countries who had provided contra assistance. The Defense Department 'commenced expedited procurement and delivery of military and other items to Honduras'. Guatemala had also provided Washington with a list of military equipment it needed. Guatemala provided end-user certificates for close to $8 million of munitions. On delivery of the arms the military receipted them and 'turned [them] over to Resistance representatives at the point of arrival'.[31]

It was vital for Washington to maintain the contras in the initial months of Reagan's second term, because the second Boland amendment provided additional aid could be requested after 28 February 1985, if the president certified that Nicaragua was aiding revolutionary movements in Central America. McFarlane informed North and the Senior Director for Policy Development, Donald R. Fortier, that the President had a 'strong wish that we not break faith with the Contras . . . [We need] to do everything possible to reverse the course of the Congress, and get the funding renewed'. North had earlier estimated the resistance could continue to function for a further six to eight months due to the largesse of 'sympathetic government(s) and/or individuals.' But US funding was essential to apply the same pressure that had been exerted in early 1984.[32]

The strategy to gain funding was put in place in mid-February. A document titled 'Public Relations Campaign for the Freedom Fighters', stated the main goals were to pressurize Congress to support funding and to improve the image of the contras. The document warned all those involved in the campaign to avoid 'the theme that the Sandinistas must be outright overthrown . . .' because Congress would oppose aid. Instead, the theme of political and military pressure was to be retained, ostensibly moving 'the regime towards negotiations, [thus] the moral high ground can still be claimed'. Listed under the themes the administration should focus on was 'the breaking off of negotiations'. Despite Washington's withdrawal from the Manzanillo process in January, the administration sought to turn the tables and blame the Sandinistas for the failure of diplomacy. It maintained that the bilateral negotiations would not be resumed until after the Sandinistas had initiated negotiations with the armed and unarmed opposition groups. Congress had stated aid could be pursued after 28 February 1985 if Washington certified the Sandinistas had engaged in certain behaviour. On that day George Bush attributed all the necessary characteristics to compel congressional consideration; he told the audience of the Austin Council on Foreign Affairs that the Sandinistas were 'tyrants bent on conquest', Nicaragua was a 'warehouse of subversion and terrorism only two hours by air from the Texas border'. Further, Bush enquired, 'Do we really want to allow the virus of international terrorism to effect the American mainland?' He reintroduced the Tomás Borge quotation, misused by Washington, to the effect that 'this revolution goes beyond our borders. Our revolution was always internationalist'. The remainder of the quotation stated that it would be enough merely to export the example of the Sandinista revolution. On the other hand, the contras were described as fighting for the same democratic ideals 'that our own forefathers fought for in the American Revolution'. He specifically rejected the recent Sandinista concessions and reiterated US demands to,

> Stop subversion; reduce the military to restore a regional balance; sever military ties with Cuba and the Soviet bloc; and begin to honor their promises to the Organization of American States to create a democratic, pluralistic, political system . . . That last point, establishing pluralism and democracy, is really the most fundamental.[33]

While the Sandinistas had conceded on several points, had held elections, judged to be free and fair by international observers, had proposed initiatives at the bilateral level as well as accepting the multilateral Contadora treaty, the United States had not moved from their position of early 1982, or that of 1981, except to add the issue of democracy. The Sandinistas were not regarded as the legitimate government of Nicaragua with the right to certain conditions. Alejandro Bendaña later argued the Sandinistas had to 'battle' their way on to the negotiating table; Washington would not deal with their legitimate concerns because Washington would not recognize the Sandinistas as politically legitimate. Hence Bendaña maintained the United States refused to 'seriously negotiate with Nicaragua'. From Nicaragua's perspective Washington's opposition to the Contadora initiative stemmed from the latter's challenge to the Monroe Doctrine; Contadora sought to remove Washington from the regional military antagonisms.[34] Washington provided its regional allies with sufficient economic and military aid to resist the regional proposals, but while military chiefs increased their power the civilian presidents eventually saw their positions threatened.

# 5 Narrowing the Focus: Contadora and Esquipulas 1986

The prospects of a negotiated settlement appeared extremely remote by mid 1985. The bilateral talks held at Manzanillo had been cut off, and Washington had imposed an economic embargo against Nicaragua in early May, declaring a national emergency for the purpose. Mexico thought the embargo was incompatible with the 'objectives of Contadora'. The United States took a harder line against the Sandinistas, and gave the contras a greater sense of gravity through the President's description of them as the 'moral equivalent of the founding fathers'; he stated he wished to see the removal of the Nicaraguan government in its present structure. The Mexican Foreign Minister, Sepúlveda, had earlier suggested: 'Negotiation implies yielding some ground in order to secure the ultimate objective which is considered essential'.[1] Yet there was no room for compromise between the administration's minimum demands and their ultimate objective.

The non-lethal humanitarian aid approved by both the House and Senate in early June 1985 was seen by the Nicaraguan government as an 'intensification of aggression' against their countries and 'a bad blow to the peace efforts of the Contadora Group.' They required specific action to be taken by the Contadora Group to contain the aggression in the region. The change of agenda derailed the process and created a vacuum which caused the situation to deteriorate. The humanitarian assistance allowed the contras to remain active in the field, with other sources of finance procured from the Iran–Contra initiatives providing their lethal assistance. Nevertheless, by July 1985 the OAS had reinforced the image that the Contadora Group was the prime negotiator in Central America.[2]

As usual negotiations were only one aspect of the US approach. Adding to the Reagan rhetoric on changing the shape of the Sandinista government, Oliver North in the NSC drafted a plan for the eventual 'defeat and demobilization of the Sandinista armed forces'. Aware that the Soviets or Cubans would not implement the Brezhnev Doctrine to 'block the overthrow of the Sandinistas', the three phase operation still had to act within the constraints of the Vietnam syndrome, avoiding the direct use of US troops. The plan intended to destroy the legitimacy of the Sandinista government and provide for increasing control by the UNO/FDN.[3]

These intentions obviously required finance, but Congress had only authorized $27 million in the June vote. The 'humanitarian' aid was enough to keep the contras intact till March 1986 without providing enough to pursue a military option. The basic intention was to put the situation on hold while Congress could express its intentions more clearly. If the covert operation was to have a legitimate future it had to demonstrate some success or viability; Congress did not want to fund an unpopular programme. More specifically Congress allocated $2 million in the bill to help implement a regional peace accord in 1986 resulting from the Contadora negotiations. This legislative attempt to give alternative policies some breathing space grew out of a wariness of the private efforts to finance the contras. The new assistance further sought to distance Congress from the military approach by precluding the Department of Defense or the CIA from involvement in the distribution of the aid. They were not, however, barred from providing intelligence or advice. Despite this implicit intention throughout the second half of 1985 Iran–Contra operatives were busy enlisting third countries within and outside Latin America to support their efforts. While Congress had placed a limit on contra funds, Oliver North vigorously worked to assure the various groups concerned that Reagan supported their cause. His activities became the focus of concern for Congress throughout the autumn of 1985 initiating the exchange of a series of letters between Congressmen Barnes and Hamilton and the staff of the National Security Adviser. Eventually the investigations into North's activities stalled in November due to a lack of available documentary evidence.[4]

Empirical evidence, however, would have easily been gathered had Congress more firmly intended halting the programme. The former DCI under President Carter, Stansfield Turner, explicitly stated at the time that the CIA 'is supporting terrorism in Nicaragua'. His assertion could be confirmed by any number of Human Rights group's findings on the covert war. The requirement of documentary evidence for the initiation of violence or connections with it on the part of United States personnel at a time when the results of the violence were clearly apparent appears to be a procedural manner of protecting their stance on the operations.[5] Nor can the covert operations be regarded as an effort to facilitate the negotiating process to pressure the Sandinistas to induce further concessions. Though this was often the case, it was not the intention of the covert operations. Had it been, Congress could have been more fully informed and included in the process. The opposite in fact was more the case: the administration used the negotiating process to facilitate their requests for covert aid. While sections of Congress were complicitous with executive strategies, other sections distanced themselves by limiting aid, and pushing for negotiated settlements. The methods by which they pursued this line had to work within the anti-communist political culture of Washington. Asserting its support for a negotiated solution Congress was troubled by Ortega's visit to the Soviet Union, Nicaragua's close ties to leftist countries, the alleged curtailment of individual liberties, and 'Sandinista . . . efforts to export its influence and ideology'. Given the United States export of influence and ideology the double standards are historically apparent. Congress outlined specific measures it required of Nicaragua before deciding on the option the United States would pursue; the expectations sounded like a victorious power dictating policy to a defeated nation. Three of the four expectation were directly related to the internal affairs of Nicaragua, which should have been the sole preserve of the Sandinista government. Nevertheless, Congress prohibited military and paramilitary operations against Nicaragua, and among several provisions both urged Reagan to 'pursue vigorously the use of diplomatic and economic measures to resolve the conflict in Nicaragua, including simultaneous negotiations' implementing the 1983 Contadora objectives, and the suspension of the economic embargo of May 1985. Further, the resumption of bilateral negotiations was encouraged, again based on Contadora. The executive, however, was given the latitude to request further aid if the president determined that negotiations had failed and submitted a statement on why they had done so.[6]

Almost simultaneously NSA McFarlane went on the record to deny that it was the US intention to overthrow the Sandinistas while others in the administration favoured such an approach. These unnamed officials cited by *The New York Times* indicated that there was no possibility of finding accord in the region while the Sandinistas were still in power. They argued the conflict went beyond Nicaragua, the strategy for the Reagan Doctrine was to 'find ways to help democratic resistance movements without sending troops'. The idea being to defeat what was perceived to be a Soviet colony: 'If these people can stand up and throw off Communism, it goes beyond Managua. It goes to the gut of our national interest.' While McFarlane insisted the covert and diplomatic efforts would work in tandem, the new Secretary of State for Inter-American Affairs, Elliot Abrams, argued that an agreement would not be upheld by the Sandinistas and hence the pressure to democratize the country to bring to government people who would adhere to a US accord. The parameters of direct US action were narrow. Bilateral talks had minimal possibility of administration acceptance; multilateral talks were rhetorically supported but undermined by continued support of the contras; another Cuba or independent 'communist' state such as Yugoslavia was unacceptable; and the direct introduction of US troops was politically intolerable. Thus the dual and contradictory policy remained in place; the contras could be used to pressure the Sandinistas in bilateral talks, in the multilateral forum their disbandment was required.[7]

The policies and authority within the administration were fragmented. When Shultz dispatched instructions to the new US ambassador to Costa Rica, Lewis Tambs, he found it necessary to instruct him on the line of command from the president through Shultz, to Elliot Abrams and then down to the ambassadorial level. Furthermore, the Secretary of State listed the aim of strengthening Costa Rica's support for the 'multilateral and comprehensive solution' to the regional conflict.[8]

## CONTADORA 1985

The apparent obfuscation of a clear statement of policy or approach to the conflict caused anxiety in a number of governments in the region and in Europe. Out of a fear of US pressure and the possibility of a direct invasion a need for an united Latin American opposition became a reality with the signing of the Lima Declaration at the inauguration of President Alán García of Peru. The Contadora Group was now joined by the Support Group made up of Argentina, Brazil, Peru, and Uruguay. Jack Child argues that these new members brought a considerable moral authority and counterpoise to the United States given that these nations were at the fore of the 'redemocratization' process earlier in the decade. Together, Contadora and its support group represented almost 90% of Latin America's economy and population. The first substantial joint communiqué stressed that unless a negotiated peaceful solution was found fundamental questions on democracy, independent development, and the stability of Latin America as a whole would be affected. To this end they called for an imminent signing of the Contadora agreement to avoid a generalized regional conflict. And for the record, they stated their 'conviction that the solution to the problems of Central America cannot be arrived at by means of force' but must be pursued through dialogue and negotiations. In fundamental opposition to the Reagan approach the group recognized that the roots of the conflict lay in 'economic and social inequality and in structures which restrict free expression and popular participation' in the political processes. The economic and the political problems would have to be tackled in tandem if a viable long term solution were to be found.[9]

The contras were not a tool in the administration's policy that could be bargained away in the search for a solution. They were an integral part of their ultimate objectives. Not only had they to demonstrate that they could prevail, assuring the western alliance and other US partners that Washington could be relied on in a time of crisis, not only had a coercive mechanism to be demonstrated to succeed in the wake of the Vietnam war, but given the new opposition, US foreign policy had to be seen to prevail and its support for its interpretation of democracy had to be shown to be widely accepted. Not only did the credibility of the United States rest on their success, given the hyperbolic rhetorical investment in their cause, but perhaps more crucially, the credibility of this administration lay in the balance. Hence the creation of the Nicaraguan Humanitarian Assistance Office to distribute the $27 million aid and to assure the 'people of Nicaragua that we will not abandon them in their struggle for freedom' according to Reagan, and the release of the State Department report *Revolution Beyond Our Borders: Sandinista Intervention in Central America* was a major attempt to further their interpretation of events in the policy and regional debates. The title, taken from a truncated and misleading extract of a speech by Tomás Borge, and the efforts at Public Diplomacy tried to portray the Sandinistas as an aggressive force in the Central American region as the vanguard of the various isthmian revolutionary movements. More to the point, and despite the lack of evidence for the claim on aggression, the report was designed to counter the charges brought by Nicaragua against the United States at the International Court of Justice. Given the withdrawal of the United States from the formal proceedings there was an added need to present their argument.[10]

The thrust of the diplomatic initiatives was moving away from Washington's approach. As Contadora neared the release of its second draft, the three core countries closely aligned to Washington in the diplomatic process released a statement trying to present Nicaragua as the cause of the regional arms race and called for measures similar to the US requirements: internal national reconciliation; reductions of arms; and international supervision. The security issues concerning the Sandinistas were not addressed. The rift between these countries, aligned with the United States and Contadora with its support group was becoming more apparent. The timing of the second draft in this atmosphere may not have been effective, even if it was more necessary given the perpetual conflict. The Monge government complained that Contadora was more interested in protecting Nicaraguan security but was slow to act against Nicaragua on border issues with Costa Rica. Nicaraguan suggestions for a buffer zone between the two countries were rejected by Costa Rica on the grounds that Nicaragua had to accept responsibility for an earlier incident. Further, the United States opposed the formation of a buffer zone, though backed by the Support Group.[11]

The second draft of the Contadora Act released on 12 September 1985 was a compromise between the September 1984 Act which Nicaragua had agreed to sign and the counterdraft presented at Tegucigalpa in October of that year. Nicaragua's Deputy Foreign Minister, Victor Tinoco, thought 'Contadora felt it . . . necessary to make concessions to the United States in order to keep the negotiating process alive'. The UN Secretary General's report on the proceedings described the changes as 'fair and viable compromises concerning the most controversial issues'. This time, however, Nicaragua refused to sign. They made it clear they accepted 100 of the 117 provisions in the agreement, but could not accept others given the continued contra activities which had been stepped up as the document was released. The Sandinistas accused the Honduran government of violating Nicaraguan airspace and attacking their territory. Additional supply planes were provided through Oliver North's operations and were due to arrive in Honduras two days before the draft was released. The supply planes were initially to be flown by US crew employed by the 'firm'. The intensified climate of aggression was seen by Nicaragua as a provocation rather than conducive to the diplomatic process.[12]

Specifically the Sandinistas considered the section on internal reconciliation as their sole preserve, hence the October offers of a resumption of bilateral talks by Harry Shlauderman were rejected, because they were tied to bilateral talks with the contras; on the support for irregular forces or terrorism the Sandinista position was that these should be disbanded before the signing of the act to provide for their minimum security conditions. Further, a lasting and stable solution could not be found unless there was a US commitment to halt the 'illegal conduct' in the region. Peace in Central America could not be effectively re-established unless the United States stopped all forms of aggression against Nicaragua; curtailed military manoeuvres which the new draft allowed under regulation; and adhered to the decisions of the International Court of Justice. An agreement with these commitments the Sandinistas stressed would have to be signed at the same time as the Contadora Act. Without these security guarantees, Nicaragua refused to limit the size of its armed forces.[13] The bottom line for the Sandinistas was that these new compromises did not guarantee the security of their revolution. Indeed its security could not be guaranteed given the positions adopted by Washington in their continued support for the contras.

The perspective on the regional conflict was vital to a viable solution. While the Reagan administration continued to place the problem in the East–West perspective, at one point trying to have Nicaragua included on the agenda for the superpower summit with the new Soviet leader Mikhail

Gorbachev in Geneva, the groups pushing for a diplomatic solution over military pressure consistently illegitimized this interpretation stressing the structural roots of the conflict. The strife to date had severely exacerbated the economic situation in the region rebounding on all countries in the region who were forced to divert more funds to their defense than their social or economic development programmes. During this period the Secretary General's report, Contadora, and Nicaragua tried to emphasise the 'unjust socio-economic structures and domestic policies' of the various countries as the original cause of the conflict. These interpretations were given support by the Canadian government and the European Community, all of which condemned the economic embargo and called for the freedom of sovereign nations to choose their own forms of development. The United States was becoming increasingly isolated on this issue. Both the use, and interpretation, of the terms democracy and economic development were part of a semantic game used to full effect to delay negotiating procedures. The draftees of the Contadora document had to be specifically guided by an attempt to avoid imprecise and ambiguous concepts open to 'confusion and erroneous interpretations'. The preamble to the draft made several mentions of the need to improve the socio-economic conditions and the prospects for more complete political participation. The importance of creating democratic systems that were representative, participatory and pluralistic was noted in several points which stressed that development plans should be allowed to proceed based on the priorities adopted by the sovereign states. The government of Nicaragua put the matter more bluntly. The United States was reluctant to explore solutions that would 'contain' as opposed to destroy the Sandinistas, even though its allies both in the region and in Europe did not share the concerns of a threat, suggests Washington wanted to destroy the revolution and mitigate the example of its initial successes in certain areas of development. Daniel Ortega argued that Washington wanted to destroy the revolution because they were a bad example as far as Washington was concerned because they were trying to form a new political and economic relationship with the United States that was 'just, equitable and respectful'. The current support for the contras had further escalated the aggression, terror destruction and genocide according to Ortega, which had cost Nicaragua 11 000 lives, severe displacement of peoples and $1.5 billion in direct and indirect losses. In 1985 60% of Nicaragua's budget was spent on defense. While a strategic defeat of the contras was undertaken during this period, rendering them more of an harassment force rather than a threat to the military security of the revolution, the United States could still maintain forces in Honduras and small groups within Nicaragua, necessitating, as William Robinson has noted, a permanent 'diversion of the country's resources from social welfare and economic development'.[14] The contras were ineffective in the military field against the Sandinista army, and the United States would not participate in bilateral negotiations or support the regional drafts, hence the covert programme remained a force to inflict continual low intensity damage on the country and prevent further viable development.

Following the Nicaragua rejection of the September 1985 Act the regional countries once again called for bilateral talks which were promptly ruled out by George Shultz. State Department personnel including Abrams and Shultz continued to interpret the situation through the East–West prism, perhaps in an effort to balance the attempts to make reject these approaches in the preceding weeks.[15] With the continued aggression suffered by Nicaragua and the increased capability of the weaponry introduced during this period, Nicaragua considered that its security interests were not being met under the current set of negotiations and requested their suspension for a period of six months till May 1986. With the introduction of surface to air missiles in the contra armory, Honduran complicity in their presence, and the statement made by Shultz to the effect that the United States would continue to support the contras even if a Contadora agreement were signed, the prospects for a secure negotiated solution for Nicaragua were dim. While Venezuela opposed the suspension of talks, Nicaragua argued that the transition of various Central American governments necessitated the suspension. Despite the rejection of the 1985 Act the Central American Historical Institute suggested that the suspension may have been a ploy for the Sandinistas to buy time. Contadora obviously opposed the US policies and allowed the Sandinistas increased manoeuvrability and legitimacy in a major international negotiating process. The suspension according to this interpretation was to stave off the complete collapse of the process; an interventionist Contadora agreement was preferable to and interventionist US policy. The former allowed for some Sandinista consent.[16]

Following the suspension of the Contadora process the United States sought to assure the Central American countries of their continued support. The new National Security Advisor, John Poindexter, assured several countries within the region of US military support. While his meeting with General Noriega in Panama did not specifically discuss the contras, he limited his criticism because of Noriega's assistance in training the contras on Panamanian territory. Thus Panama played a duplicitous role within the Contadora group. Most pertinently, however, Poindexter made it clear to Honduran military officials that their support for the resistance was essential. Further, North noted that Poindexter should inform the Central American officials that the United States intends 'to pursue a victory and that [a Central American country] will not be forced to seek a political accommodation with the Sandinistas'.[17]

The high level assurances to the Central American officials of the US resolve to pursue the covert approach was in evidence through the supply efforts of Oliver North and others. Part of his effort involved the diversion of aircraft used for 'humanitarian' deliveries to that of lethal aid. Despite congressional opposition to such assistance, considerable amounts had been supplied through various private sources and 'third country' support associated with the Iran–Contra initiatives. The diversion of Iranian funds to the contras was, according to North, a 'neat idea'. A National Security Council meeting on 10 January 1986 concluded with Reagan's request that $100 million should be sought from Congress. The vastly increased request according to North's reasoning a year earlier would indicate to Congress the 'urgency of the situation'. The drive for further aid was coupled with extensive efforts at public diplomacy to fill what was termed by Abrams as the 'information gap' in congressional understanding of 'the nature of Sandinista subversion, not only in Central America, but in South America'.[18]

## CARABALLEDA

With the increasing military pressure and the potential threat of its escalation, Daniel Ortega reversed his position on the suspension of Contadora, amidst widespread speculation that the process had completely collapsed and called for a resumption of talks in keeping with the July 1985 Contadora document, new bilateral talks between Shultz and D'Escoto, and a dialogue based on international law between the Central American governments. Days later on 12 January 1986 the Contadora and Support Groups issued the 'rousing' Caraballeda Message which was in effect a retreat to the September 1984 Contadora Act agreeable to Nicaragua. The hype surrounding the document reflected the unanimity of the public postures of the Latin countries on the need to peacefully defuse the situation before potential escalation. This time, however, in attempting to 'define the permanent' base for peace, through a Latin solution, the process would have to galvanize the specificity of the various issues in the documents. Furthermore, preparations for creating the conditions of self-determination, non-intervention, territorial integrity, and pluralistic democracy among other provisions would have to be conducted simultaneously with the signing of the document. Theoretically the onus was now on Washington to dismantle the contras as a precondition to the signing of the document; Caraballeda specifically prioritized the 'cessation of outside support for irregular forces operating in the region'.[19] Given the Reagan intention to pursue further lethal aid legitimately through Congress, the administration had to be careful not to antagonize members by rejecting or opposing this regional initiative.

Adding to the diplomatic momentum, the Central American leaders in Guatemala City for the inauguration of President Vinicio Cerezo were persuaded by him to endorse the Caraballeda message. Hence, nearly all the Latin countries and the population they represented were officially united in their call on the United States to dismantle the contras. The diplomatic tension in the early part of 1986 was played around the contradictory aims of these governments and the Reagan administration. Washington was still not prepared to let the Caraballeda declaration form the basis for new negotiations. When the Contadora ambassadors presented the document to Shultz, the US response was to insist that Nicaragua's 'broken promises' remained the heart of the problem, and that the United States would only resume bilateral talks if the Sandinistas began talks with the contras. Despite verbally supporting Contadora Washington did not mention the Caraballeda position of the contras.[20]

Despite the signing of the document at the inauguration, various Central American countries continued to assist the United States in their efforts to supply the contras. These powers, vital to the US strategy, used their leverage to expedite additional aid from Washington. February and March 1986 was spent preparing for and requesting more contra aid from Congress. Under pressure, a key aspect for administration success was the attempt to clearly demonstrate the diplomatic track had failed; Nicaragua had to be shown to be intransigent. These efforts required extensive meetings with Democrats favourable to the contra effort, and an extensive public diplomacy effort, including major speeches by Abrams, Shultz and Reagan to various fora. Moreover, the image and unity of the contras had to be improved. The propaganda focused on the ostensible democratic and civilian nature of the United Nicaraguan Opposition (UNO) and the FDN, despite public assessments to the contrary by various human rights groups.[21]

Despite press reports indicating the United States had 'stone walled' Contadora requests for further efforts at negotiation in mid February, the Reagan request for $100 million described how in their interpretation the regional and bilateral negotiations had failed. United States attempts at a negotiated solution (incredibly based on Contadora) had failed because 'Nicaragua has continued to reject meaningful negotiations.' And 'Communist attempts to circumvent and subvert Contadora, apparent from the beginning of the negotiating process, have left a clear trail of lost opportunities for peaceful reconciliation.' Pointing to the Nicaraguan request for the suspension of Contadora, Washington reasoned the Sandinistas were intransigent. The Central American and 25 other states had at the time requested a resumption of the regional process. Despite Nicaragua's acceptance of the Caraballeda message, the White House concentrated on the reservations and 'prerequisites' Nicaragua insisted on that were actually contained in the document. For its part, the White House indicated that it too supported the message in that it called for internal national reconciliation, a position consistently advocated by UNO. The Sandinista position was seemingly intransigent because they insisted on an additional agreement on non-aggression with the United States, outside the Contadora negotiating process; such an agreement would be necessary to secure their position. Negotiations with the so called Democratic Resistance were consistently ruled out by the Sandinistas, as it was questionable whether they would be a viable and united group without extensive US management. Following the new financial request these arguments were repeated by top US officials while Congress decided on the matter. Reagan's address to the nation was perhaps the most important of these engagements. The Democratic response delivered by Jim Sasser accepted many characterizations of the Sandinistas but remained concerned that the further request for $100 million in an 'undeclared' war was premature perhaps because 'the President is seizing military options before he has exhausted the hope of a peaceful solution.' The contras to facilitate the process suggested talks which the Sandinistas rejected. The Democratic Study Group concluded that the administration continuously tried to impose military solutions on Nicaragua and stated it seemed 'clear that no genuine interest in negotiating with the Sandinistas exists'.[22]

The exaggerated claims, misinformation and the extensive attempts to 'redbait' opponents of contra aid alienated many in Congress including some Republicans. Furthermore, with shifts to more civilian led governments in Latin America the Reagan policies came under increasing attack. Formal requests to desist from the military option were ignored, though such requests were supported by Europe, Canada, and Australia. The hyperbolic threat of the supposed 'sea of red, eventually lapping at our own borders' was not shared by the regional or hemispheric governments. Former US ambassador Wayne Smith wrote in *The New York Times* that as long as support for the contras continued and the US 'tragically [and] arrogantly block the diplomatic initiatives of the very countries it claims to be defending, the Administration dooms them to continued turmoil and bloodshed'. The eventual rejection of Reagan's request by a vote of 222 to 210 described by him as a major test of his presidency, represented the failure, according to Representative Thomas Foley, to convince the public that 'other avenues are fully explored'. The diplomatic option gained another, if brief, lease of life.[23]

The new presidents of Guatemala and Costa Rica, Vinicio Cerezo and Oscar Arias Sanchez respectively were much more reluctant to support the Reagan policy. Arias apparently limited his criticism of the contras after a visit from US special envoy Philip Habib, but Guatemala's leader outlined his opposition to the confrontational approach. Despite these positive opportunities the Sandinistas ruined the public relations benefits by conducting a military incursion into Honduran territory to strike contra base camps. Despite a DIA estimate that it represented a target of opportunity rather than a strategic aim, the CIA intended to take full advantage of the attack. Ignoring the DIA dissent, William Casey suggested the intelligence report did not make the point clear that this operation was part of a long planned effort to 'knock out the Contra forces quickly'. Casey instructed that copies of the report should be 'used locally' and sent to Contadora and other pertinent Latin countries. In Honduras, President Azcona was initially ignorant of the 'invasion' that had occurred 48 hours before; similarly he was ignorant of his request for $20 million in emergency aid to which the White House responded rapidly. Azcona later stated he had asked for the aid. In any case the military move dramatically improved the chances of further aid being passed through Congress at the next vote.[24]

## CONTADORA 1986

In early April as the Central Americans and Contadora ministers met in Panama, the Contadora ministers appealed to a visiting Democratic delegation to delay the House vote till another round of diplomacy had been conducted. Contadora's last substantial effort got off to a bad start. Mexico proposed a joint appeal to the United States to suspend consideration of aid to the contras though the immediate Central American neighbours of Nicaragua refused to adopt this stance disingenuously arguing that contra aid was an internal US matter. Nicaragua's Foreign Minister then refused to sign Contadora by the previously agreed deadline of 6 June 1986 unless simultaneous steps were taken to remove the US/contra threat. As long as the contras continued their attacks the diplomatic efforts would be fruitless, D'Escoto insisted that Contadora could only proceed along the Caraballeda lines. The earlier unity of the Latin American states was now fractured with the Nicaraguan dissent. The 'Panama Commitment' to intensify negotiations leading to a signing by 6 June by the core group countries exacerbated the division. The reasonable Sandinista intransigence on this procedural point was perhaps politically inept given the widely perceived boost it lent the administration. Proponents of contra aid portrayed the Sandinista position as a torpedoing of the Contadora process. Reagan argued that the Sandinistas would now only respond to the use of force given their recent decisions on the diplomatic track. The Sandinista point was eventually supported in the final communique which clearly linked countries 'with ties and interests in the region' a clear reference to the United States abstaining from support of irregular forces.[25] While this was the authoritative position, the effectual stance was a substantial boost for the administration's pursuit of further aid; diplomacy, they could argue had failed. Despite these perceptions, the Costa Rican Vice Foreign Affairs Minister, Gerado Trejos Salas affirmed that during his time in office, 1985 to May 1986, 'Washington tried by all means available to block the signing of the Contadora Peace Act'.[26]

Clear divisions in the Reagan administration intensified during the period. Nominated for the position of Deputy Director for Central Intelligence, Robert Gates argued during his hearing that in several regional conflicts in the past ten years diplomacy had not proved an effective tool. On the other hand protracted military engagement was, since Vietnam, either inappropriate or unpopular. The covert option, nevertheless, was available and appropriate despite the large scale and public nature of some of these operations. The covert classification removed the requirements for a declaration of war, and provided a 'fig leaf', maybe small, but 'sufficient to allow third parties who have parallel interests to cooperate with us'. While this not so thinly veiled reference to third country contributions signaled the intentions of the covert track in the administration, the special envoy to the region, Philip Habib, pursued another path. Confirming a conversation with Representative Slattery on the status of the contras within the Contadora framework, he wrote:

> We interpret these provisions as requiring a cessation of support to irregular forces and/or insurrectional movements from the date of signature. We do not believe these provisions would prohibit financial or other humanitarian aid for the purpose of relocating or repatriating such forces.

The administration would ostensibly abide by a Contadora agreement though not legally bound to do so, if there was simultaneous implementation of the objectives; the agreement would not be respected if Nicaragua was violating it. Slattery, described as one of the 'waverers' on the contra issue decided to give the diplomatic option another chance, though he thought the process was close to exhaustion. With the Habib letter the US and

Nicaraguan position on the contras was close and offered an impetus for further compromise. Ortega released a communiqué on 12 April stating Nicaragua would sign the Act on 6 June if the United States ceased its aggression and if the modifications on the 17 objectionable provisions were made. Thus the Latin American unity and the possibilities of a theoretical solution were close. Opponents of the diplomatic track had to discredit the Habib position, though his letter had official clearance, and had to demand further specificity on verification in Contadora. Habib's letter had ample 'escape clauses' which allowed the United States to determine whether Nicaragua was complying with any agreement, and understood 'national reconciliation' to mean negotiations with the contras, which was not the interpretation Managua or Contadora gave to the phrase. While liberals in Congress applauded the apparent shift in favour of negotiations, the right wing in Congress, the Defense Department and the National Security Council moved against the seeming concession.[27]

The Habib concession was effectively demolished and his position discredited through the month of May. Shultz, Reagan and Poindexter discussed the legislative strategy and their position aboard Air Force One on 1 May. Further, Poindexter related a conversation with Reagan in which the President indicated he wanted the contra package pushed through Congress by 9 June. If this could not be done, Reagan wanted 'to figure out a way to take action uni-laterally to provide assistance'. Poindexter noted 'he does not buy the concept of taking actions or talking about pulling out'. Reagan was ready according to this memorandum to confront Congress on the constitutional question on who controls foreign policy. The National Security Planning Group meeting on 16 May 1986 considered the various ways in which funding could be enhanced through various approaches to 'third countries', through private donations from 'Ollie's people', and from Congress. At this time funds had already been solicited from other countries to the tune of $32 million in one case, and North had $6 million from the diversion of funds from Iran. The situation was not desperate, but was presented as such given that only $2 million of the humanitarian aid remained. The contras needed funding to bridge the gap because of Congress's delay to allow further regional diplomatic activity. Administration posture on Contadora was crucial to their legislative strategy. A paper on contra funding and Contadora was prepared by North and Burghardt, from Poindexter for the meeting. According to this paper the Contadora discussions were creating some anxiety in the United States and Central America, and the lack of a clear availability of funds was influencing the core Central American thinking on Contadora, which was scheduled to resume negotiations the following day. There was 'considerable speculation that a treaty is about to be signed by the Central Americans which would "sell out" the DRF'. The paper outlined the need to maintain the contras because they would be needed to engage in the negotiations on national reconciliation, thus the argument according to this logic was that there was no point in delaying funds till after the 'Contadora process has "played out"'. Though Shultz was scheduled to talk on the Contadora process at the NSPG meeting, this paper from NSC staff was more closely aligned to the Reagan position. Within this analysis, the consistent contradiction remained: the US ostensibly supported a verifiable Contadora treaty, while insisting on the maintenance of the irregular forces the regional countries sought to remove. Finally, a Pentagon study, *Prospects for Containment: Nicaragua's Communist Government* outlined a scenario requiring a major financial ($9.1 billion) and personnel (100 000 US troops) commitment if the contras were abandoned and the United States was forced to take action. The study effectively argued that the current treaty would allow Nicaraguan transgressions:

> In short the Sandinistas likely would conclude that a Contadora-like peace accord would provide them the shield from behind which they could continue their use of subversive aggression to impose Communist regimes throughout Central America.

The administration openly divided on the issue with the NSC, Defense, CIA, with Abrams from State opposed to Contadora while Habib seemed to think the treaty was workable. The State Department indicated the study was not part of the official US policy, though it had strong support. For its part 101 members of Congress responded by urging administration support of Contadora and requesting diplomatic action on behalf of the United States to conclude the work of Contadora.[28]

## ESQUIPULAS

Within Central America the inauguration of President Oscar Arias Sanchez in Costa Rica on 8 May 1986 created some new momentum for the negotiating process. Arias did not invite Nicaraguan officials to his inauguration and presented the other heads of State a document that outlined direct interference within Nicaragua including changes to its constitution. 'Pro Democracy Declaration in Central America' was seen as presenting views on internal matters close to Washington's position. While these ideas formed the genesis of what later became the Arias peace plan the more significant action in the region was taking place in Guatemala where

President Cerezo convened the other Central American presidents creating another high level forum for discussions. The United States had warned Cerezo to make sure 'nothing emerged from the meeting that Nicaragua could sign', but he continued despite the offense. While all governments signed the resulting Esquipulas Declaration, committing themselves to signing the Contadora document, the meeting achieved nothing apart from their document, a significant part of which declared:

> That real peace in Central America can only come about as the result of an authentic pluralist, and participatory democratic process. This implies a process that promotes social justice, respect for human rights and for the sovereignty and territorial integrity of the states, as well as for the right of nations to freely determine their economic, social and political model without any external influence. It is understood that this determination is the result of the freely expressed will of each peoples.

Nevertheless, Washington had other ideas as the 6 June deadline for the signing of Contadora approached. Against many of the provisions in Esquipulas a State Department memorandum to Abrams pointed out its commitment to the contras, the support for which 'will not slacken whatever the results in Contadora'.[29]

## FINAL CONTADORA DRAFT

Despite the Esquipulas commitment and Ortega's unconditional offer to sign Contadora in late May, anticipated by North who earlier outlined the US strategy of entering a 'propaganda contest' supporting 'our friend's position' and 'denouncing the Sandinistas for refusing to negotiate', the meeting in Panama on 6 June did not produce final agreement; the three core US allies in the region thought the final text was too favourable to Nicaragua and rejected it. The 42-page June 1986 document incorporating the changes from September 1985 dealt with the 'minutiae' on verification and confidence building to adhering to the requirements of specificity and avoidance of ambiguous terminology to prevent endless debate on interpretation. In Jack Child's assessment: 'In their zeal to provide the most exhaustive possible verification and control structure, the Contadora countries outdid themselves, proving the relevance of the old saying "the perfect is the enemy of the good".' The imperative to finding a diplomatic solution must be seriously questioned given the isthmian and regional adoption of Caraballeda and the Central American declaration at Esquipulas coupled with more and more specific Contadora documents, the crucial element missing in the negotiating process was a bilateral discussion between Managua and Washington. The Reagan administration had consistently announced its supports of Contadora and consistently undermined the process by declaring its unwavering support for the contras despite the not so steady support of Congress. Washington's insistence that bilateral negotiations could resume when the Sandinistas began talks with the internal opposition, meaning the contras (actually operating from outside Nicaraguan territory, and united under pressure from Washington) was another impediment to the search for peace. A form of national reconciliation would have been dealt with under Contadora. Washington's insistence on dealing with these irregular forces outside any agreed formula and refusing to enter a process of their own allowed them to structure the failure of diplomacy. With the coincidence of the collapse of both Esquipulas and Contadora, the Reagan administration could more persuasively put their argument that diplomacy had been tried and had failed. It was time for Congress to seriously consider contra aid. William LeoGrande has aptly pointed out that the division in the Reagan administration that sought to contain the Sandinistas concentrated on the security provisions contained in Contadora. Those opposed to the existence of the Sandinistas and who sought their elimination, including the President, concentrated on the political aspects of the diplomacy including the issue of democracy, which could be unilaterally judged by Washington. For this faction Contadora was 'primarily a public relations problem'. This division was also reflected amongst the Central American countries. Azcona of Honduras rejected the Sandinista proposals on arms control through making distinctions between offensive and defensive weapons. Nicaragua's offer through 14 points in late May 1986 to limit or eliminate its offensive weapons was thus rejected. Azcona argued during a visit to Washington that it was a ploy to delay the process and distract from the vital political issues. The joint communiqué with Reagan stressed the internal process of democratization.[30]

## CONTRA AID

The rhetoric and public relations exercise in the bid to turn around the indecisive congressional voters focused on the issue of democracy, and was part of a broader move in the diplomatic dialogue that moved more and more to concentrate on the internal process of Nicaragua. Sandinista concessions were part of the effort to maintain the diplomatic process in the face of soon to be renewed military support for the contras. And as they conceded on the internal aspects despite a lack of focus or scrutiny of the other Central American countries, the success of diplomacy was heralded.

On the eve of the house vote Reagan revived the theme of his influential 1983 speech in which he invoked the Truman Doctrine resulting from what Reagan interpreted as a similar civil war; this time in Nicaragua the United States was backing the irregular forces. In Central America the tide was turning towards democracy in what Reagan called the freely elected governments of the other four isthmian countries. Security issues were not ignored when Reagan suggested that Nicaragua would be the 'first Soviet base on the mainland of North America'. Despite the absence of this intention in Moscow, the comprehensive Contadora treaty would have eliminated such a possibility. US goals he stated remained in search of a peaceful solution because 'no humane person wants to see suffering and war'. Again in this speech written by Bernard Aronson, later filling Abrams position in the Bush administration, the Sandinistas were labeled as expansionist despite no concrete proof presented in support of the contention. In what could be considered an ultimate depravity in Reagan's understanding of history, the contras were referred to as 'freedom fighters' and their efforts were compared to the revolutionary process through which the United States had come into being. Reagan's speech invoked all the figures whose rhetoric had introduced new concepts on liberty in US history. The revolutionary process, Lincoln, Truman, Kennedy, were all used to muster support for the contras; people had to be reminded that the United States was in Kennedy's words the 'watchmen on the walls of world freedom', in Lincoln's, the United States had to provide 'hope to the world for all future time', and in Reagan's it was time to tell Nicaraguans 'it is not dangerous to have friends like us. Tell them America stands with those who stand in defense of freedom.' The United States could not be shown to be divided and paralyzed and unable to act. Indeed the draft speech if Congress did pass the bill stressed the 'new bipartisan consensus' in US foreign policy, while the draft speech for a defeat called for such unity because another Cuba was intolerable and according to Reagan the contra cause was freedom, it was just, and it would triumph.[31] Reagan used the draft for the success.

Apart from the pressure of the public diplomacy, efforts were made at individual persuasion of reluctant or indecisive members which ultimately proved successful when on 25 June 1986 the House voted in favour of the bill authorizing $100 million in contra aid. The vote, 221 to 209 saw a Democratic controlled Congress approve the foreign policy of prime interest to the president. $70 million was to be spent on military assistance;

while $40 million would be available without delay though weapons could not be delivered till after 1 September. During this period the North network was delivering regular supplies of munitions paid for by third countries, the diversion of profits from Iran, and private individual contributions. A further $20 million would be released on 15 October if the President certified that there was no reasonable chance of negotiating with the Sandinistas, and the remaining $40 million would be released in February 1987, when heavy weaponry could also be provided. The bill also provided $300 million to the other four Central American republics providing some relief from the strife caused by the militarization of the region and giving them an interest in peddling the administration line and demanding economic return for doing so. The Nicaraguan Government responded immediately accusing the United States of backing illegal and brutal attacks, and demonstrating their contempt for Contadora and Support Group diplomacy. The provisions of these group messages had been ignored, especially that of Caraballeda, because it was the most proximate major statement calling for a halt to such aid. When Contadora received support from the other major 'democratic' countries of Latin America the United States had a more difficult job of presenting the various peace efforts as inadequate and backed by Nicaragua, Cuba, and the Soviet Union. The work of Contadora had to be denigrated. Latin American unity on the diplomatic level was a threat to US interests. Shortly after the formation of the Support Group in August 1985 a State Department memorandum indicated:

> We need to develop an active diplomacy now to head off efforts at Latin American solidarity aimed against the U.S. and our allies, whether they are sponsored by the support group, the Cubans, or the Nicaraguans. We need to find a way to turn pressure they bring to bear on us or our friends to our advantage.

The inability of the Contadora process to reach a successful conclusion seems also to have been anticipated by the State Department. The memorandum stated: 'Contadora remains central to our policy and our interests continue to be served by the process. Nevertheless, its collapse wouldn't be total disaster for US policy.' An internal post vote analysis indicated that one of the influences on the House moderates was the appointment of Philip Habib, who in two months, 'made the term good faith diplomatic effort, and its exhaustion, more meaningful'.[32] Either way the Reagan administration would triumph. The only significant threat to its policies and approaches was a successfully concluded peace agreement with backing from the region, the hemisphere, NATO allies, Moscow, and large segments of the non-aligned movement.

## FURTHER ISOLATION

Two days after Congress voted to support the administration the International Court of Justice passed its ruling on the case brought by Nicaragua against the United States. After lengthy proceedings in which the United States did not participate, though the Court deemed itself to still have jurisdiction, sixteen judgements were made with varying degrees of support. The Court rejected the US position on collective self defense as a justification for the contra paramilitary operations; the United States had breached customary international law violating the sovereignty of Nicaragua, using force, authorizing overflights, mining harbours, producing and disseminating operation manuals on guerilla warfare, and imposing a trade embargo. It was decided further that reparations should be paid, and the United States was obliged to refrain from these acts violating international law. Furthermore the Court unanimously recalled 'to both parties their obligation to seek a solution to their disputes by peaceful means in accordance with international law'. Informing this decision the Court called for both parties to cooperate with the 'unique contribution' made by Contadora and endorsed by the United Nations Security Council and General Assembly. In its final substantial paragraph the Court outlined the basic provisions of Contadora that were ostensibly a concern for Washington:

> The Court is aware that considerable progress has been achieved on the main objective of the process, namely agreement on texts relating to arms control and reduction, exclusion of foreign military bases or military interference and withdrawal of foreign advisers, prevention of arms traffic, stopping the support of groups aiming at the destabilization of any of the Governments concerned, guarantee of human rights and enforcement of democratic processes, as well as on co-operation for the creation of a mechanism for the verification of the agreements concerned.

The US response merely indicated that the Court did not have the relevant expertise to deal with the issues and unlike the groups authorized by the Reagan administration to investigate the issues which concluded the Sandinistas were engaged in an export of revolution. The administration's argument was that the Court did not have access to relevant material, despite testimony from David McMichael, a former CIA employee.[33]

The illegal and intransigent support for the contras effectively undermined the diplomatic processes brought by the various groups, but primarily the Contadora Group by mid-1986. Contadora would remain in existence facilitating other efforts at finding a solution, but it did not present another substantive draft. The Reagan administration wanted an end to the Sandinista revolution. The $100 million would impose further attrition on the social and economic structure of Nicaragua, while the future diplomacy would focus on more narrow objectives. Despite these clear victories for the Reagan administration its policy on Central America was in disarray. The internal record demonstrates a clear attempt to get rid of the Sandinistas, while the public face of the administration was to pursue a contradictory support for both Contadora and the contras; these goals were mutually exclusive of each other. In the post Vietnam era Reagan was inhibited from using direct US force in a protracted war, hence low intensity proxy warfare was pursued with devastating destruction and inconclusive political results. Henry Kissinger, describing the Reagan administration as 'personally offensive' to him stated in what he thought was a private symposium at the Library of Congress, that both sides were 'spouting nonsense' in the debate on Nicaragua. Kissinger, who had earlier headed the Commission on Central America, argued that either the analysis or the solution is wrong for Nicaragua, 'It cannot be that it is such a vital interest and it can be solved with $100 million.' But the parameters of presidential action were real. A *New York Times* editorial asked under the title, 'It Takes Two to Contadora' where the President stood: 'For "no more Vietnams, no more Cubas." With a war he can't win and a negotiation he can't abide. He lets the contras fight and the diplomats talk, to no discernible end.'[34] At least a discernible end that could be spoken of in the public rhetoric.

# 6 The Arias Plan 1987–1988

With the demise of Contadora greater focus started to emerge on the internal situation of Nicaragua that ultimately found its way into the Arias proposals. By mid July 1986 Ambassador Habib was discussing the internal Nicaraguan situation with the Honduran President. Azcona paid tribute to Contadora and its Support Group, but clearly indicated it was time the Central American countries took the initiative in finding solutions. With the core countries clearly aligned to Washington, this diplomatic change further isolated Nicaragua in the region. Contadora Ministers indicated that the renewed vote for aid damaged their work which consistently called for an end to support for irregular forces. Mexican Foreign Minister, Sepúlveda, was concerned the contra aid might radicalize the various positions in Central America, producing 'undesirable intransigent positions that may put an end to the plan for a peaceful coexistence'. George Shultz was already moving in this direction in his public utterances. In early August he indicated that the isthmian leaders thought the only way to bring peace to the region was without the Sandinistas, when Nicaragua had, according to their interpretation, a democratic government based on popular consent. While bilateral overtures were made by Nicaragua in the summer and autumn of 1986, no substantial diplomatic progress was made.[1] Through late 1986 to early 1988 the situation changed in Washington, Central America, and Managua. The Reagan administration was diplomatically debilitated by the findings and the continued controversies of the Iran–Contra investigations. The political space created by Washington's injury allowed the Arias government to press for an isthmian solution resulting in eventual agreement though inconsistently implemented. The Sandinistas for their part continued their strategy of concessions in the diplomatic fora and agreed to open talks with the contras in early 1988.

## IRAN–CONTRA

During this period Nicaragua engaged in a significant military buildup that was used by the Reagan administration for propaganda material, despite senior US officials and an intelligence study conceding internally that the 'overall buildup is primarily defense-oriented'. The new equipment provided political dividends when on 5 October a Sandinista army unit shot down a C-123 supply plane, which despite numerous official US denials was part of the network coordinated by Oliver North. While congressional hearings were already under preparation during the summer with requests made for all relevant documentation on the supply network, the downing and capture of one of the crew members, Eugene Hasenfus, who claimed ties to US agencies, boosted the Sandinista position. They immediately took the opportunity to protest the actions that now explicitly involved the isthmian countries in supporting the contras. With the lodgement of a strong complaint against the United States the Sandininstas called on them to abandon their aggressive stance and accept 'the path of dialogue' to resolve the situation. Nevertheless, days later the $100 million came into effect with the congressional approval and presidential authorization of the funds. Lethal aid to the contras was restored, described in a letter from Victor Tinoco to George Shultz as a 'new and dangerous chapter in the Central American crisis, a chapter of death and destruction'. The *Los Angeles Times* had earlier ridiculed the suggestion that Nicaragua was a security threat to the United States, when its population was on par with the number who worked for the US Defense Department. The alleged security threat could have been addressed through Contadora, but the *Los Angeles Times* asserted that Reagan wanted to destroy the Sandinistas, rather than find a compromise. They further argued, 'Reagan's policies have militarized all of Central America, polarized politics and threatened what little democracy exists.' Now Congress had also approved the policies supported by lethal assistance.[2]

Most of the investigations into the Iran and Contra affairs tried to limit their scope to focus on particularly narrow aspects of political or legal wrongdoing. These decisions have limited the public and institutional ability to learn from the occurrences. Culpability was narrowed significantly, thereby limiting the corrective measures required. The Iran and Contra operations were, as Theodore Draper argues, different operations in different countries, dealing with different problems: the supply of the contras and the release of US hostages held in the Middle East. Within a two month period Gutman notes the administration suffered four serious set backs significantly reducing its leverage in the regional diplomacy. Apart from the shooting down of the C-123 plane, a Lebanese magazine *Al Shiraa* revealed on 3 November that McFarlane had been in Tehran to conduct secret negotiations with representatives of their Foreign Ministry. The two demands made by Tehran's officials were that Washington should cease its military and political support of Iraq, and that Iran should be sold spare parts for their American made equipment. In the domestic political context the Republicans lost control of the Senate to the Democrats depriving Reagan of a working majority in that chamber. Finally on 25 November the Attorney General, Edwin Meese, revealed the diversion of monies from the Middle Eastern operation to the Central American operation.[3] The revelation of the diversion document further limited the scope of the inquires. Subsequent investigations concentrated on the role of individuals and did not put the structural bureaucratic problem in context, treating it as an aberration ignoring an historical pattern. Only with the findings of the Independent Council, Lawrence Walsh, and the various criminal proceedings did a more damaging picture of the administration finally emerge from an official source; by this time, the summer of 1993, seven protagonists had been pardoned by President Bush, congressional immunity had limited additional prosecutions, and the political will to take the matters further had dissipated. The narrow focus of the initial investigations acted in part as a diversion in themselves from the larger stories which remained to be told over the subsequent years. The focus on Oliver North further diminished the scope of culpability in the broader operations of circumventing congressional powers through solicitation of funds from third countries and private individuals, thought to be an 'impeachable offense', by Shultz as early as the 25 June 1984 NSPG meeting.[4]

Kornbluh and Byrne argue the official and media focus on the diversion prompted by the Meese 'revelations' on 25 November constituted an attempt to take the spotlight off the President and save Reagan and the presidency from another Watergate or 'impeachment scenario'. Their argument is supported by extracts from the memoirs of Oliver North stating that the diversion in itself was an attempt to shape public perception. North also recounts how his days in office were numbered because the Iran initiative effectively ended with the *Al Shiraa* story, and the shoot down of the contra plane led to safe houses producing telephone numbers including his. North argues: 'This only confirmed what many congressmen and journalists already knew: that while large segments of our government were explicitly prohibited from actively supporting the contras, several of us, including the President, were quietly involved in a host of other efforts to keep them alive.' The diversion provided the focal point to sustain future support for the contras though their credibility had been severely damaged through the findings and the report of Senator Kerry: ' "Private Assistance" and the Contras'.[5] Despite the damage the administration still did not intend to abandon the contras. They had to spend the $100 million, and during that period further damage limitation exercises could be devised.

Each branch of government conducted an inquiry providing various conclusions on their findings. In part their differing focus led them to investigate different aspects of the affairs, and in part the time period under scrutiny perhaps produced constrained results. The President's Special

Review Board, more commonly known as the Tower Commission, reported on their findings in late January 1987 and primarily remarked on the presidential management style, which they considered lax. The lack of accountability, oversight procedures and executive vigilance increased the possibilities of legal transgressions. Reagan's detached management and the absence of cabinet level objections allowed the operations to proceed without adequate scrutiny. The circumvention of the required process allowed bad ideas to become presidential policy; the 'NSC system will not work unless the President makes it work'. Thus the Commission's remit to focus on the operational role of the NSC concluded that staff of the NSC were out of control, though this was ultimately Reagan's responsibility, the specifics of the operations did not result from his decisions. Overall the Tower Commission exonerated Reagan with a public chastisement. Ultimately the board satisfied themselves that he did not know about the diversions of profits from the sale of arms to Iran to the contra operation. The overall impression left after their report enhanced the idea that the diversion of funds was the key question and that operatives such as North, Poindexter, and McFarlane were circumventing the system.[6]

The more comprehensive but still incomplete investigations of the Congressional Committees were constantly wracked by political compromises. They too focused narrowly; their reasoning was to avoid damaging the presidency during an internationally sensitive period. Daniel Inouye and Warren Rudman who headed the Senate Committee investigation visited George Shultz early in 1987 to indicate while they intended to pursue the truth, they were aware of the 'tense situation with the Soviets . . . and they were not out to destroy the president' or impair his ability to deal with Moscow. A meeting of the Senate Select Committee similarly indicated they did not want to induce another Watergate and hence may have sought to protect President Reagan. The Senate Committee made up of eleven senators, seven of which voted for contra aid did not vigorously pursue Reagan, as one participant concluded, he was too old with too little time left in office; impeachment bore a high cost. The chief counsel of the Senate Committee, Arthur Liman, argued that 'unless you had a smoking gun – irrefutable evidence that would cause the President to resign – to have gone down that road could have sacrificed whatever opportunity there was to try to establish some new order with the Soviet Union.' The Senators agreed that if an impeachable offense existed, it had to include the conscious knowledge of the diversion. On this aspect of investigative restraint, the Chairman of the House Committee later concluded similarly: if Reagan was to be pursued, 'you've got to kill the King'. While the Committees found Reagan bore responsibility for 'failing to take care that the law reigned supreme' they affirmed the notion that a 'cabal of zealots' was in charge of the operations primarily centred around North, Poindexter, and McFarlane, with the encouragement of William Casey. Congress found no evidence that Bush knew of the diversion, but Reagan had lied about details of the story as it unfolded, and the failure to communicate clearly with his subordinates allowed them to pursue the vague policy of keeping the contras together 'body and soul'. Thus the ultimate responsibility lay with the president. Though not wanting to pursue the issues Congress destroyed the most effective 'lines of inquiry' by granting North and Poindexter immunity, so they could 'exculpate and eliminate' the need for Bush and Reagan testimonies. Lawrence Walsh concluded his report with the observation:

> The disrespect for Congress by a popular and powerful President and his appointees was obscured when Congress accepted and tendered the concept of a runaway conspiracy of subordinate officers and avoided the unpleasant confrontation with a powerful President and his Cabinet.[7]

The Congressional enquiry did result in the declassification of thousands of documents and revealed the role of the so called Enterprise, as North described it, as an off the shelf, 'stand alone', independent of congressionally appropriated funds and hence oversight at times when executive and legislative foreign policies were not in accordance. In effect the enterprise circumvented one of the most fundamental congressional powers of appropriation. As Draper argues, Poindexter wanted to deprive Congress of any effective influence in matters of foreign policy by negating these powers. While the Congressional Committees had the task of rectifying the possibility of an 'unchecked' executive through their mandate to recommend legislative reform, of the almost 700 page report, four and a half pages dealt with such recommendations. Otherwise the report pursued individual culpability, more suited to the legal enquiry. Through a 'retrospective search for individual responsibility' the committees failed to suggest adequate reforms to the system that allowed the transgressions or out right violations not just of US law, but also of international law. The majority report ultimately decided that new laws were not needed, but that a new fidelity to constitutional constraint was more appropriate. None of the committees' recommendations were signed into law during the Reagan administration. The continued structure facilitating an imperial presidency led Draper to conclude that the affairs were not an aberration, 'they were brought on by a long process of presidential aggrandizement, congressional fecklessness, and judicial connivance'. Koh similarly found that a look at history revealed a 'consistent pattern of executive circumvention of legislative constraint' that stretched back to the Vietnam war and beyond to the Bush administration. Even before the Vietnam period of US foreign policy the NSC system of management dating from 1947 lead to a more centralized system of decision making premised on beliefs in 'permanent and universal crisis, [and] fear of communism . . .' evident in the rhetoric of the Truman Doctrine through to the speeches of Reagan on Central America. Checks and balances were not observed and the 'outdated and rarely criticized strategic vision' since the second world war assumed that national security required a global vigilance against leftist regimes. Kornbluh pointed out further deficiencies of the congressional enquiry resulted from its concentration on the smaller issues of the diversion and management style, they did not examine the 'incompatibility between a constitutional political system premised on the active consent of the governed, and an anti-democratic, autonomous, national security system predicated on secrecy, stealth, and nonaccountability'. To understand the scandal as an historical aberration, he argues, is false. While the executive had taken advantage of the system the process of congressional oversight as the watchdog over covert operations was 'toothless and blind'.[8]

The immunities granted to the principle protagonists of Iran Contra left the Walsh inquiry only 'conditionally' independent. Those prosecuted through the legal process ultimately appealed and overturned the verdicts on technicalities, or were pardoned by President Bush a month before he handed power to President Clinton. According to Walsh, the pardons completed the 'cover-up' by preempting the forthcoming trials of Casper Weinberger and Duane Clarridge. Walsh categorically rejected previous findings limiting the responsibility stating that the operations 'veered off into criminality', substantiated by evidence establishing that the affairs were not 'aberrational' as concluded by congressional investigators, 'no evidence of dissent among his Cabinet officers' was found on Reagan's determination to support the contras. North was not the scapegoat presented in the earlier investigations and by the mainstream media. The prosecuted protagonists:

> were not out-of-control mavericks who acted alone without the knowledge or assistance of others. The evidence establishes that the central NSC operatives kept their superiors – including Reagan, Bush, Shultz, Weinberger and other high officials – informed of their efforts generally, if not in detail, and their superiors either condoned or turned a blind eye to them.

Congressional duty to check executive power failed in this 'first known criminal assault' on the post-Watergate rules governing National Security officials. The lesson of Iran–Contra, Walsh concluded, was the US system required cooperation between the branches of government, with the circumvention of congressional power the legislative branch was 'defrauded'. Walsh's inquiry produced in their words a 'vast record' of official US involvement with the contras during the period when the prohibition on military aid was in effect. The contras were completely dependent on the United States. On top of US aid they received funds, weapons, ammunition, assistance, and other facilities from numerous sources through the period Washington was prohibited from aiding them. With Nicaragua defined as a test case for Reagan's foreign policy several extra-regional countries saw the benefit of helping the administration during periods of congressional bans. Israel sold weapons; Saudi Arabia and Brunei provided millions to the supply network; Guatemala, El Salvador, and Honduras provided small arms, ammunition and facilities; additional support was provided by South Africa, South Korea, and Taiwan. A conservative estimate of the resources available to the contras during the two year ban was put at $88 million. Despite these excessive funds the contras did not bring a single Nicaraguan village under their control, unlike the Salvadoran insurgents who consistently occupied significant sections of their country.[9]

Apart from the detailed findings of the Walsh report the affair effectively ended with Bush's presidential pardon of six operatives including Weinberger, Abrams, Clarridge, Fiers, George, and McFarlane. In the statement on Executive Clemency the violation of the US constitutional system conducted by these people, albeit with the knowledge of Reagan and Bush, was put down to their patriotism, whether their actions were right or wrong. In addition Bush referred to the period of the mid eighties when the resolution of the Cold War was far from clear, and debates raged on the methods 'about how that struggle should be waged'. The pardoning Bush explained was an attempt to extract political differences from the legal arena, with the implication that future criminal activities may be politically punished without legal action. If Congress was given false information, as it was at several points during the Reagan administration, the system of checks and balances could not adequately protect US citizens. The search for policy consensus often compromised the system of congressional oversight. Walsh's reaction to the Bush pardons asserted the action undermined 'the principle that no man is above the law. It demonstrates that powerful people with powerful allies can commit serious crimes in high office – deliberately abusing the public trust – without consequence'.[10] These aspects of the domestic situation in the United States did not even begin to address the consequences of these illegal activities in Nicaragua and Central America. While the contras were shown to be militarily ineffective the political pressure applied to Managua through their terrorism and sabotage activities produced devastating results.

## ARIAS AND ESQUIPULAS

While the structural information on Iran–Contra may be put together with hindsight the diplomacy that took place contemporaneously was privy to their own partial understanding of the regional events. In the wake of the scandal and the continued revelations of the Iran–Contra hearings during the summer of 1987 the manoeuvrability of the Reagan administration was constrained. Despite the demonstration of an executive contempt of congressional power the ambivalent approach of the legislature to the contras continued throughout the Reagan administration. Crucially they decided not to cut the last installment of aid in March 1987 that provided heavy weapons to the irregular forces. Nevertheless, the Central American agreement could perhaps only have emerged because of the political crisis in Washington, aided by key Democrats tired of administration policy, and cemented when a bipartisan attempt at an alternative to President Arias's plan was seen as an effort to coopt the isthmian governments.

The Arias Plan that developed through 1987 was largely based on the Contadora documents. Child has pointed out three quarters of the language in Arias was actually in Contadora. The significant features of the 'new' diplomatic move were that it came from within Central America, played down the inter-state security measures, and furnished both the Sandinistas and the Reagan administration with one of their major desires: an end to support for the contras, and pressure on the internal democratization process.[11]

The contras had proved themselves an almost totally ineffective force except in mutilation, murder and destruction of the infrastructure and economy. Investigations in late 1986 and resulting from the Iran–Contra showed contra involvement in drug trafficking, assassination, misappropriation of money, corruption, and violations of international law. Washington constantly had to refurbish their image through extensive Public Diplomacy exercises dating back to 1983. The problem in early 1987 was a public questioning of the efficacy of Reagan policies in Central America and of the contras usefulness. After years of war there were 43 000 Nicaraguan casualties by 1988 and as a critic of the Reagan administration (cited by LaFeber) observed: Washington was the only town the contras held. Now Washington had to discuss and decide on the future of the mercenary force. The objective of a military victory over the Sandinistas had slipped away since the 1986 delivery of Soviet weapons to Nicaragua which resulted in 400 contra casualties each month. More to the point, a hypothetical military victory would not necessarily produce a peaceful result in the region, with the likelihood of the Sandinistas regrouping in the mountains of Nicaragua. The US Senate held hearings in early 1987 on the policy options with regard to the contras and Nicaragua during which Abrams described US efforts at 'keeping alive the flame of freedom in today's world'. The contras according to Abrams were improving their military capability and pressuring the Sandinistas to negotiate. Washington had three options, to abandon the fight, to accept 'communist rule in Managua' or to continue the two track policy of supporting the contras as the only viable solution for a democratic negotiated settlement. Habib then provided the specific and familiar US stance on negotiations: rhetorical support for the Contadora process and the contradictory insistence on supporting the contras. A far more plausible argument was put to the Senate Committee by Kenneth Sharpe of Swarthmore College. Even if the contras were judged on their merits and not punished for the transgressions of the Reagan administration they would still encounter serious problems in terms of the objectives set in Washington. They were militarily ineffective despite over $200 million in aid; the attacks on health workers, peasants, workers, teachers and Christian social activists were counterproductive, 'more US money, arms and training will not reverse this losing bottle for the hearts and minds of the populace'. Contra involvement in 'kidnappings, indiscriminate attacks on civilians, torture and mutilation of prisoners' documented by Amnesty International and Americas Watch flew in the face of US and UNO rhetoric on respect for human rights. Contra operations were provocative in the border regions, and any cross border incursion may be used by 'top administration officials, still determined to topple the Nicaraguan government before President Reagan leaves office'. Abrams' argument on accepting the Soviets as the dominant power between Panama and Mexico was out of touch with reality. According to Sharpe, Gorbachev probably woke each morning and like Reagan says: 'we don't want another Cuba.' Soviet presence or connection did not mean Soviet control. The contra war contributed to the anti-democratic tightening of control by Managua that was in line with the measures taken by developed democracies while under attack, including US internment of Japanese Americans after Pearl Harbor. The increased pressure on Managua moved them towards an increasing reliance on Soviet weapons and aid, thus increasing their presence in the region. Sharpe argued, 'if our major concern is Nicaraguan–Soviet military ties, the contra war is counterproductive'. Without advanced offensive missile technology the Sandinistas did not pose a threat to the United States. Any attack would be their last, given the legitimate regional and US response through the Rio pact: 'Indeed the Nicaraguans, following the lead of the Contadora countries, have shown a willingness to negotiate every security concern I have just mentioned. The major obstacle to those negotiations has been the Reagan administration.'[12]

Despite congressional considerations of a moratorium on the remaining $40 million of the $100 million, Reagan requested the monies on 5 March 1987 citing the failure of Contadora to provide an effective and comprehensive agreement, the lack of internal dialogue, and that there was no 'reasonable prospect' of agreement through any 'further diplomatic measures . . . without additional assistance to the Nicaraguan democratic resistance'. The moratorium allowed a six month delay without the need to force an outright rejection of the aid. Additionally it lent credibility to the prospects for a total rejection of lethal aid for the following fiscal year. The Senate voted for the aid to be released but pressed Reagan to engage in negotiations. The threat was an absolute cut of contra aid in the autumn without any other alternatives. Congress was not willing of totally cut contra aid.[13]

Reagan's determination on contra aid demonstrated utter contempt for the peace initiative that was emerging from primarily Costa Rica's President Oscar Arias. The new aperture created by a Washington beset with scandal was used by regional foreign ministers who recognized the deteriorating situation. Contadora as well as the UN Secretary General Javier Pérez de Cuéllar identified a lack of will to implement the proposals already tabled. Arias worked with the Democratic leadership in Washington and was spurred by the new 'Group of Ten' (Contadora was joined by the secretary generals of the UN and OAS) conclusions that an isthmian agreement was possible due to Reagan's problems, and the disintegration of the UNO coalition, with the departure of the Southern Front from their political control, the resignation of Adolfo Calero and Arturo Cruz, with Robelo leaving in June, and division among the military and civilian leadership, and Ortega's desire for further bilateral talks with Washington. But such talks were proscribed by Washington till Nicaragua became by US regional standards a 'democratic' country.[14]

The genesis of the Arias Plan as explained by Goodfellow and Morrell was one of the 'greatest ironies' of the peace efforts; the meeting that was about to 'inaugurate Nicaragua's isolation' produced its salvation. An EC, Contadora and Central American meeting in Guatemala City on 9–10 February 1987 affirmed support for Contadora. The alternative provided by Arias, initially called the San José plan, emerged from discussions between Costa Rican Foreign Minister, Rodrigo Madrigal Nieto, Abrams and Habib in Miami in early January. With the idea of developing an 'Alliance of Democratic Countries' Nicaragua's isolation was almost assured. Costa Rica was boycotting the Contadora process because of Nicaragua's suit against it at the International Court of Justice. Hence, when Pérez de Cuéllar rejected this position and pushed the authority of the twenty one participating nations at the Guatemala meeting, Costa Rica's reaction was negative. The Venezuelan Foreign Minister observed Washington 'was not contributing in any manner towards achieving peace,' but Arias' insistence on democratization, his rejection of Contadora's proposal, and the exclusion of Nicaragua, that seemed totally in line with Washington's thinking, provoked the ire of Managua, where *Barricada* argued the plan was an attempt of divert attention from Contadora, and that Arias had extracted financial and political arrangements as his costs. As Nicaragua approved of Contadora, Arias indicated his alternative would not supplant the regional diplomacy. Shultz added weight to the 'democratic' thrust of the negotiations with a speech isolating Nicaragua as a Soviet 'stepping stone' in the hemisphere where ninety per cent of Latin American's enjoyed 'democratic government'. Nicaragua expressed surprise it was not invited to the San Jose meeting where Arias' proposal was revealed for the first time. Only without Nicaraguan consent the document imposed its own impotence as indicated in its final sentence requiring all five signatures. But the Core countries had not seen the document and perhaps thought they were contributing to Nicaragua's segregation. The 'Process Towards Establishing a Firm and Lasting Peace in Central America', heavily stressed national reconciliation, democratization, and free elections. The suspension of military aid by extra regional countries would also be requested. Thus the renewed subjection to a verified democratic election in Nicaragua would be the cost of a cessation of contra aid. While all isthmian countries would be subjected to the requirements of the plan, necessitating a dialogue between San Salvador and the FMLN, the bulk of the document was clearly aimed at Nicaragua. Moreover, Washington's compliance Arias posited was logical, because democratization in Nicaragua would remove the need for contra pressure.[15]

While the plan contained all the provisions to isolate and then punish Nicaragua for its anticipated rejection, it also contained clauses requiring the removal of irregular forces from the territory of the core countries. Abruptly, Duarte of El Salvador and Honduras expressed reservations on the plan and backed away from full endorsement. The intended 'united front' against Nicaragua broke up and Managua was invited to the next Esquipulas meeting in May ninety days later, which it promptly accepted. The gap between Costa Rica and Nicaragua was bridged by the mediation of Guatemala who informed Managua of the content of the meeting. The document ultimately signed in February was a non-specific statement of general principles indicating it was time Central American solutions were found. Managua was traditionally uneasy with this because the original core four countries were closely aligned with Washington. Duarte, however, had received warnings from the Salvadoran military not to enter commitments affecting their internal war, or necessitating dialogue with the FMLN. So Arias' plan met immediate obstacles from the Salvadoran military and the Reagan determination in early March, but allowed him to extricate Costa Rica from the Core Four and enter the search for peace. The Sandinistas dramatically changed their position within a week; rejecting their earlier contention that the plan was written in Washington, they now indicated there was much in it they could live with. The confusion was understandable, Arias' rhetoric mirrored that of Washington. As Goodfellow and Morrell point out Arias differed in his fidelity to the principles of diplomacy, 'concessions by both sides', were required; Washington's only concession in the April 1986 Habib letter was soon repudiated by Abrams. Arias' plan was to implement Washington's stated diplomatic position, requiring a democratic Nicaragua. This did not necessitate the removal of the Sandinistas. The plan soon received backing from Congress, and a month later from Contadora. With Guatemala and Nicaragua willing to negotiate, the key objectors to the plan were Washington, El Salvador and Honduras. Washington objected because they argued the contras must be maintained while the Sandinistas democratize. The ingredients for political pluralism were present in the Nicaraguan 1987 constitution and recognized by the Senate Committee on Foreign Relations; crucially though, Arias argued that democratization was not possible under pressure. The retired contra leaders, Cruz and Robelo, backed the plan while the military leader Enrique Bermúdez rejected it, stating that a cease-fire would amount to an effective surrender. The contras were in a period of definition according to their military leadership, while Aristide Sanchez argued they now had to win the next $100 million 'with our performance on the battlefield'.[16]

Various manoeuvres took place between this crucial defining period and the final signing by all the Central American governments in early August of a plan not substantially different from the one presented in February. By then Washington was completely isolated on the peace issue, though it tried to sustain its alternatives in the interim. The Reagan administration officially welcomed the Arias initiative in early May though expressing some reservations on the implementation procedures, but again the sticking point was his insistence on support for the 'freedom fighters'. Administration allies in Central America, especially the Duarte government forced the delay of the post-ninety-day meeting scheduled for 15 May. Duarte had made an unscheduled visit to Guatemalan President Cerezo to seek assurances there would not be surprises in the next meeting he did not know about; he had been warned by the military not to force a dialogue or reduction in US aid. El Salvador was at the time the third largest recipient of US aid after Israel and Egypt, receiving more than $500 million a year. The contras, largely based in Honduras, provided the Azcona government further concern. Apart from 15 to 20 000 contras in his country, Honduras was also host to almost 200 000 refugees from Nicaragua. His government wanted these forces and people out of the country should an agreement be signed, because Honduras could not effectively police the areas in which the contras based themselves. Thus any cease-fire had to include an agreements between the contras and the Sandinistas, which Managua objected to. Still, Arias was able to gather support in Europe and in Washington during May and June. The objectors had to be overcome, despite FMLN objections, because they thought the plan unrepresentative of local realities; Arias was mainly concerned about Washington, Honduras, and El Salvador. His position was the initial concessions would have to be made by the United States and the contras, while the process of democratization would take some time; but the State Department required simultaneous implementation of both, with democracy defined in Washington as in 1984.[17]

The diplomatic manoeuvring found the objectors on the defensive. Mexico was rumored to have formed a pressure group including Guatemala and Nicaragua to isolate the other two. US officials in the region pondered the possibility of 'a terrible moment when we find Costa Rica and Guatemala in greater agreement with Nicaragua than with Honduras and El Salvador'. The United States is thought to have brought pressure on the regional countries sending a high level delegation including Ikle, Abrams, Pentagon and NSC officials to visit El Salvador and Honduras. Within days Arias was in the White House where he too faced the top brass of the Reagan administration including Bush, Carlucci (the new NSA), Abrams, Habib, and James Baker. While Arias stood his ground, Nicaragua enjoyed the power the possibility of a peace plan gave them: 'the Americans are scared to death of the talks because . . . we might . . . offer to sign it immediately.' The situation was different in San Salvador where Duarte requested a postponement to the scheduled 25 June meeting because, he explained to his Guatemalan counterpart, of US pressure. Nicaragua initially rejected the new date but soon accepted on the condition of greater Contadora involvement. While Arias was informed by Washington that they had no intention of abandoning the contras, dooming his plan to failure, he argued that they had become 'the excuse for everything', their presence making democracy in Nicaragua impossible. With the meeting rescheduled, the Reagan administration was further isolated when Congress passed a Joint Resolution in late June applauding the bold initiative, and congratulating Arias on 'the significant contribution he has made' to end conflict and reinforce democracy in Central America. Nevertheless when Habib was directly asked during Congressional hearings in July whether the United States would allow an agreement to happen if the Central Americans agreed, Habib said, 'I just won't answer that.'[18]

## SIGNING

At the pre-summit meeting in Tegucigalpa, Honduras offered an alternative 'under the icy gaze' of Sepúlveda, which D'Escoto's suggested should be gathered together and reconciled by Contadora ministers. The changes were minor, necessitating the cease-fire agreements to be negotiated by the governments with the guerilla opposition. A more influential but short lived alternative was offered by the Reagan administration and Congressional Speaker of the House, Jim Wright, which emphasized bilateral concerns starting with the security issues the Arias plan had specifically ignored since these contributed to the earlier Contadora stalemate. Reagan requested that the plan was given to the leaders for deliberation at their Guatemala meeting. Arias immediately rejected the idea stating their meeting intended to 'exclusively' discuss his plan. Even Democrats in Washington suggested the plan was the normal 'false' procedure before a request for contra aid: 'every time they've been behind in votes, they've thrown up some peace plan . . . Every one of those negotiations has broken down after contra aid was approved.' Guatemala was not happy either, Cerezo indicated 'nobody should fall into the trap of giving too much importance' to Washington's peace plan. Central American negotiators viewed it as a diversionary tactic aimed at reducing the momentum of the initiative by offering alternatives. Not only was it diversionary, but also counterproductive; it is widely interpreted to have provided added momentum to the Central American plan because the tactic roused nationalistic reactions. Ortega, however, used it to his advantage by immediately requesting bilateral negotiations with Washington because the main concerns of their plan were aimed at Nicaragua. The gambit drew the instant rejection in Washington, where Democratic leaders criticized the White House move.[19]

The Esquipulas agreement, not technically a treaty, represented Central American unity on a narrow range of issues; yet they were crucial to begin the process. When negotiations faltered at the last minute El Salvador and Honduras were subjected to new congressional pressure. This time representatives of Senate majority leader Robert Byrd told the two governments that Democrats did not back Reagan. Furthermore, congressmen warned these two governments that they ought to back the Arias agreements or bilateral aid to them would be cutoff at the next foreign aid bill. The agreement mostly signaled a rejection of interference in their countries by the United States. It was backed by the EC, the Soviet Union, the Nonaligned Movement, Contadora, the Support Group, the UN and OAS, and by Democrats in Congress; the Reagan administration and the contras were almost totally isolated. The agreement required an amnesty, a cease-fire, pluralistic and participatory democracy (crucially the agreement set up the outlines of a verification procedure in which the meaning of democracy had to be agreed), cessation of extra regional aid, and a halt to the use of Central American territory by irregular forces.[20]

Again, while providing verbal support, there was dissension from Weinberger, reflecting the division in the administration. Reagan wanted it both ways, support for the plan and contra aid; a stance adopted simply because the latter depended on the former. Bush indicated that Washington would not leave 'the contras twisting in the wind, wondering whether they are going to be done in by a peace plan'. But Wright had insisted Reagan hold off his request for a further $270 million while the plan was still effective. The administration indicated it would wait till 30 September 1987 which was criticized by Democrats as an unrealistic time frame to allow compliance. The carrot of bilateral talks was briefly held out by Senate minority leader Bob Dole, but the stick of continued contra aid was attached. The suggestion must be seen as a ploy preparing for the legislative battle. The diplomatic track was shaken in mid August with the resignation of Habib. He had faced pressure from the right because he advocated serious negotiations, recognizing the thrust of the current plan. The administration lost the diplomat most likely to convince Congress they had a serious negotiating track, the prerequisite for contra aid. More to the point, his resignation was prompted by an order from Reagan and Abrams to desist discussions with the Sandinistas. Habib was the fourth envoy to resign in four years, all pressured because within the parameters of administration thinking they placed too much emphasis on negotiations, leaving widespread scepticism on the sincerity of Reagan's alleged concerns for peace.[21]

## VERIFICATION

Esquipulas perhaps succeeded where Contadora failed because it lacked the specificity of the former. This problem was identified when the verification process got underway. The Arias plan was necessarily vague; signing the agreement was an act of trust that fell short of the original 21 Contadora objectives. With less in the package there was less to object to. The new and only unity that existed amongst the Central American governments was their call to stop aid to the contras; on this one point the region was 'squarely in opposition to the United States' albeit under some duress. The other provisions of the agreement were open to interpretation which produced more acrimony. Nicaragua was the first country to set up a 'reconciliation commission' and moved fastest to implement the provisions of the accord. The international spot light was mostly focused on them and other countries merely gave tacit support to the verification process. When the first official report of the CIVS (International Commission for Verification and Follow Up), made up of Contadora foreign ministers, was issued in January 1988 and criticized most of the isthmian counties, favouring the position of Nicaragua, it was promptly thanked and dismissed. The Central Americans then set up their own commission taking power away from the Contadora countries.[22]

Problems emerged early when Shultz stated the agreement did not address US national security concerns and the administration still had the 'responsibility to define and assert that interest for ourselves', with the inescapable conclusion that unless security interests were addressed the effective termination of contra aid would result in a 'communist victory'. Any efforts by the Sandinistas had to be denigrated in the White House bid for contra support. The opening of the opposition paper *La Prensa* was described by the administration as 'cosmetic' and similarly an unilateral cease-fire would not meet the requirements of negotiating with the contras; the Sandinistas insisted on talking to Washington. Jim Wright became a dominant force in the debate, suggesting the United States had a problem if it saw itself as a judge on compliance when they were not asked to conduct such a role. Nevertheless, Washington increased its demands on the Sandinistas as they moved faster than the other isthmian countries to implement and comply with the plan's requirements. As the deadline for the first round of compliance drew close the Reagan administration moved away from the Arias plan and requested $270 million over an eighteen month period, despite Wright's assertion there would be no support for military aid after Arias was awarded the Nobel Peace Prize in October

1987. At the first deadline of 5 November Nicaragua had moved further than the other countries except Costa Rica. The International Verification Commission began its work in the second phase to determine compliance with the measures already taken.[23]

The report of the CIVS, never released, was watered down under pressure from the core four Central American countries. They were outnumbered on the Commission whose view tended to reflect the position predominantly of Mexico, Venezuela, and Colombia. The report was critical of all the Central American countries including Costa Rica. It did, however, make the case that Nicaragua was complying with Esquipulas more thoroughly than any other. The LASA Commission on Compliance reached a similar conclusion:

> Nicaragua has also been the country in which the greatest change has occurred the terms and timetable of the Accord. The National Reconciliation Commission in Nicaragua was the most prominent, most public, and, by most criteria, the most successful in the region. By appointing its most respected critic, Archbishop Obando y Bravo, to the commission . . . the Nicaraguan government took the considerable risk of placing itself under intolerable pressure . . .

The failure on the part of Honduras to comply was due in part the commission argued to its 'abject dependence' on the United States who they thought had 'little interest in the peace plan'.[24]

The findings of the CIVS were the main topic of the Alajuela summit in mid January 1988, but Nicaragua was the only country under scrutiny. On the day of the summit Azcona demonstrated his non compliance by stating that they would not ask the contras to leave till Nicaragua had become a democracy. Nicaragua was the only country where significant concessions were being made, but the lack of movement in the others was not under scrutiny for the 'success' of the plan. On the other hand, success for Managua was vital to head off the possibility of renewed lethal aid. Despite the CIVS findings, and in spite of internal Sandinista division over the concessions and changes, Ortega strategically succumbed to isthmian pressure and announced a set of unilateral concessions. Ortega realized a successful summit declaration required his sacrifices. The declaration affirmed that the countries had fallen short on compliance but placed all on an equal footing that belied the findings of the various commissions. The summit was a success for Nicaragua in as much as the diplomatic track was still viable. Ortega's four unilateral concessions: suspending the emergency; convoking direct talks with the contras; implementing an amnesty law; and providing a schedule for elections, were immediately used by the Reagan administration to argue that these last minute concessions implied Nicaragua had avoided compliance earlier. Abrams asserted they were a ploy to defeat the upcoming decision on contra aid. By this stage it was clear the Central Americans and the United States had to be satisfied on Nicaraguan conformity. Managua could only maintain its strategy of concessions to avert further isolation and potential US military action. Henceforth the verification and follow up procedures would be conducted by the Executive Commission of isthmian foreign ministers. The end of the regional verification signaled, according to Goodfellow and Morrell, the 'abandonment of evenhandedness', causing the process to stagnate for over a year till new measures were implemented after Reagan left office.[25]

## TALKING TO THE CONTRAS

The largest Sandinista concession in the period and the process was their agreement to hold direct talks with the contras which they had refused to do for the previous eight years. Thus greater legitimacy was given to a group that had proved itself both politically and militarily ineffective if not backed and directed by Washington. With dismal prospects for new military aid the contras were able to gain money to keep them in tact till further settlement eventuated. Nicaragua's realization that the contras would not disappear while the Reagan administration was in office, their desire to insure the defeat of future military aid bills and insure against the possibility of a direct invasion by perpetuating the negotiating process, necessitated the move towards talks aimed at a cease-fire. In this regard Honduran violation, and US obstruction of Esquipulas had to be tolerated because the system had no sanctions against violating governments.

Ortega's reluctance to talk with the contras was because they did not represent a viable force without Washington. Yet the appointment of Morris Busby as US ambassador to Managua, who had run the contra programme at the State Department, signaled White House resolve. The administration and the contras had stated they would disappear without US aid, unlike the Salvadoran FMLN who remained a viable force without massive extra-regional aid. The Sandinistas were under pressure to talk because intransigence on this point would contribute to congressional opposition; renewed US pressure began with their bid for over a quarter of a million aid. Arias visited Washington to ensure the survival of his plan by trying to reduce the prospects of contra aid. Part of his strategy was to ensure proponents of aid that Costa Rica fully intended to isolate Nicaragua if it did not meet their requirements. Such a threat was not levied against the other isthmian violators of the agreement such as Honduras, but Busby had clearly outlined Washington's opposition to the plan until Nicaragua began the direct talks. Bilateral talks were similarly tied to this condition, even the Sandinista unilateral cease-fire was spurned by both Washington and Arias. US aims remained unchanged despite the plan; a State Department official explained that over the last eight years containing the Sandinistas was not enough. Within a two day period the administration's isolation grew even more acute. Reagan's speech to the United Nations was immediately responded to by Arias' address to a joint session of Congress directly opposing the requests for aid. Simultaneously, 121 members of Congress damned Reagan's persistence:

> It is difficult . . . to escape the conclusion that you and your administration are attempting to scuttle the Central American peace plan in order to justify continued funding for the contras . . . Aside from a few pro forma positive statements, your administration has done nothing but criticize the agreement and call for more aid . . . and a continuation of their ineffective war against the Nicaraguan government.

Arias appealed for direct talks even though it was not part of the plan which Nicaragua conceded to on the condition aid was halted.[26]

Washington's demands on internal affairs provided new difficulties for the Sandinistas, prompting Jim Wright to label the demands 'ridiculous' and a violation of Nicaraguan sovereignty. Wright also added it was 'becoming increasingly difficult to avoid the conclusion that someone advising the President is trying to torpedo the peace process'. White House officials involved in Central American strategy confirmed the intention to see 'the Sandinistas out of power by the time his term ends or that at least sets in motion an irreversible process towards that end'. Managua tried vainly to offset the motion by appealing for direct talks that were denigrated by Duarte on a visit to Washington where he argued the Sandinistas should get on with contra talks as he had begun talks with the FMLN without demanding Moscow's involvement. The lack of parallel was not commented on.[27]

The strategy that emerged to block the agreement from the autumn of 1987 was to insist on direct talks with the contras as part of the process towards democratization. Reagan outlined this strategy in his speech to the OAS in October 1987. The Sandinistas refused to comply with the Reagan demands enhancing his position on Capitol Hill; the intransigence continued till the 5 November date in the compliance schedule. The Sandinista concession came on the day of the compliance meeting when the most media attention was focused on the region demonstrating flexibility in stark contrast to Washington's continued intransigence. The move effectively defused the contra bill, that now became a question not of whether military aid would be granted, but how much non military aid would be passed. The retreat was announced by Shultz who stated the aid request would be delayed till 1988. The Sandinistas continued to build up their military, reliant on Soviet supplies, which, under Gorbachev's 'new thinking', dwindled anyway. Sandinista–Contra talks proceeded intermittently throughout the year and into 1988. As a concession resulting from the Alajuela summit Ortega further damaged contra aid with the 'January surprise' of agreeing to hold direct talks with them. Despite the concession, Reagan certified a cease-fire had not been reached and pressed the contra case. By the end of January the administration dropped its request to $36.25 million, signalling a retreat, though hidden costs would have put the actual price up to $60 million. In any case the bill was rejected and executive policy rebuked, albeit by a narrow margin.[28]

The Sapoá agreement between the Sandinistas and the contras followed a period of intense fighting on the border region, with pursuit into Honduran territory. Having finished their offensive, and under pressure from Arias, the two parties agreed to a sixty day cease-fire which suspended rather than ended the war. The agreement bestowed greater legitimacy on both groups with a contra concession of referring to the Sandinistas as the Government of Nicaragua, and in turn being recognized as a political force. The agreement included directions to locate contras in safe zones, an amnesty, further dialogue, repatriations and elections. The significance of the agreement, though not specifically part of either plan, demonstrated that Contadora or Esquipulas could not work without an effective agreement between the government and the armed opposition.[29]

Despite further acrimony and manoeuvring throughout the Reagan administration the Sapoá agreement began the contra integration into the Nicaraguan political process. Goodfellow and Morrell point out the Sandinista strategy of concessions by perpetuating negotiations defused 'the momentum toward massive aid to the contras, regional war, and US intervention'.[30]

# 7 Bush and the Sandinistas 1989

The Reagan attempt to rollback the Sandinista revolution had effectively ended in February 1988 with the vote to end contra military aid. They were no longer a credible force within Washington's objectives and now had to find the most viable way to survive the transitional period. The Sandinistas too continued their negotiating strategy. After the defeat of military aid a broad coalition of support was given for non-lethal aid of $47.9 million which was passed in late March. A congressional report indicated that Reagan's 'lame duck' presidency had little influence on the debate; more important were the events in the region and some tentative agreement in Congress. Even the Sandinistas acquiesced to the aid as long as it was channelled through neutral organizations. The Sandinista–Contra negotiations towards a permanent cease-fire broke up on 9 June 1988 without agreement, probably because of division amongst the contra leadership factions. The first comprehensive Sandinista proposal was rejected while contra leader Alfredo César began secret talks with Humberto Ortega and Paul Reichler, an American legal representative to the Sandinistas. According to the Center for International Policy, César presented a list of reforms that had to be met before the contra directorate would sign any agreement. In late May the Sandinistas accepted the points, resulting in further and unconstitutional demands put forward by the Bermúdez faction of the contras. The Sandinistas prepared further concessions without accepting the May demands, but on the 9 June 1988 meeting they did not present them because they were presented with yet further contra demands. Ortega's proposals for future talks were rejected till US contra aid matched Soviet aid to Managua. While Ortega felt the contras were trying to buy time till the November 1988 US elections, after which their prospects might have improved with a Bush victory, he declared the unilateral cease-fire would continue as long as possible. The Reagan administration attributed the collapse to Sandinistas' intransigence on democratic reforms suggested in the contra document which went against Nicaragua's constitution legitimated through the Esquipulas process. The bilateral situation deteriorated further during July when both countries expelled a number of each other's diplomats, after the new US ambassador Richard Melton stated the Sandinistas did not reach the minimal standards of democracy and there would be no further compromises with them.[1] Despite the press largely blaming the contras for the breakup of the talks the Sandinistas lost the advantage when they broke up a protest in Nandaime, arresting and suspending the civil rights of several prominent opposition leaders.

With growing questions about the future viability of the contras the factions seemed to disagree whether the diplomatic or military track served their interests best. Certainly the military track dimmed the prospects for further diplomacy while Reagan was in power. Still as yet another round of congressional voting approached representatives called for a new US two track policy both involving diplomacy; directly between Washington and Managua, and also between the Sandinistas and the contras. Talks ground to a complete halt when the Sandinistas offered to hold a further round in Managua which the contras rejected. Ortega announced the Sandinistas had reached the 'limits of their flexibility', and no more substantial direct talks took place during the year.[2]

Several changes at different levels in late 1988 moved the Central American situation beyond the stalemated and stubborn Reagan determination to oust the Sandinistas. The contras were militarily ineffective and were constantly outmanoeuvred by Managua; Washington lost control as the Central Americans asserted themselves; the election of Bush and a more influential Congress initiated changes in Washington; and the results of Gorbachev's 'new thinking' and Soviet disengagement from regional conflicts were becoming apparent. The combination of these processes allowed the peace process more space and effectively contributed to the contras' demise. Despite Shultz's support for the contras at the November 1988 OAS meeting, president-elect George Bush made it clear, though not through a policy statement, that Washington's approach would change. Greater accord with Congress was intended reflecting the future Secretary of State, James Baker's 'moderate' approach. The absence of a dramatic break in policy may have been precluded because the right of the Republican party constrained such movement, and Bush could not simply break from his consistent involvement on Central America throughout the Reagan administration. In addition Bush had the same maximum aims as Reagan, though the style and substance, with reduced rhetoric and added weight behind the political options, were different. Aides made it clear the 'ideological zeal' of the Reagan–Abrams approach would be dropped. Bush immediately declared renewed contra aid would 'have a high priority' even if aides knew military aid was out of the question in the immediate future. Despite Bush's claims since 1986 and during his bid for the presidency of being out of the loop on Iran–Contra, Walsh's investigation found he was very much involved. Still, change to a pragmatic style recognizing the new constraints suited the new administration which did not accord the same significance to the region as did its predecessor. Central America was a defining point of Reagan's foreign policy, a test case in the Reagan Doctrine, for Bush, William LeoGrande argues, the region was regarded 'as the troublesome bequest of his predecessor rather than as issues that held any significance'. With other priorities Central America would ultimately return to Washington's back burner.[3]

While military aid was not ruled out, reports indicated Bush would give diplomacy a real option, though stressed bilateral negotiations were not on offer despite Ortega's immediate invitation to resume such contact. Instead Washington intended an aggressive 'containment' involving a host of political, economic, diplomatic and propaganda measures to continue the pressure on the Sandinistas. While some contra leaders ruled out the role of merely applying pressure, others signalled the end of the military option and returned to the political arena. Borge in Managua expected 'progress' from a 'man of better judgement than Reagan'. Contra leaders and their hosts in Honduras became increasingly worried about the possibility that Washington may not renew aid to them in an adequate manner; Tegucigalpa worried about running a guest house in which the guests did not have enough money, had no where else to go and remained armed within their territory. Tegucigalpa proposed the creation of a UN force made up of Canada, Spain and West Germany, an idea proposed years earlier by the Sandinistas, to patrol the border between Honduras and Nicaragua, and with less emphasis, between Honduras and El Salvador. The isthmian countries found it imperative to revive the peace plan because of possible neglect from Washington and reduced aid from the Bush administration. European finance was also specifically tied to progress on peace, thus the real possibility that Central Americans would have to bear the economic burden of the decade of destruction threatened the stability of the region when the countries could not bear the costs alone. At the inauguration of Mexican President Carlos Salinas de Gortari the Central American foreign ministers acted on the Honduran proposal and requested the help of the UN through Javier Pérez de Cuéllar. The multinational patrols would effectively contribute to the end of cross border contra operations.[4]

The call for UN participation and the revival of the peace process after a year's interruption also affected the erosion of US influence which had declined since August 1987 and the aftermath of Iran–Contra. This time the Central American unity, usually fractured, was presented in terms of direct opposition to Washington, though any advance depended at least on its acquiescence. The difference resulted from a regional agreement that the contras had to be disbanded or moved out of Honduras. President Azcona, the weakest link in the unity, and also the President with the most to worry about in terms of the 'contra disposal problem' stressed they had to leave Honduras: either they receive new military aid, he stated, and moved into Nicaragua, or 'if they don't receive aid, they will have to dissolve themselves'. Costa Rica, which had consistently denied the presence of the contras, now claimed they could no longer shoulder the financial burden after nine years, thus implicitly conceding the country had also violated Esquipulas. Similarly, Salvadoran Foreign Minister, Ricardo Acevedo Peralta, declared the irregular force a thing 'of the past'. The more pragmatic contra leaders Alfredo César and ex-leader Alfonso Robelo realized their forces had been 'strategically weakened' through Sandinista action and an inconsistent US policy. César declared the military option no longer 'viable' and announced the formation of a new 'Democratic Center Coalition' to pursue a political battle. The contras feared being ignored even as a political force if the new US administration reached an agreement with the Sandinistas. They were further isolated by the new isthmian unity centred on the Arias plan that necessitated their dissolution. The initiative seemed to come from the region when Cerezo argued they should not wait for US decisions, but said: 'we should decide ourselves what to do and present conclusions to President Bush so he has an idea what we are thinking'. To that end they scheduled a summit for mid January 1989. Simultaneously the Sandinistas lost no advantage when they proposed direct talks as soon as Bush was inaugurated. Ortega argued if the pressure was taken off Nicaragua and bilateral relations were normalized democracy would flourish in the country.[5] While this eventuality was the stated aim of both Reagan and Bush, the interpretation of 'democracy' by the former necessitated the removal of the Sandinistas, while Bush was prepared to live with them so long as continued economic, diplomatic and political pressure remained to push them towards further democratic reforms.

The Sandinistas were also under pressure to work out a political settlement because they faced several other constraints. They could not and did not contemplate taking on the United States through military conflict, and they could not totally eliminate the contra harassment without a serious risk of invoking US hostility if they invaded Honduras. With a regional sanctuary military victory over the counterrevolution was always out of the question. With the large amounts the FSLN had to spend on defense and the resultant inability to continue their revolutionary programme in the social and economic field, a strategy which allowed development was essential. Low Intensity Conflict engendered the deterioration of the economic situation which by 1988 had produced inflation rates of up to 32 000 per cent. This, coupled with European insistence that economic aid depended on headway in the regional peace initiative, and Soviet restrictions on future aid, made the diplomatic track absolutely compelling for Nicaragua. Now diplomacy offered the first real opportunity to disband the contras. The Sandinistas had appealed for this in the bilateral talks in 1981 and 1984; Contadora had consistently and ineffectively required it from their initiation in 1983 through to their final plan in 1986. Ironically, the Arias/Esquipulas process, dominated by countries who supported or hosted the contras: Costa Rica, Honduras, El Salvador and Guatemala, did most to bring about their demise, against US resistance, through a series of vague plans which would earlier have been rejected because they provided no specifics to measure compliance. Having dropped the detailed measures of Contadora which provided numerous points for objection, and having dropped the international security issues, the remaining intentions made it difficult for the United States to object without displaying the contradictions in their rhetoric on democratization and human rights.

## TO THE TESORO BEACH ACCORD

The division among the contras became explicit in late December 1988 when the two main factions headed by Alfredo César and Adolfo Calero made separate gestures towards the resumption of dialogue with the Sandinistas. Washington's efforts to unify the groups had totally failed, and the new divisions centred around the issue of negotiations which had stalled since June over disputes on venues. The division allowed the Sandinistas to reject the proposals that still demanded sweeping constitutional changes, because they claimed they did not know which group was backed by Washington. Instead, Ortega proposed a set of simultaneous talks within the region and between Nicaragua and Washington. Diplomatic efforts were further harmed with Arias' request that the scheduled meeting for mid-January, before the Bush inauguration, should be delayed till mid-February. Arias was reportedly concerned that Abrams would undermine his position even in the last few days of his job. While the delay was immediately condemned by Nicaragua, it was more a question of trying to maintain the initiative in Central America than allow it to slip into the hands of the still unclear Bush policy. The contras, however, had been pronounced 'dead' and Azcona met both Reagan and Bush to seek assurances the forces on his territory would be moved out in the near future. Despite the delay the internal opposition continued to press their voice in a protest made up of 14 main political parties. Requesting Washington abandon its embargo against Nicaragua, the parties called for greater unity amongst themselves.[6] Thus the internal coalition of parties began to solidify as economic conditions deteriorated, numbers of people leaving the country increased, and the US began to focus more on the internal opposition as well. 1988 was one of the worst years for the revolution.

The delayed meeting seemed to give the Bush administration the initiative in the region, but despite emphasizing its importance Washington did not control the process and allowed several important meetings to produce their own results that further undermined the contras. In Washington, however, their position did not deteriorate so quickly, with Bush's inauguration signaling the beginning of the bipartisan relationship that would at least prove effective in Central America. Isthmian unity was urged by Pérez de Cuéllar who conditioned the introduction of UN forces on a clear Central American mandate and an irregular force agreement to their presence. Hence, at least the United Nations Observers in Central America (ONUCA) required contra concession on their impending impotence. Right wing members of the Congressional Committees blocked three moderate nominations to replace Abrams, till Bernard Aronson was accepted due to his pro-contra activities during the Reagan administration and his Democratic background. Further confusion emanated from the administration, with different signals coming from Baker and Vice President Danforth Quayle representing the different wings of the Republican party. In any case there was at least nominal support for the peace process that solidified an agenda at the inauguration of Carlos Andréz Pérez in Caracas, Venezuela on 2 February 1989. Arias sought assurances from Quayle that the United States would 'allow us to work together,' and then used the gathering of the Central American leaders to agree on an agenda for the mid-February meeting. Contra leader Alfredo César and internal opposition figure, Violeta Chamorro also attended the inauguration which facilitated the discussion on various policy positions. César worried that Washington might conduct bilateral diplomacy with Managua and accused the latter of delaying the implementation of the peace plan. Such fears were ruled out by Quayle, who insisted on a 'serious' negotiation with the contras. With the awareness the meeting would be the last of the signatories of the 1987 agreement, it was imperative to push the process forward. A series of meetings took place with consultations at all levels, the results of which focused on Nicaragua at the exclusion of the other isthmian countries. While the lopsided process allowed continued violation of the Esquipulas process, the intense focus on Nicaragua was the only viable way to make progress. New attention and pressure on Nicaragua emerged as more important than the actual talks with the contras. A Nicaraguan initiative discussed at the informal meetings outlined a bilateral agreement with Honduras to voluntarily repatriate the contras within the multilateral framework. The further success of the process was to be measured through Nicaraguan compliance, the opening of political space in the country, and the institutionalisation of democracy to satisfy the Esquipulas group. Extracting further concessions from Managua was consistent with the various peace processes since 1984, and it now played to the interests of all countries to declare the process a success. Nicaragua needed a definitive end to the contra war to begin the process of reconstruction and address the economic problems through attracting international finance, absent due to the regional instability and European preconditions for further loans. Costa Rica had a personal stake in the process; Honduras wanted to get rid of the contras due to the domestic instability they caused; the legitimacy gained through negotiations would also favour Guatemala and El Salvador, the latter of which was still reluctant to accommodate the FMLN, and neither could curb gross human rights violations by their armed forces.[7] Thus the meeting was set for mid-February 1989, with further technical aspects discussed by the foreign ministers in New York before the summit.

The process was driven at the speed of Nicaraguan concessions and the pressure of regional actors and social democrats resulting from the Caracas meetings. Isthmian compliance was not enforced, but Managua needed to achieve results. Democrats in Congress had told the Sandinistas US objection in multilateral lending agencies such as the World Bank, the IMF, and the Inter-American Development Bank and the US embargo would only be lifted after Nicaraguan elections. While the Reagan strategy had been to apply pressure through the contras, the much more constraining factor was the economic war against Nicaragua which now necessitated concessions on democratization to lift the financial siege. The new strategy of political pressure and economic inducements at the cost of pursuing the contra war effectively produced agreement though isthmian governments fell short of the plan in different regards. Arias specifically spoke of the 'funeral of the peace process' which Nicaragua could not allow to be buried, unless 'the Sandinistas are ready for immediate moves towards democratization'. Nothing was said about democratization of the other three countries. Ortega agreed to release political prisoners, bring forward the date of elections to February 1990, and to open political space for an adequate campaign period. The sooner the Sandinistas could gain 'legitimacy' the sooner financial aid and loans would open up; the revolution could thus emerge from what Nicaraguan Ambassador to London, Francisco D'Escoto called the emergency situation. The declaration at El Tesoro, El Salvador, basically reflected Arias' original intentions on the compromise between Nicaraguan democratization and contra demobilization; the document specifically centred around Ortega's disposition on the process of 'democratization and national reconciliation'. Extra-regional governments were requested to stop aiding irregular forces, except to contribute to the goals of the document, following Ortega's earlier call on the United States to provide humanitarian assistance to repatriate the contras. With further conciliation intended, the declaration called on the international community to aid the socio-economic recovery of the region. Hence, within the realist bounds of diplomacy Nicaragua had provided a series of concessions to rebuild its economy. Francisco D'Escoto underlined the North–South aspect of the antagonism and US resistance to revolutionary change by invoking the international legal order, 'lest it be believed that certain nations – Nicaragua today, others tomorrow – are condemned to second class world citizenship on account of geographical destiny and a decrepit Cold War analysis'.[8]

While the Bush inauguration had identified the 'new breeze', if not winds of change in the international bipolar relationship, they had not yet produced a coherent stance on Nicaragua and the agreement caught the administration off guard. Despite Washington's assurances to Honduras that they took responsibility for the contras, the agreement was reached because both Nicaragua and Honduras wanted the groups disbanded; it produced an exchange of concessions that remained vague and avoided specificity to produce the first agreement since January 1988. Child notes that Guatemalan Foreign Minister, Alfonso Cabrera, explained, 'If we had tried to work out the details, we wouldn't have succeeded and the Summit would have broken down'.[9]

US officials indicated they were not expecting agreement on the request to disband the contras, because James Baker had just talked to the foreign ministers of Honduras and Costa Rica, and Washington had not yet formulated a response. The trade off between democratization and repatriation raised the old response that the Sandinistas could not be trusted to fulfil their part of the bargain. While the demobilization plan was unclear, though set to be formulated within 90 days, the election was not scheduled till 1990. The confidence of President Azcona that the United States would accept the agreement was undermined by contra leader Adolfo Calero who stated they would not concede to demobilization till democracy was implemented in Nicaragua. Bush also argued a similar line, claiming Nicaragua had a history of 'promises made, promises broken' and in this case, noting 'troubling elements' Bush did not want 'some fluffy promises' while the contras 'twisted out there without fulfillment of the commitment to democracy' by the Sandinistas. Bush wanted clarification on details and 'some certification of the election process'. But it was precisely by avoiding details the isthmian presidents were able to force an agreement. The specifics would result from the process and the momentum generated by the peace plan. While *The New York Times* described Bush's approach as a 'no track policy', that is not pushing for military aid and not endorsing regional diplomacy, the administration had to find a position between liberal and conservative elements in Washington to forge a bipartisan approach; the non military aid resulted from a compromise position. The Centre for International Policy pointed out the Bush administration should have anticipated the agreement given its observers attended the summit. The apparent surprise at the agreement reflected Washington's indecision, which according to Alfredo César was reluctant to meet contra leaders to assure them of US fidelity. There was, however, cautious optimism in the Bush approach. As Dunkerley argues:

> this more qualified approach – the fact that there was some modest space between Bush's minimum and maximum aims – revived the possibilities of diplomatic and political initiative that had previously been nullified by Reagan's consistent subjection of these unavoidable formalities to an ultimatumist veto.

But Bush needed to avoid any division in Washington that was being raised by conservative contra supporters, so without the possibility of a military solution the diplomatic efforts were supported even if their agreed process was objectionable. Washington sent Under Secretary of State, Robert Kimmit, to warn Honduras if they pressed for immediate demobilization, contra humanitarian aid would possibly be damaged and the groups would remain without funds in Honduras. With this worst case scenario posed as a threat from Washington, Honduras backed the humanitarian aid sought by the Bush administration.[10]

The confusion in Washington impeded the momentum of El Tesoro, as did the request for further aid. *The New York Times* suggested if the administration had nothing constructive to provide, 'silence would be the best course'. The Tesoro deal involved compromise Washington was not going to accept. Bush told Cerezo early in March that US 'commitment to the resistance and democracy in Nicaragua is firm'. Still, while Nicaragua had to subject itself to international scrutiny, hosting a number of inspection groups on its elections, without respective isthmian concessions, coupled with the enormous pressure the Sandinistas were under from Latin Americans, Europeans and the Soviet retrenchment, let alone the detrimental economic situation necessitating dramatic change, Washington would not compromise on the status of the contras, when even some of their political directorate indicated the armed option no longer remained. The intransigent US position required the contra presence while the specifics on democratization were being worked out. Their renewed existence in the event of Sandinista non-compliance would not have brought about greater pressure to democratize. The contras were totally ineffective in this regard during the eighties and at this point there was tremendous pressure from elsewhere and Sandinista self interest to conduct verified free elections as soon as possible. A Senate report reviewed the eight years of Reagan policy indicating they had not contributed to strengthen stable democracies, instead it had 'unintended negative consequences' of increasing the power of the various militaries. The report indicated

> a decade of civil conflict and economic decline has devastated Central America. More than 160 000 people have died in wars or unrest. By 1990, ten million people – 40% of the population – will be living in extreme poverty. The problems have deep roots in the endemic poverty and injustices that have long plagued the region.

They argued the fundamental premise was that 'peace, genuine democracy and equitable development' were inextricable. Specifically endorsing Esquipulas, the report argued for an end to hostilities in the region to stem the negative consequences of further violence.[11] The Bush insistence on ignoring the overwhelming decisions of numerous governments and groups resulted from the institutionalisation of the contra position within Washington's politics. Bush's nominees for various foreign policy positions necessitated conservative consent in Congress.

## THE BIPARTISAN ACCORD

By mid-March the Bush administration had requested $50 million contra aid at least until after the February 1990 elections, despite the Central American agreements, which would have accepted aid to demobilize but not maintain the irregular forces. While certain congressional members questioned the move as a 'face saving' device, Baker argued it was totally consistent with the peace plan, which he pointed out did not call for immediate demobilization. It was important for Bush, already being accused of policy drift on Central America, to gain some initiative and leverage, before the May deadline for the Central American ratification of the contra demobilization. In the absence of specificity, the bipartisan accords between the White House and Congress to further aid the contras till after the 1990 elections could be presented as consistent with Esquipulas, because Washington acquiesced to the voluntary repatriation to a democratic Nicaragua. The key point lay in the word democracy; under El Tesoro 'insurgent forces are supposed to voluntarily reintegrate into their homeland under safe, democratic conditions', the Washington Accord noted. The cease-fire in Washington between the White House and Congress marked a sharp departure from the Reagan administration, which had consistently sent mixed signals upsetting the diplomatic procedures due to the lack of clarity on what exactly the US position was. In 1987 Arias exploited the divisions to wrest congressional support for his plan. The Bipartisan Accord on Central America signaled a unified voice on US policy. Still the rhetoric including all of Central America employed in the Accord necessitating 'credible standards of compliance', enforcement, and verification, lent democratic legitiamcy to El Salvador, Honduras and Guatemala, when these 'standards' were clearly understood to exclusively apply to Nicaragua.[12]

The Washington Accord resulted from over 40 hours of negotiation between Baker and a number of influential congressmen. The sustenance of the contras in the immediate future was traded for an approach to the peace process that did not fully comply with the spirit of Esquipulas, but did not invoke outright US opposition. If the contras were deemed by any of four Congressional Committees to have damaged the peace process by resuming offensive action the committees maintained a veto power to halt further aid at a review scheduled for November 1989. The Nicaraguan government denounced the agreement, arguing Washington could not claim to support the peace and maintain the contras. Alejandro Bendaña hoped the aid would not be approved out of a respect for 'international law, and a minimum regard for the agreement signed by five Presidents, including some of the US's closest friends'. Further objections to the agreement were made by Senator Helms who described the process as an 'inducement to promote the dismemberment of the contras.' Later in the month the Bush administration cut funds for contra political activity in Washington, urging them to redirect their efforts to the internal process in Nicaragua. While the move was described as an effort to get the contras to 'think political' it also effectively reduced the conservative opposition to Bush's more moderate and less ideological approach.[13] While the bipartisan Accord continued contra aid, it denounced Soviet support of the Sandinistas and the FMLN, which appeared to result from concessions to the right and the East–West perspective, given the Soviet position on Nicaragua in the recent past.

## THE SOVIET UNION AND NICARAGUA

The diplomacy between February 1989 to the electoral defeat of the Sandinistas in February 1990 took place during the initiation of momentous changes in the international configuration of relations. Long before the Berlin Wall came down in late 1989, superpower diplomacy and resolution of regional conflicts which they had initiated or exacerbated was changing the context of these hostilities. The failure of the superpowers to successfully resolve the conflicts in Central America through diplomacy points to their local and structural causes. However, Gorbachev's 'new thinking' had presaged changes for both Cuba and Nicaragua, both recipients of Soviet aid estimated in the case of Nicaragua to have been about $1 billion a year split between economic and military aid.

While there was a marked difference between Reagan's and Bush's rhetoric on Soviet involvement in Central America, Moscow's role was repeatedly referred to in the Bipartisan Accord with Congress. The Bush position on external aid and its transfer through the region was replete with double standards. Though the Accord explicitly dismissed any equivalence of interests in the region with the Soviets, and the Republican Party Platform in 1988 had affirmed 'strong support of the Monroe Doctrine . . . We therefore seek not only to provide for our own security, but also to create a climate for democracy and self determination throughout the Americas'. Demonstrating a lack of analysis, Nicaragua, according to the document, had become a client state of the Soviet Union; democracy was threatened by the 'Sandinista military machine and armed subversion exported from Nicaragua, Cuba, and the Soviet Union'. That rhetoric continued into 1989, despite an agreement made in late 1988 that Moscow would cut off arms supplies to Nicaragua and pressure them to accept the election results in return for an end to the US war against them. The March 1989 Accord noted that while Moscow and Cuba supported Esquipulas, 'their continued aid and support of violence and subversion in Central America is in direct violation of that regional agreement.' But the evidence on compliance with the various Esquipulas accords weighed against the countries Washington called the Central American democracies. While the Accord provided for $4.5 million a month for the contras till February 1990, which the administration repeatedly argued was in compliance with the El Tesoro agreement, it did not adhere to the proposal to repatriate as opposed to maintain the contras; besides, the agreement was a derivation of the Arias plan prohibiting support for territorial occupation by irregular forces. Thus Honduras, with whom the Unites States remained in close connection, was not in compliance. The processes of democratization and the adherence to the human rights provisions in El Salvador and Guatemala were far from adequate. While the Bush administration criticized Moscow's support for the Sandinistas it did not move to reduce its military support to El Salvador, which had a record of gross human rights abuse.[14] The rejection of equivalence in the region allowed continued US military supply to El Salvador and Honduras, while requiring a halt to Managua's supplies.

With the domestic concentration on Perestroika, Gorbachev's foreign policy was dominated by what he called 'new thinking' from 1987. It had been a consistent Soviet position to support Nicaragua in any political way, reaffirmed by Boris Yeltsin on his visit to Nicaragua in March 1987. From that time, faced with severe shortages in the domestic economy, Gorbachev needed to reduce Soviet commitments abroad, and a dialogue began with Washington on a number of regional issues. New Thinking resulted from 'a shift in one domain of the rivalry' due, according to Fred Halliday, to 'an increase or decrease in the resources that either side can mobilize at any one time'. With Moscow under pressure, the Reagan Doctrine and its wars against revolutionary regimes weakened these states and questioned the basis of the Soviet system. George Shultz and Soviet Foreign Minister Eduard Scheverdnadze held regular meetings on regional issues which produced tentative agreements, including the Soviet withdrawal from Afghanistan. During 1987 the Soviets proposed a simultaneous termination of all military aid to Central America, which most probably would have resulted in the collapse of the Salvadoran government. Without a US response to the Soviet offer, Moscow unilaterally terminated military aid a year later. With few significant regional interests, Moscow was more amenable to a diplomatic solution which would have maintained the Sandinistas in power by removing the external threat. Nevertheless, Halliday points out that the Soviets honoured their military commitments under Gorbachev between 1986 and 1988, allowing most of their allies to conduct offensives against the forces that challenged them. The Sandinista build-up of arms between these years allowed them to conduct their operations against the contras decisively defeating them as a viable military force in early 1988. Since the Sapoa agreement, a fractured and later unilateral cease-fire remained in place. Moscow had learned from Cuba it could not afford to supply another regime isolated by the regional economy, and Nicaragua provided few additional benefits. The Sandinistas had learned, according to Nicola Miller, Soviet reluctance to help them forced an avoidance of dependency. They were provided with enough to defend their revolution, but no more. Voytek Zubek's study of New Thinking in Central America argues that most analysts agree Soviet actions were prudent and premeditated, they did not want an open confrontation with Washington, where they ran the risks of another humiliation similar to the 1962 Cuban missile crisis. Gorbachev explained in his book *Perestroika* they found 'it preposterous [to hear] allegations that Nicaragua "threatens"

US security' and that Soviet bases were going to be built there, 'which the Americans supposedly know about but which I, for one, have never heard of'. Generally New Thinking redefined Soviet interests around attempts to strengthen its national situation, retract from the international arena, and emphasize the more cost effective peaceful resolution to regional conflicts.[15]

Over a year after the 1987 Arias plan had been signed, purposefully omitting the security issues that constantly stalled Contadora, Washington was no longer in control of the peace process. Advisors to President-Elect Bush sought to reintroduce the Soviet Union as a target of its rhetoric in opposition to the Sandinistas. Advisers to the Bush transition team wanted more Soviet concessions in Central America: 'We will let the Soviets know that if they want to improve relations with us, their behaviour in Central America will be one of the factors affecting the overall content of the relationship'. The Soviet concession to halt military supplies to Nicaragua came shortly after. Without additional Sandinista military aid Washington could make a virtue of their inability to provide contra aid due to legislative opposition. The March Accord with Congress providing 'humanitarian' aid put the United States 'back in the ballgame' according to Baker. Bush further challenged the Soviet Union to demonstrate that New Thinking was more than just a 'tactical response to temporary set-backs' and opened the way for a principled approach to foreign policy. Stressing the Soviet Union had no legitimate interests in the region and had promised to support Esquipulas, Bush asserted 'Soviet military aid to the Government of Nicaragua continues at levels wholly uncalled for by any legitimate defensive needs'. The United States hence had serious reason to question their attitudes and intentions. Gorbachev's visit to Cuba was used as a test to see if they would comply with their stated position on Esquipulas.[16]

Given military aid had already stopped, Washington's stray rhetoric in the accord may have been to attain right wing support for the agreement, or may have been in retaliation for Moscow's strong criticism of continued US aid to the contras. Cuba warned Moscow not to enter into a separate deal with Washington that would undercut the peace process, legitimating Washington's support of the contras. Castro, involved in the February talks in Caracas, had an interest in supporting the Latin American position, given its desire to increase contacts between Cuba and the other regional countries as prospects of reduced Soviet aid loomed. Baker welcomed Gorbachev's renunciation of an 'export of revolution' but revived the Reaganesque charges that Moscow continued the practice in Central America. Baker urged Gorbachev to pressure 'their client states' to cease aid to irregular forces as a test of their 'behaviour'. Baker incorrectly asserted the United States was in compliance with Esquipulas because it did not provide military aid to the contras, while the Soviets and Cubans continued to violate the provisions. Gorbachev could demonstrate his fidelity to 'new thinking' in Central America by supporting Washington's Bipartisan Accord, which fell short of Esquipulas. Baker argued peace could prevail in the region if the Soviets took these steps. Castro objected to the assumption that it was a colony of the Soviet Union and that Gorbachev could control his actions. Gorbachev avoided the issue, stating Soviet moves were contingent on a similar end to US military aid. But the White House had rejected the idea of equivalence of the superpower role in this area. An opinion piece in *The New York Times* pointed out the incongruity in Washington's position. By calling for Moscow's aid to help democratize Nicaragua, Neil MacFarlane argued, 'we want them to do for us what we have failed to do in eight years of sponsoring the contras'. Linking improved relations between Moscow and Washington on Nicaragua made little sense since Moscow never had control over the Sandinistas and Washington showed little 'willingness to meet the standards it has set for the Kremlin'.[17]

The public rhetoric demonstrating solidarity belied the private diplomacy of the period. Soviet Ambassador to Washington Dobrynin put Central America on offer in the dialogue for regional issues between Baker and Scheverdnadze, which began an intensive negotiation on the region. The consequential shift in the relationship resulted from an end to the Cold War on regional issues, structural changes in the Soviet Union, and Gorbachev's 'new thinking'. Gorbachev did not support Washington's position but strongly endorsed the El Tesoro agreement, when Washington criticized it for not demonstrating new thinking. Without bases or offensive weapons in the region, the Soviets had no interest in drawing Nicaragua closer to the Soviet Union at a time of reduced economic capacity. Hence the moral high ground of endorsing elections and encouraging pluralism could only benefit Moscow. When Gorbachev wrote to Bush indicating that Soviet arms had stopped, in May 1989, Bush continued to hold Moscow responsible, but Baker started to accept their position and shifted the blame to Cuba; suggesting a change in administration thinking in which Cuba was suddenly not under Moscow's control. At the time, Cuba promised no Soviet weapons would be shipped to irregular forces in Central America and indicated a willingness to discuss the issues with Washington in either a bilateral or multilateral forum. Washington ignored the offer. Some form of outside support was politically necessary for the Bush administration to demonstrate the capability of Nicaragua's so called 'threat' to the United States. Because Washington wanted to maintain the economic blockade on Nicaragua to influence the 1990 elections through induced shortages, the Bush administration continued the 'national emergency' with respect to Nicaragua affirming that it remained 'an unusual and extraordinary threat to national security and foreign policy of the United States'.[18]

## THE TELA AGREEMENT

The process in Nicaragua and the diplomacy in Central America was slipping out of Washington's control, but the compromises already conceded by Managua, to avoid direct war, made the regime much weaker, and Washington's moves had to be minimal to still have effect on the process. The original Arias compromise still held in this latest round of diplomacy, albeit in a more refined sense: agreement on an electoral process for the agreement on contra disbandment. In early August the Sandinistas came to an agreement with twenty opposition parties after twenty two hours of negotiations to hold elections on 25 February 1990 and on the conditions under which they would be conducted. A part of the deal was that the internal parties contesting the election called for contra demobilization. Ortega urged the United States to accept the agreement made by the legitimate parties of Nicaragua. The contras as an 'irregular' force were isolated by the decision. Washington's position became even more isolated with the move because the issue of Nicaragua's elections was effectively removed from the negotiating agenda set for the Tela summit. The contras and the FMLN were the main focus of the meeting. In an attempt to pre-empt the move, US Assistant Secretary of State for Inter-American Affairs, Bernard Aronson, met the foreign ministers of the El Salvador, Guatemala, and Honduras to pressure them to slow down the demobilization process; Bush additionally telephoned both Arias and Azcona to pressure these governments, both being financially dependent on the United States. The Bush administration was caught in a dilemma according to LeoGrande: it opposed demobilization yet agreed to it indirectly by supporting the Central American Peace Plan in his own Bipartisan Accord with Congress. The latter support was conditional on the US interpretation of the Central American agreement that was now at variance with the five isthmian governments. The State Department resolved the dilemma by arguing the regional agreement required demobilization and reintegration with 'full guarantees of their security and civil, political and property rights'. Nicaragua did not guarantee these rights as yet, and the contras would remain mobilized till after the February 1990 elections.[19]

The US position put the diplomatic onus back on Managua. No matter what the Sandinistas did the United States raised their demands one step further. The compromise envisaged in Arias was again one-sided. The agreement signed in Tela, Honduras, by the five Central American presidents clearly tightened the provisions requiring the demobilization, repatriation or relocation of the contras as a priority. Chapter one of the agreement dealt with the procedures and the verification of the process, to which end it called for the creation of the Commission of Support and Verification (CIAV) by the General Secretaries of the UN and the OAS. Explicitly, the five affirmed:

> their commitment to halt the use of their own territory by people, organizations or groups to destabilize other states and the cease all types of aid to armed groups, with the exception of humanitarian aid, which might serve the purposes which the Presidents have defined for this plan.

Apart from the endorsement of Nicaragua's position, backed by the internal opposition, the Cristiani government in El Salvador benefitted from the plan which similarly made explicit reference to the FMLN and requested their cooperation in initiating an internal dialogue and a cessation of armed action. Ortega did not like this argument on equivalence between the contras and the FMLN; the former were created and supported by outside governments without occupying any territory of Nicaragua, the latter were a true guerrilla force, with outside support, but in constant occupation of parts of El Salvador. The contras, he reasoned, were an international problem, incumbent on the United States and Honduras to demobilize, whereas the FMLN were in El Salvador and was the internal responsibility of that country. Nevertheless, Ortega had to officially concede this argument to obtain a specific deadline for contra demobilization which was set at either 5 or 8 December 1989.[20]

The Bush administration continued to object to the deadline for demobilization despite warning from senior Democrats in Congress that new inter-branch acrimony might result if the administration did not adhere to the Tela agreement. The bipartisan agreement could have collapsed, given four congressional committees had a veto over continued expenditure beyond 30 November, according to the March Accord. The administration indicated it had no plans to demobilize the contras; this was echoed by their spokesman, Bosco Matamoros, who insisted democratization and demobilization were part of the same process, they would not lay down their arms under the current agreement. Democracy had to be guaranteed before demobilization; but how could democratic procedures evolve under continued contra attacks, given they had not continued their part of the cease-fire beyond the 60-day agreement at Sapoá 1988. *The New York Times* editorialized that Bush's stance might gain him the gratitude of conservatives but would do little to promote democracy in Nicaragua. But the process of contra demobilization appeared to be almost beyond Bush administration control. Reports indicated that James Baker expressing his displeasure on the emerging agreement to President Arias, told him that the accord would provoke outcry amongst right wing Republicans. The contra issue had become an internal US problem, an internal Honduran problem, a regional diplomatic problem, and a tragedy for Nicaragua. Throughout, their low intensity war continued. While the heads of state argued about whether the demobilization was to be voluntary or obligatory, it seems the latter had greater credibility due to the separate bilateral agreement between Nicaragua and Honduras for the former to drop its suit against the latter pending the demobilization process. Washington publicly expressed support for the Tela agreement, despite the reports to the contrary, by emphasizing the voluntary nature of the demobilization and inaccurately stating there was no fixed deadline for demobilization. While there was some confusion as to the exact date, it was clear demobilization should be conducted by 8 December 1989 at the latest. Administration arguments on the need to maintain irregular pressure to ensure a democratic outcome in February 1990 were dismissed by the Tela agreement. William LeoGrande pointed out at the time that the contras were counter-productive; the best guarantee to free elections was the desperate state of the economy. The Sandinistas had to provide the internal opposition with enough confidence to re-invest in the country, and had to seek international legitimacy to activate international aid. Free and fair elections were the only way to achieve these goals.[21]

As Arias said, the Presidents had 'taken the destiny of Central America in our hands', and *The New York Times* referred to a 'ringing declaration of independence from the United States'; the process remained part of Washington's political turmoil over the issue remaining from the Reagan administration. Reports emerged on the dispute between Bernard Aronson and his counterpart at the NSC, Everett Ellis Briggs. Briggs, formerly the ambassador to Honduras, 1986–1989, and earlier to Panama, 1982–1986, was an active contra supporter. He thought the Tela agreement was bad and could have been prevented through stronger diplomatic pressure. He was reported to have worked closely with Quayle to channel conservative policy on the isthmian issues and act as a counterforce to the so-called pragmatism of the Baker–Aronson line that sought accord with Congressional Democrats. The two officials were said to maintain different contacts with the contras, with Briggs working more closely with the political directorate, while Aronson worked with the younger emerging leaders.[22]

The long sought unity of the contras by Washington totally fractured in autumn 1989 when some groups came into peaceful contact with the Sandinista army; others pledged to fight on despite the accords, and in a series of events that pointed to their further demise, contras sold their weapons to the FMLN, threatened to become 'bandits', retaining their arms to earn an illegal living. As these changes further threatened the other governments of Central America the United Nations stepped up the creation of its observer group (ONUCA) to monitor the various provisions of the diplomatic agreements. Almost simultaneously the Soviet Union proposed that both superpowers become the guarantors of a mechanism to cut arms to the region; this was promptly rejected by Washington, trying to avoid any permanent legitimate role of the Soviet Union in the region.[23]

On the last day for Nicaraguans to register for the 1990 elections, the contras were in disarray with their support reduced in several quarters; on 21 October a group of their forces ambushed and killed eighteen Sandinista soldiers. Between Tela and this incident, contras had been moving back into Nicaragua to avoid the demobilization plans soon to be verified by ONUCA, and the Azcona government had moved to seal off contra areas to facilitate the process. Preempting this, 2 300 contras had stepped up their attacks mostly, on Nicaraguan civilians. Ortega responded by cancelling the unilateral cease-fire which had held since spring 1988 and promised to move against the contras. The contras had killed up to 143 people in 1989 and the figures had risen sharply at the time of the most intense voter registration. Ortega's announcement to suspend the cease-fire was met by accusations in Washington that he was desperate to scrap the forthcoming elections. Ortega, however, argued the move against the contras was to protect the electoral process which was endangered by contra attacks. The Sandinista announcement came when all the democratically elected heads of state in the Americas were meeting in Costa Rica to celebrate 100 years of Costa Rican democracy. The focus of the news from Nicaragua was the Sandinista suspension of the cease-fire as opposed to the continued contra attacks against civilians. The suspension of the cease-fire was reversible if Congress terminated contra aid. The apparent concession seemed to be an attempt to mitigate the almost unanimous criticism from the gathered heads of state at San Jose. Thus the announcement backfired diplomatically, as Javier Pérez de Cuéllar joined in the criticism of Nicaragua. The point, according to Nicaragua, was to draw attention to the constant violations perpetuated by the US-funded and Honduran-hosted groups.[24]

The announcement was presented in the United States as part of a series of gaffes by Ortega just when Nicaragua had gained the diplomatic initiative, similar to his visit to Moscow following congressional rejection of contra aid, and the break up of the Nandaime rally in 1988. On this occasion the former US Attorney General, Elliot Richardson, monitoring the Nicaraguan elections, had so far approved of the proceedings and identified the contras as a threat to the democratic process, but the symbolic effect in Washington of Ortega's announcement had more influence on Congress who passed more resolutions against Nicaragua and decided to continue funding the contras till after the elections. In the resulting political atmosphere and the near universal condemnation it was unexpedient for the Democrats to confront Bush on the contras. Nicaragua tried to explain that a sovereign government had the responsibility to protect the lives of its citizens.[25] There had not been a formal cease-fire since the collapse of the Sapoá agreement in mid 1988, and the cease-fire to date was a unilateral Sandinista concession to maintain the momentum of the diplomatic track and, indirectly, the bilateral relationship with Washington.

As the United Nations prepared to deploy its first peace-keeping mission in the Western Hemisphere, the Sandinistas did not renew their unilateral cease-fire and conducted an offensive against contra positions in mid November. Throughout the process they maintained a bilateral dialogue with the contras at the United Nations in New York. The eleven days of negotiations did not produce one contra concession, while the Sandinistas agreed to accept the evacuation only of those who had infiltrated since the Tela agreement, under CIAV observation. The Sandinistas insisted on compliance with the Tela deadline, but the new contra leadership under Israel Galeano, pointed out in a letter to Quayle they would not disarm before the elections, implying they would not comply with Tela.[26]

While the Sandinistas moved against the contras in Nicaragua, the FMLN in El Salvador, denigrating the possibility of further negotiations with the Cristiani government, launched what was called the 'final offensive' in November 1989, initiating one of the heaviest periods of fighting in the civil war. The FMLN demonstrated their organized capacity to sustain ten days of attacks on San Salvador and regional capitals before withdrawing in an organized fashion. In the midst of the offensive the Salvadoran army's murder of six Jesuits clearly demonstrated the government had not reached minimal requirements in terms of national reconciliation. Nevertheless, the focus was primarily on Nicaragua, where it was implicitly understood, by Arias included, the plan had to work in Nicaragua before it could be adequately applied elsewhere. The diplomatic repercussions of Sandinista action were detrimental to the peace process: Washington had already described the suspension of the cease-fire a 'serious blow', but the downing of a plane in an FMLN area with 24 SAM–7 Soviet missiles, was presumed to be a Sandinista attempt to resupply the Salvadoran guerillas. El Salvador broke diplomatic relations with Nicaragua, and Cristiani refused to attend the next scheduled meeting in Managua. Costa Rica blamed both the FMLN and the Sandinistas for breaching the terms of the peace accords, which gave the Cristiani government and the United States added leverage to press their cases.[27]

With the breach of the Berlin Wall, the symbolic end of the Cold War, and a superpower-negotiated end to other regional conflicts during 1988, Central America remained the anomaly because Moscow did not exert control over either the Sandinistas or the FMLN. Yet the alleged continuation of a Soviet supply of arms to Nicaragua and the FMLN, described by Baker as a 'Cold War relic', was presented as the 'biggest obstacle to an across the board improvement' in the bilateral Washington–Moscow relationship. With reference to the SAM-7 missiles, Baker accused Moscow of throwing 'fuel on the fire', and urged them to 'foster new thinking in Cuba and Central America'. At a joint summit news conference Gorbachev denied the Soviet Union continued to arm the Sandinistas.[28]

With the intense hostilities, the December emergency summit was moved to San José to impel attendance by Cristiani. The deadline for contra demobilization had passed and Ortega needed further progress to move the process towards the original Arias compromise of 1987: demobilization for democratization. Further concessions were made to allow contra electoral registration before 5 February 1990, beyond the internal deadline that had already passed. The Presidents agreed in point five to transfer the remaining aid to the contras to the CIAV, to increase the mandate of ONUCA, and called on the UN Secretary General to involve countries with links to the regional irregular forces to be involved 'more directly in the peace efforts in the framework of the Esquipulas II Agreements and subsequent declarations'. This was an appeal to pressure the United States to adhere to the Central American agreements as interpreted by the isthmian governments, not by Washington. Ortega needed this progress, Goodfellow and Morrell argue, and had to concede to several Salvadoran demands; they 'hurt Ortega, and damaged the peace process, to make a completely unbalanced pronouncement on El Salvador, but this was the price of progress on Nicaragua'. Cristiani extracted a condemnation of acts of warfare by irregular forces, thus diplomatically placing the FMLN on an equal footing with the contras, though the November offensive patently demonstrated their differences. Ortega also had to join in a call to request the CIAV to immediately begin disbanding the FMLN.[29]

The concession epitomized the imbalance in the peace process, the FMLN were an indigenous insurrection that demonstrated a clear ability to occupy large segments of El Salvador aided by popular support in the regions. Though supported by outside supplies of arms, they also captured and bought them from the US-funded Salvadoran military. They set their own political agenda and did not concede to direct extra-regional pressure. The contras could not claim any of these attributes, while they still exerted considerable influence in the electoral process in Nicaragua.

# 8 The 1990 Elections and Democracy

Strictly interpreted, the Esquipulas process must be considered a failure. Yet ironically it brought a kind of peace, perhaps more accurately described by James Dunkerley as 'pacification,' because it averted a full scale war, confined it to low intensity conflict, and wound down, but could not halt, the killing. It must be regarded as a failed process for two more reasons: though the plan and its derivatives nominally referred to all five Central American countries, Nicaragua was really the only country under scrutiny. For this reason democratization and elections in the other four did not have to meet the same rigorous standards. Despite the numerous electoral monitors the key to 'authentication' was Washington's approval, which undermined the self determination of the regional process. The Sandinistas subjected themselves to the extraordinary number of observers so Washington would have less credibility if they claimed the vote was unfair; 1984 could not occur again. The Sandinistas were scrupulous in ensuring they conceded on these provisions to meet their commitments under Esquipulas. The second major defect of the outcome was the failure to deliver the original trade off, democratization for demobilization. Quite simply the contras did not demobilize before the required dates and remained armed and active till after the election. The Sandinistas were never free of the terror committed against Nicaraguan citizens and were consequently inhibited from canvassing some rural areas. The continued conflict during the entire process deprived them of the ability to claim they were the party that had ended the war. Only Chamorro could hold out this promise.

Democratization had been a part of the various negotiations since 1982. It was included by Contadora between 1983 and 1986, but gained further importance in the proposed Arias trade off. Because it was such an elusive issue, that could not be readily quantified such as arms limits, or observed such as a demobilization process, it offered Washington the perfect issue over which to stall, delay and denigrate various talks. Democracy as originally stated in 1982 became the *sine qua non* for normalization of relations between Washington and Managua. While elections were a key aspect of Washington's understanding of democratization, in Nicaragua it was not the only test the Sandinistas would have to pass as the United States selectively applied various yardsticks to judge compliance on the issue. The Tesoro Beach accords advanced the date of Nicaragua's elections to 25 February 1990, and agreed on the demobilization of the contras. Tela put a specific dated on the latter. Washington, however, used a loose interpretation of the wording to assert their support for the regional process and undermine it by passing further contra aid. Thus while the peace process was not in Washington's total control, they were able to limit the expectations of it because they were not under any binding obligations and remained the contra paymasters. Central Americans were not allowed to decide on their future, despite a specific appeal through diplomatic language for States with 'interests' in the region to get 'more directly involved in the peace efforts' framed by Esquipulas. At that point they vehemently condemned 'warfare and terrorism' by irregular forces, and found it 'imperative to drive home in the minds of the people the necessity of ruling out force and terrorism as a means to the attainment of political ends.' Even the internal Nicaraguan opposition on which the Bush administration placed more emphasis called for demobilization in their agreement with the Sandinistas just before Tela in early August 1989.[1]

The Sandinistas maintained democracy did exist in Nicaragua and initially refused to negotiate on it with either the contras or the United States because it was an internal matter for a sovereign country. When the issue became the focus of US diplomacy and the Arias plan, the strategy of concessions necessitated the inclusion of the question. Widely observed and respected elections could not be denigrated by Washington. Though the date of the 1990 elections was changed under agreement within Esquipulas, it is important to note they were not the first elections and the 1987 Nicaraguan constitution mandated the 1990 elections a month before Arias revealed his plan in February 1987. The Sandinistas had no reason to abandon their schedule for elections except if the United States invaded the country. Otherwise, the Iran–Contra affairs, the strategic defeat of the contras in 1987, and Esquipulas had reduced the threat posed to the regime, if not Nicaraguan citizens. In 1984 Washington had pressurized Arturo Cruz to pull out of the race questioning the legitimacy of the process; the move was essentially beyond Sandinista control. This time Nicaragua requested monitors to observe the elections almost a year before they were held. Setting an international precedent, the United Nations sent 240 people under Elliot Richardson, the OAS sent 450, the Council of Freely Elected Heads of Government, under former US President Jimmy Carter added to the observation as did a number of independent observers totalling 2 578 people who descended on Nicaragua at various stages. The United Nations, aware it was extraordinary to appoint 'an American to oversee elections in a country with which the United States is virtually at war', created

ONUVEN after their study concluded the Sandinista electoral process was acceptable.[2]

John Peeler has pointed out traditionally elections in Central America have been viewed as a means to legitimate those in power, the opposition therefore, are principally concerned with discrediting the process. He argues that the 1984 Nicaraguan elections were the only ones to extend the range and breadth of participation in the system during the 1980s. Despite this independent judgement the Sandinistas could only gain further legitimacy through the verification of their process by international observers. Notwithstanding the concession of a sovereign country to subject itself to such extensive examination, the US rejection of the Tela agreement to disband the contras was designed to cast doubt on the authenticity of the process. Throughout the campaign period the contras persisted in their terrorism, most notably killing 18 Sandinista soldiers in October 1989, but also two nuns on New Years day 1990, and many others. The Canadian Observer mission concluded the United States 'is doing everything it can to disrupt the elections set for next year . . . American intervention is the main obstacle to the attainment of free and fair elections in Nicaragua'. Noam Chomsky points out the violence sent a clear message the war would continue if the Sandinistas were re-elected.[3]

Democracy as used in the diplomatic exchanges during the 1980s should not focus on the different interpretations of the word and process, but must be viewed as part of the US application of Low Intensity Conflict. Sandinista compliance was irrelevant as were the transgressions of the other governments and their procedures. Sandinista Foreign Ministry official, Alejandro Bendaña, later explained that there was never any thought of subjecting El Salvador, Honduras, Guatemala, or even Mexico to the same rigorous observation applied to Nicaragua. Gills and Rocamora argue democracy was used as a form of intervention to stave off either progressive reform or revolutionary change. Low Intensity Democracy sidelined popular aspirations while focusing on elections and the civilian governments they brought to power. Ironically, their study observes, civilian governments can pursue harmful economic and repressive social policies with 'more impunity and with less popular resistance' than authoritarian regimes. Governments that came to power through elections were more likely to get US aid, in spite of their records on human rights abuse. Democratization in this sense meant rehabilitation with Congress. In most Latin American countries Eduardo Galeano points out people 'vote but don't elect, and the ceremonies of official political life are projected . . . over the background of an atrociously anti-democratic social reality'. The electoral processes in El Salvador, Honduras and Guatemala, were conducted under pressure from

Washington as part of Reagan's crusade for democracy announced in 1982 to the British parliament; these countries were an integral part of the US strategy against Nicaragua. It could be argued these elections impeded the process of democratization, especially in El Salvador where they were used to convey legitimacy on the government, by avoiding negotiations with the FMLN and demanding their inclusion in the constitutional system.[4] While the FMLN was recognized by France and Mexico as a legitimate political force, their absence from the legal system brought their legitimacy into question. Finally, their position was denigrated in the Tela Accords where even Nicaragua coupled them with the contras.

If there was previous doubt, diplomatic or rhetorical obfuscation, the UN Truth Commission on El Salvador held government forces responsible for some 75% of the atrocities and extrajudicial killing during the 1980s. The killings were conducted by the military under the widely used ideological guise of protecting national security, or what Laurence Whitehead has 'loosely called "fascism" '. The abuse of human rights by the Sandinistas was minimal and mostly of a secondary nature in comparison with El Salvador during the 1980s. The regional negotiations allowed the electoral processes of the brutal regimes in El Salvador and Guatemala to pass as a form of democratization, though participation in these countries was severely limited. With a limited democratic content to the isthmian elections the term 'facade democracies' or Whitehead invokes the Portuguese phrase: *para os ingleses ver* – holding elections for the English to look at – is most apt. His argument, that once the process and institutions of, or lip service to democratization begins 'habituation . . . turns facades into real structures' is doubtful in the isthmian context.[5] Even with the relatively diminished power of the militaries, they still present the threat of their alternative, and the detrimental economic situation of the people in the region mitigates against their ability to exercise their democratic rights.

While Washington pressed the issue of democracy preempting any possible agreement except capitulation of the Sandinista government, Managua perpetuated the negotiating process to avert stronger action and deter congressional support for lethal aid. Without conclusion or the prospects of agreement the human and economic destruction meted out by the contras through Low Intensity Warfare continually undermined Sandinista popularity and programmes. The long process of negotiations, Mike Gonzales contends, committed the Sandinistas to a strategy of national survival that abandoned their socialist strategies. The pursuit of peace thus involved the 'progressive disengagement of the . . . revolution'. Gonzales questions the price and the nature of the peace which sought agreement with the some times repressive representatives of other nations, as opposed to the workers and peasants. While the argument may be appealing to revolutionaries and international socialists, had the Sandinistas ignored negotiations or failed to preserve the peace process, forging closer links to the FMLN or URNG, the White House would have been able to more convincingly extract the necessary support for a more aggressive approach to Managua. While during the early years of the revolution the Sandinistas made real advances in their social programmes, their ability to sustain this development was stemmed by the war and economic strangulation. Despite these gains for most people in Nicaragua, it is wrong to presume the Sandinistas pursued an orthodox Marxist class-based approach to their social and economic strategies. Dore and Weeks dispute the revolutionary rhetoric of the Sandinistas suggesting:

> The hypothesis that the Sandinistas planned from the outset to disposses the capitalists and landlords was one of the many myths of the Nicaraguan revolution whose tenacity derived from its emotional appeal to both the right and the left, and from taking at face value the rhetoric employed by the Sandinista leadership.

Yet their rhetoric contributed to Washington's belief that the Sandinista programme was Marxist–Leninist, which in the policy-making culture of Washington, derived from decades of their own self-deceiving rhetoric, represented a system that was inherently expansionist, externally aggressive, and internally repressive. Dore and Weeks argue that the Sandinista programme was first and foremost that of radical nationalism. Just over a year after the covert war began, Tomás Borge, pointed out in May 1982 the distinctive and mixed character of the revolution:

> It is still necessary to unite the widest possible strata of Nicaraguan society to confront . . . U.S. imperialism. This means that [in] this new phase, after victory . . . the main emphasis [will be] on the defense of the nation, on the struggle to have our national sovereignty respected, on the right of self-determination, and on the need to unite all Nicaraguan patriots to confront a huge and cruel enemy.[6]

Regardless of the ideological bent of the Sandinistas, Washington could not tolerate significantly independent action by a Third World regime. The use of 'democracy', understood in the context of Low Intensity Conflict was used to bring the Sandinistas back into line; thus Susanne Jonas, points out the contradiction in the use of democracy to undermine Third World sovereignty. Ultimately and ironically she points out the four Central American countries, united in the 1982 San José group around the issue of democracy, had to abandon the Reagan Doctrine and its support of the contras because this policy also undermined their sovereignty and independence. Arias asserted several times that his plan was designed to allow Central Americans to decide their own, at least diplomatic, fate. By 1987 Managua's short term economic strategies and their austerity plan were similar to their neighbours, notwithstanding their longer term objectives embodied in their revolutionary rhetoric. Because Washington could not overthrow the Sandinistas their aim was to bring about as much damage in all areas to negate the potentially positive example Nicaragua represented for other Third World regimes; simply put by Enders early in the tactics, to 'harass the government, waste it'. The Sandinista strategy of concessions did not allow for this slow destructive process. According to Chomsky's analysis of regional reaction to the elections, the Sandinistas fell for a 'scam perpetrated by Costa Rican President Oscar Arias' and the other isthmian governments. His trade off was immediately broken by Washington with diplomatic impunity. The contras continued their 'wasting' project, and the Sandinistas were compelled to liberalize their society in the face of externally supported terror. Alejandro Bendaña later wondered if they fell into a trap; were free elections political suicide for a government under siege whose social base was eroded through low intensity conflict and the economic strangulation that brought about the critical poverty in Nicaragua in the late 1980s?[7]

## THE INTERNAL OPPOSITION

The revolution undoubtedly increased political participation, considered by Carlos Vilas as one of its greatest achievements. Ironically, in some ways this contributed to its defeat. Two years after the Arias agreement and the political space created with the strategic defeat of the contras, in addition to congressional reluctance to provide lethal aid in the wake of Iran–Contra, the focus of US policy moved onto the internal opposition. Bernard Aronson explained while 'Reagan's policy was to take the political protagonists out of Nicaragua. Ours is to put them back in.' The contra directorate had made a good living out of the covert programme, but the Bush administration began to cut back on their funds for operations in Washington and the majority of Bush's administration favoured the political approach. This may have been making a virtue out of necessity; the contras were increasingly defunct and isolated, their presence was objected to by Honduras, and more broadly by the Central American governments, and the internal Nicaraguan opposition also called for their demobilization. As the Sandinistas compromised within the peace process and made concessions on democratization, congressional support was eroded, but the contras were not demobilized, perhaps out of fear of a conservative reaction in Washington, but also because they played an important role in shaping the perception of voters in Nicaragua; the covert war could be resumed if necessary.[8]

Esquipulas brought the internal political parties back to prominence with the democratization articles. The main dynamics of the political situation in Nicaragua had been the war between Managua and the contras and their antagonism with Washington. In 1989 and 1990 the political parties gained a prominence they had not had since the 1984 elections and the 1986 writing of the constitution. By 1989, when the campaign period was nearing, the parties that existed in 1984 had broken up into twenty three opposition groups. Washington created a coalition of fourteen parties; that dropped to thirteen, settled on the name United Nicaraguan Opposition (UNO), and barely stayed united during the campaign. It soon fragmented after the election, but because of the diversity of ideology and interests within the coalition, the only credible unifying factor was their opposition to the Sandinistas. LeoGrande argues the coalition would not have stayed united unless Washington had exerted its influence on the various personalities that wanted to lead it. The US embassy was said to have promoted the candidacy of Violetta Chamorro, over the competition between Enrique Bolaños and Virigilio Godoy. Independent parties outside the coalition could not hope to compete with the Sandinista structure or the US-financed UNO coalition.[9]

To some extent the contest between UNO and the Sandinistas replayed the division in the anti-Samoza revolution. Several prominent people in UNO, such as Chamorro, César and Robelo had served in the first junta with the Sandinistas between 1979 and 1982; some had defected to the contras, others remained in Nicaragua pursuing their political struggle within the constitutional system. UNO, and especially Chamorro, tried to focus their campaign along the lines of Washington's rhetoric: that the 1979 revolution was a necessary historical fact, but it had been betrayed by the Sandinistas; UNO would redress these earlier 'deceptions'. The campaign distinction was not so credible because several prominent contras also found their way into UNO, prompting Carlos Fernando Chamorro, editor of *Barricada*, to accuse his mother of going into coalition with the people who had murdered his father. With this alliance and support from the United States it was little wonder UNO failed to condemn contra violence. But the other parties within the coalition, some even to the left of the Sandinistas, attracted votes from more militant workers who felt betrayed by the Sandinista austerity programmes since 1987. The inclusion of the Moscow-oriented Communist Party and the Maoist party in the coalition reduced Sandinista ability to criticize it as a collection of right wing parties, but also reduced UNO's ability to openly advocate neo-liberal economic policies.[10]

To preempt covert destabilization of the elections and accusations that the process was not conducted freely the Sandinistas changed a 1988 law prohibiting the use of foreign funds for political purposes. The concession 'all but guaranteed the participation of the opposition in the elections', and was made on the condition that the Supreme Electoral Council received fifty percent of all donations to off set their costs. The decision to allow external funding for specific political parties, a practice which is illegal in most countries, was made through an informal agreement between Washington and Managua, mediated by Jimmy Carter. Assurances were given that covert aid would not be provided. Congress authorized the release of $9 million in October 1989, which was distributed through the semi-private National Endowment for Democracy. The programme, according to their officials, dwarfed their previous operations in both Chile and the Philippines. UNO was intimately connected with Washington through the provision of these funds. The United States not only broke the Tela agreement through the maintenance of the contras, it also broke the agreement on the provision of covert aid that the Sandinistas had made with both Washington and the opposition parties in the August 1989 accords. Though the Bush administration specifically refused to rule out covert operations, the Sandinistas felt it necessary to make the concession on overt aid. The CIA carried out operations throughout the campaign period, as did the contras. An estimated $11 million was channeled to the opposition parties covertly and in addition to the funding they received through NED. Further evidence of internal CIA activity came in late 1988 when Jim Wright indicated he had

> clear testimony from CIA people that they have deliberately done things to provoke an overreaction on the part of the government of Nicaragua . . . Agents of our government have assisted in organizing the kinds of anti-government demonstration that have been calculated to stimulate and provoke arrests.[11]

Little was left to chance or a fair process if that meant the Sandinistas could retain power.

The political and psychological effect of the US decision to invite Chamorro to the White House on 8 November was considerable. During the visit Bush promised to lift the economic embargo if Chamorro was elected, which offered the promise of relief from the poverty and desperate economic state the country was in. UNO spent the campaign period accusing the Sandinistas of economic mismanagement and incurring the wrath of Washington. Chamorro and UNO offered a way out of this awful condition by emphasizing their relations with Washington and the expected largess that would follow if they won. Kornbluh points out, Managua had in 1988 explained in their memorial to the International Court of Justice that 'no . . . reparation can revive the human lives lost, or repair the physical and psychological injuries suffered by a population that has endured an unrelenting campaign of armed attacks and economic strangulation.' The impact and costs were simply 'incalculable'.[12] The visit came with perfect timing for full impact as the contra attacks provoked Ortega to end the unilateral cease-fire, and Bush renewed the US national emergency.

Despite the many reports during the campaign that the process was both free and fair UNO began to allege unfair tactics on the part of the Sandinistas to lay the ground work for accusations of fraud. The process was overwhelmingly judged to be both free and fair. The Freely Elected Heads of Government concluded 'the Nicaraguan people were free to vote their preferences in a fair election, and the official results reflected the collective will of the nation'. The Elliot Richardson headed ONUVEN assessed the process to be 'conducted in a highly commendable manner, and no problems have been detected which might cast doubts on their fairness'. An important distinction must be made between an electoral process that was judged to be free and fair, and an election that was not fair. While the political realities of the world cannot be excluded, the election cannot be assessed in isolation from almost a decade of covert war, half a decade of economic embargo, and intense efforts at diplomatic isolation. The Freely-Elected Heads argued that because the FSLN and UNO combined obtained over 95% of the vote the country was deeply polarized, and reflected the 'extent to which the election was a referendum on Sandinista rule'. The LASA Commission argued, however, that hailing the Sandinista defeat as a victory for democracy, 'obscures the context of war in which these elections took place and the role of the US in shaping their outcome'. The United States 'played a central role in creating the conditions' for the election through the war and economic damage, the FSLN lost 'its attractiveness to the Nicaraguan people'. Indeed, 'the role of the United States in sustaining the contra war and in crippling the Nicaraguan economy' with the 'symbolic, political and financial signals of support' for UNO 'continued a long-standing pattern of US interference in Nicaraguan affairs. It made the process less purely a measure of Nicaraguan preferences, and more a reaction to US policies.' The Sandinistas remained the largest political party in Nicaragua after their defeat on 25 February 1990. With

86% of registered voters participating they obtained 41% of the vote to UNO's 55%; they retained 39 of the 92 seats in the National Assembly while UNO gained 51.[13]

James Baker stated two days before the elections that the conclusion of the monitors was one thing, but the United States reserved the right to judge the elections themselves. A similar tactic had been used in 1984 when the State Department explicitly argued it did not need to use the same yardstick to assess the elections of a country avowedly hostile to Washington. A week before the elections, however, the press began to speculate on the possibility of normalization of relations after a fair Sandinista victory. While a period of time would be necessary to assess the situation, it was stated a fair election would remove any justification for continued support for the contras. Contra leaders had begun negotiations with the Sandinistas, and the United States had begun background talks between Aronson and Tinoco.[14]

## THE SANDINISTA DEFEAT

An important question asked by Dore and Weeks on whether it is enough to contextualize the Sandinista defeat in terms of US imperialism, provides a good introduction to the attempt to explain why they lost in a procedurally fair election. These authors ask the question with the critical suggestion US policies can by no means be discounted, but they may not sufficiently elucidate the result. The construction of socialism, they argue, requires more than the use of rhetoric and invocation of ideological abstraction on the part of the Sandinistas.[15] The general reasons given are the contra war, the economy and the Sandinista response to it, and the internal structure of the Sandinista party which led to an authoritarian approach in their leadership. While it may not be enough to exclusively explain the upset with reference to external pressure, the international context did set the agenda for Sandinista reaction during the decade. Their economic mismanagement and political behaviour may need to be considered in their future. Vilas argues that neither the knee jerk reaction of the left, exclusively blaming external sources, nor the reaction of the right repudiating the Sandinistas is complete. The Sandinistas were not responsible for the brutal decade, but they did administer the country during it.[16]

While the Carter Commission argued the election was a referendum on Sandinista rule, LASA thought it more a reaction to US policies. The procedure may have been both free and fair, that is to say, the campaign, the casting and the counting of votes, but the context was anything but fair. The United States had spent extraordinary sums of money and exerted their material resources and covert operations to shape the internal political system and the external relations of the Sandinistas. Washington wanted to overthrow the Sandinistas by any means short of a direct invasion, and this prospect could not be ruled out entirely, especially after the 1983 invasion of Grenada, and 1989 invasion of Panama. Robinson has described the elections as a referendum on survival, and Kornbluh suggests the vote was the culmination of the rollback approach to Nicaragua extant for ten years. Chomsky points out the logical problem: If the Sandinistas were defeated because of the perilous state of the economy and the resultant misery, this was the exact intention of the contra attacks on soft targets such as schools, hospitals, granaries, oil facilities, and cooperatives, coupled with the US economic embargo and diplomatic pressure on other Latin American and European countries to cease their aid to Nicaragua. This aspect was directly influenced by Washington, and the elections could not be said to be either free of external influence or fair.[17] In this sense the Sandinista defeat was a victory for Washington. They had undermined the demonstration of progressive change, necessitating a different approach for others resulting from the 'lessons' of Nicaragua.

## THE CONTRA WAR

While the election results obviously represented the choice of Nicaraguans at that particular time, the vote was in part a plea to end the contra war; the people voted for a relief from the terror and misery of the past years. Nicaraguans were not permitted to make an autonomous political decision. Chomsky argues democracy had suffered as a result because a popularly elected government was replaced under duress through a proxy system of violent intervention. The tactic was explicit; as the contra leader Israel Galeano stated, the Sandinistas would not be allowed to live in peace.[18]

By 1990 the Sandinistas could not run on a progressive economic or social platform as most of the early gains of the revolution had been reversed in the late 1980s. And even though the contras had been strategically defeated without prospects for additional lethal aid they continued their aggression throughout the campaign. As long as they had sanctuary in Honduras they could maintain their ability to kill and destroy infrastructure. The strongest Sandinista argument was that they were radical nationalists who had so far successfully resisted US aggression; but they could not totally end the war because, Dore and Weeks point out, 'sporadic and localized conflicts of a terrorist sort' continued. While the United

States had obviously been the source of this negative nationalism, it had also perpetuated it through its continued intervention, mitigating any real opportunities for self determination. The ability of the Sandinistas to exploit this as an electoral issue had become largely irrelevant by 1990 precisely because of their incomplete triumph over the contras. They could not exploit any positive aspect of their achievements successfully; their social programmes had been reversed and their radical nationalism was perceived as largely irrelevant because of the low scale, but persistent, contra aggression. Ironically, the US invasion of Panama briefly revived the chances of victory centred around nationalistic positions. Alternately, LASA argues Nicaraguans may have feared that if the FSLN remained in power they too might be the target of an invasion that disproportionately killed civilians. Bush's hard line on Panama, dispelling the 'wimp' factor, allowed him political space in Washington to pursue a more political approach on Nicaragua. But even this approach was backed by intermittent aggression. Alejandro Bendaña submitted:

> While at once taking every organizational advantage of the political space that was opened and of the strict Nicaraguan compliance with the Esquipulas plan, the U.S. sent the Nicaraguan electorate a clear message: vote for the Sandinistas and you will see a continuation of the war and the economic crisis, and if you do not believe us, then look at what happened to Panama and to the North American nuns ambushed and killed weeks before the election.

In effect, the US position undercut Nicaragua's self determination and invalidated a fair choice. Another widely cited reason for defeat was the failure to suspend military conscription during the campaign, which LASA referred to as a 'tactical error.' Even though the Sandinistas probably regarded the opposition to the draft as treasonous, Vilas contends it probably had more to do with a 'parental reaction' to seeing their children involved in the war.[19]

## THE ECONOMY

In trying to assess the US reaction to the Sandinista revolution, apart from the simplicities of Reagan's ideological framework and the incredible arguments on the National Security threat posed to the United States, the revolution experimented with a mixed economic policy that maintained a significant proportion of business in the private sector while also trying to improve the circumstances of the poor. The initial results were impressive and received commendation from the World Bank. Results in the improvement of education, health care, literacy and the agrarian reform to some extent improved the options for the poor. Whether this was a part of a coherent ideological stance centred around socialist ideas is widely debated; rhetorical statements and policy implementation do not always run in accordance. Still, the experiment, whether intentionally or not, significantly increased the participation of Nicaraguan citizens in the system that tried to mix representative and participatory politics. More pertinently, perhaps, the independence and self determination the Sandinistas insisted on, later even at the expense of their revolutionary programme, incurred the wrath of Washington owing to this challenge to their traditional, if decreasing, hegemony within the region. Chomsky argues the experiment could not be allowed to succeed, not for the sake of Nicaragua alone, but because:

> still less will the US willingly tolerate a government that diverts resources to the poor majority, thus demonstrating its utter failure to recognize the right priorities, and embarking on a course that may have dangerous demonstration effects if the experiment is permitted to succeed.

The tactics and intention of the contra war was to ensure the failure of the experiment.[20]

The situation was bad during the 1984 elections, but was 'incomparably worse' six years later during the 1990 elections. The war, economic boycott, world recession, government mismanagement, hyperinflation, debt, shortages, and rampant disorganization left the Sandinistas in a precarious position. Their nationalism and opposition to the United States may have been appealing in 1984, because not all these influences existed and a loyalty to the revolution and reward through their programmes made them attractive. The economy began to stagnate in 1984, the US embargo began in 1985, by 1988 they had effectively lost control of the economy and their response introduced an austerity programme widely regarded as little different from those imposed by the IMF. Subsidies were cut back and income fell to levels experienced thirty years before. By 1988 inflation was running at about 30 000% and the response, according to Ricciardi, was decidedly monetarist 'reflecting the short run urgency of addressing at least the proximate cause of the crisis: excess money growth.' Hence the economy was opened to forces beyond popular support and without the gains normally sold with IMF type austerity plans; international finance would not respond to Sandinista measures. The Sandinistas initiated the worst of both worlds according to Vilas: they underwent the austerity without minimal gains of assistance. The higher prices associated with the strategy meant the poorest sectors of society were hit the worst. State workers and the poor could not afford the decreasing quantity of products on sale; the poor lost purchasing power first. Throughout, the Sandinistas needed to maintain a defense budget roughly about 40% of their national expenditure.[21]

The Gross Domestic Product declined 11.7%, the trade deficit was over $1.2 billion, foreign debt was $7.5 billion; by the late 1980s the country was one of the poorest in the world. Exports declined since 1979, and the government response to pay for the short fall was to print money leading to the hyperinflation of 1988. The main produce, sugar and coffee, had been devastated by the war; coffee exports suffered further with the sharp decline in its price in 1989 with the deregulation of the International Coffee Organization. By 1990 the austerity programme did bring inflation down to 1 689%, but by this time Sandinista economic policies were quite similar to those of the other isthmian countries, adding relevance to the movement for regional economic integration. The war had an horrendous effect on the economy. Ironically the 'socioeconomic transformations brought on by the revolution . . . and not a few errors in economic policy – not so much in the overall macroeconomic context as in their impact at the microeconomic level, in the day to day life of the people' contributed to the Sandinista demise. In other words their economic response hurt those who benefitted most from the revolution and were most likely to have earlier supported it. González puts it simply: The results of the austerity plan were unequally distributed; private capital was protected as 65% of the economy remained in private hands and was less susceptible to Sandinista measures. The poor were being hurt in the late 1980s by the contra war and by the Sandinista reaction. Vilas contends that the FSLN 'belief that an adjustment program could be met with popular acquiescence turned out to be a technocratic fantasy that cost the revolution dearly'.[22]

LASA judged the living standards of most Nicaraguans had declined, but it was also clear that the FSLN had not convinced potential supporters that the problem was entirely due to the United States. While their defeat was celebrated in Washington and represented an ultimate victory, despite its illegal character, progressive change would be far more complex in the future. The Sandinistas presented their defeat as a victory for imperialism and reactionary economics; though their recent policies were monetarist, it is unlikely they would have moved in this direction had it not been for the duress under which they miscalculated their response. The revolutionary rhetoric that continued, even as the austerity programme was introduced exacerbated the bitterness of those most affected. UNO derived its base of support from the poorest sectors of the organized right, while the educated middle class supported the FSLN. When the revolution fulfilled the demand of small farmers for land, the FSLN contributed to their own defeat, these groups lent more support to UNO, and Sandinista nationalism failed to convince people they had a viable programme for government, in the absence of normalized relations with Washington. Yet the Sandinistas remained the largest party after the elections. The irony played itself out in the final FSLN rally which dwarfed that of UNO. Vilas explains:

> It was not anti-communist ideology or sympathy with the counter-revolution that drove many of those who took part with such enthusiasm in the extraordinary FSLN closing rally on the night of February 21, to vote for UNO on the morning of the twenty-fifth. It was because when they returned home they had to face the empty rice dish, the vacant place of the son recruited into the army, the photo of the son killed by the contras, or the neighbor's shiny new car.[23]

The revolution undoubtedly increased the range and depth of participation in Nicaraguan society, perhaps some of it resulted from unintended aspects of their policies that broke up the large land holdings into the smaller, but still private, farms. Disaffection for the Sandinistas also resulted from the expectations created by the move towards greater participation; the limits of inclusion in decision making also alienated people. The arrogance of Sandinista decision making and the vertical nature of the party structure are frequently cited as reasons for their demise. The FSLN grew out of clandestine revolutionary groups whose structure was necessarily vertical. The reunited FSLN in 1978 remained centralized, and after the revolution this tendency made its way into the bureaucracy. The organizations involving mass participation debated the issues, but once the Sandinistas made a decision these groups were then expected to follow and implement their decisions. The disagreements within the FSLN, centred upon their earlier tripartite division, found their way into the state institutions and led to, according to Vickers, a factionalised process of decision making, sometimes leading to contradictory policies and confusion. Mass participation was encouraged but limited at certain points; Dore and Weeks suggest that the FSLN served as a barrier to mass participation. During a time of war and an economic siege it is difficult to expect otherwise, and the perhaps inevitable verticalness and the concomitant defiance of the United States contributed to the decisions that were taken without understanding the opinions of the popular base of their initial support. Ortega's campaign manager later suggested: 'We were drunk with this idea that everything was OK. We lost our capacity to converse, to listen, to criticize ourselves, the capacity to measure, and the people punished us for that.' A similar assessment was reached by an UNO legislative candidate Luis Humberto Guzmán and LASA, it was a 'vote to punish the FSLN' even though 'the expectation was that UNO would win'.[24]

## DEMOCRATIZATION

Considering the diversity of ideologies and personalities in UNO's coalition, it was difficult to present a coherent programme or a set of principles they would act on. Indeed, Chamorro once responded that she did have an economic policy, but it was a secret. The unifying factor for UNO, as its name suggests, was its opposition to the Sandinistas; the coalition represented an opportunity to stop the continued destruction and economic deterioration. Furthermore, Chamorro immediately embodied a sense of national reconciliation after the victory. The diversity of the opposition was such that it is widely considered unlikely they would have stayed united unless they had been persuaded to do so by Washington; the covert and overt funding cemented the unity.

The 1990 elections must be assessed in the international context and may not meet the requirements normally included in democratic theory. The ability of small Third World regimes to build a viable political system opposed by a superpower, subject to multinational financial arrangements, and transnational political contingencies may be severely constrained, undermining the democratic aspirations of a people, and the self determination of a country. David Held considers it necessary to question the prospects for democracy within the nation state system. National borders determine the extent of political and constitutional inclusion of a system, but as in Nicaragua's case the outcome of their revolution largely depended on forces outside their system; as, for that matter, was the systemic injustice that originally gave rise to Sandinismo and later the FSLN, and still later provoked the revolution. While Nicaragua enjoyed legal sovereignty, in practice its sovereignty was continually violated, both in the Somoza and Sandinista periods and may still be under the Chamorro government. 'Political independence,' Held contends, 'provides at best only a brief respite from the processes of marginalization in the world economy.' Nicaragua's revolution was subject to the political and economic power of Washington, which in the Westphalian world ultimately molds 'the effective deployment of rules and resources within and across borders'.

Cardinal aspects of democratic theory such as consent and legitimacy are affected by international intervention, as are

> the nature of a constituency, the meaning of representation, the proper form and scope of political participation, and the relevance of the democratic nation-state, faced with unsettling patterns of relations and constraints in the international order, as the guarantor of the rights, duties and welfare of subjects.[25]

The Sandinista experiment tried to merge the beneficial aspects of liberal and participatory democracy that were written into the 1987 constitution. While such a document did not guarantee the respect for individual rights, the Sandinistas held over 4 000 political prisoners, basic rules were set out, approved in this case by large majorities of the Assembly. The Constitution basically provided for a 'mixed' ideological framework. It brought together participatory and representative democracy, socialism and capitalism, nationalism and aspects of international law. Thus the problems associated with liberal representative democracy, most pertinently the inequalities of political power and economic power reduced the effective equality of citizens. Conversely, government by popular majorities can impair the accountability of the government to the diverse pluralistic forces; liberal democracy protects the rights of individuals more effectively. The Sandinistas were subject to compromise on these provisions which could not mutually accommodate the polarized interests in Nicaragua and the extraterritorial actors.[26]

To argue the 1990 elections were free and fair, exclusively concentrating on the electoral procedures concentrates on the representative liberal aspects of the system without giving importance to the inclusionary aspects fundamental to Nicaragua's revolution. The democracy that emerged under the Sandinistas focused on the inclusion of people within the system rather than an exclusive form of democratic representation for the more dominant economic interests of society. The quality and depth of participation was vastly increased, whether directly intended through the redistributive policies and the literacy programmes, or through the unintended inclusion of small farmers that emerged from the break up of large holdings. The ultimate test of FSLN fidelity to the system was their concession of power after their 1990 upset. By this stage it was almost inconceivable they would not transfer power because the excuses they may have used were removed through their own success against the contras or their compliance with the Central American Peace plan. The select focus on the electoral and liberal direction of democracy vitiated the scope and quality of participation, contributing to what Gills and others have called Low

Intensity Democracy, which in effect requires the non-participation of popular sectors of society and emerges from the failure of economic development. The democratic experiment which initially enabled and required citizens to participate, albeit limited by the vanguard position of the FSLN, was eventually subverted by eroding the economic base of wide inclusion.[27] Most fundamentally, the opposition had a reasonable chance and did win the election. In El Salvador, though the main competitive axis was between the government and the FMLN, the electoral process passed power between the Christian Democrats and ARENA. The FMLN extracted concessions from the government but could not participate in the system while the military continued to exercise unaccountable power.

In analyzing democratization in Nicaragua one must not lose sight of the aims and effects of the revolution, or get lost in the pervasive rhetoric on democracy. Washington's application of 'democracy' was in essence a form of anti-communism, and was used as an ideological tool in an extraregional conflict. Little seemed to be contingent on popular aspirations within the region; Central Americans and Nicaraguans in particular had not consented to the international political and economic systems, and their governments could not be subjected to total accountability because many influences on their society were beyond their control. Far from communist, Washington's problem in Nicaragua was more the Sandinista solution centred around, as Galeano has eloquently put it:

> a dangerous and contagious example of a people that lost patience. To guard a criminal social order, the neighbour governments are forced into armed insomnia. With good reason they feel themselves threatened, but threatened by their own peoples, who may find out that they'd be better off making history from below and from inside than continuing to suffer history made by others from above and from outside.

The process of democratization injected into the diplomacy was designed to restore the historical agency of those 'others' above and outside the national system. Regional and global connections contest the idea that democracy can be limited to the nation state, and Nicaragua's subjection to an economic violence, ultimately more effective than the contra war, testifies to the frontiers of citizenship, responsibility, consent, and accountability. The national community could not make decisions outside the scope, in this case of the United States, the IMF, diminishing aid from the European Community, Latin America, Moscow or the Eastern block. As Held argues, the notion of consent, vital to any representative system, immediately becomes problematical. The politics of a nation cannot be understood without reference to international financial institutions, subjected to pressure from Washington to limit their aid to Nicaragua, exacerbating the embargo and siege economy it suffered from during the 1980s. Washington sought to nullify the Sandinista experiment and place Nicaragua squarely back into the world market centred around concepts, if not the practice of, free trade. Thus free elections associated with free trade may undermine the ability of the range and depth of participation the Sandinistas tried to obtain. Electoral procedures may continue in an impeccably 'fair' manner, but may be fundamentally undemocratic because the impact of the global order is ignored. The Sandinistas tried to combine democracy with social reform to remove the unequal distribution of power experienced during the Somoza period and did for the duration of Contadora's plans find sympathy from these regional governments when they expressed concern in their first bulletin in 1983 on the 'recessive tendency of the world economy' and the

> negative effects which that phenomenon has produced . . . in terms of shifts in financing, trade, investment and employment, and noted the need to revise an international system which, in its unbalanced state, causes serious problems in developing countries.

The military forces used to contain the popular aspirations for greater inclusion and participation were yet another impediment to democratization in Central America. The idea of democracy, Peeler argues, 'posits the political equality of citizens, and political equality is only an illusion in the face of extreme economic inequality'.[28] Hence the 1990 electoral process may have advanced liberal democracy, but with Nicaragua's slow and fractured return to neo-liberal economic policies coupled with the regional integration of the market forces; governments may gain added bargaining power, but the relative poverty and exclusion of the regional and Nicaraguan citizens are augmented. Unsatisfied with history being made from 'above' and from 'outside' the tendency led to frustration with the system to the point where Sandinistas and contras joined together calling themselves recontras and resorted to extra-constitutional means to assert their desires for better conditions. The ideological stance adopted in the rhetoric of Washington and the Sandinistas was lost in these appetites.

# Conclusion

During the spring of 1986 Senator Leahy questioned Robert Gates on the appropriateness of the 'new Reagan doctrine of increasingly open and direct confrontation with the Soviet Union and its allies and friends around the world', to which Gates outlined a strategy that rested between diplomacy, which on its own he regarded as ineffective, and the use of military power, which 'would not be supported by the American people or the Congress'. At that point Gates posited the United States had two options: to develop other instruments, such as covert operations, or walk away. The strategy that lay between diplomacy and military action was the Reagan response to the constraints of the 'Vietnam syndrome' where since that war congress had been reluctant to back direct US intervention in conflicts without a clear set of goals and a very limited duration. The administration also worked within the traditional US approach to the region that alternated between patterns of hegemonic or coercive control. Previous radical challenges to the system in the western hemisphere, as Dunkerley notes, Bolivia (1952–1964), Guatemala (1944–1954), Dominican Republic (1963–1965), and Chile (1970–1973), were 'either suffocated slowly or shot to pieces'. Washington was intolerant of political diversity, and regarded such experiments as Soviet attempts at violating the Monroe doctrine. And now Reagan applied his desire to confine Marxism to the 'ash heap of history' and promote an exclusive type of 'democracy' to Nicaragua. Gates had asserted in 1984 after Reagan's re-election:

> The fact is that the Western Hemisphere is the sphere of influence of the United States. If we have decided totally to abandon the Monroe Doctrine, if in the 1980's taking strong actions to protect our interests despite the hail of criticism is too difficult, then we ought to save political capital in Washington, acknowledge our helplessnesss and stop wasting everybody's time.[1]

The resulting instrumental combination of covert operations, more accurately a form of low intensity conflict, and diplomacy had a symbiotic relationship in Washington's institutional politics: the administration argued the Sandinistas had to be induced to the negotiating table, while Congress conditioned further contra aid on the exhaustion of diplomacy. But 'hardliners', predominantly, but not exclusively, from within the National Security Council were engaged in an attempt to overthrow the Sandinista regime, hence the US approach to diplomacy is best understood within the legislative constraints and not as an attempt to reach accord with Managua.

There is little evidence to demonstrate that negotiations, in so far as seeking accommodation with the Sandinistas, were conducted. Compromise, a necessary tool of diplomacy, was not offered by Washington. The Reagan administration was neither interested in concluding an agreement based on national security for Nicaragua or the United States under the auspices of Contadora, nor did bilateral negotiations produce any US compromise. The bottom line was a Contadora treaty which would have kept the Sandinistas in power, maintaining the so called Nicaraguan 'threat of a good example', backed by the regional group's call for a restructuring of the international economic order. Washington was not only concerned about the external dimensions of the revolution, it wanted to overthrow the regime or roll back the revolution, mitigating any successful experiment or economic model.

US security concerns were exaggerated throughout; there is little evidence of Sandinista expansionism as constantly alleged, the transfers of arms till January 1981 were soon curtailed under diplomatic pressure. Any substantial Nicaraguan aggression would have been sharply dealt with under regional security agreements and the Sandinistas did not acquire advanced offensive aircraft, in the knowledge that, to do so, would have invited a direct regional response. The weaponry procured reflected their internal needs. To preclude agreement the US strategy continually raised the stakes from interdiction to democracy and Nicaraguan concessions induced further US demands. The diplomatic process served both governments, but Washington's imperative was to avoid a solution or conclusion to any set of negotiations. With the ever increasing US demands and prevarication on verification it could implausibly argue the diplomatic approach had failed to produce agreement and the covert 'inducements' needed further teeth. The arguments put forward by those interested in containing the Sandinistas gained currency only in so far as they contributed to efforts to gain added contra funding. Diplomatic action was only important if it helped convince Congress that it had reasonably pursued the option and failed.

The Central American crises and the Reagan opposition to the Sandinistas were presented as a vital component of US national security. While such arguments are ludicrous in terms of a physical threat to the United States, the administration had limited their own manoeuvrability through the use of their public diplomacy. The defining speech of April 1983, argued that the western alliance could not depend on the United States if they could not prevail in Nicaragua.[2] While neither European nor Latin American governments shared these concerns, Reagan's failure to resolve the issue on US terms became a political liability, detrimental to the gist of his doctrine. The political check on the military option and the loss of support for covert action led to the convoluted procurement of extrajudicial funds which resulted in the Iran–Contra scandals that severely damaged the NSC hardliners and the administration, opening diplomatic space for greater Central American cohesion.[3]

The Esquipulas process took advantage of the political constraints in Washington, and by 1987 there were more similarities than differences in their economic policies; the Nicaraguan experiment had been hurt and needed a swift resolution. The Central American governments knew that the poor of their countries no longer looked to Nicaragua for a 'good example' as Dunkerley argues 'because of the hammering Nicaraguans had taken as a result'. Esquipulas was a conservative agreement that offered all governments some relief, autonomy from the United States, and an isthmian trade system to pull themselves out of depression.[4] The counterrevolution took over 40 000 lives, destroyed the economy, ground down the Sandinistas through the multifaceted low intensity conflict, and they conceded power in elections scheduled in their 1987 constitution.

Before these elections Reagan had staked US prestige on removing the Sandinistas but was constrained by congressional hesitation to support such dubious policies exacerbated by the discord between the rhetoric and realities of the region. Congress mandated, at least, a demonstration of diplomacy, but substantial negotiations were mitigated by the hyperbolic use of public diplomacy which exacerbated tensions between the two governments, and distorted Sandinista objectives. The State Department through its office of Public Diplomacy consistently pointed to the alarming advances 'communist' forces were making on the American mainland, but no Soviet forces were operating in Central America, and 'no one ever unearthed a [Cuban] . . . fighting with the Sandinistas, the FMLN, or any of the Guatemalan guerrilla groups'. The tactics of public diplomacy are accurately put by Hans Morgenthau:

> the public diplomats speak to the world rather than to each other. Their aim is not to persuade each other that they could find common ground for agreement, but to persuade the world and especially their own nations that they are right and the other side is wrong and that they are and always will remain staunch defenders of the right.[5]

In the absence of ongoing bilateral talks, Nicaragua's use of public diplomacy set out to convince, not only their population, but also US audiences they were willing to compromise, as long as their sovereignty was respected. US public opinion constrained the possibility of direct action. Similarly, to avert this possibility their strategy of concessions made it difficult for the administration to convince Congress of Sandinista intransigence; each potential settlement was blocked by Washington, and Central American unanimity on contra demobilization was ignored.

The patterns of US policy toward the region, generally affirmed in recent literature, were maintained. US policy was erratic, swinging between neglect and 'overreaction to . . . crises'. It sought hegemony by keeping nationalist governments out of power, and in doing so supported repressive regimes, which 'polarized local populations and ultimately undermined regional stability and US hegemonic control'. The United States was able to repeat its mistakes in Central America 'simply because it has been able to afford to do so' in the absence of a real security threat.[6]

Carter administration officials argued the Nicaraguan revolution was not a cohesive leftist movement, and pluralism could have been maintained without contra pressure. Though the Sandinistas initiated their redistributive programmes, Viron Vaky argued economic aid would keep them in the international economy, maintaining US influence. Sandinista programmes were virtually undermined by the late 1980s, and their economic policies under austerity predominantly hurt the poor. Still, both the economic and political aspects of the revolution had to be destroyed; if the covert war savaged the people and economy, diplomacy undermined Sandinista nationalism. Chomsky argues the internal record of US diplomacy clarifies the objectives:

> High level planning documents emphasize that the major threat to U.S. interests is posed by 'nationalistic regimes' that are responsive to popular pressures for 'immediate improvement in the low living standards of the masses' and diversification of the economies.

In this interpretation the ideological basis of the regimes that break out of the traditional mold of international relations are irrelevant; independence and radical nationalism challenged the historical hegemony of the United States.[7] But within the cultural framework of US decision making, an imperative since the Truman Doctrine has been to present such challenges as linked to and orchestrated by the Soviet Union.

## FULL CIRCLE?

Serious flaws emerged in the systemic approach to the Nicaraguan revolution during the Reagan administration; the globalist perspective's irrelevance to the dynamics of the revolution, if not the source of the counterrevolution, can perhaps be seen in the on-going post-Sandinista conflicts.

When Violata Chamorro assumed power on 25 April 1990 national reconciliation was an imperative task to facilitate her other goals of consolidating democratic liberties and strengthening the economy while reducing social inequalities. Her closest deputy Antonio Lacayo realized the Sandinistas would have to play a vital role in the attempt to build a political consensus for reconstruction that would be impossible 'if the winning party does not integrate all Nicaraguan's into its project'. The FSLN were still the largest party, perhaps the most cohesive, retaining a base of support, although somewhat fractured. Chamorro's intentions did not last beyond the inauguration period.[8]

The compromises made by Lacayo with Humberto Ortega in the 'Transition Protocol' of 27 March 1990 that Ortega could retain power of the military if he left the FSLN, outraged the right of UNO, most importantly Viriglio Godoy, and the right in Washington. The coalition split immediately; its previous unity was based entirely on opposing the FSLN. The lack of a cohesive governing strategy and the absence of party loyalty created factions informally headed by Lacayo and Godoy. The fragility of the coalition and its ideological diversity exacerbated the divisions which were strategically exploited by the Sandinistas who incorporated a strategy of ruling from below. The government's brutal deflationary policies prompted strikes resulting in FSLN mediation. Within months they were in an informal coalition with Chamorro and, as Dunkerley argues, the continued search for agreement in the centre reflected a deepening of the conservative Esquipulas process.[9] The move towards further regional integration was aided by the rightist economic policies introduced by the Sandinistas in the late 1980s and was continued by Chamorro in an attempt to reintegrate the country into the international economic order, and find favour with the World Bank and the IMF. Such economic restructuring was later defended by Sergio Ramirez, who became FSLN leader in the National Assembly. Dore and Weeks argue that the bargain between Chamorro and the FSLN reflects the mixed coalition of 1979, this time assimilating 'capitalist modernization mediated by populist restraint'. While Washington lifted the economic embargo, provided $30 million in emergency aid and another $300 million which followed, this was much less than the Chamorro government expected to aid the reconstruction of a virtually destroyed society. Nicaraguan trade was regionally reintegrated and once again dependent on the United States. By 1991 unemployment increased by a third to 40%, and living standards were back at 1930s levels. Washington's assistance was constrained by the competing claims from the newly independent government of Eastern Europe and the political manoevres of the Republican right centred around Senator Jesse Helms, who influenced the White House to suspend $104 million aid to Nicaragua pending the resolution of the dispute on Humberto Ortega's position and the alliance between Chamorro and the FSLN.[10]

Contra demobilization remained contentious and dangerous when they failed to meet several agreed deadlines to surrender their arms in return for some economic benefits. The contras were cautious about demobilization precisely because Ortega retained control of the army. Though the process of demobilization was broken and discontinuous, Chamorro succeeded in reducing those with arms, either from the Sandinista army or the contras, by 100 000 troops in the first year of government. By early 1991, however, groups of ex-contras rearmed and demanded greater material benefits. Their initial action was more demonstrative than substantive, but after the assassination of former contra leader Enrique Bermúdez, their action was stepped up and by April 1991 groups had clashed with the army; soon after their numbers were estimated between 300 to 1 100. By this stage Sandinistas had also taken offensive action when the UNO controlled Assembly threatened to repossess houses and land the Sandinistas signed over to themselves after their defeat. Close to the end of 1991 former Sandinistas became more militant, forming groups called the 'Recompas' to fight the Recontras. Tentative agreement was found between the groups to settle matters peacefully, but even three years into the new government Nicaragua threatened to split into several small conflicts.[11]

The confused divisions were not confined to the armed groups. Political factions shifted alliances between the Chamorro government and Lacayo, the Godoy centred right of UNO, and the Sandinistas. Initial division resulted from attempts to 'roll back' the agrarian reforms, headed by Godoy and Alfredo César, the former contra leader and now head of the Assembly. The FSLN boycotted the Assembly, blocking legislation by depriving it of a quorum. Their compromise with Chamorro to defuse tension for limitations on the privatization process, strengthened the alliance which by early 1992 had developed into an open suggestion that the FSLN and the Chamorro faction should stand together in the 1996 polls. Later in 1992 César took direct control of the Assembly in an implicit legislative 'coup' while the Sandinistas were absent. Some power returned to the FSLN in early 1993 when the Supreme Court gave them control of the Assembly and UNO officially declared themselves in opposition. The accord between the FSLN and Chamorro did not last and by late 1993 Ortega became a sharp critic of her government, warning of the rebirth of 'somocismo'.[12]

The consensus on the political framework had not been achieved which is vital for the consolidation of democracy in Nicaragua. The termination of the redistributive policies from the late 1980s will effectively deprive the poorer sectors of society from exercising their democratic rights and the long term prospects for stability remain slim. Nicaragua joined the economic repercussions of the Esquipulas process of regional integration which were formalized by the creation of the Central American Economic Community in 1990–1991. The common economic policies revolve around orthodox stabilization programmes where market 'solutions' are applied to social problems, with the normal results of macroeconomic growth stimulated by free trade and the attendant return to a fall in real wages, increased poverty, and diminished social benefits.[13]

Months into the Clinton administration the new Secretary of State for Inter-American Affairs, Alexander Watson, told the Subcommittee for Western Hemisphere Affairs, 'US values are shared to an unprecedented degree by nearly every country in the region' and the United States must 'avail itself of this unique historic opportunity to enhance and deepen the commitment of all nations of the hemisphere to the core values of US foreign policy'. There were calls for further regional integration and for the isthmus to 'dock up beside NAFTA.' Yet it is precisely these economic policies that create the regional inequalities, reducing the effective power of the poor. More generally the 1991 Inter-American Development Bank reported on the regional conditions that may lead to a 'further deterioration of the already highly uneven income distribution in most countries in the region [which] could effectively block recovery by creating political and social unrest'. The potential return of the situation of volatile instability caused by poverty still looms; Dunkerley persuasively argues the 'pacification' of Central America, and Nicaragua in particular was tenuous. Earlier, the International Commission for Central America argued:

> The most ominous external possibility is that when Central American wars end and the region is no longer an area of geo-political crisis, economic aid will be withdrawn and openings for Central American exports closed off. It would be an enormous tragedy if Central America's search for peace were to condemn the region to economic stagnation and eventually another cycle of violence.

Through Reagan's redefinition of the problem focusing on the wrong question, of communism rather than poverty, to satisfy a propulsion of US power towards the end of the cold war, the isthmus went through a devastating decade without resolving the basic systemic problems.[14]

Orthodox stabilization and modernization policies often devastate the conditions of the poor. A clear advantage of the end of the Cold War is that their response can no longer be explained through east–west explanations, masking the tension between North and South. While the end of history thesis argues for a greater homogenisation in the world economy, Xabier Gorostiaga reminds us the pattern of development under 'modernization' and the northern way of life cannot be extended globally because of the structural constraints and the 'contradiction between the demands for progressive accumulation intrinsic to this model and the increasing concentration in the North to the exclusion of the majority in the South'. Governments who seek greater redistribution within their societies still face the distributive system of the international economic order; the left, or radical nationalist have to 'govern against the current'. The economic orthodoxy and the ideological conformity around concepts of neo-liberal democracy, which moves towards greater exclusion at both economic and political levels, compelling an almost uniform system is, as Isaiah Berlin posits 'almost always the road to inhumanity'. When people are subjected 'to a single ideology, no matter how reasonable or imaginative,' their freedom and vitality is taken; the 'richest development of human potentialities' occurs under conditions of freedom and a greater plurality of governing methods.[15]

The Sandinistas attempted a revolutionary experiment destroyed by the United States because of its inability to allow a modicum of pluralism in its hegemonic reactions to change and economic redistribution. Even when the economic aspects of the revolution were destroyed Sandinista nationalism had to be devastated as an example to those who challenge systemic imperatives. While the diplomatic rhetoric employed the intolerance of the superpower discourse, the low intensity war destroyed the unrelated experiment.[16]

# Notes and References

## Introduction

1. Republican Party Platform, '1980 Republican Platform Text,' *Congressional Quarterly Weekly Report* 38, no. 29 (19 July 1980), pp. 2054, 2030, 2052; Roy Gutman, *Banana Diplomacy: The Making of American Policy in Nicaragua 1981–1987*, (New York: Simon and Schuster, 1988), pp. 19–20.
2. James David Barber, 'President Reagan's Character: An Assessment,' in *Perspectives on American Foreign Policy: Selected Readings*, eds. Charles W. Kegley Jr., and Eugene R. Wittkopf, (New York: St. Martin's Press, 1983), p. 496; Walter LaFeber, *America, Russia, and the Cold War 1945–1990*, 6th ed., (New York: McGraw-Hill, Inc., 1991), p. 302; The Committee of Santa Fe, L. Francis Bouchey, Roger Fontaine, David C. Jordan, Lt. General Gordon Sumner, and Lewis Tambs, *A New Inter-American Policy for the Eighties*, (Washington, D.C.: Council for Inter-American Security, 1980), pp. 1, 3, 46, 52.
3. Jeane Kirkpatrick, 'Dictatorships and Double Standards,' *Commentary* 68, (November 1979): pp. 34, 37; Walter LaFeber, *Inevitable Revolutions: The United States in Central America*, (New York: W. W. Norton & Company, 1984), pp. 278–279.
4. Christopher Hitchens, 'A Dynasty Divided,' *The Independent Magazine* (London), no. 76 (17 February 1990): p. 25; Gabriel Kolko, *Confronting the Third World: United States Foreign Policy, 1945–1980*, (New York: Pantheon Books, 1988), pp. 284–285.
5. Peter Kornbluh, *Nicaragua: The Price of Intervention*, (Washington, D.C.: Institute for Policy Studies, 1987), p. 14; Theodore Roosevelt, fourth annual message to Congress, reprinted as 'Roosevelt Corollary of the Monroe Doctrine, December 6, 1904,' document 28, in Thomas P. Brockway, ed., *Basic Documents in United States Foreign Policy* (Princeton: D. Van Nostrand Company, Inc., 1957), 72–74; for a contextual history of the doctrine, see Cecil V. Crabb, Jr., *The Doctrines of American Foreign Policy* (Baton Rouge: Louisiana State University Press, 1982), pp. 9–55; see also Walter LaFeber, *The American Age: United States Foreign Policy at Home and Abroad since 1750* (New York: W. W. Norton & Company, 1989), pp. 230–235.
6. Kolko, *Confronting the Third World*, p. 287; Robert Pastor, cited in James DeFronzo, *Revolutions and Revolutionary Movements*, (Boulder: Westview Press, 1991), p. 210; Noam Chomsky, *Deterring Democracy*, (London: Verso, 1991), p. 258.
7. James Dunkerley, *Power in the Isthmus: A Political History of Modern Central America*, (London: Verso, 1988): pp. 270–271; US Congress, House, Committee on Foreign Affairs, Subcommittee on Inter-American Affairs *Central America at the Crossroads: hearings before the Committee on Foreign Affairs, Subcommittee on Inter-American Affairs*, 96th Cong., lst sess., 11–12 September 1979, pp. 24–25, 29.

President Carter had previously stated:

> I believe that our position with regard to Nicaragua is appropriate. By no means do I attribute the change in Nicaragua to Cuba. I believe the Nicaraguan people are discerning enough to make their own decisions, and our efforts will be appropriately applied, without intervention, so that the voice of the Nicaraguan people can be heard in shaping their own affairs.

(Jimmy Carter cited in Manlio Tirado, 'The United States and the Sandinista Revolution,' in Richard L. Harris and Carlos M. Vilas, *Nicaragua: A Revolution Under Siege*, [London: Zed Books, 1985], p. 203).

8. Dunkerley, *Power in the Isthmus*, p. 271. The Sandinistas moved early to remove the threat of the forces to their left, because they had independent military power. The 'ultra-leftism' of the Trotskyist organization was often depicted as 'at the service of imperialism.' Leaders from the Nicaraguan Communist Party (PCN) were briefly gaoled and the party was banned from attending the Council of State. Dunkerley points out that their possession of an independent militia was the principle reason for their confinement. When their force was removed, their criticism was tolerated. In the 1984 elections, the PCN won two seats in the National Assembly. (Dunkerley, *Power in the Isthmus*, pp. 327–328, note 6). During the 1990 elections the Communist Party ran as part of the fourteen party coalition, The United Nicaraguan Opposition (UNO), supported by the United States; William M. LeoGrande, Douglas C. Bennett, Morris J. Blachman and Kenneth E. Sharpe, 'Grappling with Central America: From Carter to Reagan,' in Morris J. Blachman and others, *Confronting Revolution: Security Through Diplomacy in Central America* (New York: Pantheon Books, 1986), pp. 300–301; Viron Vaky, cited in Kolko, *Confronting the Third World*, p. 287. The premise, Vaky argued, was that the die had not been cast in Nicaragua. With support for 'non-Marxist elements' the internal situation could 'evolve toward a Mexican rather than a Cuban model.' Tied to the 'West's political economy, a Marxist system can be prevented from consolidating' (Viron P. Vaky, 'Hemispheric Relations: "Everything is Part of Everything Else,"' *Foreign Affairs* 59, no. 3, [1981], p. 622); Mark P. Sullivan, *Nicaragua: An Overview of US Policy 1979–1986*, Congressional Research Service Report for Congress 87–855 F, (Washington, D.C.: The Library of Congress, 13 October 1987): pp. 4–8; Noam Chomsky, *Deterring Democracy*, p. 313.
9. Ian Smart, 'The Adopted Image: Assumptions about International Relations,' *International Journal* (Toronto) 39, no. 2 (Spring 1984): p. 251; William M. LeoGrande, Douglas C. Bennett, Morris J. Blachman and Kenneth E. Sharpe, 'Grappling with Central America: From Carter to Reagan,' in Morris J. Blachman and others, *Confronting Revolution*, p. 297; Lars Schoultz, *National Security and United States Policy towards Latin America*, (Princeton University Press, 1987), pp. 143–222, 13 note 18.
10. Lars Schoultz, *National Security and United States Policy towards Latin America*, pp. 20–21.
11. John A. Booth, and Thomas W. Walker, *Understanding Central America* (Boulder: Westview Press, 1989), pp. 55–60. For further literature on the historical background and the Soviet presence in Central America see: Walter

LaFeber, *Inevitable Revolutions: The United States in Central America* (New York: W. W. Norton and Company, 1993); Jenny Pearce in *Under the Eagle: US Intervention in Central America and the Caribbean* (London: Latin America Bureau, 1981); Richard Millet's *Guardians of the Dynasty: A History of the US Created Guardia Nacional De Nicaragua and the Somoza Family*, (New York: Orbis Books, 1977); Ralph Lee Woodward, Jr., *Central America: A Nation Divided*, (New York: Oxford University Press, 1976); John A. Booth, *The End and the Beginning: The Nicaraguan Revolution*, (Boulder: Westview Press, 1982); Thomas W. Walker, *Nicaragua: The Land of Sandino*, (Boulder: Westview Press, 1981); George Black, *Triumph of the People: The Sandinista Revolution in Nicaragua*, (London: Zed Press, 1981). Karl Bermann, *Under the Big Stick: Nicaragua and the United States since 1848*, (Boston: South End Press, 1986). On the Soviet presence: Cole Blasier, *The Giant's Rival: The USSR and Latin America*, (Pittsburgh University Press, 1983); *The Hovering Giant: US Responses to Revolutionary Change in Latin America*, (University of Pittsburgh Press, 1983); Nicola Miller's *Soviet Relations with Latin America, 1959–1987*, (Cambridge University Press, 1989); Wayne S. Smith, *The Russians Aren't Coming: New Soviet Policy in Latin America*, (Boulder: Lynne Rienner Publishers, 1992); Howard J. Wiarda and Mark Falcoff's, *The Communist Challenge in the Caribbean and Central America*, (Washington, D.C.: American Enterprise Institute, 1987).

12. Booth and Walker, *Understanding Central America*, pp. 117–120. It should be noted that the Sandinistas initially turned to the United States to standardize their military after the revolution. The Pentagon endorsed the idea, but Carter during an election campaign opted for the politically beneficial option and rejected the request. (John A. Booth, and Thomas W. Walker, *Understanding Central America*, p. 120). Ironically, had the administration pursued this course, the United States would have had some power over the Nicaraguan military, by way of controlling, to some extent, the replacement of and spare parts for their equipment. Skidmore and Smith argue that in the post World War II period, following the foundation of both the Rio Pact in 1947 and the Organization of American States in 1948, the military and political alliances commenced a trade of US military equipment and services in exchange for strategic raw materials. They state: 'The implications of these new defense arrangements were far reaching. The US was tying Latin America's armed forces into the US web – once possessing American equipment, they would depend on the US for parts, replacements, and ammunition.' (Thomas E. Skidmore, and Peter H. Smith, *Modern Latin America*, 2nd ed. [New York: Oxford University Press, 1989], p. 350).
13. Cole Blasier, *The Hovering Giant: US Responses to Revolutionary Change in Latin America* (University of Pittsburgh Press, 1983): p. 233; Lawrence A. Pezzullo, Baltimore, Maryland, letter to author, 18 September 1990; Viron P. Vaky quoted by Lars Schoultz, *National Security*, p. 45.
14. Raymond Bonner, *Weakness and Deceit: US Policy and El Salvador*, (London: Hamish Hamilton, 1985), pp. 244–254; Lars Schoultz, *National Security*, pp. 9–10, 63.
15. See, for example, Ronald Reagan, 'Central America: Defending Our Vital Interests,' *Department of State Bulletin* 83, no. 2075 (June 1983): pp. 1–5;

US Congress. Senate. Democratic Policy Committee, *Foreign Aid to Central America FY 1981–1987*, Special Report, no. 1 (Washington, D.C.: Democratic Policy Committee, 12 February 1987), pp. 83, 81, 5–7; Joshua Cohen and Joel Rogers, *Inequity and Intervention: The Federal Budget and Central America* (Boston: South End Press, 1986), p. 22.

16. Transcript of a Press Conference by President Reagan, 'US Objectives in Nicaragua,' 21 February 1985, document 538, *American Foreign Policy Current Documents 1985* (Washington, D.C.: Department of State, 1986), pp. 966–967; US Senate Select Committee On Secret Military Assistance to Iran And the Nicaraguan Opposition, and the US House of Representatives Select Committee to Investigate Covert Arms Transactions with Iran, *Report of the Congressional Committee Investigating the Iran–Contra Affair*, 100th Cong., lst Sess., 13 November 1987, pp. 45–46.
17. William M. LeoGrande, 'Rollback or Containment? The United States, Nicaragua, and the Search for Peace in Central America,' *International Security* 11, no. 2 (Fall 1986): pp. 89–90.
18. William M. LeoGrande, *Central America and the Polls: A Study of US Public Opinion Polls an US Foreign Policy Toward El Salvador and Nicaragua under the Reagan Administration*, Special Report, (Washington, D.C.: Washington Office on Latin America, March 1987), pp. 41–42; Thomas W. Walker, 'Introduction,' in Thomas W. Walker, ed., *Revolution and Counterrevolution in Nicaragua*, (Boulder: Westview Press, 1991), p. 3; Michael Reid, 'Truth Commission Points Finger at Salvadoran Military,' The *Guardian* (London), 16 March 1993; Guy Gugliotta and Douglas Farah, 'Salvadoran Findings Raise Questions for Reagan, Bush,' *Austin American-Statesman*, 21 March 1993, reprinted in *Central America NewsPak* 8, no. 3, issue 185, 8–21 March 1993.
19. Initially, on entering office, Reagan moved to reduce the role of the National Security Advisor. Congressional hearings held in 1980 indicated that former holders of the office testified that it would be desirable to return the strength of the office to pre-Nixon years. Richard Nixon had elevated Henry Kissinger to a position that overshadowed the Secretary of State. Initially, also, the intention was to centre foreign policy around the Department of State. The attempt by the Secretary of State, Alexander Haig, to formalize his new strength, provoked others, closer to Reagan to balance the power. Edwin Meese, counsellor to the President; Michael Deaver, an assistant to the president; and James Baker, chief of staff, resisted the attempts to allow the State Department to overshadow the White House in the politically important area of foreign policy. Conflict between the National Security Advisor, Richard Allen, and Alexander Haig, soon became apparent in the media. Alexander George suggests that it is not surprising that conflicts emerged:

> Reagan had entered the White House without a well developed set of position papers on security matters and foreign policy, such as challengers for office usually prepare during their presidential campaigns. Indeed, his campaign advisers had decided not to attempt to articulate specific positions in order not to expose the latent disagreements among his supporters.

(Alexander L. George, 'Presidential Management Styles and Models,' in Charles W. Kegley, Jr., and Eugene R. Wittkopf, eds., *Perspectives on*

*American Foreign Policy: Selected Readings*, [New York: St. Martin's Press, 1983], pp. 484–485). The Staff of the National Security Advisor grew rapidly during the Reagan presidency. In many cases the functions of the staff duplicated those of the Department of State (Theodore Draper, *A Very Thin Line: The Iran–Contra Affairs*, [New York: Hill and Wang, 1991], p. 6).

## 1 Diplomacy and Counterrevolution 1981–1982

1. Letter from US Assistant Secretary of State for Inter-American Affairs (IAA) Thomas O. Enders to Comandante Daniel Ortega Saavedra, 31 August 1981, document 1.8, in Bruce Michael Bagley, Roberto Alvarez, and Katherine J. Hagedorn, eds., *Contadora and the Central American Peace Process: Selected Documents*, SAIS Papers in International Affairs, No. 8 (Boulder: Westview Press, 1985), p. 22. [Hereafter cited as Bagley, *Contadora Documents*]; Alexander M. Haig, *Caveat: Realism, Reagan, and Foreign Policy* (London: Weidenfeld and Nicolson, 1984), pp. 118, 124; Juan de Onis, 'State Department Says Salvador Rebels Get Fewer Arms,' *New York Times*, 24 February 1981; John Goshko and Don Oberdorfer, 'Haig Calls Arms Smuggling to El Salvador "No Longer Acceptable,"' *Washington Post*, 28 February 1981, quoted in Robert A. Pastor, *Condemned to Repetition: The United States and Nicaragua* (Princeton University Press, 1987), p. 232.
2. Juan de Onis, 'US Halts Nicaragua Aid Over Help for Guerrillas,' *New York Times*, 23 January 1981; Haig, *Caveat*, pp. 99–100; Jaime Wheelock, speech at National Conference in Solidarity with Nicaragua, Managua on 26–31 January 1981, in Tomás Borge, and others, *Sandinistas Speak: Speeches, Writings, and Interviews with Leaders of Nicaragua's Revolution* (New York: Pathfinder Press, 1986), p. 117; Holly Sklar, *Washington's War on Nicaragua* (Boston: South End Press, 1988), pp. 65–66.
3. Lawrence Pezzullo, Baltimore, Maryland, letter to author, 18 September 1990; June Carolyn Erlick, 'Pezzullo Asked to Stay on in Nicaragua,' *Miami Herald*, 22 January 1981.
4. Memorandum from Assistant Secretary for Inter-American Affairs, John Bushnell, to Secretary of State, Alexander Haig, 'Arms Shipments to El Salvador – Getting the Word Out,' 2 February 1981, cited in Peter Kornbluh, *Nicaragua: The Price of Intervention* (Washington, D.C.: Institute for Policy Studies, 1987), pp. 184, 262 note 95; United States Department of State, Special Report No. 80, 'Communist Interference in El Salvador', White Paper, 23 February 1981, in Warner Poelchau, ed., *White Paper Whitewash: Interviews with Philip Agee on the CIA and El Salvador* (New York: Deep Cover Books, 1981), p. Al; James Petras, 'Blots on the White Paper: The Reinvention Of The "Red Menace",' *The Nation*, 28 March 1981, reprinted in Marvin E. Gettleman and others, eds., *El Salvador: Central America in the New Cold War* [New York: Grove Press, 1981], p. 243; for further refutation, see Warner Poelchau, ed., *White Paper, Whitewash* [New York: Deep Cover Books, 1981], pp. 75–101; Piero Gleijeses, 'Tilting at Windmills: Reagan in Central America,' *Occasional Papers in International Affairs* (Washington, D.C.: The Johns Hopkins Foreign Policy Institute, April 1982); Juan de Onis, 'State Dept. Says Salvador Rebels Get Fewer Arms,' *New*

*York Times*, 24 February 1981; Raymond Bonner, *Weakness And Deceit: US Policy and El Salvador* (New York: Times Books, 1984), p. 267.

5. Lawrence Pezzullo, Baltimore, Maryland, letter to author, 18 September 1990; Bob Woodward, *Veil: The Secret Wars of the CIA, 1981–1987* (New York: Pocket Books, 1987), pp. 114–115; Ronald Reagan, 'Parallel Between El Salvador and Vietnam,' 24 February 1981, document 671 in *American Foreign Policy Current Documents 1981* (Washington, D.C.: Department of State, 1984), p. 1237, [hereafter cited as *Current Documents 1981*]; Judgement of The International Court Of Justice, *Nicaragua v. The United States of America* (The Hague: International Court Of Justice, 27 June 1986), p. 63, paragraph 134, p. 75, paragraph 160, [Hereafter cited as *International Court of Justice*].

6. Bonner, *Weakness And Deceit*, pp. 236, 264; Richard Whittle, 'Reagan Weighs Military Aid To Counter Soviet, Cuban 'Interference' In El Salvador,' *Congressional Quarterly Weekly Report* 39, no. 9 (28 February 1981), p. 388; William M. LeoGrande, *Central America and the Polls: A study of US public opinion polls on US foreign policy toward El Salvador and Nicaragua under the Reagan administration*, (Washington, D.C.: Washington Office on Latin America, March 1987), pp. 4, 20; Alexander Haig, 'Interview on the 'MacNeil/Lehrer Report,' *Department of State Bulletin* 81, no. 2050 (May 1981): p. 1; Alexander Haig, 'Interviews at Breakfast Meetings,' *Department of State Bulletin* 81, no. 2050 (May 1981): p. 11; Lawrence Pezzullo, Baltimore, Maryland, letter to author, 18 September 1990; Alexander M. Haig, *Caveat*, p. 131; Wayne Smith, *The Closest of Enemies*, (New York: W. W. Norton, 1987), p. 244.

7. Robert C. McFarlane, memorandum to The Secretary [of State], 'Covert Action Proposal for Central America,' 27 February 1981, in US House of Representatives Select Committee to Investigate Covert Arms Transactions with Iran and US Senate Select Committee On Secret Military assistance to Iran And the Nicaraguan Opposition, *Report of the Congressional Committees Investigating the Iran–Contra Affair*, Appendix A: Volume 1, Source Documents, 100th Cong., lst sess., 13 November 1987 (Washington, D.C.: Government Printing Office, 1988), pp. 4–5, [Hereafter cited as *Iran–Contra Affair*, Appendix A: Volume 1, Source Documents]; Ronald Reagan, presidential finding on Central America, 9 March 1981, in US House of Representatives Select Committee to Investigate Covert Arms Transactions with Iran and U.S. Senate Select Committee On Secret Military assistance to Iran And the Nicaraguan Opposition, *Report of the Congressional Committees Investigating the Iran–Contra Affair*, Appendix A: Volume 2, Source Documents, 100th Cong., lst sess., 13 November 1987 (Washington, D.C.: Government Printing Office, 1988), p. 1156, [Hereafter cited as *Iran–Contra Affair*, Appendix A: Volume 2, Source Documents].

8. Department Statement, 'US Suspends Economic Aid to Nicaragua,' *Department of State Bulletin* 81, no. 2050 (May 1981), p. 71; Special to the New York Times, 'US Halts Economic Aid to Nicaragua,' *New York Times*, 2 April 1981; Lawrence Pezzullo, Baltimore, Maryland, letter to author, 18 September 1990; Official Communiqué Nicaraguan Government, 2 April 1981, [unofficial translation] in *Documents on US Tolerance of Terrorist Activities Within the United States Against Nicaragua*, p. 16, from the Central

American Historical Institute, Georgetown University, Washington, D.C.; US Congress, Senate, Committee on Foreign Relations, *The Situation in El Salvador: Hearing before the Committee on Foreign Relations*, 97th Cong., lst sess., 18 March and 9 April 1981, p. 178.

9. Lawrence Pezzullo, Baltimore, Maryland, letter to author, 18 September 1990.

10. Eddie Adams, 'How Latin Guerillas Train on Our Soil,' *Parade*, 15 March 1981; Jo Thomas, 'Nicaraguans Train in Florida as Guerillas,' *New York Times*, 17 March 1981; Miguel D'Escoto letter to Alexander Haig, 20 March 1981 and Haig letter to D'Escoto, undated, both contained in '*Documents on US Tolerance* . . . pp. 14–15. It is not clear whether these documents are drafts of letters or letters actually sent; Representative Gerry E. Studds to Acting Assistant Secretary of State for Inter-American Affairs John A. Bushnell, in *Foreign Assistance Legislation For Fiscal Year 1982 (Part 7), Hearings and Markup before the Subcommittee on Inter-American Affairs of the Committee on Foreign Affairs*, 97th Cong., lst sess., 23, 26, 30 March and 8 April 1981, p. 267; Letter from the Nicaraguan Democratic Union to President-elect Reagan quoted in, Alan Riding, 'Rightist Exiles Plan Invasion of Nicaragua,' *New York Times*, 2 April 1981; Richard V. Allen, Assistant to the President-elect for National Security Affairs letter to Edmundo Chamorro R., Member of the National Council of the Nicaraguan Democratic Union, 6 January 1981, in *Documents on US Tolerance* . . . p. 13.

11. US Congress, House, Committee on Foreign Affairs, *Central America, 1981: Report to the Committee on Foreign Affairs*, 97th Cong., lst sess., March 1981, p. 7; Alan Riding, 'Rightist Exiles Plan Invasion of Nicaragua,' *New York Times*, 2 April 1981; Department of State Information Memorandum from Thomas Enders to the deputy secretary, 6 May 1981, quoted in Peter Kornbluh, *Nicaragua*, p. 9; Central American Historical Institute (CAHI), *US–Nicaraguan Relations: Chronology of Policy and Impact, January 1981–January 1984* (Washington, D.C.: CAHI, 1984), p. 2.

12. Gerald F. Seib, 'The Nicaraguan Balancing Act,' *Wall Street Journal*, 13 July 1981; Nick Kotz and Morton Kondracke, 'How to Avoid Another Cuba,' *The New Republic* 184, no. 25 (20 June 1981), p. 22.

13. Juan M. Vasquez, 'Nicaraguans Seek Improved US Relations,' *Los Angeles Times*, 26 July 1981; Roy Gutman, *Banana Diplomacy: The Making Of American Policy In Nicaragua 1981–1987*, (New York: Simon and Schuster, 1988), p. 66.

14. Gutman, *Banana Diplomacy*, pp. 69, 67; *International Court of Justice*, p. 65, paragraph 136.

15. Constantine C. Menges, *Inside The National Security Council: The True Story Of The Making And Unmaking Of Reagan's Foreign Policy* (New York: Simon and Schuster, 1988), pp. 104–105. Pezzullo confirmed that internal matters were not discussed during the August 1981 talks. (Lawrence Pezzullo, Baltimore, Maryland, letter to author, 18 September 1990); Don Oberdorfer, 'US, in Secret Dialogue, Sought Rapprochement With Nicaragua,' *Washington Post*, 10 December 1981; Gutman, *Banana Diplomacy*, p. 70; Woodward, *Veil*, p. 176; Alan Riding, 'US Official, in Nicaragua, Ties Aid to Policy Shifts,' *New York Times*, 13 August 1981; Dial Torgerson, 'US Talks Leave Nicaraguans Hopeful,' *Los Angeles Times*, 13 August 1981;

Lawrence Pezzullo, Baltimore, Maryland, letter to author, 18 September 1990.

16. Alan Riding, 'Nicaragua Hopes Next US Envoy Equals the Last,' *New York Times*, 24 August 1981; Lawrence Pezzullo, Baltimore, Maryland, letter to author, 18 September 1990; Letter from the Permanent Representatives of France and Mexico to the President of the United Nations, Security Council, document S/14659, 28 August 1981, document 2.1, in Bagley, *Contadora Documents*, pp. 152–153; 'Caracas Declaration' in Robert S. Leiken and Barry Rubin, eds., *Central American Crisis Reader*, (New York: Summit Books, 1987), pp. 629–630; Christopher Dickey, 'Managua's Remaining Pluralists Worried by Tough US Stance,' *Washington Post*, 24 August 1981; Thomas Enders letter to Daniel Ortega, of 31 August 1981, document 1.8, in Bagley, *Contadora Documents*, p. 23; Thomas Enders letter to Daniel Ortega, of 8 September 1981, document 1.9, in Bagley, *Contadora Documents*, p. 25; Gutman, *Banana Diplomacy*, p. 73; Roy Gutman, 'America's Diplomatic Charade,' *Foreign Policy*, no. 56 (Fall 1984): p. 7.

17. Letter and Draft Proposal from Thomas Enders to Daniel Ortega, of 16 September 1981, document 1.10, in Bagley, *Contadora Documents*, pp. 25–27; Letter from Miguel D'Escoto to Alexander Haig, of 19 September 1981, document 1.11, in Bagley, *Contadora Documents*, pp. 27–28; Letter from Miguel D'Escoto to the President of the Security Council, of 25 September 1981, United Nations, Security Council, document S/14710, 26 September 1981, 81–24456 2926f (E), microfiche.

18. Thomas Enders letter to Miguel D'Escoto, of 28 September 1981, document 1.12, in Bagley, *Contadora Documents*, pp. 28–29; Gutman, *Banana Diplomacy*, p. 74; Gutman, 'America's Diplomatic Charade,' *Foreign Policy*, no. 56 (Fall 1984): p. 8.

19. Daniel Ortega, speech to the United Nations General Assembly, 7 October 1981, in Tomás Borge and others, *Sandinistas Speak*, pp. 141–154; United States Deputy Representative to the United Nations, Kenneth Adelman, Statement in the General Assembly, in Right of Reply to Nicaragua, 8 October 1981, United States Mission to the United Nations, Press Release USUN 63(81), 8 October 1981; Nicaraguan Ministry of Foreign Affairs, September 1982, document 1.19, in Bagley, *Contadora Documents*, p. 49.

20. Ronald Reagan, 'Possibility of US Military Intervention in the Caribbean and in El Salvador,' 16 November 1981, document 706, *Current Documents 1981*, p. 1352; James McCartney, 'Haig says US might intervene in Nicaragua,' *Miami Herald*, 13 November 1981.

21. Nina M. Serafino, *Contra Aid, FY82–FY88: Summary And Chronology Of Major Congressional Action On Key Legislation Concerning US Aid To The Anti-Sandinista Guerillas*, Congressional Research Service (CRS), Report for Congress 88–563 F (Washington, D.C.: The Library of Congress, 18 August 1981), p. 3, citing the *Miami Herald*, 5 June 1983; Sklar, *Washington's War on Nicaragua*, p. 100; Woodward, *Veil*, pp. 188, 185.

22. Ronald Reagan, presidential finding on Central America, 1 December 1981, *Iran–Contra Affair*, Appendix A: Volume 2, Source Documents, p. 1157; US Senate Select Committee On Secret Military Assistance to Iran And the Nicaraguan Opposition and US House of Representatives Select Committee to Investigate Covert Arms Transactions with Iran, *Report of the*

*Congressional Committees Investigating the Iran–Contra Affair* (Washington, D.C.: US Government Printing Office, 1987), p. 379, [Hereafter cited as *The Iran–Contra Report*]. Section 662 Of The Foreign Assistance Act Of 1961 (22 U.S.C. 2422), The Hughes Ryan amendment states that:

> No funds appropriated under the authority of this or any other Act may be expended by or on behalf of the Central Intelligence Agency for operations in foreign countries, other than activities intended solely for obtaining necessary intelligence, unless and until the President finds that each such operation is important to the national security of the United States. Each such operation shall be considered a significant anticipated intelligence activity for the purpose of section 501 of the National Security Act of 1947.

Permanent Select Committee on Intelligence of the House of Representatives, *Compilation of Intelligence Laws and Related Laws and Executive Orders of Interest to the National Intelligence Community,* 100th Cong., lst sess., March 1987, (Washington, D.C.: US Government Printing Office, 1987), p. 259; Woodward, *Veil*, p. 203; Piero Gleijeses, 'Tilting at Windmills: Reagan in Central America,' *Occasional Papers in International Affairs* (Washington, D.C.: The Johns Hopkins Foreign Policy Institute, April 1982), p. 34, note 3; Theodore Draper, *A Very Thin Line: The Iran–Contra Affairs* (New York: Hill and Wang, 1991), p. 16.

23. Robert McFarlane cited in Frank McNeil, *War and Peace in Central America*, (New York: Charles Scribner's Sons, 1988), p. 145.
24. Don Oberdorfer, 'US, in Secret Dialogue, Sought Rapprochement With Nicaragua,' *Washington Post*, 10 December 1981; Thomas O. Enders, 'Strategic Situation in Central America and the Caribbean,' Statement before the Subcommittee on Western Hemisphere Affairs of the Senate Foreign Relations Committee, 14 December 1981, as *Current Policy*, no. 352 (14 December 1981): pp. 2–3; on the strategy of concessions see, William Goodfellow and James Morrell, 'From Contadora to Esquipulas to Sapoá and Beyond,' in Thomas W. Walker, ed. *Revolution and Counterrevolution in Nicaragua* (Boulder: Westview Press, 1991), pp. 369–393.
25. Barry Rubin, *Secrets of State: The State Department and The Struggle Over US Foreign Policy* (New York: Oxford University Press, 1985, 1987), p. 205; Statement by the Principal Deputy Press Secretary on the Resignation of Richard V. Allen and the Designation of William P. Clark for the Position, 4 January 1982, exhibit JMP–105, in Testimony of John M. Poindexter, *Iran–Contra Investigation*, Joint Hearings before the House Select Committee To Investigate Covert Arms Transactions With Iran and the Senate Select Committee On Secret Military Assistance to Iran and The Nicaraguan Opposition, 100th Cong., lst sess., 100–8, 15–17, 20–21 July 1987, p. 893, [Hereafter, *Testimony, Iran–Contra Committees*]; Statement on the Issuance of a Presidential Directive, 12 January 1982, 'National Security Council Structure,' exhibit JMF–104, Testimony of John M. Poindexter, *Testimony, Iran–Contra Committees*, 100–8, pp. 888–889.
26. Miguel D'Escoto to Robert MacNeil on the *MacNeil–Lehrer Report*, 4 February 1982, WNET/Thirteen, Transcript # 1659, pp. 1–4. MacNeil makes the second charge that the United States does not want to 'discover the lack

of proof,' to which D'Escoto replies 'exactly.' On the transfer of arms, D'Escoto's stated in his affidavit: 'Such allegations are false, and constitute nothing more than a pretext for the US to continue its unlawful military and paramilitary activities against Nicaragua intended to overthrow my government.' He asserts that since the revolution the 'policy and practice has been to prevent our national territory from being used as a conduit for arms or other military supplies intended for other governments or rebel groups.' (Miguel D'Escoto Brockmann, affidavit, [21 April 1984, Ministerio Del Exterior, Managua, Nicaragua], p. 1). In Miguel D'Escoto's memorial to the International Court of Justice he explained: 'As a small underdeveloped country with extremely limited resources, and with no modern or sophisticated detection equipment, it is not easy for us to seal off our borders to all unwanted and illegal traffic.' The Court remarked in passing that:

> if this evidence really existed, the United States could be expected to have taken advantage of it in order to forestall or disrupt the traffic observed; it could presumably for example arrange for the deployment of a strong patrol force in El Salvador and Honduras, along the frontiers of these states with Nicaragua. It is difficult to accept that it should have continued to carry out military and paramilitary activities against Nicaragua if their only purpose was, as alleged, to serve as a riposte in the exercise of the right of collective self-defense. If, on the other hand, this evidence does not exist, that, as the Court has pointed out, implies that the arms traffic is so insignificant and casual that it escapes detection even by the sophisticated techniques employed for the purpose, and that, *a fortiori*, it could also have been carried on unbeknown to the Government of Nicaragua, as that Government claims. These two conclusions mutually support each other.

(*International Court of Justice*, pp. 70–74, paragraphs 147, 152, 155, 156).

27. Affidavit Of Edgar Chamorro, (City of Washington, District of Columbia, 5 September 1985), p. 6.
28. National Security Council document, 'US Policy in Central America and Cuba through F.Y. '84, Summary Paper,' as 'National Security Council Document on Policy in Central America and Cuba,' *New York Times*, 7 April 1983. (Hereafter cited as NSC, Summary Paper).
29. Comite Organizativo Permanente De Partidos Politicos De America Latina (COPPPAL), 'Declaration From Managua,' 20 February 1982, document 6.1, in Bagley, *Contadora Documents*, pp. 254–255.
30. Declaration by Representatives of Costa Rica, El Salvador, Honduras, Columbia, Venezuela, and the United States, in Tegucigalpa, 29 January 1982, document 667, *American Foreign Policy Current Documents 1982* (Washington, D.C.: Department of State, 1985), pp. 1369–1371, [Hereafter cited as *Current Documents 1982*].
31. The peace proposal is set out in 'Letter dated 24 February 1982 from the Charge D'Affaires A. I. of the Permanent Mission of Nicaragua to the United Nations addressed to the Secretary General,' from Ambassador Alejandro Bendaña, United Nations, Security Council, S/14891, 24 February 1982.

32. López Portillo speech in Managua, 21 February 1982, document 671, *Current Documents 1982*, pp. 1379–1381; and document 1.29, in Bagley, *Contadora Documents*, pp. 100–102; Sandinista promise to the OAS cited in *International Court of Justice*, p. 122, paragraph 261; the Sandinista political platform as reissued 12 July 1979, by the provisional Sandinista government in exile, as appendix I, to Richard Araujo, 'The Nicaraguan Connection: A Threat to Central America,' *Backgrounder*, no. 168, The Heritage Foundation, 24 February 1982; Ronald Reagan speech to the OAS, 24 February 1982, cited in Gutman, *Banana Diplomacy*, p. 94.
33. Congressional letter cited in Sklar, *Washington's War On Nicaragua*, p. 109; Fidel Castro letter to José López Portillo, 24 February 1982, document 1.30, in Bagley, *Contadora Documents*, 102; Gutman, 'America's Diplomatic Charade,' *Foreign Policy*, p. 12; Department of State Press Briefing, 8 April 1982, 'US Proposals to Nicaragua,' document 686, *Current Documents 1982*, pp. 1437–38; US Congress, House, Committee on Appropriations, Subcommittee on Foreign Operations, *Foreign Assistance and Related Programs Appropriations for 1983*, Hearing before the Committee on Appropriations, Subcommittee on Foreign Operations, 97th Cong., 2nd sess., 1982, 115, cited in Cynthia Arnson, *Crossroads: Congress, The Reagan Administration, and Central America* (New York: Pantheon, 1989), pp. 100–101; Edward Boland quoted in Staff Report, Subcommittee on Oversight and Evaluation, Permanent Select Committee on Intelligence, *US Intelligence Performance on Central America: Achievements and Selected Instances of Concern*, 97th Cong., 2nd sess., 22 September 1982, p. 3; Press Briefing by Secretary of State Haig, New York, 6 March 1982, 'US–Mexican Discussions on the Situation in Central America,' document 675, *Current Documents 1982*, p. 1401.
34. NSC Summary Paper, op. cit.; Kornbluh, *Nicaragua*, p. 55; Smith, *The Closest of Enemies*, p. 255.
35. Department of State Press Briefing, 8 April 1982, 'US Proposals to Nicaragua,' document 686, *Current Documents 1982*, p. 1438.
36. Casey interview, document 676, *Current Documents 1982*, p. 1404; transcript of the statements on the military buildup in Nicaragua given at the Department of State by Bobby R. Inman, Deputy Director of Central Intelligence, and John T. Hughes, Deputy Director for Intelligence and External Affairs for the Defense Intelligence Agency, as 'Transcript of Statements at State Dept. on the Military Buildup in Nicaragua,' *New York Times*, 10 March 1982; Bob Woodward, claims that Casey 'hoped for a Cuban Missile Crisis-scale blast of publicity' (Woodward, *Veil*, p. 208); Kenneth E. Sharpe, 'Serious Diplomacy On Nicaragua Needed,' *New York Times*, 17 March 1982.
37. Democratic Policy Committee, *Foreign Aid to Central America FY 1981–1987*, Special Report, (Washington, D.C.: Senate Democratic Policy Committee, 12 February 1987), pp. 6, 81, 15–19; Marc Edelman, 'Lifelines: Nicaragua and the Socialist Countries,' *NACLA: Report on the Americas* 19, no. 3 (May/June 1985), p. 50; International Institute for Strategic Studies (IISS), *The Military Balance 1982–1983* (London: IISS, 1982), pp. 123, 104–6.

38. In more detail, Buchanan insinuated that the briefing had distorted the actual situation in Central America. During his testimony he stated, 'with your permission I wish to violate the rules of military briefers. I bought with me a detailed map of the region. This is the sort of map men engaged in mortal combat use – not the sort used in budget battles.' He pointed out that the Soviet T–55 tank could only realistically use one route to attack Honduras: the Pan American highway. The route is 290 miles long, giving ample time for US satellites or Honduran reconnaissance planes to detect the movements. In one specific thirty mile stretch the tanks would have to climb from 500 to 5000 feet, yet the maximum gradient for the T–55 tank is thirty degrees. 'Under optimum conditions,' he surmises 'including level terrain, it would take ten hours for the tanks to travel from Managua to Tegucigalpa . . . they probably would never make it.' On the tanks he concluded that their real usefulness lies in internal 'crowd control in their major cities.' (Prepared statement of Lt. Col. John H. Buchanan, USMC (retired) before the Subcommittee on Inter-American Affairs, Committee on Foreign Affairs, US House of Representatives on US Aid to Honduras, [Washington, D.C., 21 September 1982], reprinted as 'Honduras/Nicaragua – War Without Winners,' in 'Central America: Guns Of December,' *NACLA: Report on the Americas* 26, no. 5 (September/October 1982): pp. 3–5, 9; US Congress. House. Permanent Select Committee on Intelligence, Subcommittee on Oversight and Evaluation, *US Intelligence Performance On Central America: Achievements and Selected Instances of Concern: Staff Report*, 97th Cong., 2nd sess., 22 September 1982, p. 21; Daniel Ortega Saavedra to the United Nations Security Council, 25 March 1982, Republic of Nicaragua, Permanent Mission to the United Nations, Press Release, 25 March 1982, pp. 7, 11.
39. Smith, *The Closest of Enemies*, pp. 254, 256; NSC Summary Paper, op. cit.; Vladimir I. Stanchenko, 'United States–USSR–Latin America: Soviet Role in Central America,' Paper delivered at the Jean Donovan Conference, University College, Cork, 26–27 January, 1990, p. 10; Nicola Miller, *Soviet Relations With Latin America 1959–1987*, (Cambridge University Press, 1989), p. 198.
40. Patrick E. Tyler and Bob Woodward, 'US Plans Covert Operations To Disrupt Nicaraguan Economy,' *Washington Post*, 10 March 1982; Gutman, *Banana Diplomacy*, p. 104; Defense Intelligence Agency, *Weekly Intelligence Summary*, 16 July 1982, cited in Sklar, *Washington's War on Nicaragua*, pp. 116–7; Governing Junta of National Reconstruction of the Republic of Nicaragua, *Annex*, United Nations, Security Council, S/14909, 15 March 1982, pp. 1–2; NSC Summary Paper, op. cit.
41. Gutman, 'America's Diplomatic Charade,' *Foreign Policy*, pp. 12–13; Gutman, *Banana Diplomacy*, pp. 95–6; Department of State Press Briefing, 8 April 1982, 'US Proposals to Nicaragua,' document 686, *Current Documents 1982*, p. 1438; Response from Nicaragua to the US proposal of 10 April 1982, issued 7 May 1982, document 1.15 in Bagley, *Contadora Documents*, p. 38.
42. Carl G. Jacobsen, *Soviet Attitudes Towards, Aid to, and Contacts With Central American Revolutionaries*, (Washington, D.C.: for the Department of State, June 1984), p. 3; Lord Chitnis, *The Election in El Salvador in March 1982*, Report for the Parliamentary Human Rights Group, (London: House of

Commons, 1982), p. 18; Thomas O. Enders, 'Building the Peace in Central America,' speech 20 August 1982, *Current Policy*, no. 414, (Washington, D.C.: US Department of State, 20 August 1982), p. 2.

Cynthia Arnson has pointed out that the language of the Administration's certification to Congress for the release of aid to El Salvador was changed shortly after Reagan assumed office. The certification originally stated that the Salvadoran government 'has achieved' control over the security forces. Under Reagan the language read, 'is achieving' control. Thus she points out, the Administration could focus on *process* rather than *accomplishment* [emphasis in original] (Arnson, *Crossroads*, p. 85, footnote). In Enders' speech at the Commonwealth club he explains:

> Why is political violence *declining* in El Salvador? It has partly been a matter of the consolidation of the new *reforming* government, which has *gradually* contained guerilla violence and *increased* its authority over security forces, *gradually creating* a climate in which violence is *less and less* expedient, even if it is *still not adequately deterred and controlled and punished* [emphasis added].

(Thomas O. Enders, 'Building the Peace in Central America,' speech before the Commonwealth Club, San Francisco, California, *Current Policy*, no. 414, [Washington, D.C.: US Department of State, 20 August 1982], p. 2). While the number of deaths did decline in this period, there is no evidence that violence had become less expedient for the security forces. It was 1990 before a high ranking officer was arrested in El Salvador for human rights abuse.

43. Sergio Ramirez, 'US Working People Can Stop Intervention in Central America,' 4 March 1982, Sandinista Leaders, *Nicaragua: The Sandinista People's Revolution*, (New York: Pathfinder Press, 1985), p. 5; Menges, *Inside the National Security Council*, p. 105.

44. Smith, *Closest of Enemies*, p. 257; Secretary of State Haig, press briefing U.N. Plaza Hotel, New York, 6 March 1982, 'US–Mexican Discussions on the Situation in Central America,' document 675, *Current Documents 1982*, p. 1400; Haig at the U.N. Plaza Hotel, New York, 15 March 1982, 'US Policy in Central America,' document 680, *Current Documents 1982*, pp. 1427, 1429; Alan Riding, 'Diplomats Say Havana Wants Wide US Talks,' *New York Times*, 26 March 1982; Thomas O. Enders and Walter J. Stoessel, 'Excerpts From Statements on Cuba and Caribbean By Enders and Stoessel,' *New York Times*, 26 March 1982.
45. Daniel Ortega address to the United Nations Security Council, 25 March 1982, Press Release, Republic of Nicaragua, Permanent Mission to the United Nations, 25 March 1982, pp. 5–7, 11.
46. NSC Summary Paper, op. cit.
47. Barbara Crossette, 'Nicaragua Accepts US Plan For Talks on Reconciliation,' *New York Times*, 15 April 1982; John M. Goshko, 'US Stalling On Negotiations With Nicaragua,' *Washington Post*, 17 April 1982; United Press International, 'Report of "Stall" Denied by US,' *Washington Post*, 18 April 1982; Don Oberdorfer, 'Managua, in Turnabout, Seeks US Talks,' *Washington Post*, 25 April 1982; Tomas Borge, speech 1 May 1982, Managua, in Leiken and Rubin (eds.), *The Central American Crisis Reader*, p. 234;

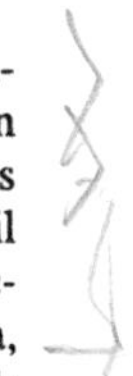

Special, 'US Is Said to Rule Out a Plan for Sandinist Talks,' *New York Times*, 1 May 1982; United States Department of State, *Revolution Beyond Our Borders: Sandinista Intervention in Central America*, Special Report, no. 132 (Washington, D.C.: Department of State, September 1985), p. 23.

48. Response from Nicaragua to the US proposal of 10 April 1982, issued 7 May 1982, document 1.15, in Bagley, *Contadora Documents*, pp. 34–39.
49. Alan Riding, 'Mexicans Pessimistic on Talks Between US and Caribbean Leftists,' *New York Times*, 10 May 1982.
50. Eden Pastora, 'The Watchful Eye,' in Leiken and Rubin, eds., *The Central American Crisis Reader*, pp. 252–54; Secret National Security Council Memorandum for William P. Clark from Donald Gregg, 'Proposed Covert Action Finding on Nicaragua,' Intelligence NSC/ICS 400178, 12 July 1982, *Iran–Contra Affair*, Appendix A: Vol. 1, Source Documents, 100th Cong., lst sess., 13 November 1987, pp. 1018–1022; *Iran–Contra Report*, p. 32; Haig, *Caveat*, pp. 306–7, 312–15.

## 2 Contadora: Latin America Repudiates Washington 1983

1. Mexican President José López Portillo and Venezuelan President Luis Herrera Campins' letter to President Reagan, 7 September 1982, document 2.2, in Bagley, *Contadora Documents*, pp. 153–155. The letter quotes in full a section from Enders' speech to the Commonwealth Club:

   > The Obstacles to peace in Central America stand more clearly exposed with every new crisis. Central America has deep political divisions, among nations as well as within them. It suffers severe economic troubles, with the world recession devastating economies already weakened by high oil prices and internal inefficiencies. And it is fragmented by social tensions, with population growth straining public services and popular aspirations outrunning the historically possible.

   Letter from President Reagan to Mexican President López Portillo, undated, as 'Bringing Peace to Central America,' document 696, *American Foreign Policy Current Documents 1982*, pp. 1464–1465; McNeil, *War and Peace in Central America*, p. 168. Frank McNeil, then the US ambassador to Costa Rica, stated that he latter learned that Venezuela would have attended, over Mexican objections, if the US delegation had been headed by the Secretary of State, 'opening up endless speculative possibilities' (McNeil, *War and Peace in Central America*, p. 168).
2. Memorandum from ARA, Ambassador Motley to all ARA Officers on 'ARA Public Diplomacy Effort,' 27 September 1982, United States Department of State, as document 00062, fiche 11, *The Iran–Contra Affair*, Washington, D.C.: National Security Archive, 1990 [hereafter cited as National Security Archive 1990]; Points made by Nicaragua in response to the López Portillo–Herrera Campins initiative, presented by The Ministry of Foreign Affairs, Managua, 24 September 1982, as document 1.20, in Bagley, *Contadora Documents*, pp. 54–56.
3. Foreign Ministers, Forum for Peace, 'Declaration on Democracy in Central America,' 4 October 1982, as document 699, *Current Documents 1982*, pp. 1470–1473.

4. Letter from 106 Congressmen, sponsored by David E. Bonior, Jim Leach, Michael D. Barnes, Millicent Fenwick, to Ronald Reagan, and joint news release, 6 October 1982, copy with author; CAHI, *Chronology*, p. 10; Don Bohning, 'War of minds underlies US peace effort,' *Miami Herald*, 24 October 1982.
5. John Brecher, John Walcott, David Martin, & Beth Nissen, 'A Secret War For Nicaragua,' *Newsweek*, (International edition), 8 November 1982, pp. 42, 46–47; Affidavit of Edgar Chamorro, City of Washington, District of Columbia, 5 September 1985, pp. 8–10. Herein after cited as *Chamorro Affidavit*; Harkin Amendment in Congressional Record, 97th Cong., 2nd sess., 8 December 1982, p. H9148, as footnote 24 to document 705, *Current Documents 1982*, p. 1495; Arnson, *Crossroads*, p. 106; *Iran–Contra Report*, pp. 395–396; the amendment was part of HJ Res. 631 (PL 97–377), Nina Serafino, *Contra Aid FY82–FY88*, Congressional Research Service, (Washington, D.C.: US Congress, 18 August 1988).
6. *Iran–Contra Report*, p. 396.
7. *Chamorro Affidavit*, p. 10; Bernard Weinraub, 'Congress Renews Curbs On Actions Against Nicaragua,' *New York Times*, 23 December 1982.
8. The Foreign Minister involved were for Panama: Mr. Juan José Amada III; Colombia: Mr. Rodrigo Lloreda Caicedo; Mexico: Mr. Bernardo Sepúlveda Amor; Venezuela: Mr. José Alberto Zambrano Velasco. Their Information Bulletin, issued Isla Contadora, 9 January 1983, United Nations, General Assembly, A/38/68, 12 January 1983, pp. 2–3; US Department of State, *'Revolution Beyond Our Borders' Sandinista Intervention in Central America*, Special Report no. 132 (Washington, D.C.: Department of State, September 1985), p. 26; Daniel Ortega, Opening Address, as appendix I, United Nations General Assembly and Security Council, A/38/106–S/15628, 1 March 1983, pp. 24–25; Alan Riding, 'Sandinists Accuse US Of Terrorism,' *New York Times*, 13 January 1983; President Reagan signed on 14 January 1983, a National Security Decision Directive (NSDD) 77. The document titled 'Management Of Public Diplomacy Relative To National Security,' included among its activities:

   > aid, training and organizational support for foreign governments and private groups to encourage the growth of democratic political institutions and practices. This will require close collaboration with other foreign policy efforts – diplomatic, economic, military – as well as a close relationship with those sectors of the American society – labor, business, universities, philanthropy, political parties, press – that are or could be more engaged in parallel efforts overseas. This group will undertake to build up the US government capability to promote democracy, as annunciated in the President's speech in London on June 1982. Furthermore, this committee will initiate plans, programs and strategies designed to counter totalitarian ideologies and aggressive political action moves undertaken by the Soviet Union or Soviet surrogates.

   (National Security Decision Directive 77, 'Management Of Public Diplomacy Relative To National Security,' 14 January 1983, document 00068, fiche 11, [The National Security Archive 1990]; Kornbluh, *Nicaragua*, p. 160;

Peter Kornbluh, 'Reagan's Propaganda Ministry,' *Propaganda Review*, no. 2, [Summer 1988], p. 25).

9. Nicaraguan Democratic Force Peace Initiative, 13 January 1983, appendix C, in Edgar Chamorro, *Packaging The Contras: A Case of CIA Disinformation*, Monograph Series Number 2 (New York: Institute for Media Analysis, Inc., 1987), pp. 77, 15–16; *Chamorro Affidavit*, p. 10.
10. US Congress, Senate, Committee on Foreign Relations, Subcommittee on Western Hemisphere Affairs, *Security and Development Assistance: Hearing before the Committee on Foreign Relations, Subcommittee on Western Hemisphere Affairs*, 98th Cong., lst sess., 14 March 1983, 643, pp. 646–647; George Shultz, 'Strengthening Democracy in Central America,' *Current Policy*, no. 468, 16 March 1983.
11. US Congress, *Security and Development Assistance*, pp. 656–658, 661–662, 670–671; Jeane Kirkpatrick, US Representative at the United Nations, before the UN Security Council, 'Somocismo and Sandinismo Turn Out Not To Be Unlike Each Other,' 23 March 1983, document 615, *American Foreign Policy Current Documents 1983*, (Washington, D.C.: Department of State, 1985), pp. 1291–1296.
12. Jeane Kirkpatrick, to the UN Security Council, 'The United States Government Has No Aggressive Designs Against the Government of Nicaragua,' 25 March 1983, document 616, *Current Documents 1983*, p. 1298; Alfonso Chardy, 'Diplomatic, military options prepared for Managua crisis,' *Miami Herald*, 20 April 1983.
13. President Reagan, 'Central America: Defending Our Vital Interests,' address before a joint session of Congress, 27 April 1983, *Department of State Bulletin* 83, no. 2075 (June 1983), pp. 1–5.
14. Senator Christopher J. Dodd, 'Text of Democratic Response To Reagan Speech to Congress,' 27 April 1983, *Congressional Quarterly Weekly Report* 41, no. 17 (30 April 1983), pp. 856–857.
15. Alan Riding, 'Sandinists, Worried About Rebels, Accuse Honduran Troops of Raid,' *New York Times*, 26 March 1983; Stephen Kinzer, 'Honduras Denies Sandinist Charges,' *New York Times*, 26 March 1983; The *Washington Post* quoted a contra leader: 'The people . . . are not fighting to stop the weapons. We are fighting to liberate Nicaragua' cited *Iran–Contra Report*, p. 52 note 15; Robert F. Turner, memorandum for President's Intelligence Oversight Board, 'Preliminary Analysis of Legal Objections to Certain alleged CIA Covert Activities in Central America,' 6 April 1983, *Iran–Contra Affair*, appendix A, vol. 2, source documents, 100th Cong., lst sess., 13 November 1987, pp. 1126, 1141–1146. A month later the Department of Defense was not completely satisfied with the process of assessing the legality of the covert operations, or their participation in them. A memorandum to the Secretary of Defense from John O. Marsh, stated: 'with increasing frequency, due largely to the Presidential Finding relating to Central America, the CIA has been requesting DOD support which should be considered significant and raises some difficult policy and legal questions.' Marsh recommended that the legal issues should be dealt with in an ongoing systematic manner instead of on an *ad hoc* basis. The Boland amendment, he noted, is also applicable to the Department of Defense. Marsh stated:

> Support requests must be reviewed to determine whether they are within the legal parameters of the Finding which the request seeks to implement. For example, I was concerned that the support requested pursuant to project [deleted] . . . was beyond the scope and intent of the underlying Finding which related to [deleted]. Thus, while I executed the approval memorandum, I conditioned my approval upon an *a priori* notification to Congress of the exact nature of the operation given conflicting mission statements in the transmittal memoranda between the participating agencies. For this, and various other reasons, the Army raised objections to the support request and it was eventually withdrawn by the CIA.

(Memorandum for the Secretary of Defense, from John O. Marsh, Jr., 'Sensitive DOD Support to CIA Special Activities,' 9 May 1983, document 00097, fiche 16, National Security Archive; Margot Hornblower and Patrick E. Tyler, 'House Panel Votes Ban on US Aid In Nicaragua War,' *Washington Post*, 13 April 1983; Martin Tolchin, 'Key House Member Fears US Breaks Law On Nicaragua,' *New York Times*, 14 April 1983; President Reagan news conference, 'We Are Complying With the Law,' document 621, 14 April 1983, *Current Documents 1983*, pp. 1308–1310.

16. John Fenton, 'Congress Directing Attention To Central America Policies,' *Congressional Quarterly Weekly Report* 41, no. 17 (30 April 1983), pp. 819–823; Secretary of State George Shultz letter to Clarence D. Long, 26 April 1983, excerpts printed in *Congressional Quarterly Weekly Report* 41, no. 17 (30 April 1983), p. 823; National Security Council memorandum from Walter Raymond, Jr., to William P. Clark, 'Central American Public Diplomacy,' 18 May 1983, document 00102, fiche 17, The National Security Archive 1990.
17. Alfonso Chardy, 'House Panel assails CIA's Latin role,' *Miami Herald*, 16 May 1983; *New York Times*, quoted in *CAHI Chronology*, 21; Woodward, *Veil*, p. 279.
18. Associated Press, '4 Latin Officials on Peace Tour,' *New York Times*, 13 April 1983; Transcript of a Joint Press Conference by the Secretary of State, Shultz, and the Secretary of the Treasury, Regan, 17 April 1983, as 'The Relationship Between Mexico and the United States,' document 622, *Current Documents 1983*, pp. 1310–1312; Contadora, 'Information Bulletin,' 21 April 1983, United Nations, General Assembly and Security Council, document A/38/164–S/15727, 25 April 1983, fiche 83–10031 0956b (E).
19. Alfonso Chardy, 'Diplomatic, military options prepared for Managua crisis,' *Miami Herald*, 20 April 1983; Statement by Commander Daniel Ortega, Coordinator of the Government of National Reconstruction of Nicaragua, 25 April 1983, Embassy of Nicaragua, Washington, D.C., *Press Release*, no. 13, 26 April 1983; *New York Times*, 21 April 1983, quoted in *CAHI Chronology*, 19; *O Estado de Sao Paulo*, quoted in C. Jacobsen, *Soviet Attitudes Towards, Aid To, And Contacts With Central American Revolutionaries*, (Washington, D.C.: [for] Department of State, June 1984), p. 15, and Jacobsen's remarks, p. 16; $250 million of arms was transferred from the Soviet Union to Nicaragua between 1981 and 1985, $10 million from France, $5 million from Czechoslovakia, and $380 from 'other' sources.

Peru received $140 million more than Nicaragua from the Soviet Union; it did not receive the same rhetorical or officially published attention from Washington. (US Arms Control and Disarmament Agency, *World Military Expenditures and Arms Transfers 1986*, [Washington, D.C.: Government Printing Office, released April 1987], p. 145).

Figures from the International Institute of Strategic Studies in London show that Nicaragua's total forces, during the years 1983–1985, are consistently larger than any of El Salvador, Honduras, and Guatemala, but also consistently less than the combined forces of these countries (International Institute for Strategic Studies, *The Military Balance 1983–1984*, [London: IISS, 1983], pp. 110–112; International Institute for Strategic Studies, *The Military Balance 1984–1985*, [London: IISS, 1984], pp. 121–123; International Institute for Strategic Studies, *The Military Balance 1985–1986*, [London: IISS, 1985], pp. 148–152).

The Washington based Center for Defense Information quotes US government figures for Soviet bloc military deliveries as '$45 million in 1981, $90 million in 1982, $115 million in 1983, and $250 million in 1984, before falling sharply in 1985 to $75 million.' A joint publication by the Department of State and Department of Defense put the figures at significantly higher levels. US military aid to El Salvador and Honduras, the two countries north of Nicaragua, are, apart from 1981, higher than Soviet aid to Nicaragua. (Center for Defense Information, 'Soviet Geopolitical Momentum: Myth or Menace?' *The Defense Monitor* 15, no. 5, [Washington, D.C.: Center for Defense Information, 1986], p. 30; the Department of State and the Department of Defense, *The Sandinista Military Buildup: An Update*, [Washington, D.C.: Department of State Publication 9432, 1987], p. 16; Democratic Policy Committee, *Foreign Aid to Central America FY 1981–1987* [Washington, D.C.: Senate Democratic Policy Committee, 12 February 1987], pp. 79–80).

The figures above do not account for US aid to the contras, and do not account for the amount of influence applied by donor countries. Though the Reagan administration would characterize Nicaragua as a Soviet proxy, and refer to a Soviet-Cuban axis, the Center for Defense Information, directed by retired US military personnel does not note Nicaragua as a country with 'Significant Soviet Influence'. They argue,

> Soviet Influence is limited. Cuban influence is extensive, and while the Soviets reap some benefits from Cuba's influence, the two are not the same. . . . the Soviets have little, if any, input into Nicaraguan decision-making . . .

(Center for Defense Information, 'Soviet Geopolitical Momentum: Myth or Menace?' *The Defense Monitor* 15, no. 5, [Washington, D.C.: Center for Defense Information, 1986], pp. 3, 30). Joachim Krause, assents, that while the Soviet Union has influenced events outside Europe, 'it is far from clear to what extent the Kremlin succeeds in influencing those whom it supports.' (Joachim Krause, 'Soviet Military Aid to the Third World,' *Aussen Politik* 34, 4/1983, p. 402).

20. Woodward, *Veil*, p. 138; Menges, *Inside The National Security Council*, pp. 67, 106.

21. US Congress, *Security and Development Assistance*, p. 647; Menges, *Inside The National Security Council*, pp. 106–107.
22. Gutman, *Banana Diplomacy*, p. 162; US Congress, *Security and Development Assistance*, p. 681; Woodward, *Veil*, pp. 258–260; McNeil, *War and Peace in Central America*, p. 138; Policy makers believed Enders was reassigned not so much because he did not support the administration's policies, but because he had

> antagonized close Reagan advisers, especially national security adviser William P. Clark and United Nations Ambassador Jeane J. Kirkpatrick. Some hard-line conservatives in the administration and on Capitol Hill had been questioning Enders' team loyalty since February . . .

(John Felton, 'Congress Ponders Shake-ups In Central America Policy,' *Congressional Quarterly Weekly Report* 41, no. 22 [4 June 1983], p. 1109).
23. McNeil, *War and Peace in Central America*, p. 171; Barry Rubin, *Secrets of State*, [New York: Oxford University Press, 1985], pp. 225–226).
24. George P. Shultz, memorandum for the President, 'Managing Our Central American Strategy,' 25 May 1983, document 00106, fiche 18, The National Security Archive 1990.
25. Terri Shaw, '3 US Diplomats Expelled From Nicaragua,' *Washington Post*, 7 June 1983; Philip Taubman, '21 Nicaraguans In 6 Consulates Expelled by US,' *New York Times*, 8 June 1983; Philip Taubman, 'Nicaraguan Embassy Is a Study in Turmoil,' *New York Times*, 9 June 1983.
26. Philip Taubman, '21 Nicaraguans In 6 Consulates Expelled by US,' *New York Times* 8 June 1983; Stephen Kinzer, 'US Envoy Meets Sandinists And Opposition in Managua,' *New York Times*, 11 June 1983; Associated Press, 'Nicaragua Terms Stone Trip Propaganda for Aggression,' *Washington Post*, 16 June 1983.
27. John Felton, 'Republicans Against Aid Ban To Nicaraguan Rebel Troops,' *Congressional Quarterly Weekly Report* 41, no. 25 (25 June 1983), p. 1293; William P. Clark for the President memorandum to William J. Casey, 'Increased Funding Level for Nicaraguan/[deleted] Covert Action Program,' 13 July 1983, document 00151, fiche 24, The National Security Archive, 1990; *Iran–Contra Report*, p. 34; Otto J. Reich memorandum to Lawrence Eagleburger, 'Public Diplomacy (Central America),' document 00111, fiche 18, The National Security Archive, 1990; Memorandum for the Joint Chief of Staff, 'DOD Support for DCI,' 25 July 1983, *Iran–Contra Affair*, appendix A, vol. 1, Source Documents, 100th Cong., lst sess., 13 November 1987, pp. 62–63, 55; *Iran Contra Report*, p. 35.
28. Walter Raymond memorandum to William Clark, 'Central American Covert Action,' 8 July 1983, document 00129, fiche 21, The National Security Archive, 1990; Kenneth deGraffenreide, Al Sapia–Bosch, Oliver North, memorandum to William Clark, 'Increased Funding Level for Nicaraguan/[deleted] Covert Action,' 11 July 1983, document 00131, fiche 21, The National Security Archive 1990.
29. Marlise Simons, 'Nicaragua Aides Hoping Regional Effort Will Forestall a Reputed US Plot,' *New York Times*, 17 July 1983; Declaration by Presidents Miguel De La Madrid H., Belisario Betancur, Ricardo De La Espriella, and

Luis Herrera Campins, issued Cancun, Mexico, 17 July 1983, press release, Embassy of Mexico, Washington, D.C., pp. 1–5; Contadora VI and Central American Countries, 18 July 1983 in 'Communication from the Contadora Group on peace efforts in Central America,' Annex II, OEA/Ser.P, AG/CG/doc.6/83, 16 November 1983, to Organization of American States, General Assembly, OEA/Ser.P, AG/doc.1707/83, 17 November 1983, Thirteenth Regular Session, 14 November 1983, Washington, D.C., p. 32; Richard J. Meislin, '4 Latin Presidents Urge Steps To End Conflict in Region,' *New York Times*, 18 July 1983.

30. Commander Daniel Ortega Saavedra, Peace Proposal presented in Leon, 19 July 1983, Embassy of Nicaragua, Washington, D.C., (unofficial translation); US Presidential Statement, 20 July 1983, document 1.5, in Bagley, *Contadora Documents*, pp. 11–12; Assistant Secretary of State for Inter-American Affairs, Motley, address to the Foreign Policy Association, New York, 19 January 1984, 'The Situation in Central America,' document 496, *American Foreign Policy Current Documents 1984* (Washington, D.C.: Department of State, 1986), p. 997; Tomás Borge Martinez, 'The US and Nicaragua,' *Washington Post*, 31 July 1983; Editorial, 'A Peace Scare From Managua,' *New York Times*, 22 July 1983; Charles Mohr, 'Salvador Rebels Reported to Get Little Arms Aid,' *New York Times*, 31 July 1983; Special, 'State Department Comments,' *New York Times*, 31 July 1983; Steven R. Weisman, 'Reagan Denies Aim Is Bigger Presence In Latin Countries,' *New York Times*, 27 July 1983; Barbara Crossette, 'Castro Says US Seeks to Deploy Troops Under Guise of Maneuvers,' *New York Times*, 27 July 1983; William P. Clark for the President memorandum to Cabinet members, 'National Security Decision Directive on Enhanced US Military Activity and Assistance in the Central American region (NSDD–100),' 29 July 1983, document 00164, fiche 26, The National Security Archive 1990; Partial Text of NSDD–100, signed by Ronald Reagan, 'Enhanced US Military Activity And Assistance For The Central American Region,' 28 July 1983, document 00165, fiche 26, The National Security Archive, 1990; President Reagan, address to International Longshoresmen's Association, 'Saving Freedom in Central America,' 18 July 1983, *Current Policy*, no. 499, (Washington, D.C.: Department of State, 1983), p. 3; Steven R. Weisman, 'Reagan Weighs New Latin Panel Under Kissinger,' *New York Times*, 18 July 1983; Francis X. Clines, 'Reagan Names 12 to Latin Panel; House Holds Secret Debate on Aid,' *New York Times*, 20 July 1983; Barbara Crossette, 'What Hopes for the Contadora Process?' *New York Times*, 19 June 1983; Francis X. Clines, 'Reagan Names 12 to Latin Panel; House Holds Secret Debate on Aid,' *New York Times*, 20 July 1983.

31. John Felton, 'House Quashes Covert Nicaragua Aid,' *Congressional Quarterly Weekly Report* 41, no. 30 (30 July 1983), pp. 1535–1537; 'Communication from the Contadora Group on Peace Efforts in Central America,' Annex II, OEA/Ser.P, AG/CG/doc.6/83, 16 November 1983, to Organization of American States, General Assembly, OEA/Ser.P, AG/doc.1707/83, 17 November 1983, Thirteenth Regular Session, 14 November 1983, Washington, D.C., p. 33; Richard J. Meislin, '9 Latin Ministers Fail to Achieve Accord On Region,' *New York Times*, 31 July 1983; Walter LaFeber, *The*

*Panama Canal: The Crisis in Historical Perspective*, (New York: Oxford University Press, 1989), pp. 199–200.

32. Edgardo Paz Barnica, letter to Contadora Foreign Ministers, undated, after the completion of the 5 August 1983 Contadora meeting, document 1.34, in Bagley, *Contadora Documents*, pp. 131–135; Edgar Chamorro cited in *New York Times*, 30 July 1983; FDN, ARDE, MISURA, 'Declaracion Sobre Centroamerica,' quoted in CAHI, *Chronology*, pp. 28–29; Heath J. Meriwether and William R. Long, 'Advisers, but not Government, Negotiable, Nicaragua says,' *Miami Herald*, 13 August 1983; Ambassador Vernon Walters, Meeting of the Outreach Group, 'Myths About Central America,' 24 August 1983, document 635, *Current Documents 1983* pp. 1349–1350; Tom J. Farer, 'Manage The Revolution,' *Foreign Policy*, no. 52 (Fall 1983): p. 111.

33. Associated Press, 'US Official Cancels His Visit To Nicaragua After a Rebuff,' *New York Times*, 4 September 1983; Contadora communiqué issued in Panama, Embajada de Mexico, 9 September 1983; Contadora, 'Document of Objectives,' 9 September 1983, document 3.6, in Bagley, *Contadora Documents*, pp. 176–180; Bruce Michael Bagley and Juan Gabriel Tokatlian, *Contadora: The Limits of Negotiation*, Foreign Policy Institute Case Studies, no. 9 (Washington, D.C.: The Johns Hopkins Foreign Policy Institute, 1987), p. 26; Secretary of State, George P. Shultz, memorandum for the President, 'Central America Dialogue: Status and Prospects,' 6 September 1983, document 00186, fiche 29, The National Security Archive, 1990.

34. *Washington Post* cited in CAHI, *Chronology*, p. 31; *Chamorro Affidavit*, pp. 16–17.

35. Under Secretary for Defense for Policy, Ikle, address to Baltimore Council on Foreign Relations, 'We Seek Victory for the Forces of Democracy,' 12 September 1983, document 637, *Current Documents 1983*, pp. 1357–1360; *Washington Post*, 25 November 1983, quoted by Kornbluh, *Nicaragua*, p. 46. Presidential finding on Nicaragua, signed by Ronald Reagan, The White House, Washington, D.C.: 19 September 1983, copy in the files of The National Security Archive, Washington, D.C.; Clark forwarded this finding to Reagan on the 17th of September and received approval. (William P. Clark, memorandum for the President, 'Finding on Nicaraguan Covert Action,' exhibit GPS–2, *Iran–Contra Investigation*, 100th Cong., lst sess., 100–9, 23–24, 28–29 July 1987, p. 470; *International Court of Justice*, paragraph 260–261, p. 122.

36. Robert A. Pastor, *Condemned To Repetition*, p. 245; *Iran–Contra Report*, p. 35.

37. Comandante Daniel Ortega, letter to Presidents of the Contadora countries, 26 September 1983, document 1.22, in Bagley, *Contadora Documents*, pp. 59–60; *New York Times* 11 November 1983, in CAHI, *Chronology*, p. 33; Phil Gunson and Greg Chamberlin, *The Dictionary Of Contemporary Politics Of Central America And The Caribbean* (London: Routledge, 1991), p. 89; Woodward, *Veil*, pp. 317–319; Menges, *Inside the National Security Council*, pp. 61–62; Gutman, *Banana Diplomacy*, pp. 173–175; Rubin, *Secrets of State*, p. 228.

38. Hedrick Smith, 'State Dept. Official Plans to Visit Nicaragua,' *New York*

*Times*, 11 October 1983; Richard J. Meislin, 'State Dept. Aide Visits Nicaragua for Discussions,' *New York Times*, 15 October 1983; Richard J. Meislin, 'US–Nicaraguan Talks Make No Breakthrough,' *New York Times*, 16 October 1983; Department of State Press Briefing, on background by a senior Department of State Official, 17 October 1983, 'The Only Way This Thing's Going To Work Is Everything Together,' document 641, *Current Documents 1983*, pp. 1364–1370; Official Proposal of Nicaragua Within the Framework of the Contadora Process, 'Juridicial Foundation to Guarantee International Peace and Security of the States of Central America,' 15 October 1983, document 1.23, in Bagley, *Contadora Documents*, pp. 61, 64, the complete texts are printed between pp. 61–83; Patrick E. Tyler, 'Sandinistas Propose 4 Security Accords to US' *Washington Post*, 21 October 1983; Joanne Omang, 'US Calls Nicaraguan Offer Deficient,' *Washington Post*, 22 October 1983; Editorial, 'The Wrong Nicaragua Policy,' *Washington Post*, 23 October 1983.

39. Department of State, '*Revolution Beyond Our Borders*': *Sandinista Intervention in Central America*, Special Report no. 132 (Washington, D.C.: Department of State, September 1985), p. 28; 'Communication from the Contadora Group on peace efforts in Central America,' Annex II, OEA/Ser.P, AG/CG/doc.6/83, 16 November 1983, to Organization of American States, General Assembly, OEA/Ser.P, AG/doc.1707/83, 17 November 1983, Thirteenth Regular Session, 14 November 1983, Washington, D.C., p. 35.

40. Hedrick Smith, 'House Again Votes Against Financing Nicaragua Rebels,' *New York Times*, 21 October 1983; *New York Times*, 29 October 1983 cited in CAHI, *Chronology*, p. 36; Tomás Borge, interview by Newsweek International, *Newsweek* (14 November 1983), p. 24; Robert J. McCartney, 'Nicaraguans Act to Revive Peace Dialogue,' *Washington Post*, 11 November 1983; Stephen Kinzer, 'Pro-Sandinista Press Spurns Talks,' *New York Times*, 15 November 1983.

41. UN General Assembly Resolution 38/10, 11 November 1983, document 4.7, in Bagley, *Contadora Documents*, pp. 233–236.

42. John Felton, 'White House Gets Better Half Of a Covert Aid Compromise,' *Congressional Quarterly Weekly Report* 41, no. 47 (26 November 1983): pp. 2486–2487; OAS Resolution adopted at the seventh plenary session, 18 November 1983, as Annex II, Note by the Secretary General, 'The Situation In Central America,' United Nations Security Council, S/16208, 9 December 1983, fiche 83–34752 09058 (E), p. 6; Tomás Borge interview by Newsweek International *Newsweek* (14 November 1983): p. 24; Hedrick Smith, 'US Policy on Nicaragua: Keep the Pressure On,' *New York Times*, 1 December 1983; Sections 108 and 109 of Public Law 98–215, approved 9 December 1983, document 651, *Current Documents 1983*, p. 1388.

43. 'More Sandinista Peace Initiatives,' Central America Report 10, no. 47 (Guatemala City, 2 December 1983), pp. 369–370; Alfonso Chardy, 'Stone hopes to unite "contras",' *Miami Herald*, 1 December 1983; Stephen Kinzer, 'Nicaraguan Rebels Ask Peace Talks,' *New York Times*, 2 December 1983; *New York Times*, 6 December 1983 cited in CAHI, *Chronology*, p. 40; Note by the Secretary General, 'The Situation In Central America,' United Nations Security Council, S/16208, 9 December 1983, fiche 83–34752 09058 (E), p. 1.

44. *Washington Post*, 6 January 1984, cited in CAHI, *Chronology*, p. 41; Contadora Bulletin and 'Norms for the Implementation of the Commitments of the Document of Objectives,' 8 January 1984, unofficial translation, Embassy of Mexico, Washington, D.C., pp. 1–5; Ambassador Leonardo Kam, Deputy Permanent Representative of Panama, to the United Nations Secretary General, 9 January 1984, United Nations, General Assembly and Security Council, A/39/71–S/16262, 10 January 1984, fiche 84–00741 1477b (E), pp. 4–6; Richard Stone memorandum to The Secretary, 'Trip Report: Western Europe,' 28 October 1983, document 00223, fiche 35, The National Security Archive, 1990.

    In June 1983 the European Community had placed itself squarely behind the Contadora initiative in their Stuttgart Communiqué. Initiated by the Dutch, the communiqué read in part:

    > They are convinced that the problems of Central America cannot be solved by military means, but only by a political solution springing from the region itself and respecting the principles of non interference and inviolability of frontiers. They, therefore, fully support the current initiative of the Contadora Group.

    (European Community, 'Joint Communiqué at Stuttgart,' June 1983, in Robert S. Leiken and Barry Rubin, eds., *The Central American Crisis Reader*, [New York: Summit Books, 1987], p. 661); *Chamorro Affidavit*, pp. 18–19.
45. Assistant Secretary of State for Inter-American Affairs, Motley, address to the Foreign Policy Association, New York, 19 January 1984, 'The Situation in Central America,' document 496, *Current Documents 1984*, pp. 996–999; John Felton, 'Kissinger Panel Backs Central America Policy,' *Congressional Quarterly Weekly Report* 42, no. 2 (14 January 1984): pp. 39–41; George J. Church, 'More of Everything,' *Time*, 23 January 1984; Gutman, *Banana Diplomacy*, pp. 167–168, 173, 180; Gutman, 'America's Diplomatic Charade,' *Foreign Policy*, no. 56 (Fall 1984): p. 20.
46. Gutman, *Banana Diplomacy*, pp. 293, 180–181.

## 3 Manzanillo and Contadora 1984

1. Carlos Fuentes, 'Are You Listening, Henry Kissinger?' An open letter to the Commission on Central America, *Harper's* 268, no. 1604 (January 1984): p. 36; Jim Morrell and William Jesse Biddle, 'Central America: The Financial War,' *International Policy Report* (Washington, D.C.: Center for International Policy, March 1983), passim; President Reagan, message to Congress, 'Central America Democracy, Peace, and Development Initiative Act of 1984,' 17 February 1984, document 502, *American Foreign Policy Current Documents 1984* (Washington, D.C.: Department of State, 1986), p. 1014; Secretary of State, Shultz, statement to the Senate Foreign Relations Committee, 'The President's Program for Central America,' 22 February 1984, document 503, *Current Documents 1984*, pp. 1015–1016; Oliver L. North, Alton Keel, memorandum to Robert C. McFarlane, 'Additional Resources for our Anti-Sandinista Program,' 7 February 1984, document 00313, fiche 49, The National Security Archive, 1990.

2. Jacobsen, *Soviet Attitudes*, pp. 17, 31; Jozef Goldblat and Victor Millan, 'Arms Control in Central America,' *Arms Control* 8, no. 1 (May 1987), pp. 76–78; Vladimir I. Stanchenko, 'Soviet Views of the Caribbean and Central America 1959–1991,' (Cork: Irish Institute of International Relations); Vladimir I. Stanchenko, interview by author, 15 February 1992, Cork, Ireland, tape recording; Stephen Kinzer, 'Soviet Help to Sandinistas: No Blank Check,' *New York Times*, 28 March 1984; Center for Defense Information, 'Soviet Geopolitical Momentum: Myth or Menace?' *The Defense Monitor* 15, no. 5 (Washington, D.C.: Center For Defense Information, 1986), p. 31.

   The Church was not only influential in Central America, the United States Catholic Conference sought to influence their government. Rev. Bryan Hahir appearing before the Subcommittee on Western Hemisphere Affairs of the Senate Foreign Relations Committee, testified that the United States had a great capacity to shape the future direction of Central America. The United States had not paid enough attention to diplomatic opportunities:

   > At the present time the dynamic of US policy is not sensitive to the diplomatic potential of the moment . . . [R]ealizing our diplomatic potential means placing the political resolution of the Central American conflict ahead of military objectives – it requires a diplomatic strategy in which the political perspective controls military measures. United States policy presently does not manifest this order of values; there is not a convincing daily demonstration of a primacy of concern for diplomatic initiatives aimed at a political resolution in the region.

   (Bagley, *Contadora Documents*, document 8.6, p. 296).
3. President Ronald Reagan, memorandum for, Shultz, Weinberger, Casey, and Vessey, 'Central America Legislative Strategy – Additional Funding for Nicaraguan Democratic Opposition Forces,' 21 February 1984, *Iran–Contra Affair*, Appendix A: Volume 1, Source Documents, pp. 212–213; FDN, 'Plan for Peace and National Conciliation,' proposal to Nicaraguan Government of National Reconstruction, 21 February 1984, in Bagley, *Contadora Documents*, document 7.8, pp. 279–280; US Congress, House, Committee on Foreign Affairs, *Legislation Concerning Latin America: Columbia, The Contadora Process, And El Salvador: Markup before the Committee on Foreign Affairs*, 98th Cong., 2nd sess., 5 April 1984, appendix 1, pp. 15–17; Robert C. McFarlane, memorandum for the President, 'Central America Legislative Strategy – Additional Funding for the Anti-Sandinista Forces,' 21 February 1984, document 00340, fiche 53, The National Security Archive, 1990.
4. United Nations, *Chronicle* 21, no. 3 (March 1984): pp. 7–8; Oliver L. North, Constantine Menges, memorandum for Robert C. McFarlane, 'Special Activities in Nicaragua,' 2 March 1984, from the files of the National Security Archive, Washington, D.C.; Embassy of Nicaragua, Press Release, 'Nicaragua Alerts of CIA Plan To Mine Corinto, Nicaragua's Main Port,' Washington, D.C., 5 March 1984; Governing Junta of National Reconstruction, message addressed to the people of Nicaragua and the world, annex to Javier Chamorro Mora, Nicaraguan Ambassador to the United Nations, 13 March 1984, United Nations, Security Council, document S/16413, fiche 84–06750 1178q (E), pp. 2–4.

5. Secretary of State, Shultz, Report to Congress, 'US Peace Efforts in Central America,' 15 March 1984, document 508, *Current Documents 1984*, pp. 1036–1042.
6. Langhorne A. Motley, Assistant Secretary for Inter-American Affairs, before the Subcommittee on Foreign Operations of the House Committee on Appropriations, prepared statement, 'A National Response to the Crisis in Central America,' *Current Policy*, no. 559 (27 March 1984), pp. 4, 7.
7. William J. Casey, letter to Robert C. McFarlane, 'Supply [obscured] Assistance to Nicaragua Program,' 27 March 1984, exhibit CG–58, *Iran–Contra Investigation*, 100th Cong., lst sess., 100–11, 4–6 August 1987, p. 943; *Iran–Contra Affair* appendix C, Chronology of Events, 100th Cong., lst sess., 13 November 1987, p. 7; *The Iran–Contra Report*, p. 37.
8. Secretary of State, Shultz, note to Secretary-General of the United Nations, Pérez de Cuéllar, 'Modification of US Acceptance of the Compulsory Jurisdiction of the International Court of Justice,' 6 April 1984, document 515, *Current Documents 1984*, p. 1051; Nicaragua Ambassador to the United Nations, Chamorro Mora, letter to the president of the Security Council, 29 March 1984, United Nations, Security Council, document S/16449, fiche 84–08038 1224u (E); Draft Resolution, United Nations Security Council, document S/16463, 4 April 1984, fiche 84–08606, pp. 1–2; Central American Historical Institute, (CAHI) *Update*, no. 14 (2–8 April 1984), p. 2.
9. CAHI, *Update*, no. 14 (2–8 April 1984), p. 2.
10. Philip Taubman, 'Americans on Ship Said to Supervise Nicaragua Mining,' *New York Times*, 8 April 1984; Richard Halloran, 'US Said to Draw Latin Troops Plan,' *New York Times*, 8 April 1984; Reuters, 'Moscow Assails US,' *New York Times*, 8 April 1984.
11. Barry Goldwater, letter to William J. Casey, 9 April 1984, *Iran–Contra Investigation*, 100th Cong., lst sess., 100–11, 4–6 August 1987, pp. 1069–1070; US Congress, Senate, Senate Select Committee on Intelligence, *January 1, 1983 to December 31, 1984: Report of the Senate Select Committee on Intelligence*, 98th Cong., 2nd sess., 10 October 1984, pp. 7–9.
12. CAHI, *Update*, no. 14 (2–8) April 1984), pp. 3–4; Statement by the President's Principal Deputy Press Secretary, Speakes, 'US Policy in Central America,' 10 April 1984, document 516, *Current Documents 1984*, pp. 1052–1053; Deputy Secretary of State, Dam, to House Foreign Affairs Committee, 'The United States, Nicaragua, and the International Court of Justice,' 11 April 1984, document 517, *Current Documents 1984*, p. 1054; Jeane Kirkpatrick and Henry Kissinger interviewed on *ABC News: This Week With David Brinkley* (15 April 1984), pp. 21, 5, 11; George J. Church, 'Explosion Over Nicaragua,' *Time* (23 April 1984), p. 10; Democratic Study Group, *An Act of War*, Special Report, no. 98–18 (11 April 1984), p. 9; Richard Falk, 'Curbing a Lawless Government,' *Progressive* 48, no. 6 (June 1984): p. 13; Special, 'Sandinista Accuses Rebels of Vast Economic Damage,' *New York Times*, 29 April 1984; Martin Tolchin, 'House Vote Opposes Mining of Nicaraguan Ports,' *New York Times*, 13 April 1984; David Shribman, 'Poll Finds A Lack Of Public Support For Latin Policy,' *New York Times*, 29 April 1984.
13. George Russell, 'Last Exit to Costa Rica,' *Time*, (16 April 1984), p. 10; CIA cables, outgoing, 10 April 1984, and 1 May 1984, as exhibit DRC–19–14,

and DRC–19–18, respectively *Iran–Contra Investigation*, 100th Cong., 1st sess., 100–11, 4–6 August 1987, pp. 505, 509; *The Iran–Contra Report*, p. 38; Sklar, *Washington's War on Nicaragua*, p. 224.

14. *International Court of Justice*, text of ruling, reprinted as 'US "Should Cease and Refrain",' *Washington Post*, 11 May 1984; *International Court of Justice*, paragraph 292, pp. 138–139.

15. George J. Church, 'Explosion Over Nicaragua,' *Time* (23 April 1984), p. 6; Frank J. Smist, Jr., *Congress Oversees the United States Intelligence Community, 1947–1989*, (Knoxville: University of Tennessee Press, 1990), pp. 97–99, 247–248; George J. Church, 'No Place Left to Hide?' *Time* (30 April 1984), p. 31; *Iran–Contra Report*, p. 396; Barry M. Blechman, *The Politics of National Security: Congress and US Defense Policy* (New York: Oxford University Press, 1990), p. 137.

16. John Felton, '"Contadora" Talks Prompt Praise – and Debate,' *Congressional Quarterly Weekly Report* 42, no. 19 (12 May 1984): pp. 1094–1095; Assistant Secretary of State for Inter-American Affairs, Motley, before a Subcommittee of the House Foreign Affairs Committee, 'US Objectives in Central America,' 2 May 1984, document 521, *Current Documents 1984*, pp. 1061–1063; US Congress, House, Committee on Foreign Affairs, *Legislation Concerning Latin America: Columbia, The Contadora Process, And El Salvador: Markup of the Committee on Foreign Affairs*, 98th Cong., 2nd sess., 5 April 1984, p. 16; *International Court of Justice*, 27 June 1986, paragraphs 195, 233, 239, 231, 238, pp. 93, 109–110, 112. El Salvador made a declaration of intervention in mid-August 1984. (Republic of El Salvador, *Case Concerning Military and Paramilitary Activities in and Against Nicaragua*, Declaration of Intervention, General list no. 70 [The Hague: International Court of Justice, 15 August 1984]).

17. Remarks by Presidents Reagan and de la Madrid at the White House, 'Excerpts From Remarks by the Two Presidents,' *New York Times*, 16 May 1984; Alfonso Chardy, 'Reagan: Hands Off Nicaragua,' *Miami Herald*, 23 June 1984; Ambassador Bernardo Sepúlveda Amor, interview by author, 20 March 1991, London, tape recording, Embassy of Mexico.

18. Robert C. McFarlane, memorandum for the President, 'Nicaragua and El Salvador Funding,' 18 May 1984, document 00428, fiche 66, The National Security Archive, 1990; Ronald Reagan memorandum for George P. Shultz, Caspar W. Weinberger, William J. Casey, John W. Vessey, 'Funding for the Nicaraguan Program and El Salvador,' undated, attached to above memorandum, document 00427, fiche 66, The National Security Archive, 1990.

19. Ambassador Bernardo Sepúlveda Amor, interview by author, 20 March 1991, London, tape recording, Embassy of Mexico.

20. Secretary of State, Shultz, statement, 'US Concerns With Nicaragua,' 1 June 1984, document 526, *Current Documents 1984*, pp. 1076–1077; Joanne Omang, 'Shultz Meets With Ortega In Managua,' *Washington Post*, 2 June 1984; Robert J. McCartney, 'Managua Wary Of Initiative By Washington,' *Washington Post*, 3 June 1984.

    Nicaragua's stance of not negotiating on internal matters is substantially supported by the International Court of Justice.

> It appears to the Court to be clearly established first, that the United States intended, by its support of the *contras*, to coerce the Government

of Nicaragua in respect to matters in which each State is permitted, by the principle of State sovereignty, to decide freely; and secondly that the intention of the *contras* themselves was to overthrow the present Government of Nicaragua. The Court considers that in international law, if one State, with a view to the coercion of another State, supports and assist armed bands in that State whose purpose is to overthrow the government of that State, that amounts to an intervention by the one State in the internal affairs of the other . . .

(*International Court of Justice*, paragraph 241, pp. 113–114).

21. Ambassador Bernardo Sepúlveda Amor, interview by author, 20 March 1991, London, tape recording, Embassy of Mexico; Special, '"Dissatisfaction" Voiced,' *New York Times*, 3 June 1984; Francis X. Clines, 'Nicaragua Policy Is Affirmed By US After Shultz Trip,' *New York Times*, 3 June 1984; Bill Keller, 'Democrats Laud Nicaragua Move, but They Question the Motives,' *New York Times*, 14 June 1984; Mark P. Sullivan, *Nicaragua: An Overview of US Policy 1979–1986*, Congressional Research Service Report for Congress 87–855 F (Washington, D.C.: The Library of Congress, 13 October 1987), p. 20; CAHI, *Update*, no. 19 (14–20 May 1984): p. 4; Anonymous, 'An Israeli Connection?' *Time* (7 May 1984), p. 27; Report of the Congressional Committees Investigating the *Iran–Contra Affair* Appendix C, Chronology of Events, 100th Cong., lst sess., 13 November 1987, p. 9.
22. National Security Planning Group Meeting, National Security Council, Washington, D.C., 25 June 1984, on file at the National Security Archive, Washington, D.C., pp. 1–4.
23. NSPG meeting, National Security Council, 25 June 1984, pp. 4–8.
24. NSPG meeting, National Security Council, 25 June 1984, pp. 9–10.
25. NSPG meeting, National Security Council, 25 June 1984, pp. 9–11; 13.
26. President Reagan, memorandum to George P. Shultz, Caspar W. Weinberger, William J. Casey, Jeane J. Kirkpatrick, and John W. Vessey, 'Central America: NSPG Meeting of June 25, 1984,' 25 June 1984, document 00462, fiche 72, The National Security Archive 1990.
27. US Congress, House, Committee on Foreign Affairs, Subcommittee on Western Hemisphere Affairs, *The Role Of The US Southern Command In Central America: hearing before the Committee on Foreign Affairs, Subcommittee on Western Hemisphere Affairs*, 98th Cong., 2nd sess., 1 August 1984, pp. 27, 29–30; *Chamorro Affidavit*, pp. 19–20; Clifford Krauss, 'Honduran, Nicaraguan Patrols Proposed By Sandinista Leader to Halt Guerillas,' *Wall Street Journal*, 13 August 1984.
28. Denis Volman, 'Sandinistas and foes begin informal talks,' *Christian Science Monitor*, 1 August 1984; Tim Coone, 'Contras fail to find a political voice,' *Financial Times* (London), 1 August 1984; Arturo J. Cruz, interview, 'The Vote Is for Outside Consumption,' *Newsweek* (6 August 1984), p. 48.
29. Nina M. Serafino, *Contra Aid, FY82–FY88: Summary and Chronology of Major Congressional Action on Key Legislation Concerning US Aid to the Anti-Sandinista Guerillas*, CRS Report 88–563 F, Congressional Research Service (Washington, D.C.: Library of Congress, 18 August 1988), p. 6; Philip Taubman, 'House Votes to Deny Help To Nicaraguan Insurgents,' *New York Times*, 3 August 1984; Clifford Krauss, 'Honduran, Nicaraguan Patrols Proposed By Sandinista Leader to Halt Guerillas,' *Wall Street*

*Journal*, 13 August 1984; Associated Press, 'US Denies Nicaraguan Claim Of CIA Assassination Plot,' *Washington Post*, 14 August 1984; CIA's Nicaragua Manual, *Psychological Operations in Guerilla Warfare*, (New York: Vintage Books, 1985); Leslie Cockburn, *Out of Control: The Story of the Reagan Administration's Secret War in Nicaragua, the Illegal Arms Pipeline, and the Contra Drug Connection* (London: Bloomsbury, 1988), p. 7; Robert J. McCartney, 'Nicaraguan Hails "Fluid" Talks with US on Security,' *Washington Post*, 12 August 1984.

30. US Proposal at Manzanillo, presented orally at the fourth meeting 15–16 August 1984, and in writing at the fifth meeting 5–6 September 1984, 'Timetable of Reciprocal Unilateral Measures,' as Appendix I, in Gutman, *Banana Diplomacy*, pp. 378–381; Representatives Jim Leach, George Miller, Michael D. Barnes, Don Edwards, Mark O. Hatfield, Edward M. Kennedy, *US Policy in Central America: Against the Law*? Report to Arms Control and Foreign Policy Caucus (Washington, D.C.: US Congress, 11 September 1984), p. 7; *Chamorro Affidavit*, p. 23; United States Department of State, *'Revolution Beyond Our Borders': Sandinista Intervention in Central America*, Special Report No. 132 (Washington, D.C.: Department of State, September 1985), p. 29; Associated Press, 'US Warns Nicaragua on Airport,' *New York Times*, 18 August 1984.

Chamorro's affidavit was not enough to convince the International Court of Justice who argued that it was not satisfied that the United States created the contras [paragraph 108]. For legal purposes the Court had to determine whether the relationship between the contras and the United States was one of dependence and one of control. The Court cited an Intelligence committee as stating that the only means of control the United States could exercise over the contras was the cessation of aid. It noted that this, paradoxically, underlines the potential control. Yet 'there is no clear evidence of the United States having actually exercised such a degree of control in all fields as to justify treating the contras as acting on its behalf' [paragraph 109]. The contras could commit acts without the control of the United States [paragraph 115]. In legal terms, human rights violations could not be imputable to the United States [paragraph 116]. This argument was partly based on the supposition that after the US funds were cut off in late 1984, the contra activities continued, thus the contras were not completely dependent on the United States [paragraph 110]. (*International Court of Justice*, paragraphs 108, 109, 115, 116, 110, pp. 50–51, 53–54). Documents released a year after this Court ruling during the Iran–Contra Affair demonstrate that the funds procured for the contras were in the main solicited by US officials. Moreover, counterrevolutionary forces existed immediately following the 1979 revolution in Nicaragua, and were organized initially by Argentine forces. These forces were soon nurtured by the CIA, official funding began in late 1981, though the CIA was directed to carry out activities in Central America from March 1981. Chamorro's allegation is that the United States created the FDN as an organization, as opposed to the contras in general. On the political and diplomatic level there was a significant degree of control of the contras, even if particular operations were not controlled. During the time frame covered by the first Presidential finding from December 1981 to September 1983, the US rational was that the contras were an interdiction force. If the US Congress believed administration claims that the intent of the contra operation was to interdict weapons, then Congress must have assumed US control over these forces; after all there was sufficient evidence in the US media that the intent of the contras was to overthrow the Sandinistas. Chamorro's affidavit states that US officials told contra leaders that this was also the administration's intention: 'Mr. Lehman assured us that President Reagan remained committed to removing the Sandinistas from power' (*Chamorro Affidavit*, p. 19). (On the early years of the contras see: Kornbluh, *Nicaragua*, pp. 25–46; Edgar Chamorro, *Packaging the Contras: A Case of CIA Disinformation*, Monograph Series No. 2, [New York: Institute for Media Analysis, Inc., 1987], pp. 4–7; R. Pardo-Maurer, *The Contras, 1980–1989: A Special Kind of Politics* [New York: Praeger, 1990], pp. 1–7).

31. William Orme, 'Mexico Says 4th Session of US–Nicaraguan Talks "Substantive",' *Washington Post*, 18 August 1984; NSPG meeting, National Security Council, 25 June 1984, p. 3.
32. William Orme, 'Mexico Says 4th Session of US–Nicaraguan Talks "Substantive",' *Washington Post*, 18 August 1984; Ambassador Bernardo Sepúlveda Amor, interview by author, 20 March 1991, London, tape recording, Embassy of Mexico.
33. Communication from the Foreign Ministers of the Contadora Group, 'The Contadora Act on Peace and Cooperation in Central America,' 7 September 1984, document 533, *Current Documents 1984*, pp. 1082–1083; The 'Contadora Act For Peace And Cooperation in Central America,' 7 September 1984, is reprinted in Bagley, *Contadora Documents*, document 3.10, pp. 188–217; Bruce M. Bagley, 'The Failure of Diplomacy,' in Bruce M. Bagley, ed., *Contadora and the Diplomacy of Peace in Central America, Volume I: The United States, Central America, and Contadora*, SAIS Papers in Latin American Studies (Boulder: Westview Press, 1987), p. 190; Associated Press, 'Nicaragua Spurns Plea for Regional Disarmament,' *New York Times*, 9 September 1984; George P. Shultz, letter to European Community Foreign Ministers, 7 September 1984, copy with author.
34. Menges, *Inside the National Security Council*, pp. 140–141.
35. Jim Morrell and William Goodfellow, 'Contadora: Under The Gun,' *International Policy Report* (Washington, D.C.: Center for International Policy, May 1986), pp. 3, 5; Commandante Daniel Ortega, to Presidents of Contadora, 21 September 1984, document 1.24, Bagley, *Contadora Documents*, pp. 83–85; Menges, Inside the *National Security Council*, p. 142; Gutman, *Banana Diplomacy*, pp. 229–230; Dunkerley, *Power in the Isthmus*, p. 318.
36. Gutman, *Banana Diplomacy*, p. 229; Philip Taubman, 'US Reported to Fear Sandinista Publicity Coup,' *New York Times*, 24 September 1984; Joanne Omang, 'Nicaraguan Acquiescence on Peace Plan Puts US on Defensive,' *Washington Post*, 27 September 1984; US Department of State, '*Revolution Beyond Our Borders*', p. 28; US Department of State, *Negotiations in Central America 1981–1987*, publication 9551, Office of Public Diplomacy, (Washington, D.C.: Department of State October 1987), p. 4; Terry Karl, 'Mexico, Venezuela, and the Contadora Initiative,' in Morris J. Blachman, William M. LeoGrande, Kenneth E. Sharpe, eds., *Confronting Revolution: Security Through Diplomacy in Central America* (New York: Pantheon Books, 1986), p. 413, note 47; Commandante Daniel Ortega, to Presidents

of Contadora, 21 September 1984, document 1.24, Bagley, *Contadora Documents*, pp. 83–85.

37. Menges, *Inside the National Security Council*, pp. 142–144; Stephen Kinzer, 'Managua Takes a Trick With the Contadora Card,' *New York Times*, 30 September 1984; Gutman, *Banana Diplomacy*, pp. 230–231.
38. Ambassador Bernardo Sepúlveda Amor, interview by author, 20 March 1991, London, tape recording, Embassy of Mexico.
39. Joint Communiqué by Foreign Ministers of the European Community, Spain, Portugal, Contadora states and Central American states, 'Cooperation Between Central America and Europe,' San José, 29 September 1984, document 534, *Current Documents 1984*, p. 1084; George P. Shultz, letter to European Community Foreign Ministers, 7 September 1984, copy with author.
40. Secret/Sensitive, Background paper for NSC meeting on Central America, October 30, 1984, copy with author; Ambassador Bernardo Sepúlveda Amor, interview by author, 20 March 1991, London, tape recording, Embassy of Mexico.
41. Legal Advisor of the Department of State, Robinson, prepared statement to the International Court of Justice, The Hague, 'US Argument Against Nicaraguan Claim,' 15 October 1984, document 540, *Current Documents 1984*, pp. 1095–1099; *International Court of Justice*, paragraphs 290, 291, pp. 135–136; Roy Gutman, 'America's Diplomatic Charade,' *Foreign Policy*, no. 56 (Fall 1984): p. 22; Philip Taubman, 'Latin Peace Plan: Why the US Balks,' *New York Times*, 3 October 1984; Kenneth E. Sharpe, 'The US–Nicaragua Duel of Words,' *Los Angeles Times*, 3 October 1984.
42. Gutman, *Banana Diplomacy*, pp. 208–210; Doyle McManus, Don Shannon, 'Nicaraguan Leader Sees Impasse in Talks With US,' *Los Angeles Times*, 4 October 1984.
43. *Iran–Contra Report*, p. 41; National Security Decision Directive, 'Arms Interdiction in Central America,' attached as Tab I to Oliver L. North, memorandum to Robert C. McFarlane, 'Draft National Security Decision Directive (NSDD) on Arms Interdiction in Central America,' 9 October 1984, *Iran–Contra Affair*, Appendix A: Volume 1, Source Documents, pp. 247–249.
44. Dale Tate, John Felton, Pat Towell, 'Last-Minute Appropriations Bill Tripped Up,' *Congressional Quarterly Weekly Report* 42, no. 40 (6 October 1984), p. 2420; Serafino, *Contra Aid, FY82–FY88*, p. 6; US Congress, House, 98th Cong., 2nd sess., *Congressional Record*, 10 October 1984, p. H 11980; US Congress, House, *Activities in Nicaragua*, 98th Cong., 2nd sess., *Congressional Record*, 11 October 1984, p. H 12206, reprinted as exhibit 27, *Iran–Contra Investigation*, 100th Cong., lst sess., 5–8 May 1987, pp. 588–592.
45. *Iran–Contra Report*, pp. 41–42; Public Law 98–473, 98th Congress, Joint Resolution, Section 8066 (a), 12 October 1984, as exhibit BGS–23, *Iran–Contra Investigation*, 100th Cong., lst sess., 2–5, 8–9 June 1987, p. 1270; Theodore Draper, *A Very Thin Line: The Iran–Contra Affairs* (New York: Hill and Wang, 1991), pp. 25–26.
46. Secretary of State, Shultz, press conference, Panama City, 'The United States and the Contadora Process,' 11 October 1984, document 537, *Current Documents 1984*, p. 1089; Walter LaFeber, *The Panama Canal: The Crisis in Historical Perspective* (New York: Oxford University Press, 1989), pp.

196–197; Simon Tisdall, 'Noriega is found guilty,' The *Guardian* (London), 10 April 1992; United States of America v. Oliver North, fact 45, p. 17, document 04305, fiche 663, The National Security Archive, 1990; Secret/Sensitive, Background paper for NSC meeting on Central America, October 30, 1984, copy with author.

47. Foreign Ministers of Costa Rica, El Salvador, and Honduras, joint communique, Tegucigalpa, 'Revision of the Contadora Act on Peace and Cooperation in Central America,' 20 October 1984, document 541, *Current Documents 1984*, pp. 1102–1103; US Department of State, *The Contadora Process*, Resource Book, annex 3, (Washington, D.C.: US Department of State, January 1985), pp. 1–3; Tom J. Farer, 'Contadora: The Hidden Agenda,' *Foreign Policy*, no. 85 (Summer 1985): p. 71.
48. 'Contadora Act on Peace and Cooperation in Central America – As Revised at the Meeting of Central American Ministers for Foreign Affairs,' Tegicigalpa, 20 October 1984, annex to letter from the Permanent representatives of Costa Rica, El Salvador, and Honduras to the Secretary General, United Nations General Assembly, A/39/630, 2 November 1984, 84–26254 1400q (E); Secret/Sensitive, Background paper for NSC meeting on Central America, October 30, 1984, copy with author; United States Department of State, '*Revolution Beyond Our Borders*', p. 29; Farer, 'Contadora: The Hidden Agenda,' *Foreign Policy*, p. 71.
49. Secret/Sensitive, Background paper for NSC meeting on Central America, October 30, 1984, copy with author.
50. Sandinista Proposal at Manzanillo, in Gutman, *Banana Diplomacy*, appendix II, pp. 382–384; Jim Morrell and William Goodfellow, 'Contadora: Under The Gun,' *International Policy Report* (Washington, D.C.: Center for International Policy, May 1986), p. 3; Norman Kempster, Doyle McManus, 'US Move on Latin Pact Backfires,' *Los Angeles Times*, 6 October 1984.
51. J. Philip Taubman, 'Nicaraguan Talks Are Said To Stall,' *New York Times*, 2 November 1984.

## 4 Undermining Democracy: Elections 1984

1. John A. Booth, 'Elections and Democracy in Central America: A Framework for Analysis,' in John A. Booth and Mitchell A. Seligson eds., *Elections and Democracy in Central America* (Chapel Hill: The University of North Carolina Press, 1989), pp. 8–9, 33–34.
2. Susanne Jonas, 'Elections and Transition: The Guatemalan and Nicaraguan Cases,' in Booth and Seligson, eds., *Elections and Democracy in Central America*, p. 148; Alejandro Bendaña, 'Building a Negotiation Strategy: 'Lessons' from the Nicaraguan Experience,' Papers from the 1991 Catholic Institute for International Relations (CIIR) Conference, 'Negotiating For Change: The Struggle for Peace with Justice,' Regents College, London, 18–19 January 1991, p. 59.
3. Seventeenth Meeting of Consultation of Ministers of Foreign Affairs, Organization of American States, resolution of 23 June 1979, and Junta of the Government of National Reconstruction, telegram sent from Costa Rica to the Organization of American States, 12 July 1979, both cited by *International Court of Justice*, 27 June 1986, paragraph 167, pp. 78–79.

4. The Report of the Latin American Studies Association, Delegation to observe the Nicaraguan General Election of 4 November 1984, *The Electoral Process in Nicaragua: Domestic and International Influences* (Pittsburgh: Latin American Studies Association, 19 November 1984), pp. Summary of Findings, 19, 29–30, (Hereinafter, *LASA Report 1984*); Philip Taubman, 'Key Aides Dispute US Role in Nicaraguan Vote,' *New York Times*, 21 October 1984; Roy Gutman, 'How the 1984 Vote Was Sabotaged,' *The Nation* 246, no. 18 (7 May 1988), pp. 642–643; Gutman, *Banana Diplomacy*, pp. 247–253; Gutman, 'How the 1984 Vote was Sabotaged,' *The Nation*, 8 (7 May 1988): cover, pp. 642–643; Secret/Sensitive, Background paper for NSC meeting on Central America, October 30, 1984, copy with author; Alma Guillermopreito and David Hoffman, 'Document Describes How US 'Blocked' A Contadora Treaty,' *Washington Post*, 6 November 1984.

   High level American officials also visited another significant opposition leader, Virgilio Godoy, who withdrew from the race two weeks before the elections. His visitors included Langhorne Motley, Harry Shlauderman, and US ambassador to Nicaragua Harry Bergold. Godoy denied any connection between these visits and his decision to withdraw, and described the timing as 'unfortunate.' LASA quotes an associate of his who stated that he thought he was 'subject to terrible pressure from the Embassy' (*LASA Report 1984*, p. 30). Godoy became Nicaragua's Vice President in 1990, as part of the US supported coalition UNO.
5. *LASA Report 1984*, summary and p. 32.
6. Parliamentary Human Rights Group, Report of a British Parliamentary Delegation to Nicaragua to observe the Presidential and National Assembly elections, 4 November 1984, pp. 27–28; Thorvald Stoltenberg, Managua, 5 November 1984, *Report to Willy Brandt, President of the Socialist International, on the Nicaraguan Elections, November 4, 1984, by Thorvald Stoltenberg, Socialist International Special Representative to Nicaragua*, Socialist International Press Release no. 14/84, London, 12 November 1984, pp. 1–2.
7. *LASA Report 1984*, summary; Parliamentary Human Rights Group, London, p. 27.
8. John Hughes, transcript of the Department of State daily press briefing, 'The Nicaraguan Elections,' 5 November 1984, document 545, *Current Documents 1984*, pp. 1106–1107.
9. *LASA Report 1984*, pp. 31–32.
10. Francis X. Clines, 'US Says Study Found Manual Broke No Law,' *New York Times*, 11 November 1984; Mark P. Sullivan, *Nicaragua: An Overview of US Policy 1979–1986*, Congressional Research Service Report for Congress 87–855 F (Washington, D.C.: The Library of Congress, 13 October 1987), pp. 22–23; The Manual is reproduced as CIA's Nicaragua Manual, *Psychological Operations in Guerilla Warfare*, (New York: Vintage Books, 1985); The Senate Intelligence Committee investigated the issue. A brief report on it is found in US Congress, Senate, Select Committee on Intelligence, *January 1, 1983, to December 31, 1984: Report of the Select Committee on Intelligence*, 98th Cong., 2nd sess., 10 October 1984, pp. 12–13; *Chamorro Affidavit*, pp. 21–22.

Leslie Cockburn points out that the officials involved were not junior officials, and their re-assignments were not demotions. Duane Clarridge, who had commissioned the manual was transferred to take charge of the European desk of the CIA Operations Directorate, his deputy, Vincent Cannistraro was transferred to the staff office of Oliver North at the NSC, and Joe Fernandez was made station chief in Costa Rica (Leslie Cockburn, *Out of Control: The Story of the Reagan Administration's Secret War in Nicaragua, the Illegal Arms Pipeline, and the Contra Drug Connection* [London: Bloomsbury, 1988], p. 7).

11. Alfonso Chardy, 'Reagan: Hands off Nicaragua,' *Miami Herald*, 23 June 1984; Philip Taubman, 'US Warns Soviet It Won't Tolerate MIG's in Nicaragua,' *New York Times*, 8 November 1984; International Institute for Strategic Studies, *The Military Balance 1984–1985* (London: International Institute for International Studies, 1984), pp. 121–123; Stephen Kinzer, 'Sandinista Accuses Reagan,' *New York Times*, 11 November 1984; *LASA Report 1984*, p. 31; Philip Taubman, 'Military Moves Considered,' *New York Times*, 11 November 1984.
12. President Reagan, 'US Policy Toward Central America,' 4 November 1984, document 544, *Current Documents 1984*, p. 1106; Stephen Kinzer, 'Sandinista Accuses Reagan,' *New York Times*, 11 November 1984; Oliver L. North, memorandum to Robert C. McFarlane, 'Clarifying Who Said What to Whom,' 7 November 1984, document 00624, fiche 96, The National Security Archive, 1990.
13. Contadora Group Joint Communiqué from Brazilia, 'Observations on the Tegucigalpa Revision of the Contadora Act on Peace and Cooperation in Central America,' 14 November 1984, document 548, *Current Documents 1984*, pp. 1110–1111; Resolution adopted by the General Assembly of the Organization of American States, in Brazilia, 'Organization of American States Support for the Contadora Group's Efforts,' 17 November 1984, document 549, *Current Documents 1984*, pp. 1111–1112; International Court of Justice, judgement, The Hague, 'Court Ruling in Favor of Nicaragua on Jurisdiction Claim and Admissibility of its Applications,' 26 November 1984, document 550, *Current Documents 1984*, pp. 1112–1113; John Poindexter note to Bud McFarlane, 'A proposal for Resolving Inter-agency Conflict,' 23 November 1984, exhibit JMP–4, *Iran–Contra Investigation*, 100th Cong., lst sess., 15–17, 20–21 July 1987, pp. 414, 416.
14. Oliver L. North, memorandum to Robert C. McFarlane, 'Confusion in the Nicaraguan Resistance,' 4 December 1984, *Iran–Contra Investigation*, 100th Cong., lst sess., 100–7, Part III, 7–10, 13–14 July 1987, pp. 1004–1005; Oliver L. North, memorandum for Robert C. McFarlane, 'Assistance for the Nicaraguan Resistance,' 4 December 1984, document 00644, fiche 99, The National Security Archive, 1990; The *Iran–Contra Report*, p. 42; United States of America v. Oliver North, in The United States District Court for the District of Columbia, document on facts admitted to be true, facts 44 and 45, pp. 16–17, document 04305, fiche 663, The National Security Archive, 1990.
15. William J. Casey, Director of Central Intelligence, memorandum for Deputy Director for Central Intelligence; Deputy Director of Operations; Chief,

Latin America Division; Chief, Central America Task Force; 'Analysis of the Nicaraguan Revolution,' 6 December 1984, document 00646, fiche 99, The National Security Archive, 1990; Robert M. Gates, Deputy Director for Intelligence, memorandum for Director of Central Intelligence, 'Nicaragua,' 14 December 1984, exhibit CG–79, *Iran–Contra Investigation*, 100th Cong., lst sess., 4–6 August 1987, pp. 1039–1043; reprinted in full in US Congress. Senate. Select Committee on Intelligence, *Nomination of Robert M. Gates* 100th cong., 2nd sess., 16–20 September 1991, vol. 1, pp. 731–735; see also Louis Wolf, 'The Confirmation of Robert Gates,' *Covert Action Information Bulletin*, no. 39 (Winter 1991–1992): pp. 65–66; Martin Walker, 'CIA to grow despite end of cold war,' The *Guardian* (London), 21 September 1991, and Martin Walker, 'CIA nominee hints at targeting old allies,' The *Guardian Weekly* (Manchester), 29 September 1991.

16. Gordon D. Mott, 'Nicaragua Presses US for Progress in Talks,' *New York Times*, 9 December 1984; US Congress, House, Permanent Select Committee on Intelligence, *Activities of the Permanent Select Committee on Intelligence*, 98th Cong., 2nd sess., 2 January 1985, pp. 15–16.
17. Oliver L. North, memorandum to Robert C. McFarlane, 'Central America Trip Notebook for Your Visits to Guatemala, El Salvador, Panama, Costa Rica, and Honduras: January 17–19, 1985,' 15 January 1985, Top Secret National Security Council document, in files of the National Security Archive, Washington, D.C.; United States of America v. Oliver North, fact 49, p. 19, document 04305, fiche 663, The National Security Archive, 1990.
18. Oliver L. North, memorandum to Robert C. McFarlane, 'Nicaragua Options,' and 'Tab 1 – Nicaragua Options Notebook,' 15 January 1985, document 00725, fiche 111, The National Security Archive, 1990; United States of America v. Oliver North, fact 47, p. 18, document 04305, fiche 663, The National Security Archive, 1990.
19. United States of America v. Oliver North, fact 47, p. 19, document 04305, fiche 663, The National Security Archive, 1990; Declaration of Ministers for Foreign Affairs of the Contadora Group Meeting of 8 and 9 January 1985, Panama, 9 January 1985, to the Secretary General, 10 January 1985, United Nations General Assembly and Security Council document A/39/856–S/16889, 10 January 1985.
20. Richard Harwood, 'Nicaraguan Leader Says US attitude Negates Peace Drive,' *Washington Post*, 17 January 1985; Philip Taubman, 'US Says It Has Halted Talks With Nicaragua,' *New York Times*, 19 January 1985; Roy Gutman, *Banana Diplomacy*, p. 263.
21. Philip Taubman, 'US Says It Has Halted Talks With Nicaragua,' *New York Times*, 19 January 1985; US Department of State, *'Revolution Beyond Our Borders'*, p. 30.
22. Ambassador Bernardo Sepúlveda Amor, interview by author, 20 March 1991, London, tape recording, Embassy of Mexico.
23. Department of State, statement, 'US Withdrawal From Proceedings in Nicaragua Case,' 18 January 1985, document 535, *American Foreign Policy Current Documents 1985* (Washington, D.C.: Department of State, 1986), pp. 956–957; *International Court of Justice*, paragraph 195, p. 93.
24. Oliver L. North, memorandum for John M. Poindexter, 'Nicaraguan SNIE,' 28 January 1985, *Iran–Contra Affair*, Appendix A: Volume 1, Source

Documents, pp. 308–309; Bureau of Intelligence and Research, Current Reports, 1 February 1985, exhibit JKS–7, *Iran–Contra Investigation*, 100th Cong., 1st sess., 20–21, 27–28 May 1987, p. 475; Oliver L. North, memorandum to Robert C. McFarlane, 'Nicaraguan Arms Shipments,' 6 February 1985, document 00803, fiche 123, The National Security Archive, 1990; Oliver L. North, memorandum for Robert C. McFarlane, 'Cable to President Suazo of Honduras,' 6 February 1985, exhibit CG–69, *Iran–Contra Investigation*, 100th Cong., 1st sess., 4–6 August 1987, p. 1007; Robert C. McFarlane, memorandum for George P. Shultz, Caspar W. Weinberger, William J. Casey, and John W. Vessey, 'Cable to President Suazo of Honduras,' 7 February 1985, document 00807, fiche 123, The National Security Archive, 1990; ARA–Tony Motley, Action Memorandum to The Secretary, 'Honduran Actions With Respect to Nicaraguan Resistance Forces,' 7 February 1985, document 00808, fiche 124, The National Security Archive, 1990; White House to COS [Chief of Station] Tegucigalpa, eyes only for Station Chief and Ambassador, 'Possible Sandinista Attack Against Las Vegas, Honduras,' cable signed by Ronald Reagan, document 00806, fiche 123, The National Security Archive, 1990; United States of America v. Oliver North, fact 51, pp. 20–21, document 04305, fiche 663, The National Security Archive, 1990.

25. Mark Seibel, 'Ortega asks resumption of US talks,' *Miami Herald*, 10 February 1985; Robert J. McCartney, 'Nicaraguans Said to Change Stance in Talks,' *Washington Post*, 10 February 1985.

West European support for the Sandinistas was contingent on a number of factors, not least their relationship with Washington. The conflict in Central America was constantly related to larger issues; the United States could not prevail in the world, if it could not prevail in Central America, the reasoning held. While Europe recognized Washington's interests, they did not believe that the Sandinistas represented an extraordinary threat to the United States. The Central American situation was transformed into an alliance concern by Reagan's 'obsession' of fighting what he perceived to be 'communism' in the area. Political scientist Richard Payne argues:

> Whereas the United States claimed that its strategies in Central America protected Western interests against the Soviet threat, many West Europeans did not share America's perception of the threat from Moscow. On the contrary, the allies generally believed the United States itself was a threat to Western interests. Confrontation with Moscow in Central America and elsewhere in the Third World was largely detrimental to the allies' interests. Yet Central America in general and Nicaragua in particular became an alliance concern because Reagan decided to make West European support for his policy in the region his first test of alliance solidarity.

Yet Europe viewed their involvement as a release valve for 'pressure generated by tragic miscalculations and hubris on both sides.' European countries avoided direct confrontation with Washington, except for France, but still they pursued policies independent of Washington, either individually, or collectively in the European Community. Europe actively encouraged negotiations on several occasions (Richard J. Payne, *The West European*

*Allies, The Third World, and US Foreign Policy: Post-Cold War Challenges* [New York: Praeger, 1991], pp. 147–148, 153, 156).

26. Entire text of 'Presidential Message,' attached to Nicholas Platt, Executive Secretary, Department of State memorandum to Robert C. McFarlane, 'Presidential Message to President Suazo of Honduras,' 14 February 1985, document 00843, fiche 129, The National Security Archive, 1990; Robert C. McFarlane, memorandum to The President, 'Approach to the Hondurans regarding the Nicaraguan Resistance,' 19 February 1985, and Text of Ronald Reagan letter to His Excellency Dr. Roberto Suazo Cordova, President of the Republic of Honduras, document 00855, fiche 131, The National Security Archive, 1990.
27. Official communique of the Government of Nicaragua, contained in a letter from Ambassador Julio Icaza Gallard, to the Secretary General, 15 February 1985, United Nations, General Assembly, A/39/868, 19 February 1985, pp. 4–5.
28. Senior Administration Official, transcript of a White House Press Briefing, Santa Barbara, California, 'US Policy in Central America,' 16 February 1985, document 537, *Current Documents 1985*, pp. 960–965.
29. Transcript of a Press Conference by President Reagan, 'US Objectives in Nicaragua,' 21 February 1985, document 538, *Current Documents 1985*, pp. 966–967; Hedrick Smith, 'President Asserts Goal Is To Remove Sandinista Regime,' *New York Times*, 22 February 1985; Joel Brinkley, 'Nicaraguan Says Reagan Threats Killed Peace Bid,' *New York Times*, 26 February 1985.
30. Members of the Arms Control and Foreign Policy Caucus, *Who Are The Contras? An Analysis of the Makeup of the Military Leadership of the Rebel Forces, and the Nature of the Private American Groups Providing Them Financial and Material Support* (Washington, D.C.: Arms Control and Foreign Policy Caucus, 18 April 1985), pp. 1–4.
31. United States of America v. Oliver North, facts 57 and 59, pp. 23–24, document 04305, fiche 663, The National Security Archive, 1990.
32. *Iran–Contra Report*, pp. 45–46.
33. 'Public Relations Campaign for the Freedom Fighters,' 19 February 1985, pp. 1–2, exhibit RWO–4, *Iran–Contra Investigation*, 100th Cong., 1st sess., 11–14, 19 May 1987, pp. 783–784; Mark P. Sullivan, *Nicaragua: An Overview of US Policy 1979–1986*, Congressional Research Service Report for Congress 87–855 F (Washington, D.C.: The Library of Congress, 13 October 1987), p. 24; Vice President Bush, 'Nicaragua: A Threat to Democracy,' 28 February 1985, *Department of State Bulletin* 85, no. 2098 (May 1985): pp. 22–24.
34. Alejandro Bendaña, 'Building a Negotiation Strategy: 'Lessons' from the Nicaraguan Experience,' Papers from the 1991 CIIR Conference, 'Negotiating For Change' Regent's College, London, 18/19 January 1991, p. 59; Robert J. McCartney, 'Nicaraguans Said to Change Stance in Talks,' *Washington Post*, 10 February 1985.

## 5 Narrowing the Focus: Contadora and Esquipulas 1986

1. William M. LeoGrande, 'Rollback or Containment: The United States, Nicaragua, and the Search for Peace in Central America,' *International*

*Security* 11, no. 2 (Fall 1986): p. 111; Sklar, *Washington's War on Nicaragua*, p. 261; Bernardo Sepúlveda Amor quoted by Jim Morrell, 'Contadora: The Tready on Balance,' *International Policy Report*, June 1985, p. 4.

2. Nina M. Serafino, *Contra Aid, FY82–FY88: Summary and Chronology of Major Congressional Action on Key Legislation Concerning US Aid to the Anti-Sandinista Guerillas*, CRS Report 88–563 F, Congressional Research Service (Washington, D.C.: Library of Congress, 18 August 1988), p. 7; Nicaraguan representative to Contadora, reprinted in Vice Ministers for Foreign Affairs of the Contadora Group, 19 June 1985, United Nations, Security Council and General Assembly document A/40/401–S/17301, 24 June 1985, fiche 85–18720 1645m (E), p. 2. Having rejected an administration request for aid in April 1985, the turnabout in Congress was popularly attributed to the Ortega trip to Moscow at the same time. Thus by June Congress was prepared to authorize $27 million in 'humanitarian' aid (Arnson, *Crossroads*, pp. 184–185); 'Contadora is Back on the Road,' *Central America Report* 12, no. 27 (19 July 1985): pp. 209–210.
3. Oliver North, 'US Political/Military Strategy for Nicaragua,' ca. 15 July 1985, document 16 in Peter Kornbluh and Malcolm Byrne, *The Iran–Contra Scandal: The Declassified History* (New York: The New Press, 1993), pp. 50–52.
4. John Felton, 'Congress Clears Foreign Aid Authorization Bill,' *Congressional Quarterly Weekly Report* 43, no. 31 (3 August 1985), pp. 1540–42; United States of America v. Oliver North, pp. 10–11, document 04305, fiche 663, National Security Archive 1990; Joanne Omang, 'McFarlane Aide Facilitates Policy,' *Washington Post* 11 August 1985; Shari Cohen, 'Hill Probes Into 'Contra' Funds Stalled Over Lack of Evidence,' *Congressional Quarterly Weekly Report* 43, no. 46 (16 November 1985), p. 2388.
5. Stansfield Turner interview by Claudia Dreifus, 'Errors of Enthusiasm,' *The Progressive* 49, no. 8 (August 1985), p. 34.
6. International Security and Development Cooperation Act of 1985, 8 August 1985, document 568, *American Foreign Policy Current Documents 1985* (Washington, D.C.: US Department of State, 1986), pp. 1021–1028. The possibilities of bilateral talks were not entirely ruled out, but were linked to the administration request for contra aid. Further preconditions were also placed on the resumption of bilateral contacts (Richard J. Meislin, 'Shultz Rejects Resumption Of Talks With Sandinistas,' and Joel Brinkley, 'US Reverses Stand,' *New York Times*, 27 July 1985; see also, George P. Shultz, statement to the US–Mexican Binational Commission, Mexico City, 25 July 1985, document 565, *Current Documents 1985*, pp. 1016–1017.
7. A further problem was emerging. As one administration official put it, 'you could solve the security issue without internal reconciliation, but what do you do then about 20 000 contras in Honduras?' Shirley Christian, 'Reagan Aides See No Possibility of US Accord With Sandinistas,' *New York Times*, 18 August 1985.
8. George P. Shultz to Lewis A. Tambs, 14 August 1985, document 01424, fiche 215, The National Security Archive, 1990.
9. Jack Child, *The Central American Peace Process, 1983–1991: Sheathing Swords, Building Confidence*, (Boulder: Lynne Rienner, 1992), p. 34; Goodfellow and Morrell, 'From Contadora to Esquipulas,' p. 374; Contadora

and Support Group Communiqué, Cartagena, 25 August 1985, United Nations General Assembly and Security Council, A/40/582–S/17420, fiche 85–23777 1507t (E).

10. Ronald Reagan, 'Establishment of the Nicaraguan Humanitarian Assistance Office,' 30 August 1985, as document 571, *Current Documents 1985*, pp. 1032–1033; Department of State, *'Revolution Beyond Our Borders': Sandinista Intervention in Central America*, Special Report, no. 132 (Washington, D.C.: US Department of State, September 1985); Alfonso Chardy, 'US 'White Paper' Accuses Nicaragua of Aiding Rebels,' *Miami Herald*, 14 September 1985.

11. Statement by the Foreign Ministers of Costa Rica, El Salvador, and Honduras, San José, 4 September 1985, document 572, *Current Documents 1985*, pp. 1034–1035; Central American Historical Institute, 'Contadora Support Group Obstacle to US Policy in Central America,' *Update*, 12 September 1985, pp. 1–4; Child, *Peace Process*, p. 35; Report of the Secretary General United Nations, General Assembly and Security Council, A/40/737–S/17549, 9 October 1985, fiche 85–26643 2047d (E), p. 8.

12. Goodfellow, 'The Diplomatic Front,' p. 151; Report of the Secretary General, United Nations, General Assembly and Security Council, A/40/737–S/17549, 9 October 1985, fiche 85–26643 2047d (E), p. 2; Nicaraguan Presidential Communiqué, 13 September 1985, annex to UN General Assembly and Security Council document A/40/641–S/17469, 16 September 1985, fiche 85–25126 1710s (E), p. 2; Oliver North to Felix Rodriguez, 20 September 1985, as exhibit OLN–332, *Iran–Contra Investigation*, 100th Cong., 1st sess., 100–7, Part III, 7–10, 13–14 July 1987, pp. 1362–1363.

13. President of Nicaragua letter to the Contadora and Support Groups, 11 November 1985, annex to UN General Assembly and Security Council document A/40/894–S/17634, 15 November 1985, fiche 85–32903 2145d (E), pp. 6–7; Vernon Walters, 'Situation in Nicaragua,' *Department of State Bulletin* 86, no. 2108 (March 1986), p. 55; 'Sandinistas Tie Accord To an End to US Role,' *New York Times* 12 November 1985.

14. Alfonso Chardy draft article, 'US Policy Still Focuses on Contras, Reagan Searches for New Pressures,' Herald Washington Bureau, 15 November 1985; Report of the Secretary General, United Nations, General Assembly and Security Council, A/40/737–S/17549, 9 October 1985, fiche 85–26643 2047d (E), p. 3; Contadora letter to Secretary General, 26 September 1985, annex 1, Report of the Secretary General, United Nations, General Assembly and Security Council, A/40/737–S/17549, 9 October 1985, fiche 85–26643 2047d (E), p. 10, and annex VI, p. 73; Joint Political Communique by the European Community, Contadora, and Central American states, Luxembourg, 12 November 1985, document 580, *Current Documents 1985*, p. 1053; Child, *Peace Process*, p. 35; Preamble to *Contadora Act on Peace and Cooperation in Central America*, annex V, Report of the Secretary General, United Nations, General Assembly and Security Council, A/40/737–S/17549, 9 October 1985, fiche 85–26643 2047d (E), pp. 34–37; President of Nicaragua letter to the Contadora and Support Groups, 11 November 1985, annex to UN General Assembly and Security Council document A/40/894–S/17634, 15 November 1985, fiche 85–32903 2145d (E), pp. 2–4; William I. Robinson, *A Faustian Bargain: US Intervention in the Nicaraguan*

*Elections and American Foreign Policy in the Post-Cold War Era* (Boulder: Westview, 1992) p. 36.

15. Alan Riding, '8 Latin Countries Call for US–Nicaraguan Talks,' *New York Times* 4 December 1985; Alan Riding, 'US Rules Our New Nicaraguan Talks,' *New York Times* 3 December 1985; Elliot Abrams, Statement to the Subcommittee of the House Foreign Affairs Committee, 5 December 1985 and George Shultz, press conference, 6 December 1985, as documents 583 and 584 respectively, *Current Documents 1985*, pp. 1062–1066.
16. Daniel Ortega letter to UN Secretary General, 5 December 1985, annex to UN General Assembly and Security Council document A/40/993–S/17674, 6 December 1985, fiche 85–36583 1539p (E), p. 3; Victor Tinoco protest note to George Shultz, 6 December 1985, annex to UN General Assembly and Security Council document A/40/994–S/17675, 6 December 1985, fiche 85–36548 1812u (E), p. 2; US Department of State, *Negotiations in Central America 1981–1987* (Washington, D.C.: US Department of State, October 1987), p. 6; Central American Historical Institute, *Update* (31 December 1985), p. 3.
17. US Congress. Senate. Committee on Foreign Relations. Subcommittee on Terrorism, Narcotics and International Communications. *Drugs, Law Enforcement, and Foreign Policy: Panama*, Part 2, 100th Cong., 2nd Sess, 8–11 February 1988, pp. 158–164; United States of America v. Oliver North, document 04305, fiche 663, National Security Archive 1990; *Iran–Contra Report*, p. 64.
18. *Iran–Contra Report*, pp. 64–65; Gutman, *Banana Diplomacy*, pp. 320, 322; Shirley Christian, 'Administration Awaits Sign From Congress on Rebel Aid,' *New York Times*, 3 January 1986.
19. Daniel Ortega to Contadora and Support Group, 9 January 1986, annex to UN General Assembly and Security Council document A/40/1074–S/17733, 13 January 1986, fiche 86–00813 2228d (E), pp. 2–3; LeoGrande, 'Rollback or Containment,' p. 114; Editorial, *New York Times*, 8 January 1986; Caraballeda Message for Peace, Security and Democracy in Central America, annex to UN General Assembly and Security Council document A/40/1075–S/17736, 14 January 1986, fiche 86–00907 2283h (E), pp. 2–4; Goodfellow and Morrell, 'From Contadora to Esquipulas,' p. 374.
20. Statement, Department of State spokesman (Kalb), 17 January 1986, document 448, *American Foreign Policy Current Documents 1986* (Washington, D.C.: US Department of State, 1987), p. 731; Doyle McManus, 'US Rejects Call for New Nicaraguan Talks,' *Los Angeles Times*, 17 January 1986.
21. Richard A. Gephardt letter to Ronald Reagan, 16 January 1986; Elliot Abrams letter to Richard Lugar, Chairman of the Senate Foreign Relations Committee, on composition of the Nicaraguan Resistance, 24 February 1986, document 450, *Current Documents 1986*, pp. 735–737; On this topic see also, Arms Control and Foreign Policy Caucus, *The Contra High Command*, US Congress, March 1986, whose conclusions are quite different; for an overview of the human rights situation see Amnesty International, *Nicaragua: The Human Rights Record, 1986–1989* (London: Amnesty International Publications, 1989).
22. Joanne Omang, 'Latin Peace Talk Move Vetoed,' *Washington Post*, 16 February 1986; Ronald Reagan to the Congress of the United States, 25

February 1986; Ronald Reagan letter to Thomas P. O'Neill, 24 February 1986; The White House, *Report on Nicaragua*, 4 February 1986, outlining the 'efforts to promote a settlement in Central America and in Nicaragua'; for administration efforts to persuade Congress on contra aid see chronologically: George Shultz statement before the Senate Foreign Relations Committee, 27 February 1986, *Department of State Bulletin* 86, no. 2109 (April 1986), pp. 32–39; George Shultz to the Veterans of Foreign Wars, Washington, *Current Policy*, no. 801 (3 March 1986); Elliot Abrams, to House Subcommittee on Western Hemisphere Affairs, 5 March 1986, *Department of State Bulletin* 86, no. 2109 (April 1986), p. 83; Ronald Reagan address to the nation, *Current Policy*, no. 805 (16 March 1986); Democratic response by Jim Sasser, *Congressional Quarterly Weekly Report* 44, no. 12 (22 March 1986), p. 672; Steven Roberts, 'Talks, Not Guns, Democrat Urges,' *New York Times*, 17 March 1986; Transcript of Interview with President at the White House, *New York Times*, 23 March 1986; Jack Nelson, 'Contras' Offer to Talk Rejected by Sandinistas,' *Los Angeles Times*, 25 March 1986; Democratic Study Group, 'Responses to Reagan Rhetoric,' *Special Report*, no. 99–32, (11 March 1986), p. 9.

23. Arnson, *Crossroads*, pp. 191–193; Robert J. McCartney, 'Latin Mood Shifts Against Washington,' *Washington Post*, 17 March 1986; Wayne S. Smith, 'Why Not Try Diplomacy Instead?' *New York Times*, 19 March 1986; Steven B. Roberts, 'Reagan Defeated in House on Aiding Nicaragua Rebels,' *New York Times*, 21 March 1986.
24. William R. Long, 'New Central American Leaders Reluctant to Back US Policy on Nicaragua,' *Los Angeles Times*, 21 March 1986; Directorate of Intelligence ADDI memorandum to DCI, 3 April 1986, US Congress. Senate. House. Senate Select Committee on Secret Military Assistance to Iran and the Nicaraguan Opposition, and the House Select Committee to Investigate Covert Arms Transactions With Iran. *Iran–Contra Investigation*. Appendix A: Volume 2, Source Documents. 100th Cong., 1st sess., 13 November 1987, p. 1097; William Casey, DCI memorandum to Chief, Central American Task Force, 3 April 1986, document 02606, fiche 393, National Security Archive 1990; Central American Report 13, no. 12 (4 April 1986), pp. 89–90.
25. Tim Golden, 'Reluctant Nicaraguans threaten Outcome of Regional Peace Talks,' *Miami Herald*, 7 April 1986; Goodfellow, 'The Diplomatic Front,' p. 152; Goodfellow and Morrell, 'From Contadora to Esquipulas,' p. 374; Bruce Bagley, 'The Failure of Diplomacy,' in *Contadora and the Diplomacy of Peace in Central America* (Boulder: Westview, 1987), p. 197; Edward Cody, 'Latin Talks Founder Over Contras Fate,' *Washington Post*, 8 April 1986; Sara Fritz and Doyle McManus, 'Failure of Talks Viewed as Boost for Contras Aid,' *Los Angeles Times*, 9 April 1986; Robert Shogan and Eleanor Clift, 'Reagan Pushes for Contras Aid, Cites Talks Failure,' *Los Angeles Times*, 10 April 1986; Editorial, 'Nicaragua's No,' *Miami Herald*, 10 April 1986; Democratic Study Group, *Special Report*, no. 99–33 (9 April 1986), p. 11.
26. Gerardo Trejos Salas cited in Noam Chomsky, *The Culture of Terrorism* (London: Pluto Press, 1988), p. 135.

27. Nomination of Robert M. Gates, US Congress. Senate. Select Committee on Intelligence, 99th Cong., 2nd sess., 10 April 1986, pp. 46–47; Philip C. Habib, letter to Representative Jim Slattery, 11 April 1986; John Felton, 'The Contadora Card: Impasse May Affect Vote,' *Congressional Quarterly Weekly Report* 44, no. 15 (12 April 1986), p. 787; Central American Historical Institute, *Update*, no. 98 (17 April 1986), p. 1; LeoGrande, 'Rollback or Containment,' p. 117; Goodfellow, 'The Diplomatic Front,' p. 153.
28. John Poindexter note to NSDRF, 2 May 1986, Exhibit OLN–284, *Iran–Contra Investigation*, 100th Cong., 1st sess., 100–7, Part III, 7–10, 13–14 July 1987, p. 1141; Lawrence Walsh, *Final Report of the Independent Counsel for Iran/Contra Matters* (Washington, D.C.: United States Court of Appeals for the District of Columbia Circuit, 4 August 1993), pp. 7–8; *Iran–Contra Report*, pp. 70–71; John M. Poindexter, secret paper on NSPG meeting, 15 May 1986, document 02830, fiche 427, National Security Archive 1990; LeoGrande, 'Rollback or Containment,' p. 117; Leslie H. Gelb, 'Pentagon Fears Major War If Latins Sign Peace Accord,' *New York Times*, 20 May 1986; Bernard Gwertzman, 'Pentagon Report Irks State Department,' *New York Times*, 21 May 1986.
29. Havana International Service, 'Arias Document 'Open Meddling' in Nicaragua,' 9 May 1986 in *FBIS* 12 May 1986, pp. Q1–Q2; Jim Morrell, 'Contadora Vows to Continue,' *International Policy Report*, (August 1986), p. 6; Esquipulas Declaration, 25 May 1986, unofficial translation from the Center for International Policy; Goodfellow and Morrell, 'From Contadora to Esquipulas,' p. 374; Richard Melton to Elliot Abrams, 22 May 1986, exhibit EA–7, *Iran–Contra Investigation*, 100th Cong., 1st sess., 100–5, 2–5, 8–9 June 1987, p. 591.
30. Goodfellow, 'The Diplomatic Front,' p. 154; John M. Poindexter, secret paper on NSPG meeting, 15 May 1986, document 02830, fiche 427, National Security Archive 1990; Child, *Peace Process*, p. 38; Goodfellow and Morrell, 'From Contadora to Esquipulas,' p. 375; LeoGrande, 'Rollback or Containment,' p. 119; Central American Historical Institute, *Update*, no. 104, 11 June 1986, p. 4.
31. Ronald Reagan, address to the nation, *Current Policy*, no. 850, 24 June 1986; Drafts of Presidential statements both dated 25 June 1986, in Source Documents A 1, pp. 494–496; Bruce Cameron memorandum to Spitz Channell, 1 July 1986, Exhibit GPS–81, *Iran–Contra Investigation*, 100th Cong., 1st sess., 100–9, 23–24, 28–29 July 1987, p. 1055.
32. Linda Greenhouse, 'House Votes, 221–209, To Aid Rebel Forces in Nicaragua; Major Victory for Reagan,' *New York Times*, 26 June 1986; John Felton, 'For Reagan, a Key House Win on 'Contra' Aid,' *Congressional Quarterly Weekly Report* 44, no. 26 (28 June 1986), p. 1443; Javier Chamorro Mora note to George Shultz, 25 June 1986 annex to UN General Assembly and Security Council document A/40/1135–S/18189, 30 June 1986, fiche 86–17531 2856b (E); Arnson, *Crossroads*, pp. 197–198; Central American Historical Institute, *Update*, no. 98 (17 April 1986), pp. 4–5; Bruce Cameron memorandum to Spitz Channell, 1 July 1986, Exhibit GPS–81, *Iran–Contra Investigation*, 100th Cong., 1st sess., 100–9, 23–24, 28–29 July 1987, p. 1055.

33. *International Court of Justice*, final decisions, pp. 137–141, and paragraph 291, p. 136; Department of State Daily Press briefing, 27 June 1986, document 463, *Current Documents 1986*, pp. 771–773.
34. AP. '"Off Record" Kissinger Talk Isn't,' *New York Times*, 20 April 1986; editorial, 'It Takes Two to Contadora,' *New York Times*, 22 May 1986.

## 6 The Arias Plan 1987–1988

1. ACAN, Panama City, 11 July 1986 in *FBIS*, VI, 14 July 1986, p. P13; Jim Morrell, 'Contadora Vows to Continue,' *International Policy Report*, August 1986, p. 6; Excelsior, Mexico City, 9 July 1986, in *FBIS*, VI 14 July 1986, p. M2; Norman Kempster, 'Nicaragua's Neighbors All Agree That Sandinista Regime Must Go, Shultz Says,' *Los Angeles Times*, 8 August 1986; Kevin Klose, 'Ortega Seeks New Talks With US Aides, Vatican,' *Washington Post*, 3 August 1986.
2. John A. Booth, 'War and the Nicaraguan Revolution,' *Current History*, December 1986, p. 406; US Congress. House. Adverse Report, 99–724, part 1, 99th Cong., 2nd sess., 30 July 1986; Ambassador Nora Astorga letter to George Shultz, 9 October 1986, UN General Assembly and Security Council, A/41/692–S/18387, 9 October 1986, fiche 86–25251 3026b (E), p. 2; Nina M. Serafino, *Contra Aid, FY82–FY88*, 18 August 1988, p. 10; Victor Hugo Tinoco letter to George Shultz, 21 October 1986, UN General Assembly and Security Council, A/41/741–S/18419, 22 October 1986, fiche 86–26735 6314f (E); Editorial, 'Sharing the Blame,' *Los Angeles Times*, 15 August 1986.
3. Theodore Draper, *A Very Thin Line*, p. 3; *Al Shiraa* article excerpted in, Daniel Pipes, 'Breaking the Iran/Contra Story,' *Orbis* 31, no. 1 (Spring 1987), pp. 135–136; Gutman, *Banana Diplomacy*, pp. 338–339; Edwin Meese press briefing, 25 November 1986, *Current Documents 1986*, pp. 776–786.
4. NSPG meeting, National Security Council, 25 June 1984, on file at the National Security Archive, Washington, D.C., p. 9.
5. Peter Kornbluh and Malcolm Byrne, *The Iran–Contra Scandal*, (New York: The New Press, 1993), pp. xv–xvi; Oliver North, *Under Fire: An American Story*, (New York: HarperCollins, 1991), pp. 6–9; Senator John Kerry, A staff report, '"Private Assistance" and the Contras,' 14 October 1986, Office of Senator John Kerry, US Congress.
6. John Tower, Edmund Muskie, and Brent Scowcroft, *The Tower Commission Report: Full Text of the President's Special Review Board*, (New York: Bantam Books, 1987), pp. 78–79, 89; Kornbluh and Byrne, *The Iran–Contra Scandal*, p. xx; Steven Pressman, 'The Contra Connection,' *Congressional Quarterly Weekly Report* 45, no. 9 (28 February 1987), p. 355.
7. George P. Shultz, *Turmoil and Triumph: My Years as Secretary of State*, (New York: Charles Scribner's Sons, 1993), p. 901; Kornbluh and Byrne, *The Iran–Contra Scandal*, p. xx; Seymore M. Hersh. 'The Iran–Contra Committees: Did They Protect Reagan?' *The New York Times Magazine*, 29 April 1990, p. 64; *Iran–Contra Report*, pp. 20–22; Walter LaFeber, *Inevitable Revolutions*, p. 338; Lawrence E. Walsh, *Final Report*, p. 561.
8. *Iran–Contra Report*, pp. 332–333; Draper, *A Very Thin Line*, pp. 581–582; Harold Honju Koh, *The National Security Constitution: Power Sharing After The Iran–Contra Affair*, (New Haven: Yale University Press, 1990), pp. 16,

21, 22, 38–39; Kenneth E. Sharpe, 'The Real Cause of Irangate,' *Foreign Policy*, no. 68 (Fall 1987), pp. 21, 41; Peter Kornbluh, 'The Iran–Contra Scandal: A Postmortem,' *World Policy Journal* 5, no. 1, (1987–1988), pp. 131, 134–135.

9. Kornbluh and Byrne, *The Iran–Contra Scandal*, p. xxi; Walsh, *Final Report*, pp. 561–566; William M. LeoGrande, 'Arms for Hostages, Cash for the Contras,' *Close-Up* 10, no. 1 (Winter 1987), pp. 1–4; Doyle McManus, 'Dateline Washington: Gipperdammerung,' *Foreign Policy*, no. 66 (Spring 1987), pp. 157, 167; LaFeber, *Inevitable Revolutions*, p. 336.
10. George Bush, Grant of Executive Clemency, 24 December 1992, document 100 in Kornbluh and Byrne, *The Iran–Contra Scandal*, pp. 374–376; Walsh, *Final Report*, p. 561; Lawrence Walsh statement, 24 December 1992, document 101 in Kornbluh and Byrne, *The Iran–Contra Scandal*, p. 377.
11. Child, *Peace Process*, p. 45; James Dunkerley, *The Pacification of Central America*, (London: Verso, 1994), p. 45.
12. Peter Kornbluh, *The Price of Intervention*, pp. 198–205; Peter Kornbluh, 'The Selling of the FDN,' *The Nation* 244, no. 2 (17 January 1987), pp. 40–44; Robert Parry and Peter Kornbluh, 'Iran–Contra's Untold Story,' *Foreign Policy*, no. 72 (Fall 1988), 3–30; Chamorro, *Packaging the Contras*, passim; Allan Nairn, 'The Contras' Little List,' *The Progressive* 51, no. 3 (March 1987), 24–26; LaFeber, *Inevitable Revolutions*, p. 339; Elliot Abrams, 'Development of US–Nicaraguan Policy,' *Department of State Bulletin* 87, no. 2122 (May 1987), pp. 75, 80; US Congress. Senate. Committee on Foreign Relations, prepared statement of Kenneth E. Sharpe, in 'United States Policy Options with Respect to Nicaragua and Aid to the Contras,' 100th Cong., 1st sess., 28 January and 5 February 1987, pp. 210–224.
13. Legislative Update, 'The Money Continues to Flow,' Coalition for a New Foreign Policy, 5 March 1987, p. 1; Democratic Study Group, 'The Contra Aid Moratorium,' *Fact Sheet*, no. 100–2, 10 March 1987; Ronald Reagan, Presidential Determination no. 87–10, memorandum for the Secretary of State, 5 March 1987, in Communication from the Assistant Secretary of State, Legislative and Intergovernmental affairs, 100th Cong., 1st sess., 5 March 1987, p. 3; Steven Pressman, 'House, in a Symbolic Action, Votes Contra Aid Moratorium,' *Congressional Quarterly Weekly Report* 45, no. 11 (14 March 1987), p. 460; John Felton, 'Contra Aid Survives in Senate, But Outlook for More Is Dim,' *Congressional Quarterly Weekly Report* 45, no. 12 (21 March 1987), pp. 511–512; Linda Robinson, 'Peace in Central America?' *Foreign Affairs* 66, no. 3, (American and the World, 1987–1988), p. 592.
14. 'Contadora Evaluates Trip; Contras Begin to Crumble,' *Central America Report (CAR)* XIV, no. 4 (30 January 1987), pp. 25–26; Democratic Study Group, 'Contra Aid: An Update,' *Special Report*, no. 100–5, (4 March 1987), pp. 9–12; AFP, 'Cruz Resigns from UNO, Continues Struggle,' 7 February 1987, *FBIS* VI, 9 February 1987, p. P34; Wire Service, 'Ortega Tells Diplomats He Wants New US Talks,' *Miami Herald*, 20 January 1987.
15. Goodfellow and Morrell, 'From Contadora to Esquipulas,' p. 375; 'The EEC–Contadora–Central America Encounter,' *CAR* XIV, no. 6 (13 February 1987), p. 41; 'Peace Plans Proliferate,' *CAR* XIV, no. 2 (16 January 1987), p. 9; Freddy Balzan, 'Habib–Abrams and the Arias Plan,' *Barricada*

10 February 1987, in *FBIS*, 12 February 1987, p. P6; Havana radio in *FBIS* 12 February 1987, p. Q2; Jim Morrell, 'Contadora Eludes US' *International Policy Report*, (January/February 1987), p. 3; George Shultz, 'Nicaragua: The Moral and Strategic Stakes,' *Current Policy*, no. 918 (12 February 1987), pp. 1–3; Joanne Omang, 'Contras, US May Back Cease-fire Plan, Authors Say,' *Washington Post*, 13 February 1987; Presidents of Costa Rica, El Salvador, Guatemala, and Honduras, 'A Time for Peace,' 15 February 1987, San José, Costa Rica; Peter Ford, 'Ortega to be Invited to Discuss Peace Plan,' *Financial Times* (London), 17 February 1987.

16. Goodfellow and Morrell, 'From Contadora to Esquipulas,' pp. 376–377; Richard Boudreaux, 'Nicaragua Willing to Join Peace Conference,' *Los Angeles Times*, 19 February 1987; 'Arias Fails; Contadora Prevails,' *CAR* XIV, no. 7 (20 February 1987), pp. 49–50; Stephen Kinzer, 'Nicaragua Warms to Latest Peace Plan,' *New York Times*, 22 February 1987; US Congress. Senate. 'The Central American Peace and Economic Cooperation Act of 1987,' Report 100–12, 100th Cong., 1st sess., 6 March 1987, p. 3; Laurence Whitehead, 'The Costa Rican Initiative in Central America,' *Government and Opposition* 22, no. 4 (Autumn 1987), p. 459; CAHI, *Update*, no. 7 (13 March 1987), p. 7; James LeMoyne, 'With Rebels in Nicaragua: Battle Ready,' *New York Times*, 3 March 1987.

17. Ronald Reagan, 'Promoting Freedom and Democracy in Central America,' *Current Policy*, no. 952 (3 May 1987), pp. 2–3; 'Arias Plan Faces Overhaul,' *CAR* XIV, no. 17 (8 May 1987), pp. 129–130; Gutman, *Banana Diplomacy*, p. 344; Linda Robinson, 'Peace in Central America?' *Foreign Affairs*, p. 604; 'Arias Plan: Few Buyers,' *CAR* XIV, no. 20 (29 May 1987), p. 153; Child, *Peace Process*, 46; 'Arias Primer,' *International Policy Report*, (June 1987), p. 6; Department of State incoming telegram, May 1987, *Iran–Contra Affair*, Appendix A: Volume 1, Source Documents, pp. 1394–1395; Acting Secretary of State, Whitehead, 11 June 1987, document 488, *American Foreign Policy Current Documents 1987*, Washington, D.C.: US Department of State, 1988), pp. 742–743.

18. 'Northern Winds Affect Esquipulas Course,' *CAR* XIV, no. 23 (19 June 1987), pp. 177–178; James LeMoyne, 'Duarte Asks for a Delay In Latin Chiefs' Meeting,' *New York Times*, 16 June 1987; Child, *Peace Process*, p. 46; Goodfellow and Morrell, 'From Contadora to Esquipulas,' p. 377; Chomsky, *The Culture of Terrorism*, p. 140; 'Ortega Says Yes, Esquipulas II in On Again,' *CAR* XIV, no. 24 (26 June 1987), pp. 185–186; Oscar Arias interview with John Moody, 'We Have to be Realistic,' *Time Magazine*, 29 June 1987, p. 30; Concurrent Resolution, H.CON.RES. 146, 23 June 1987 in US Congress. House, Consideration of Miscellaneous Bills and Resolutions, 100th Cong., 1st sess., 1988; Centre for International Policy notes on 9 July 1987 hearings with Habib, copy with author.

19. 'Regional Leaders Take a Giant Step Towards Peace,' *CAR* XIV, no. 31 (14 August 1987), pp. 241–242; Goodfellow and Morrell, 'From Contadora to Esquipulas,' p. 378; Texto, A Peace Plan, 5 August 1987, USIS Guatemala; Ronald Reagan, announcement, 5 August 1987, *Department of State Bulletin* 87, no. 2127 (October 1987), p. 54; AFP, 5 August 1987 in *FBIS*, 6 August 1987, p. El; Pat Towell, 'Will Peace Plans Head Off Fight Over New Contra Aid?' *Congressional Quarterly Weekly Report* 45, no. 32 (8 August 1987),

p. 1784; William Branigin, 'Ortega Calls for Talks,' and John M. Goshko, 'US–Nicaraguan Talks Rejected,' both in *Washington Post*, August 1987; Edward Walsh, 'Despite Skeptics, Wright Pushes Latin Peace Plan,' *Washington Post*, 9 August 1987.

20. Child, *Peace Process*, p. 47; 'Procedure for the Establishment of a Firm and Lasting Peace in Central America,' annex to UN General Assembly and Security Council document A/42/521–S/19085, 31 August 1987; 'Regional Leaders Take a Giant Step Towards Peace,' *CAR* XIV, no. 31 (14 August 1987), p. 242.

21. Caspar Weinberger, statement, 11 August 1987, document 494, *Current Documents 1987*, pp. 754–755; Elaine Sciolino, 'Weinberger Opposes Aspects of Latin Peace Plan,' *New York Times*, 12 August 1987; John M. Goshko, 'US Denies Being Hostile To Regional Peace Plan,' *Washington Post*, 11 August 1987; Pat Towell, 'Will Peace Plans Head Off Fight Over New Contra Aid?' *Congressional Quarterly Weekly Report* 45, no. 32 (8 August 1987), p. 1784; John M. Goshko, 'Dole Suggests Separate US Steps In Pursuit of Central America Peace,' *Washington Post*, 13 August 1987; Editorial, 'The Habib/Stone/Motley/Enders Exit,' *New York Times*, 18 August 1987; Walter LaFeber, *Inevitable Revolutions*, p. 343; John M. Goshko, 'US Envoys Meet on Latin Peace Plan,' *Washington Post*, 18 August 1987; John M. Goshko, 'Kissinger Calls Habib Departure Damaging,' *Washington Post*, 16 August 1987; Stephen S. Rosenfeld, 'How Serious the Quest for Peace in Central America,' *Washington Post*, 21 August 1987.

22. Latin American Studies Association, *Extraordinary Opportunities . . . and Risks*, Final Report of the LASA Commission on Compliance with the Central America Peace Accord, (15 March 1988), p. 2; Goodfellow and Morrell, 'From Contadora to Esquipulas,' p. 379; Stephen Kinzer, 'Ortega Names a Reconciliation Panel Under Pact,' *New York Times*, 26 August 1987; Child, *Peace Process*, pp. 51–53.

23. George Shultz, statement, 10 September 1987, document 497, *Current Documents 1987*, pp. 757, 761; Neil A. Lewis, 'US Terms Managua Moves "Cosmetic",' *New York Times*, 24 September 1987; Washington Office on Latin America, 'Peace Plan Monitor,' 21 September 1987, p. 5; John Felton, 'New Contra Politics: Wright the Dominant Force,' *Congressional Quarterly Weekly Report* 45, no. 44 (31 October 1987), pp. 2664–2665; Washington Office on Latin America, 'Peace Plan Monitor,' no. 2, 5 October 1987, pp. 1–2; Washington Office on Latin America, 'Peace Plan Monitor,' no. 3, 22 October 1987, pp. 1–2; 'Compliance,' *International Policy Report*, 5 November 1987, p. 5; US Congress. House, Committee on Foreign Affairs, 'The Central American Peace Process,' 20–21 October 1987, 100th Cong., 1st sess., pp. 93–123; Paul Lewis, 'UN Sends Monitoring Team for Latin Accord,' *New York Times*, 22 October 1987; Democratic Study Group, 'The Central American Peace Process: Phase Two Begins,' *Special Report*, no. 100–21, 5 November 1987, p. 2.

24. Goodfellow and Morrell, 'From Contadora to Esquipulas,' p. 380; Child, *Peace Process*, pp. 51–53; LASA, *Extraordinary Opportunities*, pp. 35–37.

25. William Branigin, 'Central American Presidents Meet to assess Plan for Peace,' *Washington Post*, 16 January 1988; Goodfellow and Morrell, 'From Contadora to Esquipulas,' p. 381; Child, *Peace Process*, p. 53; Joint

Declaration, Alajuela, Costa Rica, 16 January 1988 in Selected Documents, no. 36, US Department of State, 1989, p. 6; Stephen Kinzer, 'Sandinista Strains,' *New York Times*, 21 January 1988; 'Central American Summit. Assessing Progress of Peace Plan,' *CAR* XV, no. 3 (22 January 1988), p. 17; Daniel Ortega, 'Text of Ortega's Declaration Of Concessions on Peace Plan,' *Washington Post*, 18 January 1988; Fitzwater statement, 19 January 1988, document 431, *American Foreign Policy Current Documents 1988*, (Washington, D.C.: US Department of State, 1989), p. 716; AP, 'Nicaragua Peace Concessions are a Ploy, US Official Says,' *Miami Herald*, 19 January 1988.

26. Gutman, *Banana Diplomacy*, p. 352; John M. Goshko, 'Shultz Presses Managua To Deal With Contras,' *Washington Post*, 29 September 1987; Joel Brinkley, 'Reagan, Faulting Peace Bid, Insists on New Contra Aid,' *New York Times*, 26 September 1987; Steven Pressman, 'Arias Sounds Call for Peace, End to Contra Aid,' *Congressional Quarterly Weekly Report* 45, no. 39 (26 September 1987), pp. 2297–2298; Alfonso Chardy, 'US Tells Central Americans its Conditions for Peace Plan,' *Miami Herald*, 25 September 1987; Ellen Hume, 'White House Rejects Ortega Cease-Fire; Costa Rica Chief Calls Plan Insufficient,' *Wall Street Journal* (New York), 23 September 1987; Alfonso Chardy, 'Peace Plan Hasn't Altered US Policy on Nicaragua,' *Miami Herald*, 20 September 1987; Ronald Reagan, 'Reagan U.N. Speech Focuses on World Peace,' *Congressional Quarterly Weekly Report* 45, no. 39 (26 September 1987), pp. 2327–2328; Oscar Arias, 'Excerpts From Arias Talk,' *New York Times*, 23 September 1987; Tom Kenworthy, 'Democrats Accuse Reagan Of Undercutting Peace Plan,' *New York Times*, 22 September 1987; Julia Preston, 'Central American Foreign Ministers Meet on Pact,' *Washington Post*, 28 October 1987.
27. Joel Brinkley, 'Wright, In Shift, Denounces Reagan Over Sandinistas,' *New York Times*, 6 October 1987; Alfonso Chardy, 'Aides: Reagan Remains Critical of Peace Accord,' *Miami Herald*, 7 October 1987; Paul Lewis, 'Ortega Calls for Direct Talks With US,' *New York Times*, 9 October 1987; Neil A. Lewis, 'New Strategy by US Stress Nicaragua Talks,' *New York Times*, 15 October 1987.
28. Ronald Reagan, address to OAS, *Current Policy*, no. 1007 (7 October 1987), p. 2; Alfonso Chardy and Don Bohning, 'Sandinistas Refusal Aids Contra Fund Drive,' *Miami Herald*, 2 November 1987; Peter Ford, 'Nicaragua Toughens Stance as Peace Plan Deadline Nears,' *Christian Science Monitor*, 2 November 1987; Stephen Kinzer, 'Sandinistas Agree to Indirect Talks on Cease-Fire Bid,' *New York Times*, 6 November 1987; John Felton, 'Reversal by Nicaraguan Leader Darkens Picture for Contra Aid,' *Congressional Quarterly Weekly Report* 45, no. 45 (7 November 1987), p. 2720; John M. Goshko, 'Shultz Pledges Delay In Contra Aid Request,' *Washington Post*, 11 November 1987; James LeMoyne, 'Nicaragua Agrees to Talk Directly with the Contras,' *New York Times*, 17 January 1988; Michael Wines, 'US Expecting a 'January Surprise' From Nicaragua,' *Los Angeles Times*, 15 January 1988; John Felton, 'Contra–Aid Denial Shifts Burden to Democrats,' *Congressional Quarterly Weekly Report* 46, no. 6 (6 February 1988), 235; Ronald Reagan, letter to House and Senate in *Congressional Quarterly Weekly Report* 46, no. 4 (23 January 1988), p. 165; The White House, Office of the Press Secretary, 27 January 1988, copy with author.

29. Stephen Kinzer, 'Sandinista–Contra Cease-Fire Termed Major Breakthrough By Nicaragua's Rival Factions,' *New York Times*, 25 March 1988; Sapoa Agreement, 'Text of Nicaraguan Agreement on Cease-Fire,' *New York Times*, 25 March 1988; Child, *Peace Process*, p. 54.
30. Goodfellow and Morrell, 'From Contadora to Esquipulas,' p. 383.

## 7 Bush and the Sandinistas 1989

1. US Congress. House, Committee on Foreign Affairs, 'Congress and Foreign Policy 1988,' 100th Cong., 1st sess., pp. 6, 53; John Felton, 'Solemn Congress Approves Contra–Aid Package,' *Congressional Quarterly Weekly Report* 46, no. 14 (2 April 1988), p. 839; Center for International Policy, 'The Nicaraguan Cease-Fire Talks: A Documentary Survey,' Washington, D.C.: 13 June 1988, pp. 1–2; Sam Dillon, 'Ortega Proposes New Peace Talks,' *Miami Herald*, 20 June 1988; Julia Preston, 'Leader Says US Behind Collapse of Talks,' *Washington Post*, 12 June 1988; Bill McAllister, 'Reagan Blames Sandinistas For Collapse of Peace Talks,' *Washington Post*, 11 June 1988; Department Statement, 'Reciprocal Expulsion of Nicaraguan Diplomats,' *Department of State Bulletin* 88, no. 2138 (September 1988), p. 69; US Congress. Senate, Select Committee on Intelligence, 'The Expulsion of American Diplomats from Nicaragua,' 100th Cong., 2nd sess., 14 July 1988; Central American Historical Institute, *Update* 7, no. 27 (17 August 1988), p. 1.
2. Paul S. Reichler, 'More Contra Aid: Torching the Talks,' *New York Times*, 4 August 1988; Wire Services, 'Contras Reject Ortega's Peace Talks Proposal,' *Los Angeles Times*, 13 August 1988; Richard Boudreaux, 'Ortega Shuts Door on Contra Talks,' *Los Angeles Times*, 14 August 1988.
3. Lindsey Gruson, 'Shultz, at OAS Supports Contras,' *New York Times*, 15 November 1988; Robert Pear, 'Bush Aides Speak of New Policy Of Diplomacy in Central America,' *New York Times*, 20 November 1988; John M. Goshko, 'Latin Leaders Watching for Hints of Bush Policy,' *Washington Post*, in USIA PDQ index and text database, 13 November 1988; Robert Pear, 'Baker at the State Dept: Pragmatism Over Zeal,' *New York Times*, 15 November 1988; Walsh, *Final Report*, p. 473; William LeoGrande, 'From Reagan to Bush: The Transition in US Policy Towards Central America,' *Journal of Latin American Studies* 22, no. 3 (October 1990), pp. 620–621.
4. Stephen Kinzer, 'Nicaragua and Rebels Expect Fresh Effort From Bush to Resolve Conflicts,' *New York Times*, 20 November 1988; Robert Pear, 'Bush Aides Speak of New Policy Of Diplomacy in Central American,' *New York Times*, 20 November 1988; William I. Robinson, 'George Bush and Nicaragua,' *Central America Information Bulletin* 5, no. 36 (16 November 1988), p. 1; Combined Dispatches, 'Ortega Seeks Negotiations with Next US President,' *Washington Times* in USIA PDQ index and text database, 9 November 1988; 'What Future for Contras,' *Central America Report* XV, no. 41 (21 October 1988); Central American Foreign Ministers letter to Javier Pérez de Cuéllar, Mexico City, 30 November 1988, annex to Centre for International Policy, *International Policy Update*, 1 December 1988; Goodfellow and Morrell, 'From Contadora to Esquipulas,' p. 384; Child, *Peace Process*, p. 63.

5. Child, *Peace Process*, p. 71; Stephen Kinzer, 'In US and in Latin America, Contras Seem to be History,' *New York Times*, 14 December 1988; 'What Future for Contras,' *Central America Report* XV, no. 41 (21 October 1988); Larry Rohter, 'Central American Countries to Revive Peace Effort,' *New York Times*, 4 December 1988; Stephen Kinzer, 'Ortega Prepares Peace Bid to US' *New York Times*, 18 December 1988; Richard Boudreaux, 'Sandinistas Reportedly Plan Peace Initiative for Bush,' *Los Angeles Times*, 13 December 1988.
6. Richard Boudreaux, 'Ortega Rejects Talks on 2 Rival Contra Truce Plans,' *Los Angeles Times*, 1 January 1989; Stephen Kinzer, 'Contra Leaders Disagree on Peace Plan,' *New York Times*, 1 January 1989; Reuter, 'Ortega Attacks Peace Summit Postponement,' The *Sunday Times* (London), 8 January 1989; Isabel Hilton, 'Central American Summit Postponed,' *The Independent* (London), 11 January 1989; Julia Preston, 'Central America Looks To Bush for Solutions,' *Washington Post*, 22 January 1989; Stephen Kinzer, 'Anti-Sandinistas Say US Should End Embargo,' *New York Times*, 12 January 1989; David Adams, 'Nicaragua Opposition on the Move,' *The Independent* (London), 16 January 1989.
7. George Bush, 'In the Footsteps of Washington on 'Democracy's Front Porch,' *The Independent* (London), 21 January 1989; Child, *Peace Process*, p. 64; John Lichfield, 'Bush to Nominate a Hard Liner to Control Latin America Policy,' *The Independent* (London), 2 February 1989; Robert Pear, 'Bush Backing Democrat for Post On Latin America in State Dept.,' *New York Times*, 2 February 1989; Norma Romano-Benner, 'Arias Optimistic About US Support for Peace Plan,' USIA Text Link, 3 February 1989; Alan Riding, 'Quayle in Caracas to Hail New Chief,' *New York Times*, 2 February 1989; Simon Fisher, 'Venezuela's New Leader Draws a Record Gathering,' *The Independent* (London), 2 February 1989; 'Central American Peace Process Revives,' *International Policy Update*, 4 February 1989, pp. 1–8; Washington Office on Latin America, 'New Possibilities for Central American Peace After Caracas,' *Peace Plan Monitor*, no. 6, (7 February 1989), pp. 1–4.
8. Goodfellow and Morrell, 'From Contadora to Esquipulas,' p. 385; David Adams, 'Ortega Calls the Shots at Summit,' The *Independent* (London), 13 February 1989; Lindsey Gruson, 'A Showdown on Nicaragua,' *International Herald Tribune* (Paris), 14 February 1989; Francisco D'Escoto letter to CIIR, 22 February 1989; William Branigin, 'Summit in El Salvador Focuses on Peace Plan,' *Washington Post*, in USIA, Text Link, 14 February 1989; Joint Declaration of the Central American Presidents, El Tesoro, El Salvador, 14 February 1989, Nicaraguan Embassy, London, pp. 1–4; David Adams, 'US Urged to Aid Return of Contras,' The *Independent* (London), 9 February 1989.
9. Goodfellow and Morrell, 'From Contadora to Esquipulas,' p. 386; Child, *Peace Process*, p. 65.
10. Robert Pear, 'Latin Agreement Raises Eyebrows at White House,' *New York Times*, 16 February 1989; Mark A. Uhlig, 'A Latin Peace Plan Not So Broad: Ball in Nicaragua's Court,' *New York Times*, 16 February 1989; ACAN, 'Azcona Sure US to Accept Contra Decision,' *FBIS* LAT–89–030, 15 February 1989, p. 2; Chris Norton, 'Contras Seek Democracy before

Demobilization,' The *Independent* (London), 16 February 1989; Lindsey Gruson, 'Despite Pact, Contras Vow to Fight On,' *New York Times*, 18 February 1989; Bernard Weinraub, 'Bush, Uneasy About Latin Pact, Wants Contra Humanitarian Aid,' *New York Times*, 17 February 1989; Editorial, 'Why Not Help the Nicaraguan Deal?' *New York Times*, 17 February 1989; John Lichfield, 'White House Trips Up Over New Plans to Disarm Contras,' *The Independent* (London), 18 February 1989; Centre for International Policy, 'El Salvador Presidential Summit Advances Peace Process,' *International Policy Update*, 21 February 1989; Robert Pear, 'Contras Chafing at US Indecision,' *New York Times*, 23 February 1989; Dunkerley, *Pacification*, p. 27; LeoGrande, 'From Reagan to Bush,' pp. 598–601.

11. Editorial, 'The Shout from Central America,' *New York Times*, 26 February 1989; Alex Brummer, 'Bush Committed to Further Contra Aid,' The *Guardian* (London), 3 March 1989; Robert Pear, 'Report is Urging an Overhaul of US Latin Policy,' *New York Times*, 9 March 1989; International Commission for Central America Recovery and Development, *Poverty, Conflict and Hope: A Turning Point in Central America*, US Congress. Senate, Committee on Foreign Relations, 101st Cong., 1st sess., March 1989, pp. xix, 113–114.
12. Robert Pear, 'Bush to Ask New Aid for Contras in Honduras,' *New York Times*, 13 March 1989; Robert Pear, 'Bush Effort to Aid Contras Is Seen As Inconsistent with Peace Plan,' *New York Times*, 15 March 1989; Bipartisan Accord on Central America with supporting Bush and Baker statements of 24 March 1989 in US Department of State, 'US Support for Democracy and Peace in Central America,' Selected Documents, no. 36, pp. 1–3.
13. Robert Pear, 'Tentative Accord Set in Washington on Aid to Contras,' *New York Times*, 24 March 1989; Bernard Weinraub, 'Bush and Congress Sign Policy Accord on Aid to the Contras,' *New York Times*, 25 March 1989; Mark A. Uhlig, 'Sandinistas Assail Renewed Rebel Aid,' *New York Times*, 25 March 1989; David E. Rosenbaum, 'Congress Appears to Support Contra Aid Plan,' *New York Times*, 25 March 1989; Thomas L. Friedman, 'Contras' Leaders Urged to return Home for Election,' *New York Times*, 29 March 1989; Martin Walker, 'Bush Urges Contras to Return Home,' The *Guardian* (London), 30 March 1989.
14. Bipartisan Accord on Central America with supporting Bush and Baker statements of 24 March 1989 in US Department of State, 'US Support for Democracy and Peace in Central America,' Selected Documents, no. 36, pp. 2–3; Text of GOP Document: Republican Platform, *Congressional Quarterly Weekly Report* 46, no. 34 (20 August 1988), p. 2389; LaFeber, *Inevitable Revolutions*, p. 348; Russell Dybvik, USIA, Text Link, 28 March 1989.
15. W. Raymond Duncan and Carolyn McGiffert Ekedahl, *Moscow and the Third World Under Gorbachev* (Boulder: Westview Press, 1990), pp. 191, 196; LaFeber, *Inevitable Revolutions*, p. 348; Fred Halliday, *Cold War, Third World: An Essay on Soviet–American Relations*, (London: Hutchinson Radius, 1989), pp. 137–138, 141; Miller, *Soviet Relations with Latin America 1959–1987*, (Cambridge: Cambridge University Press, 1989), pp. 203–204, 216; Kiva Maidanik, 'On the Real Soviet Policy Towards Central America,

Past and Present,' and Donna Rich–Kaplowitz, 'The US Response to Soviet and Cuban Policies in Central America,' both in Wayne S. Smith, ed. *The Russians Aren't Coming' New Soviet Policy in Latin America*, (Boulder: Lynne Rienner, 1992), pp. 93, 110; Voytek Zubek, 'Soviet "New Thinking" and the Central American Crisis,' *Journal of Interamerican Studies and World Affairs* 29, no. 3 (Fall 1987), p. 89; Mikhail Gorbachev, *Perestroika: New Thinking for Our Country and the World*, (New York: Harper and Row, 1987), p. 175.

16. Robert Pear, 'Bush Aides Speak of New Policy Of Diplomacy in Central America,' *New York Times*, 20 November 1988; Vice President Dan Quayle address, 'Gorbachev Urged to Adopt Bush Strategy for Central America,' USIA Text Link, 14 April 1989; Bipartisan Accord on Central America with supporting Bush and Baker statements of 24 March 1989 in US Department of State, 'US Support for Democracy and Peace in Central America,' Selected Documents, no. 36, pp. 2–3.
17. Jonathan Steele, 'Moscow Ties the Knot,' The *Guardian* (London), 1 April 1989; Bill Keller, Gorbachev–Castro Face Off: A Clash of Style and Policies,' *New York Times*, 2 April 1989; James Baker, press briefing, 5 April 1989, document 451, *Current Documents 1989*, pp. 694–695; Special, 'Baker Calls Latin Plan A Test for the Kremlin,' *New York Times*, 13 April 1989; Bill Keller, 'Gorbachev Eclipsed,' *New York Times*, 6 April 1989; Bernard Weinraub, 'US Dismisses Call by Gorbachev To End Latin America Arms Aid,' *New York Times*, 6 April 1989; S. Neil MacFarlane, 'Bush's Missing Link in Nicaragua,' *New York Times*, 6 April 1989.
18. Child, *Peace Process*, pp. 68–69; Kiva Maidanik, 'On the Real Soviet Policy Towards Central America, Past and Present,' in Smith, ed. *The Russians Aren't Coming*, pp. 93–94; Duncan and Ekedahl, *Moscow and the Third World*, p. 191; Donna Rich–Kaplowitz, 'The US Response to Soviet and Cuban Policies in Central America,' in Smith, ed. *The Russians Aren't Coming*, p. 110; Martin Walker, 'Bush Beefs Up Monroe Doctrine,' The *Guardian* (London), 3 May 1989; Martin Walker, 'Bush Doubts Soviet Pledge on Managua,' The *Guardian* (London), 17 May 1989; John Lichfield, 'White House Questions Nicaragua Aid Claim,' The *Independent* (London), 17 May 1989; President Bush, notice on emergency, 21 April 1989, document 453, *Current Documents 1989*, p. 697.
19. AP., 'Managua Rivals Urge End to Contras,' *New York Times*, 5 August 1989; Goodfellow and Morrell, 'From Contadora to Esquipulas,' p. 388; LeoGrande, 'From Reagan to Bush,' p. 601; Child, *Peace Process*, p. 69; Robert Pear, 'US Official Presses for an Extension for Contras,' *New York Times*, 3 August 1989.
20. Central American Presidents, Agreement signed at Tela, Honduras, 8 August 1989, in *New York Times*, 9 August 1989; Child, *Peace Process*, p. 70.
21. Robert Pear, 'Democrats Warn US Must Support Contras Eviction,' *New York Times*, 9 August 1989; Editorial, 'Mr. Bush, Alone on Nicaragua,' *New York Times* 8 August 1989; William Branigin and Lee Hockstader, '5 Presidents Agree to Disband Contras,' *Washington Post*, 8 August 1989; Alexander Sullivan and Edmund Scherr, 'US Supports Tela Accord on Peace in Central America,' USIA, Text Link, 8 August 1989; William LeoGrande, 'How to Dispose of the Contras,' *New York Times*, 9 August 1989.

22. Mark A. Uhlig, 'The Contras: Lost Cause?' *New York Times*, 10 August 1989; Larry Rohter, 'Central America Goes Its Own Way,' *New York Times*, 13 August 1989; Robert Pear, 'Clash of Experts Blurs Policy on Central America,' *New York Times*, 24 August 1989.
23. AP, 'Nicaragua Foes Come Face to Face and Chat,' *New York Times*, 27 August 1989; Paul Lewis, 'Contras Said to Sell Arms to Salvador Rebels,' *New York Times*, 15 October 1989; Simon Tisdall, 'Contras Sell Weapons to Leftwingers,' The *Guardian* (London), 16 October 1989; Child, *Peace Process*, p. 72; Peter James Spielmann, 'UN Force Due For Central America,' The *Independent* (London), 13 October 1989; Martin Walker, 'US Snubs Soviet Initiative in Central America,' The *Guardian* (London), 6 October 1989; Mark A. Uhlig, 'Soviets Reducing Arms for Managua,' *New York Times*, 11 October 1989.
24. Child, *Peace Process*, p. 71; AP, 'Contra Ambush Kills 18 Nicaraguan Troops,' *New York Times*, 23 October 1989; Goodfellow and Morrell, 'From Contadora to Esquipulas,' p. 389; David Adams, 'Ortega War Pledge Sours American Democracy Fiesta,' The *Observer* (London), 29 October 1989; Lindsey Gruson, 'Ortega Declares He Will Abandon Nicaraguan Truce,' *New York Times*, 28 October 1989; Mark A. Uhlig, 'Nicaraguans Begin Sweep Against Contra Stronghold,' *New York Times*, 28 October 1989; Lindsey Gruson, 'Ortega Modifies Stand on Ending Civil War Truce,' *New York Times*, 29 October 1989; Mark A. Uhlig, 'Ortega's Foray: A Stunning Misstep,' *New York Times*, 30 October 1989.
25. Mark A. Uhlig, 'Ortega's Foray: A Stunning Misstep,' *New York Times*, 30 October 1989; LeoGrande, 'From Reagan to Bush,' pp. 602–603; Nicholas Young and Martin Walker, 'Managua Suspends Truce With Contras,' The *Guardian* (London), 2 November 1989; Daniel Ortega Saavedra, 'Why I Ended the Ceasefire,' *New York Times*, 2 November 1989; Robert Pear, 'Anger With Ortega Unites Policy Makers in US,' *New York Times*, 2 November 1989.
26. Paul Lewis, 'UN to Send Observers,' *New York Times*, 8 November 1989; Goodfellow and Morrell, 'From Contadora to Esquipulas,' p. 390; Paul Lewis, 'New Contra Chiefs Say Disarming Before Election Would Be Foolish,' *New York Times*, 11 November 1989; AP, 'Managua Offer,' The *Independent* (London), 22 November 1989.
27. Dunkerley, *Pacification*, pp. 68–69; Goodfellow and Morrell, 'From Contadora to Esquipulas,' pp. 390–391; Department of State, statement, 1 November 1989, document 458, *Current Documents 1989*, p. 704; Lindsey Gruson, 'Plane in Salvador With Soviet Arms Crashes and 4 Die,' *New York Times*, 26 November 1989; Simon Tisdall, 'White House in New Crisis with Managua,' The *Guardian* (London), 27 November 1989; Noll Scott, 'Sandinistas Blamed for Accord Breach,' The *Guardian* (London), 29 November 1989.
28. Peter Pringle, 'Bush to Raise 'Cold War Relics' at Malta Summit,' The *Independent* (London), 30 November 1989.
29. Goodfellow and Morrell, 'From Contadora to Esquipulas,' pp. 390–391; LeoGrande, 'From Reagan to Bush,' pp. 602–603; Presidents of Central America, Declaration of San Isidro de Coronado, 12 December 1989, document 460, *Current Documents 1989*, pp. 706–708.

## 8 The 1990 Elections and Democracy

1. Dunkerley, *Pacification*, p. 27; Presidents of Central America, declaration at San Isidro de Coronado, Costa Rica, 12 December 1989, document 460, *Current Documents 1989*, pp. 706–707; Child, *Peace Process*, p. 75; Political Accords between Daniel Ortega and the legally constituted parties gathered at the Olof Palme Convention Center, 3–4 August 1989, Appendix 5, Council of Freely-Elected Heads of Government, *Observing Nicaragua's Elections, 1989–1990*, (Atlanta: Carter Center, 1990), p. 50.
2. J. D. Gannon, 'Conflicting Views of Democracy at Core of Nicaraguan Talks,' *Christian Science Monitor*, 27 May 1988; Noam Chomsky, *Deterring Democracy*, (London: Verso, 1991), p. 305; Jonas, 'Elections and Transitions: The Guatemala and Nicaraguan Cases,' in Booth and Seligson, eds., *Elections and Democracy in Central America*, p. 147; Andrew A. Reding, 'The Evolution of Governmental Institutions,' in Thomas W. Walker, ed. *Revolution and Counterrevolution in Nicaragua*, (Boulder: Westview Press, 1991), pp. 39, 42; Child, *Peace Process*, p. 75; Dunkerley, *Pacification*, p. 36; List of Observers in the 1990 Election, appendix 2, UN Secretary General, The Situation in Central America: Threats to International Peace and Security and Peace Initiatives, General Assembly, A/44/927, 30 March 1990, fiche 90–06213 1635d (E), p. 17.
3. John A. Peeler, 'Democracy and Elections in Central America: Autumn of the Oligarchs?' in Booth and Seligson, eds., *Elections and Democracy*, pp. 192–193, 187; Reuter, 'Contras Blamed for Nun Killings,' The *Guardian* (London), 29 January 1990; Chomsky, *Deterring Democracy*, pp. 298–299.
4. Barry Gills and Joel Rocamora, 'Low Intensity Democracy,' *Third World Quarterly* 13, no. 3, (1992), pp. 505–506; Alejandro Bendaña, 'Building a Negotiating Strategy: Lessons from the Nicaraguan Experience,' CIIR Conference Papers, 'Negotiating for Change: The Struggle for Peace with Justice,' Regents College, London, 18–19 January 1991, p. 62; Eduardo Galeano, *We Say No: Chronicles 1963–1992*, (New York: W. W. Norton, 1992), p. 202; Philip J. Williams, 'Elections and Democratization in Nicaragua: The 1990 Elections in Perspective,' *Journal of Interamerican Studies and World Affairs* 32, no. 4, (Winter 1990), pp. 13–14.
5. Michael Reid, 'Truth Commission Points Finger at Salvadoran Military,' The *Guardian* (London), 16 March 1993; Guy Gugliotta and Douglas Farah, 'Salvadoran Findings Raise Questions for Reagan, Bush,' *Austin American–Statesman*, 21 March 1993, reprinted in *Central America NewsPak* 8, no. 3, issue 185, 8–21 March 1993; Laurence Whitehead, 'The Alternatives to "Liberal Democracy": A Latin American Perspective,' in David Held ed., *Prospects for Democracy: North, South, East, West*, (Cambridge: Polity Press, 1993), pp. 315–316; Dunkerley, *Pacification*, p. 51.
6. Mike Gonzales, *Nicaragua: What Went Wrong*? (London: Bookmarks, 1990), pp. 116, 114, 112; Harvey Williams, 'The Social Programs,' in Walker, ed. *Revolution and Counterrevolution* pp. 205–206; Elizabeth Dore and John Weeks, *The Red and the Black: The Sandinistas and the Nicaraguan Revolution*, (London: Institute of Latin American Studies, 1992), pp. 13, 21; George R. Vickers, 'A Spider's Web,' *NACLA: Report on the Americas* XXIV, no. 1 (June 1990), p. 25.

7. Jonas, 'Elections and Transitions,' pp. 148–149; Woodward, *Veil*, pp. 188, 185; Mesoamerica cited by Chomsky, *Deterring Democracy*, p. 307; Bendaña, 'Building a Negotiating Strategy,' p. 62.
8. Carlos M. Vilas, 'What Went Wrong,' *NACLA: Report on the Americas* XXIV, no. 1 (June 1990), p. 18; Eric Weaver and William Barnes, 'Opposition Parties and Coalitions,' in Walker ed., p. 135; William I. Robinson, *A Faustian Bargain: US Intervention in the Nicaraguan Elections and American Foreign Policy in the Post-Cold War Era*, (Boulder: Westview Press, 1992), p. 47; Peter Kornbluh, 'The US Role in the Counterrevolution,' in Walker, ed. *Revolution and Counterrevolution*, p. 342; Bendaña, 'Building a Negotiating Strategy,' p. 61; Williams, 'Elections and Democratization in Nicaragua,' p. 20.
9. Weaver and Barnes 'Opposition Parties and Coalitions,' p. 134; LeoGrande, 'From Reagan to Bush,' p. 604; Reding, 'The Evolution of Governmental Institutions,' p. 40; Mark A. Uhlig, 'Tense Days for Nicaraguan Opposition,' *New York Times*, 19 August 1989.
10. Weaver and Barnes 'Opposition Parties and Coalitions,' pp. 136–137; Christopher Hitchens, 'A Dynasty Divided,' The *Independent Magazine* (London), 17 February 1990, p. 25; Dunkerley, *Pacification*, p. 38; Williams, 'Elections and Democratization in Nicaragua,' p. 26.
11. Williams, 'Elections and Democratization in Nicaragua,' pp. 21–22; LeoGrande, 'From Reagan to Bush,' pp. 604–605; Robinson, *A Faustian Bargain*, pp. 111–114; Accords 3–4 August 1989, Appendix 5, Council of Freely-Elected Heads of Government, *Observing Nicaragua's Elections, 1989–1990*, p. 50; Reding, 'The Evolution of Governmental Institutions,' p. 40; Kornbluh, 'The US Role in the Counterrevolution,' p. 343.
12. Reding, 'The Evolution of Governmental Institutions,' p. 41; Chomsky, *Deterring Democracy*, p. 299, Williams, 'Elections and Democratization in Nicaragua,' p. 23; Republic of Nicaragua, Memorial on Compensation, 29 March 1988, cited by Kornbluh, 'The US Role in the Counterrevolution,' p. 345.
13. Ralph I. Fine and Kenneth E. Sharpe, 'Nicaragua: The Sour-Grapes Brigade,' *New York Times*, 21 February 1990; Tom Gibb, 'Nicaragua Fears Poll Violence,' The *Observer* (London), 18 February 1990; Robert Pear, 'UN Team Reports on Nicaragua Vote,' *New York Times*, 7 February 1990; Simon Tisdall, 'UN Praise for Nicaragua in Run-up to Poll,' The *Guardian* (London), 8 February 1990; Michael McCaughan, 'UN Plays the Role of Umpire as Bush Dollars Flow for Election Razzmatazz,' *Irish Times* (Dublin), 23 January 1990; Mark A. Uhlig, 'Carter Applauds Nicaraguans On Election-Monitoring Plan,' *New York Times*, 30 January 1990; Williams, 'Elections and Democratization in Nicaragua,' p. 27; Council of Freely-Elected Heads of Government, *Observing Nicaragua's Elections, 1989–1990*, p. 12; Elliot L. Richardson, Fifth report to the Secretary General by the United Nations Observer Mission to verify the electoral process in Nicaragua, annex to UN Secretary General, The Situation in Central America: Threats to International Peace and Security and Peace Initiatives, General Assembly, A/44/927, 30 March 1990, fiche 90–06213 1635d (E), p. 12; The Latin American Studies Association, Report of the Commission to Observe the 1990 Nicaraguan Election, *Electoral Democracy: Under International Pressure* (University of Pittsburgh, 15 March 1990), pp. 1–4.

14. Robinson, *A Faustian Bargain*, p. 149; Robert Pear, 'US to weigh New Ties If Ortega Wins Election,' *New York Times*, 18 February 1990; Alma Guillermoprieto, 'Former Rebels Seeks Deal with Sandinistas,' The *Guardian* (London), 19 February 1990; LeoGrande, 'From Reagan to Bush,' p. 605; John Lichfield, 'US–Sandinista Ties Remain Unthinkable,' The *Independent* (London), 22 February 1990); Douglas Tweedale, 'Fair Vote Will Lead to Ties with US,' The *Independent* (London), 24 February 1990; Tom Gibb, 'Bush Prepares to Bargain with Sandinistas,' The *Observer* (London), 25 February 1990.
15. Dore and Weeks, *The Red and the Black*, p. 2.
16. Vilas, 'What Went Wrong,' p. 11.
17. Freely-Elected Heads, *Observing Nicaragua's Elections, 1989–1990*, p. 12; LASA, *Electoral Democracy: Under International Pressure*, p. 2; Robinson, *A Faustian Bargain*, p. 148; Kornbluh, 'The US Role in the Counterrevolution,' p. 344; Chomsky, *Deterring Democracy*, pp. 318–321.
18. Chomsky, *Deterring Democracy*, pp. 307, 296.
19. Dore and Weeks, *The Red and the Black*, pp. 30–31; Elizabeth Dore, 'Panama, Key to Ortega's campaign,' *New York Times*, 30 January 1990; LASA, *Electoral Democracy: Under International Pressure*, p. 40; Bendaña, 'Building a Negotiating Strategy,' p. 61; Vilas, 'What Went Wrong,' p. 11.
20. Dore and Weeks, *The Red and the Black*, pp. 1, 29; Chomsky, *Deterring Democracy*, p. 300.
21. Dunkerley, *Pacification*, p. 35; Williams, 'Elections and Democratization in Nicaragua,' p. 22; Joseph Ricciardi, 'Economic Policy,' in Walker, ed. *Revolution and Counterrevolution*, pp. 263–264.
22. LaFeber, *Inevitable Revolutions*, pp. 348, 350; Dunkerley, *Pacification*, p. 13–14; Vilas, 'What Went Wrong,' p. 12–13; Gonzales, *Nicaragua: What Went Wrong*? 108–109.
23. LASA, *Electoral Democracy: Under International Pressure*, p. 40; Dore and Weeks, *The Red and the Black*, pp. 1, 29; Trish O'Kane, 'The New Old Order,' *NACLA: Report on the Americas* XXIV, no. 1 (June 1990), p. 29; Vilas, 'What Went Wrong,' p. 15.
24. Dore and Weeks, *The Red and the Black*, pp. 13, 1; Vickers, 'A Spider's Web,' p. 20; Williams, 'The Social Programs,' in Walker, pp. 205–206; Galeano, *We Say No*, p. 201; Robinson, *A Faustian Bargain*, p. 154; LASA, *Electoral Democracy: Under International Pressure*, pp. 40–41.
25. David Held, *Prospects for Democracy*, pp. 27, 31–32.
26. LaFeber, *Inevitable Revolutions*, p. 351; Shelly McConnell, 'Rules of the Game: Nicaragua's Contentious Constitutional Debate,' *NACLA: Report on the Americas* XXVII, no. 2, (September/October 1993), pp. 20–21; Peeler, 'Democracy and Elections in Central America: Autumn of the Oligarchs?' p. 196.
27. Williams, 'Elections and Democratization in Nicaragua,' pp. 14–15; Barry Gills, Joel Rocamora, and Richard Wilson eds., *Low Intensity Democracy: Political Power in the New World Order*, (London: Pluto Press, 1993), p. 3, passim; Robinson, *A Faustian Bargain*, p. 152.
28. Galeano, *We Say No*, p. 195; Held, *Prospects for Democracy*, pp. 25–27, 13–15; Gills and Rocamora, 'Low Intensity Democracy,' *Third World*

*Quarterly*, pp. 502–503; Robinson, *A Faustian Bargain*, p. 158; Contadora Foreign Ministers, information bulletin, 9 January 1983, document 3.1, in Bagley, *Contadora Documents*, pp. 164–166; Peeler, 'Democracy and Elections in Central America: Autumn of the Oligarchs?' p. 194.

## Conclusion

1. US Congress, Senate, Select Committee on Intelligence, *Nomination of Robert M. Gates: Hearing before the Senate Select Committee on Intelligence*, 99th Cong., 2nd sess., 10 April 1986, pp. 45–46; David Ryan, 'Asserting US Power, 1970–1994,' in Phillip Davies (ed.), *Trends in American Politics, 1975–1995* (Manchester: Manchester University Press, 1995), forthcoming; Augusto Varas, 'From Coercion to Partnership: A New Paradigm for Security Cooperation in the Western Hemisphere,' in Jonathan Hartlyn, Lars Schoultz and Augusto Varas (eds.), *The United States and Latin America in the 1990s: Beyond the Cold War*, (Chapel Hill: University of North Carolina Press, 1992), p. 49; James Dunkerley, 'Reflections on the Nicaraguan Election,' *New Left Review*, no. 182, (July/August 1990), p. 46; Robert Gates memorandum for the Director of Central Intelligence, 14 December 1984, in US Congress. Senate, Select Committee on Intelligence, *Nomination of Robert Gates*, Hearings, 100th Cong., 1st sess., 16–20 September 1991, p. 734.
2. President Reagan asked Congress, who he imputed was also responsible for foreign policy:

   > If Central America were to fall, what would the consequences be for our position in Asia, Europe, and for alliances such as NATO? If the United States cannot respond to a threat near our own borders, why should Europeans or Asians believe that we are seriously concerned about threats to them? If the Soviets can assume that nothing short of an attack on the United States will provoke an American response, which ally, which friend, will trust us then?
   >
   > The Congress shares both the power and the responsibility for our foreign policy.

   (Ronald Reagan, 'Text of Reagan Address on Central America,' *Congressional Quarterly Weekly Report* 41, no. 17 [30 April 1983], p. 855).
3. Richard Halloran, 'US Said to Draw Latin Troops Plan,' *New York Times*, 8 April 1984; Immanuel Wallerstein, *Geopolitics and Geoculture: Essays on the Changing World System*, (Cambridge University Press, 1991), p. 34.
4. Dunkerley, *Pacification*, pp. 46–47.
5. Hans J. Morgenthau and Kenneth W. Thompson, *Politics Among Nations: The Struggle for Power and Peace*, 6th ed., (New York: Alfred A. Knopf, 1985), p. 578.
6. Cheryl L. Eschbach, 'Explaining US Policy Toward Central America and the Caribbean,' *Latin American Research Review* 25, no. 2 (1990), pp. 204–206.
7. Noam Chomsky, 'The Third World in the New World Order,' paper delivered at CIIR conference, 18–19 January 1991, Regents College London, p. 1;

William M. LeoGrande, Douglas C. Bennett, Morris J. Blachman and Kenneth E. Sharpe, 'Grappling with Central America: From Carter to Reagan,' and also their essay 'The Failure of the Hegemonic Strategic Vision,' both in Morris J. Blachman and others, *Confronting Revolution*, pp. 300–301, 329; Viron P. Vaky, 'Hemispheric Relations: "Everything is Part of Everything Else,"' *Foreign Affairs* 59, no. 3 (1981), p. 622, cited in Kolko, *Confronting the Third World*, p. 287.

8. Violeta Chamorro, Inaugural Address, 25 April 1990, Appendix 29 in Council of Freely-Elected Heads of Government, *Observing Nicaragua's Elections*, 1989–1990, p. 117; Trish O'Kane, 'The New Old Order,' *NACLA: Report on the Americas* XXIV, no. 1 (June 1990), p. 36.
9. Dunkerley, *Pacification*, pp. 59–60; Dore and Weeks, *The Red and the Black*, pp. 32, 35; Dunkerley, 'Reflections on the Nicaraguan Election,' p. 40; Williams, 'Elections and Democratization in Nicaragua,' p. 26.
10. Dore and Weeks, *The Red and the Black*, p. 34; LaFeber, *Inevitable Revolutions*, pp. 352–353; James Baker, 'Foreign Policy Priorities and US Assistance,' *Current Policy*, no. 1274 (1 May 1990), pp. 8–9, and James Baker, 'Assistance and Reform: Eastern Europe and Central America,' *Current Policy*, no. 1289 (4 July 1990), pp. 1–3; Dunkerley, 'Reflections on the Nicaraguan Election,' p. 40; Dunkerley, *Pacification*, p. 57.
11. Child, *Peace Process*, pp. 100–104, 120–126; Dunkerley, *Pacification*, pp. 57–58; LaFeber, *Inevitable Revolutions*, p. 352.
12. Dunkerley, *Pacification*, pp. 62–65.
13. Williams, 'Elections and Democratization in Nicaragua,' p. 30; Peeler, 'Democracy and Elections in Central America: Autumn of the Oligarchs?' p. 185; Dunkerley, *Pacification*, p. 14; Editor, 'A Market Solution for the Americas?' *NACLA: Report on the Americas* XXVI, no. 4 (February 1993), pp. 16–17.
14. Alexander Watson, statement before the Subcommittee for Western Hemisphere Affairs, 6 October 1993, USIA printout; Editor, 'A Market Solution for the Americas?' pp. 16–17; Dunkerley, *Pacification*, p. 57; International Commission for Central America Recovery and Development, *Poverty, Conflict and Hope: A Turning Point in Central America*, US Congress. Senate, Committee on Foreign Relations, 101st Cong., 1st sess., March 1989, p. 114. Though Secretary of State Warren Christopher stated the approach taken 'too often in our history, we have turned our attention to Latin America in times of crisis, and we have turned our back when the crisis passes' was short sighted and self defeating, the hemisphere of free trade the Clinton administration intends to build will still not address inequalities that spur revolt (Text of Warren Christopher's speech delivered by Deputy Secretary Wharton, 'Forging a True Partnership Of the Americas,' to the Council of the Americas, 3 May 1993 in *US Department of State Dispatch* 4, no. 18 [3 May 1993], p. 305).
15. Francis Fukuyama, *The End of History and the Last Man*, (Harmondsworth: Penguin, 1992), p. 235; Xabier Gorostiaga, cited in Mariano Aguirre, 'Military Intervention in the Third World in the 1990s,' in Chester Hartman and Pedro Vilanova, eds., *Paradigms Lost: The Post Cold War Era*, (London: Pluto Press, 1992), p. 49; Jose Arico, 'Rethink Everything,' *Report on the Americas: The Latin American Left, A Painful Rebirth*, NACLA 25, no. 5

(May 1992), p. 22; Isaiah Berlin, 'The Pursuit of the Ideal,' and 'The Decline of Utopian Ideas in the West,' in his *The Crooked Timber of Humanity: Chapters In The History of Ideas*, Henry Hardy, ed., (London: Fontana Press, 1990), pp. 17–19, 46.

16. Gabriel Kolko, *Confronting the Third World*, p. 297.

# Selected Bibliography

## PRIMARY SOURCES

### International Court of Justice

Documents and decisions from the case Nicaragua v. United States of America:
Chamorro, Edgar. *Affidavit.* Washington, D.C.: 5 September 1985.

D'Escoto, Miguel. *Affidavit.* Managua, Nicaragua: Ministerio Del Exterior, 21 April 1984.

International Court of Justice. *Case Concerning Military and Paramilitary Activities in and Against Nicaragua.* Declaration of Intervention of the Republic of El Salvador. The Hague: International Court of Justice, Order of 4 October 1984.

International Court of Justice. Public sitting in the Case Concerning the Military and Paramilitary Activities in and against Nicaragua (Nicaragua v. United States of America). President Nagendra Singh presiding. CR 85/20. 13 September 1985.

——. Public sitting in the Case Concerning the Military and Paramilitary Activities in and against Nicaragua (Nicaragua v. United States of America). President Nagendra Singh presiding. CR 85/21. 16 September 1985.

Judgement of the International Court of Justice. *Nicaragua v. The United States of America.* The Hague: International Court of Justice, 27 June 1986.

Republic of El Salvador. *Case Concerning Military and Paramilitary Activities in and Against Nicaragua.* Declaration of Intervention. General List no. 70, The Hague: International Court of Justice, 15 August 1984.

### United Nations

A systematic review of the Index for United Nations documents on microfiche was conducted for the years 1981 to 1990. Documents used include those from Assembly sessions 38 to 43. The two main categories of UN documents concerning this study are those of the General Assembly, and the Security Council. Each document is given a number that reflects this division. The Assembly documents appear as, for example, A/40/499; 40 indicating the session, and 499 the document number. Security Council documents appear as S/14891. Documents presented in both forums appear as A/40/894–S/17634. These documents were usually taken from the UN microfiche collection, hence a fiche number is also included in the notes: 82–04635 0081r (E). Most of the Nicaraguan diplomatic letters are contained in these documents.

### US Government Documents

Hundreds of documents were released during the public hearings on the Iran–Contra affair held in Washington, D.C., during the summer of 1987. Three additional volumes of documents were released in 1988 with just short of 5000 pages. One volume of documents is specifically related to Oliver L. North:

US Congress. Senate. House. Senate Select Committee on Secret Military Assistance to Iran and the Nicaraguan Opposition, and the House Select Committee to Investigate Covert Arms Transactions With Iran. *Iran–Contra Investigation. Joint Hearings before the Senate Select Committee on Secret Military Assistance to Iran and the Nicaraguan Opposition, and the House Select Committee to Investigate Covert Arms Transactions With Iran.* 100th Cong., 1st sess, 100–7, Part III, 7–10, 13–14 July 1987.

——. Appendix A: Volume 1, Source Documents. 100th Cong., 1st sess., 13 November 1987.

——. Appendix A: Volume 2, Source Documents. 100th Cong., 1st sess., 13 November 1987.

A collection of over 20000 pages of documents was complied by the National Security Archive, Washington, D.C. They have reproduced copies of the executive department documents that are less excised than previously released versions by the White House. In addition the collection contains additional information derived from the Intelligence Committees of Congress, the office of the Independent Council, the Tower Commission, as well as documents provided by private and government individuals. The National Security Archive also made hundreds of its own Freedom of Information Act requests. The collection is:

*The Iran–Contra Affair: The Making of US Policy.* Washington, D.C.: The National Security Archive, 1990.

## US Government Publications

US Congress. House. Committee on Foreign Affairs. *Report: Central America, 1981.* 97th Cong., 1st sess., March 1981.

——. *Legislation Concerning Latin America: Colombia, The Contadora Process, and El Salvador: Markup before the Committee on Foreign Affairs.* 98th Cong., 2nd sess., 5 April 1984.

——. *Supporting the Contadora Process: Report of the Committee on Foreign Affairs.* 99th Cong., 2nd sess., 26 February 1986.

——. *Adverse Report: President's Request for Assistance for the Nicaraguan Democratic Resistance.* 99th Cong., 2nd sess., 11 March 1986.

——. *Further Assistance to Nicaraguan Democratic Resistance.* Communication from The Assistant Secretary of State, Legislative and Intergovernmental Affairs, transmitting, a copy of Presidential determination no. 87–10, with a Report on Nicaragua, Pursuant to Sections 211(e) and 214 of the Military Construction Act, 1987 as contained in Public Law 99–500. 100th Cong., 1st sess., 5 March 1987.

——. *Consideration of Miscellaneous Bills and Resolutions: Markup before the Committee on Foreign Affairs.* 100th Cong., 1st sess., 28 July, 6, 14 October, 5 November 1987.

——. *Congress and Foreign Policy 1988: Report.* 101st Cong., 1989.

US Congress. House. Committee on Foreign Affairs. Subcommittees on Arms Control, International Security and Science, and the Western Hemisphere Affairs. *The Sale of F–5E/F Aircraft to Honduras: Committee on Foreign Affairs. Subcommittees on Arms Control, International Security and Science, and the Western Hemisphere Affairs.* 100th Cong., 1st sess., 19 May, 4 June 1987.

US Congress. House. Committee on Foreign Affairs. Subcommittees on International Economic Policy and Trade, and Western Hemisphere Affairs. *Review of the United States Economic Embargo Against Nicaragua and Humanitarian Exports: Hearing before Committee on Foreign Affairs. Subcommittees on International Economic Policy and Trade, and Western Hemisphere Affairs.* 100th Cong., 1st sess., 15 December 1987.

US Congress. House. Committee on Foreign Affairs. Subcommittee on Inter-American Affairs. *Central America at the Crossroads: Hearing before Committee on Foreign Affairs. Subcommittee on Inter-American Affairs.* 96th Cong., 1st sess., 11–12 September 1979.

——. *Assessment of Conditions in Central America: Hearing before Committee on Foreign Affairs. Subcommittee on Inter-American Affairs.* 96th Cong., 2nd sess., 29 April, 20 May 1980.

——. *Foreign Assistance Legislation for Fiscal Year 1982 (Part 7): Hearing before Committee on Foreign Affairs. Subcommittee on Inter-American Affairs.* 97th Cong., 1st sess., 23, 26, 30 March, and 8 April 1981.

——. *The Caribbean Basin Policy: Hearing before Committee on Foreign Affairs. Subcommittee on Inter-American Affairs.* 97th Cong., 1st sess., 14, 21, 28 July 1981.

US Congress. House. Committee on Foreign Affairs. Subcommittee on International Economic Policy and Trade. *Central American Development Organization: Hearing before the Committee on Foreign Affairs. Subcommittee on International Economic Policy and Trade.* 100th Cong., 2nd sess., 13 April 1988.

US Congress. House. Committee on Foreign Affairs. Subcommittee on Western Hemisphere Affairs. *US Policy in Honduras and Nicaragua: Hearing before Committee on Foreign Affairs. Subcommittee on Western Hemisphere Affairs.* 98th Cong., 1st sess., 15 March 1983.

——. *The Role of the US Southern Command in Central America: Hearing before Committee on Foreign Affairs. Subcommittee on Western Hemisphere Affairs.* 98th Cong., 2nd sess., 1 August 1984.

——. *Nicaraguan Incursion Into Honduras: Hearing before Committee on Foreign Affairs. Subcommittee on Western Hemisphere Affairs.* 99th Cong., 2nd sess., 8 April 1986.

——. *The Downing of a United States Plane in Nicaragua and United States Involvement in the Contra War: Hearing before Committee on Foreign Affairs. Subcommittee on Western Hemisphere Affairs.* 99th Cong., 2nd sess., 15 October 1986.

——. *Recent Events Concerning the Arias Peace Proposal: Hearing and Markup on H. Con. Res. 146 before Committee on Foreign Affairs. Subcommittee on Western Hemisphere Affairs.* 100th Cong., 1st sess., 9, 15, 28 July 1987.

——. *Update on the Central America Peace Process: Hearing before Committee on Foreign Affairs. Subcommittee on Western Hemisphere Affairs.* 100th Cong., 1st sess., 13 October 1987.

——. *The Central American Peace Process: Hearing before Committee on Foreign Affairs. Subcommittee on Western Hemisphere Affairs.* 100th Cong., 1st sess., 20, 21 October 1987.

——. *The Implementation of the Humanitarian Assistance Package for Central America: Hearing before Committee on Foreign Affairs. Subcommittee on Western Hemisphere Affairs.* 100th Cong., 2nd sess., 2 June 1988.

——. *The Status of Democratic Transitions in Central America: Hearing before Committee on Foreign Affairs. Subcommittee on Western Hemisphere Affairs.* 100th Cong., 2nd sess., 23, 28 June 1988.

——. *Nicaragua and the United States: A New Era?: Hearing before Committee on Foreign Affairs. Subcommittee on Western Hemisphere Affairs.* 100th Cong., 1st sess., 13 April 1989.

——. *From Duarte to Cristiani: Where is El Salvador Headed?: Hearing before Committee on Foreign Affairs. Subcommittee on Western Hemisphere Affairs.* 100th Cong., 1st sess., 13 July 1989.

US Congress. House. Permanent Select Committee on Intelligence. *US Intelligence Agencies and Activities: The Performance of the Intelligence Community: Hearing before the Select Committee on Intelligence.* 94th Cong., 1st sess., 11–12, 18, 25, 30 September, 7, 30–31 October 1975.

——. *Congressional Oversight of Covert Activities: Hearing before the Permanent Select Committee on Intelligence.* 98th Cong., 1st sess., 20–22 September 1983.

——. *Joint Resolution Relating to the Additional Authority and Assistance for the Nicaraguan Democratic Resistance Requested by the President: Adverse Report.* 99th Cong., 2nd sess., 12 March 1986.

——. *Compilation of Intelligence Laws and Related Laws and Executive Orders of Interest to the National Intelligence Community.* 100th Cong., 1st sess., March 1987.

US Congress. House. Permanent Select Committee on Intelligence. Subcommittee on Oversight and Evaluation. *Staff Report: US Intelligence Performance on Central America: Achievements and Selected Instances of Concern.* 97th Cong., 2nd sess., 22 September 1982.

US Congress. Senate. Committee on Foreign Relations. *The Situation in El Salvador: Hearing before the Committee on Foreign Relations.* 97th Cong., 1st sess., 18 March, 9 April 1981.

——. *US Policy in the Western Hemisphere: Hearing before the Committee on Foreign Relations.* 97th Cong., 2nd sess., 1, 20, 27, 28 April, and 4, 26 May 1982.

——. *National Bipartisan Report on Central America: Hearing before the Committee on Foreign Relations.* 98th Cong., 2nd sess., 7, 8 February 1984.

——. *Security and Development Assistance: Hearing before the Committee on Foreign Relations.* 99th Cong., 1st sess., 15, 20–22, 26 February 1985.

——. *United States Policy Options with Respect to Nicaragua and Aid to the Contras: Hearing before the Committee on Foreign Relations.* 100th Cong., 1st sess., 28 January, 5 February 1987.

——. *The Central American Peace and Economic Cooperation Act of 1987: Report to the Committee on Foreign Relations.* 100th Cong., 1st sess., 6 March 1987.

——. *Poverty, Conflict and Hope: A Turning Point in Central America: Report by the International Commission for Central America Recovery and Development for the Committee on Foreign Relations.* 101st Cong., 1st sess., March 1989.

US Congress. Senate. Committee on Foreign Relations. Subcommittee on Terrorism, Narcotics and International Operations. *Drugs, Law Enforcement and Foreign Policy: A Report of the Committee on Foreign Relations. Subcommittee on Terrorism, Narcotics and International Operations.* 100th Cong., 2nd sess., December 1988.

US Congress. Senate. Committee on Foreign Relations. Subcommittee on Western Hemisphere Affairs. *Security and Development Assistance: Hearing before the Committee on Foreign Relations. Subcommittee on Western Hemisphere Affairs.* 98th Cong., 1st sess., 14 March 1983.

US Congress. Senate. Select Committee on Intelligence. *Nomination of William J. Casey: Hearing before Select Committee on Intelligence.* 97th Cong., 1st sess., 13 January 1981.

——. *Report: January 1, 1981 to December 31, 1982.* 98th Cong., 1st sess., 28 February 1983.

——. *Report: January 1, 1983, to December 31, 1984.* 98th Cong., 2nd sess., 10 October 1984.

——. *Nomination of Robert M. Gates to be Deputy Director of Central Intelligence: Hearing before the Select Committee on Intelligence.* 99th Cong., 2nd sess., 10 April 1986.

——. *Preliminary Inquiry Into the Sale of Arms to Iran and Possible Diversion of Funds to the Nicaraguan Resistance: Report of the Select Committee on Intelligence.* 100th Cong., 1st sess., 2 February 1987.

——. *The Expulsion of American Diplomats from Nicaragua: Hearing before Select Committee on Intelligence.* 100th Cong., 2nd sess., 14 July 1988.

——. *Nomination of Robert M. Gates.* 100th Cong., 1st sess., 16–20 September 1991.

US Congress. Senate. House. Senate Select Committee on Secret Military Assistance to Iran and the Nicaraguan Opposition, and the House Select Committee to Investigate Covert Arms Transactions With Iran. *Iran–Contra Investigation. Joint Hearings before the Senate Select Committee on Secret Military Assistance to Iran and the Nicaraguan Opposition, and the House Select Committee to Investigate Covert Arms Transactions With Iran.* 100th Cong., 1st sess., 100–1, 5–8 May 1987.

——. 100th Cong., 1st sess., 100–2, 11–14, 19 May 1987.

——. 100th Cong., 1st sess., 100–3, 20–21, 27–28 May 1987.

——. 100th Cong., 1st sess., 100–4, 29 May 1987.

——. 100th Cong., 1st sess., 100–5, 2–5, 8–9 June 1987.

——. 100th Cong., 1st sess., 100–6, 23–25 June 1987.

——. 100th Cong., 1st sess., 100–7, Part I, 7–10 July 1987.

——. 100th Cong., 1st sess., 100–7, Part II, 10, 13–14 July 1987.

——. 100th Cong., 1st sess., 100–7, Part III, 7–10, 13–14 July 1987.

——. 100th Cong., 1st sess., 100–8, 15, 16, 17, 20, 21 July 1987.

——. 100th Cong., 1st sess., 100–9, 23, 24, 28, and 29 July 1987.

——. 100th Cong., 1st sess., 100–10, 30–31 July, 3 August 1987.

——. 100th Cong., 1st sess., 100–11, 4, 5, 6 August 1987.

——. *Report of the Congressional Committees Investigating the Iran–Contra Affair.* 100th Cong., 1st sess., 17 November 1987.

——. Appendix A: Volume 1, Source Documents. 100th Cong., 1st sess., 13 November 1987.

——. Appendix A: Volume 2, Source Documents. 100th Cong., 1st sess., 13 November 1987.

——. Appendix C: Chronology of Events. 100th Cong., 1st sess., 13 November 1987.

Kerry, John. *'Private Assistance' and the Contras: A Staff Report.* Washington, D.C.: US Congress. Senate, 1986.

## Arms Control and Disarmament Agency

US Arms Control and Disarmament Agency. *World Military Expenditures and Arms Transfers 1986*. Washington, D.C.: Government Printing Office, April 1987.

## Arms Control and Foreign Policy Caucus

Arms Control and Foreign Policy Caucus. *Who Are the Contras? An Analysis of the Makeup of the Military Leadership of the Rebel Forces, and The Nature of the Private American Groups Providing them Financial and Material Support*. Washington, D.C.: Arms Control and Foreign Policy Caucus, 18 April 1985.

Arms Control and Foreign Policy Caucus. *The Contra High Command: An Independent Analysis of The Military Leadership of the FDN*. Washington, D.C.: Arms Control and Foreign Policy Caucus, March 1986.

Leach, Jim, George Miller, Michael D. Barnes, Don Edwards, Mark O. Hatfield, and Edward M. Kennedy. *US Policy in Central America: Against the Law?: An Analysis of Possible Violations of 30 United States and International Laws*. Washington, D.C.: Arms Control and Foreign Policy Caucus, 11 September 1984.

## Congressional Research Service

Serafino, Nina. *The Contadora Initiative: Implications for Congress*. Foreign Affairs and National Defense Division, Congressional Research Service, Order Code IB85109, 10 September 1987.

——. *US Assistance to Nicaraguan Guerillas: Issues for the Congress*. Foreign Affairs and National Defense Division, Congressional Research Service, Order Code IB84139, 1 March 1988.

——. *Contra Aid, FY82 – FY888: Summary and Chronology of Major Congressional Action on Key Legislation Concerning US Aid to the Anti-Sandinista Guerillas*. Foreign Affairs and National Defense Division, Congressional Research Service, 88–563 F, 18 August 1988.

——. *Central American Peace Prospects: US Interests and Response*. Foreign Affairs and National Defense Division, Congressional Research Service, IB87200, 19 January 1989.

Sullivan, Mark P. *Nicaragua: An Overview of US Policy 1979–1986*. Foreign Affairs and National Defense Division, Congressional Research Service, 87–855 F, 13 October 1987.

## US Department of State

Abrams, Elliot. 'Permanent Dictatorship in Nicaragua,' *Department of State Bulletin* 86, no. 2109 (April 1986): 83.

——. 'FY 1989 Assistance Requests for Latin America and the Caribbean,' *Department of State Bulletin* 88, no. 2139 (October 1988): 72–82.

Abrams, Elliot, and Philip Habib. 'Development of US–Nicaragua Policy,' *Current Policy*, no. 915. Washington, D.C.: US Department of State, 5 February 1987.

Bush, George. 'Nicaragua: A Threat to Democracy,' *Department of State Bulletin* 85, no. 2098 (May 1985): 22–24.

Bushnell, John A. 'Central America Review,' *Department of State Bulletin* 81, no. 2049 (April 1981): 40–42.

Enders, Thomas O. 'Arms Transfers to Latin America,' *Current Policy*, no. 349, Washington, D.C.: US Department of State, 22 October 1981.

——. 'Strategic Situation in Central America and the Caribbean,' *Current Policy*, no. 352, Washington, D.C.: US Department of State, 14 December 1981.

——. 'Building the Peace in Central America,' *Current Policy*, no. 414, Washington, D.C.: US Department of State, 20 August 1982.

——. 'Nicaragua: Threat to Peace in Central America,' *Current Policy*, no. 476, Washington, D.C.: US Department of State, 12 April 1983.

Jacobsen, Carl G. *Soviet Attitudes Towards, Aid To, and Contacts With Central American Revolutionaries (June 1984)*, by C. G. Jacobsen. Washington, D.C.: US Department of State, 1984.

Michel, James H. 'US Policy on Central America: The Need for Consensus,' *Current Policy*, no. 828, Washington, D.C.: US Department of State, 17 April 1986.

Middendorf II, J. William. 'Nicaragua: The Stolen Revolution,' *Department of State Bulletin* 85, no. 2099 (June 1985): 83–86.

Motley, Langhorne, A. 'A National Response to the Crisis in Central America,' *Current Policy*, no. 559, Washington, D.C.: US Department of State. 27 March 1984.

——. 'The New Opportunity for Peace in Nicaragua,' *Current Policy*, no. 687, Washington, D.C.: US Department of State, 17 April 1985.

Reagan, Ronald. 'Central America: Defending Our Vital Interests,' *Current Policy*, no. 482, Washington, D.C.: US Department of State, 27 April 1983.

——. 'Saving Freedom in Central America,' *Current Policy*, no. 499, Washington, D.C.: US Department of State, 18 July 1983.

——. 'President Reagan Supports Nicaraguan Peace Process,' *Current Policy*, no. 682. Washington, D.C.: US Department of State, 4 April 1985.

——. 'Central America and US Security,' *Current Policy*, no. 805 (16 March 1986).

——. 'Why Democracy Matters in Central America,' *Current Policy*, no. 850, Washington, D.C.: US Department of State, 24 June 1986.

——. 'Promoting Freedom and Democracy in Central America,' *Current Policy*, no. 952, Washington, D.C.: US Department of State, 3 May 1987.

——. 'Central America at a Critical Juncture,' *Current Policy*, no. 1007, Washington, D.C.: US Department of State, 7 October 1987.

Shultz, George. 'Strengthening Democracy in Central America,' *Current Policy*, no. 468, Washington, D.C.: US Department of State, 16 March 1983.

——. 'The United States and Central America; A Moment of Decision,' *Current Policy*, no. 691, Washington, D.C.: US Department of State, 22 April 1985.

——. 'Nicaragua and the Future of Central America,' *Current Policy*, no. 801, Washington, D.C.: US Department of State, 3 March 1986.

——. 'Power in the Service of Peace in Central America,' *Current Policy*, no. 1010, Washington, D.C.: US Department of State, 13 October 1987.

——. 'Peace, Democracy, and Security in Central America,' *Current Policy*, no. 998, Washington, D.C.: US Department of State, 10 September 1987.

US Department of State. *Communist Interference in El Salvador*. Special Report, no. 80, Washington, D.C.: US Department of State, 23 February 1981.

——. *American Foreign Policy Current Documents 1981*. Washington, D.C.: US Department of State, 1984.

——. *American Foreign Policy Current Documents 1982*. Washington, D.C.: US Department of State, 1984.
——. *American Foreign Policy Current Documents 1983*. Washington, D.C.: US Department of State, 1985.
——. *The Contadora Process: Resource Book*. Washington, D.C.: US Department of State, 1985.
——. *The Nicaraguan Peace Process: A Documentary Record*. Special Report no. 126. Washington, D.C.: US Department of State, April 1985.
——. *'Revolution Beyond Our Borders': Sandinista Intervention in Central America*. Special Report no. 132, Washington, D.C.: US Department of State, September 1985.
——. *American Foreign Policy Current Documents 1984*. Washington, D.C.: US Department of State, 1986.
——. *American Foreign Policy Current Documents 1985*. Washington, D.C.: US Department of State, 1986.
——. *Human Rights in Nicaragua under the Sandinistas: From Revolution to Repression*. Washington, D.C.: US Department of State, 1986.
——. *Negotiations in Central America 1981–1987*. (Revised Edition). Washington, D.C.: US Department of State, 1987.
——. *American Foreign Policy Current Documents 1986*. Washington, D.C.: US Department of State, 1987.
——. 'US Policy in Central America,' *Selected Documents*, no. 29. Washington, D.C.: US Department of State, July 1988.
——. *American Foreign Policy Current Documents 1987*. Washington, D.C.: US Department of State, 1988.
——. 'US Support for Democracy and Peace in Central America,' *Selected Documents*, no. 36. Washington, D.C.: US Department of State, (14 February–24 March 1989).
——. *American Foreign Policy Current Documents 1988*. Washington, D.C.: US Department of State, 1989.
US Department of State and US Department of Defense. *The Sandinista Military Build-Up: An Update (October 1987)*. Washington, D.C.: US Department of State, US Department of Defense, 1987.
Walsh, Lawrence E. *Final Report of the Independent Counsel for Iran/Contra Matters*. (3 Volumes). (Washington, D.C.: United States Court of Appeals, 4 August 1993).

## BOOKS AND ARTICLES

Abrams, Elliot. 'The Deal in Central America,' *Commentary* 87, no. 5 (May 1989): 29–32.
Arnson, Cynthia. *Crossroads: Congress, The Reagan Administration, and Central America*. New York: Pantheon Books, 1989.
Bagley, Bruce Michael. 'Contadora: The Failure of Diplomacy,' *Journal of Inter-american Studies and World Affairs*, 28, no. 3 (Fall 1986): 1–32.
Bagley, Bruce M., ed. *Contadora and the Diplomacy of Peace in Central America*. Vol. 1, *The United States, Central America, and Contadora*. Boulder: Westview Press, 1987.

Bagley, Bruce M., Roberto Alvarez, and Katherine J. Hagedorn, eds. *Contadora and the Central American Peace Process: Selected Documents*. SAIS Papers in International Affairs. Boulder: Westview Press, 1985.

Bagley, Bruce Michael, and Juan Gabriel Tokatlian. *Contadora: The Limits of Negotiation*. FPI Case Studies, no. 9, Washington, D.C.: The Johns Hopkins University, 1987.

Bendaña, Alejandro. 'The Foreign Policy of the Nicaraguan Revolution,' in Thomas W. Walker ed. *Nicaragua in Revolution*. New York: Praeger Publishers, 1982.

——. 'Building a Negotiation Strategy: "Lessons" from the Nicaraguan Experience,' conference paper, *Negotiating for Change: The Struggle for Peace with Justice*, conference paper (London: Catholic Institute for International Relations, 1991), 57–59.

Bermann, Karl. *Under the Big Stick: Nicaragua and the United States Since 1848*. Boston: South End Press, 1986.

Blachman, Morris J., William M. LeoGrande, and Kenneth E. Sharpe, eds. *Confronting Revolution: Security Through Diplomacy in Central America*. New York: Pantheon Books, 1986.

Booth, John A., and Mitchell A. Seligson, eds. *Elections and Democracy in Central America*. Chapel Hill: The University of North Carolina Press, 1989.

Booth, John A., and Thomas W. Walker. *Understanding Central America*. Boulder: Westview Press, 1989.

Center for Defense Information (Washington, D.C.). 'Soviet Geopolitical Momentum: Myth or Menace? Trends of Soviet Influence Around the World from 1945 to 1986,' *The Defense Monitor* 15, no. 5 (1986): 1–32.

——. 'US Invasion of Nicaragua: Appraising the Option,' *The Defense Monitor* 16, no. 5 (1987): 1–8.

Center for International Policy. 'Fear of Signing: The Maneuvering Around the Arias Peace Plan,' *International Policy Report*, Washington, D.C.: Center for International Policy (July 1987): 1–7.

——. 'The Central American Peace Accord,' *International Policy Report*, Washington, D.C.: Center for International Policy (September 1987): 1–5.

——. 'Central America Negotiations Update,' *International Policy Report*, Washington, D.C.: Center for International Policy (7 October 1987): 1–8.

——. 'Compliance: The Central American Peace Accord,' *International Policy Report*, Washington, D.C.: Center for International Policy (5 November 1987): 1–5.

——. 'Central Americans Call on US to End Aid to Contras,' Washington, D.C.: Center for International Policy (14 January 1988): 1–3.

——. 'The Nicaraguan Cease-Fire Talks: A Documentary Survey,' Washington, D.C.: Center for International Policy (13 June 1988): 1–8.

——. 'The Central American Peace Accord,' Washington, D.C.: Center for International Policy (July 1988): 1–6.

——. 'Nicaraguan Peace Talks Resume,' Washington, D.C.: Center for International Policy (21 September 1988): 1–4.

——. 'Major Breakthrough for Peace Process in Central America,' Washington, D.C.: Center for International Policy (1 December 1988): 1–4.

Child, Jack. *The Central American Peace Process, 1983–1991: Sheathing Swords, Building Confidence*. Boulder: Lynne Rienner, 1992.

Child, Jack ed. *Conflict in Central America: Approaches to Peace and Security*. London: C. Hurst & Company, 1986.

Chomsky, Noam. *Turning The Tide: US Intervention in Central America and the Struggle for Peace*. London: Pluto Press, 1985.
——. *On Power and Ideology: The Managua Lectures*. Boston: South End Press, 1987.
——. *The Culture of Terrorism*. London: Pluto Press, 1988.
——. *Deterring Democracy*. London: Verso, 1991.
Dore, Elizabeth, and John Weeks. *The Red and the Black: The Sandinistas and the Nicaraguan Revolution*. Research Paper 28. London: Institute of Latin American Studies, 1992.
Draper, Theodore. *A Very Thin Line: The Iran–Contra Affairs*. New York: Hill and Wang, 1991.
Dunkerley, James. *Power in the Isthmus: A Political History of Modern Central America*. London: Verso, 1988.
——. *The Pacification of Central America: Political Change in the Isthmus, 1987–1993*. London: Verso, 1994.
Farer, Tom J. 'At Sea in Central America: Can We Negotiate Our Way to Shore?' in Robert S. Leiken (ed.), *Central America: Anatomy of Conflict*, New York: Pergamon Press, 1984, 279–296.
——. 'Contadora: The Hidden Agenda,' *Foreign Policy*, no. 59 (Summer 1985): 59–72.
Gilbert, Dennis. *Sandinistas: The Party and the Revolution*. Cambridge, Massachusetts: Basil Blackwell, 1988.
Gutman, Roy. 'America's Diplomatic Charade,' *Foreign Policy*, no. 56 (Fall 1984): 3–23.
——. 'Central America and Consensus Decision-making,' Washington, D.C.: School of Advanced International Studies Conference, 3–4 February 1986. Photocopied.
——. *Banana Diplomacy: The Making of American Policy in Nicaragua, 1981–1987*. New York: Simon and Schuster, 1988.
——. 'How the 1984 Vote Was Sabotaged,' *The Nation* 246, no. 18 (7 May 1988): cover and, 642–645.
Harris, Richard L., and Carlos M. Vilas, eds. *Nicaragua: A Revolution Under Siege*. London: Zed Books Ltd., 1985.
Held, David, ed. *Prospects for Democracy: North, South, East, West*. Cambridge: Polity Press, 1993.
Kolko, Gabriel. *Confronting the Third World: United States Foreign Policy, 1945–1980*. New York: Pantheon Books, 1988.
Kornbluh, Peter. *Nicaragua: The Price of Intervention*. Washington, D.C.: Institute for Policy Studies, 1987.
——. 'The Iran–Contra Scandal: A Postmortem,' *World Policy Journal* 5, no. 1 (1987–1988): 129–150.
Kornbluh, Peter and Malcolm Byrne, (eds). *The Iran–Contra Scandal: The Declassified History*. New York: The New Press, 1993.
LaFeber, Walter. *Inevitable Revolutions: The United States in Central America*. New York: W. W. Norton & Company, 1993.
Latin American Studies Association. Commission on Compliance with the Central American Peace Accord. *Extraordinary Opportunities . . . and New Risks*. Pittsburgh: Latin American Studies Association, 15 March 1988.
——. LASA Delegation to Observe the Nicaraguan General Election of November 4, 1984. *The Electoral Process in Nicaragua: Domestic and International Influences*. Pittsburgh: Latin American Studies Association, 19 November 1984.

——. Commission to Observe the 1990 Nicaraguan Election. *Electoral Democracy: Under International Pressure*. Pittsburgh: Latin American Studies Association, 15 March 1990.

Leiken, Robert S., and Barry Rubin, eds. *The Central American Crisis Reader*. New York: Summit Books, 1987.

LeoGrande, William M. 'Rollback or Containment: The United States, Nicaragua, and the Search for Peace in Central America,' *International Security* 11, no. 2 (Fall 1986): 89–120.

McNeil, Frank. *War and Peace in Central America*. New York: Charles Scribner's Sons, 1988.

Melrose, Dianna. *Nicaragua: The Threat of a Good Example?* Oxford: Oxfam, 1985.

Menges, Constantine. *Inside the National Security Council: The True Story of The Making and Unmaking of Reagan's Foreign Policy*. New York: Simon and Schuster, 1988.

Morrell, Jim, 'Contadora: The Treaty on Balance,' *International Policy Report*, Washington, D.C.: Center for International Policy (June 1985): 1–7.

——. 'Nicaragua's War Economy,' *International Policy Report*, Washington, D.C.: Center for International Policy (November 1985): 1–7.

——. 'Redlining Nicaragua: How the US Politicized the Inter-American Bank,' *International Policy Report*, Washington, D.C.: Center for International Policy (December 1985): 1–7.

——. 'Contadora Vows to Continue,' *International Policy Report*, Washington, D.C.: Center for International Policy (August 1986): 1–7.

——. 'Contadora Eludes US,' *International Policy Report*, Washington, D.C.: Center for International Policy, (January/February 1987): 1–7.

——. 'The Nine Lives of the Central American Peace Process,' *International Policy Report*, Washington, D.C.: Center for International Policy, (February 1989): 1–7.

Morrell, Jim, and William Jesse Biddle. 'Central America: The Financial War,' *International Policy Report*, Washington, D.C.: Center for International Policy (March 1983): 1–11.

Morrell, Jim, and William Goodfellow, 'Contadora: Under the Gun,' *International Policy Report*, Washington, D.C.: Center for International Policy (May 1986): 1–7.

Pastor, Robert A. *Condemned To Repetition: The United States And Nicaragua*. Princeton University Press, 1987.

——. 'Securing a Democratic Hemisphere,' *Foreign Policy* no. 73 (Winter 1988–1989): 41–59.

——. 'The Making of a Free Election,' *Journal of Democracy* 1, no. 3 (Summer 1990): 13–25.

Robinson, William I. *A Faustian Bargain: US Intervention in the Nicaraguan Elections and American Foreign Policy in the Cold War*. Boulder: Westview Press, 1992.

Schoultz, Lars. *National Security and United States Policy toward Latin America*. Princeton University Press, 1987.

Sepúlveda Amor, Bernardo. *Relacion De Contadora*. Mexico: Fondo De Cultura Economica, 1988.

Sklar, Holly. *Washington's War on Nicaragua*. Boston: South End Press, 1988.

Smith, Wayne S. 'US Central American Policy: The Worst-Alternative Syndrome,' *SAIS Review* 3, no. 2 (Summer–Fall 1983): 11–26.

——. *The Closest of Enemies: A Personal and Diplomatic Account of US–Cuban Relations Since 1957*. New York: W. W. Norton, 1987.

——. 'Lies About Nicaragua,' *Foreign Policy*, no. 67 (Summer 1987): 87–103.

Smith, Wayne S. ed. *The Russians Aren't Coming: New Soviet Policy in Latin America*. Boulder: Lynne Rienner Publishers, 1992.

Walker, Thomas W., ed. *Nicaragua in Revolution*. New York: Praeger Publishers, 1982.

——. *Reagan versus the Sandinistas: The Undeclared War on Nicaragua*. Boulder: Westview Press, 1987.

——. *Revolution and Counterrevolution in Nicaragua*. Boulder: Westview Press, 1991.

Woodward, Bob. *Veil: The Secret Wars of the CIA, 1981–1987*. New York: Pocket Books, 1987.

# Index


Abrams, Elliot 9, 109–10, 114–16, 121–2, 124, 134, 136–7, 139–40, 142, 145, 149, 152–3
Acevedo Peralta, Ricardo 151
Adelman, Kenneth 20
Afghanistan 10, 67, 160
Al Shiraa 129–30
Alajuela summit 144, 147
Alexander, Bill 51
Algeria 61
Allen, Richard 17, 23, 200
Americas Watch 136
Amnesty International 136
Andréz Pérez, Carlos 67, 153
Angola 10
Arce, Bayardo 18
ARENA 187
Argentina 21, 110, 224n30
Arias Peace Plan (also known as the Central American Peace Plan) 12, 26, 121, 128, 135, 135, 137, 139, 141–3, 146, 151–2, 161, 163–4, 168, 170–1, 186
Arias Sanchez, Oscar 118, 121, 128, 135, 137–41, 145–7, 152–4, 158, 163, 165, 167, 175
Aronson, Bernard 124, 153, 163, 165–6, 175, 179
Assembly, Nicaraguan 91
Australia 117
Azcona, Jose 118, 123, 128, 140, 144, 150, 152, 155, 163, 166

Baez, Bill 90
Baker, James 15, 55, 140, 149, 153, 155, 157, 158, 161–2, 165, 168, 179, 200n19
Barnes, Michael 21, 43, 58, 83, 108
Batista, Fulgencio 7
Belize 24
Bendaña, Alejandro 89, 106, 158, 172, 175, 181
Bergold, Harry 99, 228n4
Berlin, Isaiah 196
Bermudez, Enrique 139, 148, 194
Betancur, Belisario 64
Binns, Jack R. 9
Bipartisan Accords 157–9, 161–4
Bipartisan Commission on Central America (Kissinger Commission) 51, 58, 67, 127
Bishop, Maurice 57
Blasier, Cole 7
Boland, Edward 26, 38–9, 43, 57, 60, 66–7, 84–6, 93
  Boland amendment 38–9, 43, 67, 83–4, 93, 105, 134, 212n15
  Boland–Zablocki bill 50
Bolaños, Enrique 176
Bolivia 7–8, 189
Bonner, Raymond 8
Booth, John 6–7, 88
Borge, Tomás 27, 34, 52, 57, 106, 111, 150, 174
Brandt, Willy 89
Brazil 110
Brezhnev, Leonid 30
  Brezhnev Doctrine 53, 107
Briggs, Everett Ellis 165, 166
Britain 31, 64, 91, 102, 173
Brunei 134
Buchanan, John 28–9, 208
Burghardt, Raymond 120
Busby, Morris 145–6
Bush, George 106, 130, 132–4, 140, 142, 148–53, 155–7, 159, 161, 163, 165, 177–8, 181
Bush administration 124, 133, 153, 155–9, 163, 164–5, 171, 175, 177
Bushnell, John 14
Byrd, Robert 142
Byrne, Malcolm 130

Cabrera, Alfonso 155
Calero, Adolfo 94–5, 137, 152, 155
Cambodia 8, 10
Canada 113, 117, 150, 172

Cancun Declaration 50, 52
Cannistraro, Vincent 229
Caraballeda Message 115–18, 122, 125
Caracas 153–4, 161
Carlucci, Frank 140
Carter, Jimmy 6, 8, 10, 13, 55, 171, 177, 179, 198n7, 199n12
  Carter Administation 1–5, 7–8, 28, 192
Casco, Rita Delia 13
Casey, William 27, 35, 43–4, 46, 49, 64–5, 72, 83, 90, 95–6, 118, 132
Castañeda, Jorge 26, 32–3, 35–6
Castro, Fidel 4, 7–8, 26, 33, 50, 161, 162
Catholic Church 2, 61, 220n2
Center for International Policy 148, 156
Central America 2–3, 6–10, 13–14, 16–17, 20–4, 27–30, 32–6, 39, 41–5, 47–9, 51–3, 56–7, 62–73, 75, 77–83, 85, 88, 94, 96–9, 102, 104–5, 107, 110–12, 114–18, 120–5, 127–8, 130, 133, 134–5, 137–9, 141–5, 149–50, 153, 157–66, 168, 170–2, 175, 187–8, 190–2, 195, 208n38, 210n1, 212n15, 219n44, 220n2, 224n30, 231n25, 251n2
  *see also individual countries*
Central American Democratic Community 24
Central American Economic Community 195
Central American Historical Institute (CAHI) 114
Central American Peace Plan *see* Arias Peace Plan
Central Intelligence Agency (CIA) 15–16, 21–4, 27–8, 32, 38–41, 43, 49, 54–5, 58, 61, 65–6, 75–7, 80, 83–4, 90, 93, 96–8, 101–2, 108, 118, 121, 126, 177, 205n22, 212n15, 213n15, 224n30, 229n10
Cerezo, Vinicio 116, 118, 122, 140–1, 151, 156
César, Alfredo 148, 151–3, 156, 176, 194
Chamorro de Barrios, Violetta 4, 153, 170, 176–8, 185, 193, 194
Chamorro, Carlos Fernando 176
Chamorro, Edgar 23, 38–9, 41, 54, 58, 74, 76, 93, 224n30, 225n30
Cheysson, Claude 65
Child, Jack 110, 122, 135, 155
Chile 95, 177, 189
China 95
Chitnis, Lord 31
Chomsky, Noam 172, 175, 180, 182, 192
Christian Democratic Party (El Salvador) 31–2, 92, 187
Christopher, Warren 252n14
Clark, William 23, 31, 33, 46–7, 50–1, 55, 215n22
Clarridge, Duane 54, 133–4, 229n10
Clement, Peter 61
Clinton, Bill 133
  Clinton administration 195, 252n14
Coard, Bernard 57
Cockburn, Leslie 229
Colombia 24, 40, 47, 144
Commission of Support and Verification (CIAV) 164, 167–8
Communism 6–7, 9–11, 13, 28, 63, 66, 73, 79, 88, 92, 104, 108–9, 116, 121, 136, 143, 177, 184, 187, 195
CONDECA 97
Congress 3, 8, 12, 21–3, 26–8, 30, 33–9, 41–4, 46–52, 54–5, 57, 60–2, 64–5, 67, 69, 71–3, 75, 77, 83, 86, 96–8, 101–2, 105–9, 115–18, 120–1, 123–6, 129–30, 132–5, 137, 139, 141–2, 145–6, 148–9, 153–4, 157, 159, 161, 163–7, 172–3, 176–7, 189, 190–2, 200n19, 209n42, 213n15, 225n30, 251n2
  House Foreign Affairs Committee 21, 49; Subcommittee on Western Hemisphere Affairs 43, 83, 195

Congress – (*Continued*)
House Foreign Operations Appropriations Subcommittee 15, 44, 63
House Permanent Select Committee on Intelligence 26, 29, 38, 44, 49, 65–6, 93, 96
Congressional Budget Office 10
Contadora 12, 36, 39, 40–1, 45–6, 50–8, 60–7, 69–73, 76–82, 84–7, 94–100, 102–4, 106–29, 135–43, 147, 152, 161, 170, 188, 190, 219n44
Contras 4, 10, 12–13, 17, 21–3, 25–6, 33–4, 36–9, 41–2, 43, 46, 48–50, 52–4, 56–7, 61, 63–5, 71–9, 83–5, 93–5, 97–102, 104–10, 112–24, 126–32, 134–47, 148–73, 175–6, 178–82, 186, 189–90, 192, 194, 214n19, 222n20, 223n20, 224n30, 225n30, 233n7
Coordinadora Democratica (CDN) 74, 89–90, 92
Costa Rica 7, 24–6, 28, 35, 44, 47, 60, 75–6, 78–9, 85, 89–90, 102–3, 110–11, 118–19, 121, 137–40, 144–5, 151–2, 154–5, 166, 168, 175
Council of Freely Elected Heads of Government 171, 178–9
Cristiani, Alfredo 164, 167–8
Cruz, Arturo 13, 18, 20, 74, 89–91, 94, 137, 139, 171
Cuba 2–8, 13–16, 21, 24, 26–30, 33, 41–2, 48, 51, 53–4, 58–9, 64, 67, 73, 75–6, 80–2, 93, 96, 100, 103, 106–7, 109, 124–5, 136, 159, 160–2, 168, 191, 198n7, 214n19
Czechoslovakia 213

Dam, Kenneth 66
Deaver, Michael 200n19
Defense Intelligence Agency 27, 29–30, 118
Democracy/Democratization 10, 19, 22, 24–5, 31, 35–7, 40–1, 44, 46, 48, 51, 53, 69, 71–6, 78, 85, 88–9, 91–2, 101–2, 106–7, 109–11, 113, 122–3, 125–6, 128–9, 135–41, 144, 146, 148, 151–2, 154–9, 162, 164–7, 170–4, 176, 178, 180, 185–90, 193, 195–6, 211n8
Democratic Revolutionary Alliance (ARDE) 44, 62, 75–6, 96
Democratic Study Group 117
Department of Defense 38, 41, 49, 80, 84, 98, 101, 105, 108, 120–1, 129, 212, 214
Department of State 8, 14, 16, 19, 23, 26–7, 31–2, 34–5, 40–1, 45–6, 49, 56, 65, 67, 70, 73, 76, 79–80, 85, 87–8, 90, 92–5, 98–9, 101, 104, 114, 121–2, 125, 140, 145–6, 163, 179, 191, 200n19, 214n19
D'Escoto, Miguel 17, 19–20, 23, 48, 52, 55–6, 70, 78, 115, 118, 141, 206n26
D'Escoto, Francisco 154–5
Dobrynin, Anotoly 15, 162
Dodd, Christopher 41, 43, 71, 83
Dole, Bob 142
Dominican Republic 189
Dore, Elizabeth 174, 179–80, 184, 193
Draper, Theodore 22, 84, 129, 132
Duarte, José Napoleon 79, 138–9, 140, 146
Dunkerley, James 4, 79, 156, 170, 189, 191, 193, 195

Eagleburger, Lawrence 46
Economic aid 5, 7–10, 13, 16, 19–20, 32, 41, 63, 97, 106, 151
Economic embargo 107, 109, 113, 126
Economic Support Fund 9–10, 13, 101
Egypt 140
Eisenhower, Ike 9
Elections 3, 25, 31–2, 35–6, 40, 48, 53, 74–7, 84–5, 88, 90–4, 99, 102, 104, 106, 138, 144, 147, 154–5, 157, 162–3, 165–7, 169–73, 175–80, 185–6, 188, 191, 199, 228n4

El Salvador 1–2, 5, 7, 9, 11, 13, 15–16, 18–19, 22–4, 26, 28, 31–3, 41, 44–6, 48, 51, 53, 56–8, 60–2, 68–9, 74, 76, 78–80, 84–5, 88, 92–3, 96, 100, 134, 138–40, 142, 150, 152, 154, 158–9, 160, 163–4, 167–9, 172–3, 187, 206n26, 209n42, 214n19
Enders, Thomas 8–9, 13–14, 17–23, 26, 30–4, 40–1, 46–7, 49, 70, 175, 209, 210, 215
Esquipulas 107, 121–3, 135, 138, 142–5, 147–8, 151–4, 157–9, 161–2, 168, 170–1, 176, 181, 191, 193, 195
Europe 10, 14, 23, 30, 45, 51, 58, 60–1, 72, 78–82, 102, 110, 113, 117, 137, 140, 142, 150–1, 154, 156, 180, 187, 190, 194, 219n44, 229n10, 231n25, 251n2
Exile camps (US) 17, 19–20

Falk, Richard 66
Farabundo Marti National Liberation Front (FMLN) 5, 7–8, 14, 22–3, 26–7, 33, 41, 44, 46, 48, 53, 56, 68–9, 75–6, 79, 84, 86, 134, 138–40, 145–6, 154, 158, 163–4, 166–8, 173–4, 187, 191
Farer, Tom 86
Fernandez, Joseph 40, 229
Fiers, Alan 97, 134
Fokin, Yuri 30
Foley, Tom 117
Fortier, Donald 98, 105
Forum for Peace (San José Conference) 37–8, 47
France 23, 28, 50, 60, 64–5, 173, 231n25
Fuentes, Carlos 60

Galeano, Eduardo 172, 187
Galeano, Israel 167, 180
García, Alan 110
Gates, Robert 96, 119, 189
George, Alexander 200
George, Clair 134
Gills, Barry 172, 186
Glenn, John 41
Godoy, Virigilio 176, 193–4, 228n4
Goldwater, Barry 26, 43, 44, 65
Gonzales, Mike 173, 183
Goodfellow, William 137, 139, 145, 147, 168
Gorbachev, Mikhail 112, 113, 136, 147, 149, 159, 160–2, 168
Gorman, Paul 65
Gorostiaga, Xabier 196
Government of National Reconstruction 4–5
Grenada 57, 180
Guatemala 1–2, 7–8, 24, 28, 36, 61, 76, 78, 86, 88, 93, 95, 97, 105, 116, 118, 121, 134, 137–41, 152, 154–5, 158–9, 163, 172–3, 189, 191, 214n19
Guatemalan National Revolutionary Union 7, 174
Gutierrez, Augustin 76
Guttierez, Carlos 79
Gutman, Roy 1, 18, 20, 55, 90, 129

Habib, Philip 118–21, 125, 128, 136, 138–42
Hahir, Bryan 220n2
Haig, Alexander 9, 13–15, 19–21, 23, 26, 29, 31–5, 200n19
Halliday, Fred 160
Hamilton, Lee 108
Harkin, Tom 38
  Harkin amendment 38–9
Hasenfus, Eugene 129
Held, David 185, 187
Helms, Jesse 1, 18, 158, 194
Herrera Campins, Luis 36, 210n1
Hinton, Deane R. 9, 27, 47
Hitchens, Christopher 2
Honduras 1, 7, 9, 17–18, 24–6, 28–9, 36–8, 41, 52–3, 56–7, 60–2, 72, 74–6, 78–80, 85, 93, 97, 101–2, 105, 112–14, 118, 123, 128, 134, 138–42, 144–7, 150–2, 154–6, 158–60, 163–6, 172, 175, 180, 206n26, 208n38, 214n19, 233n7
Hughes, John 27–8, 65, 92
Hughes–Ryan Law 22, 205n22

Human rights 9, 24, 32, 108, 116, 126, 136, 152, 154, 159, 172–3, 224n30
Humberto Guzman, Luis 185

Ikle, Fred 41, 65, 83, 140
Inman, Robert 21, 27
Inouye, Daniel 83, 131
Inter-American Development Bank 154, 195
Inter-American Treaty of Reciprocal Assistance 20
International Commission for Verification and Follow Up (CIVS) 143–4
International Court of Justice 11, 15, 55, 64–6, 68, 82, 100, 111–112, 126, 138, 178, 206n26, 222n20, 224n30
International Monetary Fund (IMF) 154, 182, 187, 193
Iran 120, 125, 129–131
Iran–Contra Affair 21, 107–8, 115, 120, 128–9, 131, 133–5, 149–50, 171, 175, 191, 224n30
Iran–Contra Report 35, 39, 49, 55, 64, 131
Iraq 129
Israel 134, 140

Jacobsen, Carl 45, 61
Japan 60–1
Japanese Americans 136
Jesuits 167
Johnstone, Craig 20, 30, 90
Joint Chiefs of Staff 98, 101
Jonas, Susanne 88, 174

Kassebaum, Nancy 41
Kennedy, John F. 27, 42–3, 124
Kerry, John 130
Khrushchev, Nikita 27
Kimmit, Robert 156
Kirkpatrick, Jeane 2, 9, 23, 41–2, 81, 83, 90, 95, 215n22
Kissinger, Henry 8–9, 51, 60, 127, 200
Kissinger Commission 28, 51, 58, 60, 67, 127
Koh, Harold Hongju 132
Kornbluh, Peter 130, 133, 178, 180

Lacayo, Antonio 193–4
LaFeber, Walter 1–2, 135
Latin America 2–3, 6–7, 9, 14, 21, 23, 36, 46–7, 66, 91, 108, 110, 115–18, 120, 125, 138, 156, 161, 172, 180, 187, 190, 196
Latin American Studies Association (LASA) 90–2, 94, 144, 178–9, 181, 183, 185, 228n4
Lau, Ricardo 105
Leahy, Patrick 189
LeoGrande, William 11, 123, 150, 163, 165, 176
Libya 45
Lima Declaration 110
Liman, Arthur 131
Lincoln, Abraham 124
Lloreda Caicedo 58
Long, Clarence 44, 60
López Campos, Julio 31
López Portillo, José 25, 36, 210n1
Low Intensity Conflict 42, 127, 151, 165, 170, 172–5, 189, 191

MacFarlane, Neil 162
Madrid, Miguel de la 37, 57, 68–70
Madrigal Nieto, Rodrigo 137
Managua 10–11, 18–20, 22, 26, 28, 38, 51, 54, 57, 61, 70–1, 74, 78, 82–3, 88, 90, 100, 103, 120, 123, 128, 135–6, 138–40, 144–6, 148–50, 154, 160, 163–4, 168, 170, 173–4, 176–8, 190
Manzanillo 60, 70–1, 74–7, 79–80, 83, 87, 96–9, 102, 105, 107
Marroquin Najera, Mario 86
Martinez Salsamendi, Carlos 29
Marxism 4–7, 14, 43, 51, 67, 73, 98, 103, 174, 189
Matamoros, Bosco 164
McFarlane, Robert 22, 46, 50, 55, 60, 62, 64, 69, 71, 73, 80, 83, 94–5, 97–8, 101–2, 105, 109, 129, 131–2, 134
McMichael, David 15, 126
McNeil, Frank 47

Meese, Edwin 1, 130, 200n19
Mejia Victores, Oscar 86
Melton, Richard 148
Menges, Constantine 19, 32, 46, 55, 62, 65, 78–80, 83, 90, 95
Mexico 2, 7–8, 26, 30, 32–7, 39–40, 45–8, 50, 57, 60, 64, 68–72, 76, 81, 86, 99, 107, 118, 128, 136, 140, 144, 150, 172–3
Middle East 10, 129, 130
MiG aircraft 93–4
Military aid 7, 9–10, 16, 28, 32, 63, 88, 106, 124, 134, 136, 138, 145, 148, 150–1, 156, 160–1
Miller, Nicola 160
Mitterrand, François 65
Monge, Luis Alberto 45, 111
Morgenthau, Hans 191
Morrell, James 137, 139, 145, 147, 168
Moscow 7, 15, 50, 61, 124, 126, 131, 146, 159–62, 167–8, 177, 187, 231
Motley, Langhorne 9, 37, 49, 55–6, 58, 63–4, 67, 83, 101, 228n4
Monroe Doctrine 2–3, 53, 106, 159, 189
Moynihan, Daniel Patrick 57

National Endowment for Democracy 177
National Guard 6, 17–18, 23, 104–5
National Security Council (NSC) 3, 21, 24, 26, 30, 32, 34, 46, 50, 55, 62, 69, 70, 77–8, 80–1, 83–6, 90, 94–6, 98, 107, 115, 121, 131, 133, 140, 165, 189, 191, 229n10
National Security Planning Group 71, 83, 120–1, 130
Negroponte, John D. 9, 101–2
Nicaragua *passim*
Nicaraguan Democratic Union 17
Nicaraguan Democratic Force (FDN) 23–4, 38–40, 52, 54, 58, 61, 72, 75–6, 93–5, 101, 104–5, 107, 116, 121, 224n30
Nicaraguan Humanitarian Assistance Office 111
Nicaraguan Socialist Party 7
Nixon, Richard 200n19
Noriega, Manuel 95, 114
North American Free Trade Agreement (NAFTA) 195
North Atlantic Treaty Organization (NATO) 7, 31, 42, 126, 251n2
North, Oliver 10, 50, 60, 62, 64–5, 69, 83–4, 90, 94–8, 100–2, 105, 107–8, 112, 114–15, 120, 122, 125, 129–33, 229n10
Nutting, Wallace 38

Obando y Bravo, Archbishop 144
O'Neill, Thomas 60, 73
Organization of American States 19–20, 25, 52, 63, 88–9, 92, 94, 101, 106–7, 137, 142, 146, 149, 164, 171, 199
Ortega, Humberto 148, 193–4
Ortega Saavedra, Daniel 13, 18–19, 22, 25, 29, 33, 45, 51, 55, 57, 70, 75, 79, 83, 93–4, 98, 109, 113, 115, 120, 122, 137, 141, 144–5, 147–52, 154–5, 163–4, 166–8, 178, 184, 194

Panama 2, 24, 38–40, 52, 64, 85, 114, 118, 136, 165, 180, 181
Parliamentary Human Rights Group (UK) 31
Pastor, Robert 3, 55
Pastora, Eden 35, 44
Payne, Richard 231n25
Paz Barnica, Edgar 47, 52
Pearl Harbor 136
Peeler, John 172, 188
Pentagon 121, 140, 199n12
Perestroika 160
Pérez de Cuéllar, Javier 58, 112–13, 137–8, 150, 153, 166, 168
Permanent Conference of Political Parties in Latin America (COPPPAL) 24–5
Peru 110, 214n19
Pezzullo, Lawrence 4, 8–9, 13–17, 19
Philippines 9, 177
Poindexter, John 84, 94, 100–1, 114, 120, 131–2

Poverty 6, 9, 32, 64, 91, 157, 175, 177, 183, 188, 195
*Psychological Operations in Guerilla Warfare* 75, 93
Public diplomacy 13, 31, 37, 40–2, 44, 49, 90, 111, 115, 135, 190–1
President's Special Review Board (Tower Commission) 130–1

Quainton, Anthony E. 9, 23, 26–7, 31, 34, 88
Quayle, Danforth 153, 165, 167

Ramirez, Sergio 27, 32, 102, 193
Raymond, Walter 50
Reagan, Ronald 1, 5–6, 8–10, 12–17, 21, 23, 25–6, 36, 37, 42, 44, 46–7, 49–51, 53–4, 60, 65–6, 69–70, 72–4, 79–80, 83–5, 88–9, 93–4, 97, 102, 104–5, 107–11, 115–21, 123–5, 127, 129–35, 137, 139, 141–2, 145–52, 154, 156–7, 159, 161, 173, 175, 189–91, 195, 200, 209–10, 215, 225, 231, 251
  Reagan Administration 2, 8–15, 18–19, 22, 26, 28–30, 36, 39–41, 44–7, 50–1, 53, 57, 62, 64–5, 67, 70–2, 77, 81, 83, 87–90, 92–7, 99, 104, 110, 112, 116, 119–21, 123, 125–8, 130, 132, 134–7, 139–42, 145–9, 153, 158, 165, 190, 192, 209, 214, 225
  Reagan Doctrine 10–12, 53, 88, 109, 150, 160, 174, 189, 190
Reich, Otto 49, 59
Reichler, Paul 148
Ricciardi, Joseph 182
Richardson, Elliot 167, 171, 178
Rio Treaty 61, 100–1, 137, 199
Robelo, Alfonso 4, 137, 139, 151, 176
Robinson, William 113, 180
Rocamora, Joel 172
Rodriguez, Carlos Rafael 33
Romberg, Alan 80
Roosevelt, Theodore 3
Rudman, Warren 131

Salinas de Gortari, Carlos 150
Sanchez, Aristide 139
Sanchez, Nestor 65
San José peace initiative 36–7, 39–40, 47
Sandinistas (FSLN) 1–8, 10–12, 14–15, 17–26, 28–30, 32, 34–5, 38–42, 44–6, 48–50, 52, 54–5, 58, 61–5, 67, 70, 74–81, 83, 85, 87–94, 97–101, 103–9, 111–19, 121–9, 135–6, 139–40, 142–52, 154–68, 170–94, 196, 199n12, 225n30, 231n25
Sandino, Augusto 4, 21
Santa Fe, Committee of 2
Sapoá talks 147, 160, 165, 167
Sasser, Jim 117
Saudi Arabia 72, 134
Scheverdnadze, Eduard 160, 162
Schoultz, Lars 6, 8–10
Senate 65, 69, 71, 83, 107, 129, 136–7, 142, 157
  Senate Committee on Foreign Relations 16, 27, 139, 220n2
  Senate Democratic Policy Committee 10
  Senate Intelligence Committee 26, 44, 65, 93
Sepúlveda Amor, Bernardo 45, 50–1, 70–1, 77–8, 80–2, 99, 107, 128, 141
Sharpe, Kenneth 28, 136
Shlauderman, Harry 63, 70–2, 75, 79, 83, 87, 112, 228n4
Shultz, George 35, 41, 44–8, 53, 55, 58, 62–3, 70–3, 78, 81, 83, 85, 93, 101, 110, 114–16, 120–1, 128–31, 133, 138, 143, 147, 149, 160
Slattery, Jim 119
Smith, Wayne 15, 27, 29, 33, 117
Socialism 7
Socialist International 89–91
Somoza Debayle, Anastasio 2–4, 6, 17, 89, 104, 176, 185, 188, 194

South Africa 66, 134
South Korea 9, 134
Soviet Union 1–7, 10, 13–14, 16, 20–1, 24, 26–30, 33, 41–3, 45, 48, 51, 53, 55, 57, 59–61, 67, 72–3, 75, 79–83, 88, 93, 96–8, 100–1, 103, 106–7, 109, 124–5, 131, 136, 138, 142, 147–9, 151, 156, 158–62, 166, 168, 189, 191–2, 208n38, 211n8, 213n19, 214n19, 231n25, 251n2
Spain 50, 102, 150
Speakes, Larry 65
Stanchenko, Vladimir 30
Stockholm International Peace Reaserch Institute 60
Stone, Richard 44, 49, 55, 57–9, 63
Studds, Gerry 17
Suazo Cordova, Robert 101, 102
Support Group 110–11, 115, 125, 128, 142

Taiwan 9, 95, 134
Tambs, Lewis 110
Tegucigalpa Draft 85–6, 94, 112
Tehran 129
Tela Agreement 163–7, 171–3, 177
Tesoro Accords 152, 154, 156–7, 159, 162, 171
Thatcher, Margaret 102
Third World 10, 51, 174–5, 185, 231n25
Tinoco, Victor Hugo 31, 47, 71, 79, 83, 87, 99, 104, 112, 129, 179
Tower Commission, *see* President's Special Review Board
Trejos Salas, Gerado 119
Truman Doctrine 42, 124, 133, 192
Truman, Harry 124
Tsongas, Paul 67
Turner, Stansfield 108

United Nations 9, 11, 20, 29, 32, 34, 58, 61, 65, 81, 83, 112, 137, 142, 146, 150, 153, 164, 166–7, 171
  United Nations Charter 52, 82, 100
  United Nations General Assembly 57, 126
  United Nations Security Council 20, 33, 41, 56, 62, 64, 80, 126
United Nations Observer Group for the Verification of Elections in Nicaragua (ONUVEN) 172, 178
United Nations Observer Group in Central America (ONUCA) 166, 168
United Nations Truth Commission 11, 173
United Nicaraguan Opposition (UNO) 107, 116–17, 136–7, 176–9, 183–5, 193–4
United States *passim*
United States Southern Command 38
Uruguay 110

Vaky, Viron 4–5, 8, 192
Venezuela 24, 36–7, 39–40, 47, 114, 138, 144, 153
Verification 122, 142–3, 145, 158, 164, 172
Vickers, George 184
Vietnam 10–11, 42, 65, 107, 111, 119, 127, 133, 189
Vilas, Carlos 175, 179, 181–4

Walker, Thomas 6–7
Wallop, Malcolm 67
Walsh, Lawrence 130, 132–4, 149
Walters, Vernon 33, 53
Watergate 130–1, 133
Watson, Alexander 195
Weeks, John 174, 179–80, 184, 193
Weinberger, Caspar 72, 73, 83, 95, 133–4, 142
West Germany 102, 150
Wheelock, Jamie 13
White Paper ('Communist Interference in Central America') 14
White, Robert 9, 14–16
Whitehead, Lawrence 6, 173
Winsor, Curtin 79

Woodward, Bob 19, 21, 47
World Bank 154, 182, 193
Wright, Jim 50, 52, 141–3, 146, 177
Wright–Reagan Plan 141

Yeltsin, Boris 160
Yugoslavia 109

Zorinski, Edward 47
Zubek, Voytek 160